Better Homes and Gardens®

ANNUAL
Recipes
2007

SHERBET FRUIT POPS
page 169

Meredith Books
Des Moines, Iowa

GRILLED PEACH PIE
page 126

Who knew you could grill a pie? Or that there were so many refreshing ways to flavor lemonade, season corn on the cob, dress up deviled eggs, or customize a batch of brownies? How about this—did you know a matzo crust was all it took to make a fast supper of roasted salmon really shine?

"Who knew?" is the phrase I hope you're thinking again and again as you flip through the pages in this year's *Better Homes and Gardens®* *Annual Recipes*. Last February we completely revamped our food section with you and your family as our top priority. We know that time is short, but we also know that nutritious homecooked food is still essential. And it's fun to prepare! With those thoughts in mind, we set out to provide you with creative and inspiring, all-new ways to get fresh, vibrant, and definitely doable food on the table night after night for the people you love.

Among the more than 400 recipes from the 2007 issues of *Better Homes and Gardens®* magazine, you'll find a dish (or two or three) to suit every event and occasion imaginable. We also give you plenty of inspired extras to make every meal you prepare easier, better tasting, and more memorable for your family and friends. And because we know that healthful eating is important to you, we've included a new section of Good and Healthy recipes—easy, mouthwatering ways to infuse nutrition into your daily routine. Don't forget to check out our two new runaway hits with readers. Everyday Easy recipes provide you fresh, simple (and always delicious!) ways to feed your family fast. Ten to Try gives you 10 ideas to make your favorite foods—like deviled eggs and dipped strawberries—into an extra special dish.

Though we've made a lot of changes on our pages, two things remain constant. The first one, our Prize Tested Recipes® contest, is celebrating its 70th anniversary as one of the best-loved segments in our magazine. As much as our readers love this section, we actually love it more! It allows our readers to share their most cherished, tried-and-true recipes while helping us keep in touch with what today's readers really want to cook.

The other constant is the Better Homes and Gardens® Test Kitchen's commitment to testing and perfecting the recipes we publish. There's no "who knew" about the reliability of our recipes—you'll always know that each and every one will work the first time and every time you make it.

From our kitchen to yours—enjoy!

Gayle Butler

GAYLE BUTLER, EDITOR IN CHIEF
Better Homes and Gardens® magazine

Better Homes and Gardens. Annual Recipes 2007
Editor: Jessica Saari
Contributing Editors: Janet Figg, Joyce Trollope
Contributing Writer: Winifred Moranville
Associate Design Director: Som Inthalangsy
Copy Chief: Terri Fredrickson
Copy Editor: Kevin Cox
Publishing Operations Manager: Karen Schirm
Senior Editor, Asset and Information Management: Phillip Morgan
Edit and Design Production Coordinator: Mary Lee Gavin
Editorial Assistant: Cheryl Eckert
Book Production Managers: Pam Kvitne, Marjorie J. Schenkelberg, Mark Weaver
Desktop Publishing Specialist: Cari Leigh Johnson
Contributing Copy Editor: Amanda Knief
Contributing Proofreaders: Jill Blacksmith, Callie Dunbar,
    Gretchen Kauffman, Susan J. Kling
Contributing Indexer: Elizabeth T. Parson
Test Kitchen Director: Lynn Blanchard
Test Kitchen Product Supervisor: Maryellyn Krantz

Meredith. Books
Editor in Chief: Gregory H. Kayko
Executive Director, Design: Matt Strelecki
Managing Editor: Amy Tincher-Durik
Executive Editor: Jennifer Darling
Senior Editor/Group Manager: Jan Miller
Senior Associate Design Director: Ken Carlson

Executive Director, Marketing and New Business: Kevin Kacere
Director, Marketing and Publicity: Amy Nichols
Executive Director, Sales: Ken Zagor
Director, Operations: George A. Susral
Director, Production: Douglas M. Johnston
Business Director: Jim Leonard

Senior Vice President: Karla Jeffries
Vice President and General Manager: Douglas J. Guendel

Better Homes and Gardens. Magazine
Editor in Chief: Gayle Goodson Butler
Executive Editor: Kitty Morgan
Creative Director: Bradford W.S. Hong
Managing Editor: Lamont D. Olson
Art Director: Michael D. Belknap
Deputy Editor, Food and Entertaining: Nancy Wall Hopkins
Associate Editors: Richard Swearinger, Stephen J. Exel
Editorial Assistant: Anna Anderson

Meredith Publishing Group
President: Jack Griffin
Executive Vice President: Doug Olson
Vice President, Corporate Solutions: Michael Brownstein
Vice President, Manufacturing: Bruce Heston
Vice President, Consumer Marketing: David Ball
Consumer Product Marketing Director: Steve Swanson
Consumer Product Marketing Manager: Wendy Merical
Business Manager: Darren Tollefson

Meredith Corporation
Chairman of the Board: William T. Kerr
President and Chief Executive Officer: Stephen M. Lacy

In Memoriam: E.T. Meredith III (1933–2003)

Test Kitchen

Our seal assures you that every recipe in *Better Homes and Gardens. Annual Recipes 2007* has been tested in the Better Homes and Gardens. Test Kitchen. This means that each recipe is practical and reliable, and meets our high standards of taste appeal. We guarantee your satisfaction with this book for as long as you own it.

All of us at Meredith. Books are dedicated to providing you with information and ideas to enhance your home. We welcome your comments and suggestions. Write to us at: Meredith Books Editorial Department, 1716 Locust St., Des Moines, IA 50309–3023. Title is available by mail. To order editions from past years, call 800/439-4119.

Pictured on the front cover: Fresh Pear and Cranberry Pie, page 259

Pictured on the back cover (from top, left to right): Asian Noodle Slaw, page 89; Easy Mixed Grill, page 33; Almond Pound Cake, page 95; Ginger Peach Glazed Chicken, page 148; assorted pancakes, pages 12–18; Steak and Grilled Nectarines, page 123; Ice Bucket Cherry Sundaes, page 126; Catfish with Summer Succotash, page 157.

INSIDE-OUT BLTS
page 30

**PEANUT BUTTER-
BANANA TRIFLES**
page 207

Get ready for a year of great times around the table! Packed into these 336 pages is an entire year's worth of recipes—all designed to help ease your day and simplify your life while making every meal richer and more meaningful for you and your family. Whether you're looking for creative new takes on Saturday-morning pancakes, healthful after-school snacks, beautiful-but-doable weeknight dinners, or something utterly inspired to do with a bushel of fall apples, this is your month-by-month resource for up-to-date, down-to-earth ideas.

● Seasonally Inspired Recipes: Each chapter kicks off with creative, inspired ways to cook with the foods that best enhance the month's meals. Spring greens add sparkle to recipes in April, while July's pages make the most of midsummer's first crop of eggplant and green beans. Chocolate works its magic into our Valentine's Day dinner, while quick-cooking seafood is a natural for easygoing August nights.

● Everyday Easy: We know at the top of your mind is what to serve for dinner tonight. We give you dozens of answers with fresh, simple, and delightful recipes that call on just five ingredients plus a few gimmick-free pantry staples. Taking just 20 minutes, these recipes are hearty, filling, fast—and easy on the budget.

● Good and Healthy: Nutrient-packed smoothies, fiber-rich grains, wholesome berries, nourishing nuts, healthful snacks, and more! Here's where you'll find up-to-date information, delicious recipes, and practical ideas for bringing good nutrition into your everyday life.

● Ten to Try: Go Greek with your mac 'n' cheese. Slip some lavender into your lemonade. Slather chutney on your corn on the cob. We start with one basic crowd-pleasing food—from deviled eggs to caramel apples—and give you 10 fresh spins on the classic.

● Build a Better: From nachos and artichoke dip to garden wraps and green bean casserole, we'll show you simple see-and-do secrets for making something you love even better.

● Recipe Icons: To help you quickly find what you're seeking, many recipes include icons that tell you if they're Fast (30 minutes or less), Kid-Friendly, or Low Fat (for the nutrition guidelines, see page 335).

● Prizewinning Recipes: Starting on page 272, you'll find all the published winners in our monthly Prize Tested Recipes® contest, along with the honor roll recipes—those that didn't make it into the magazine but were too delectable to keep out of the book.

2007 CONTENTS

SWEET-AND-FIERY POLENTA FRIES
page 34

POTATO AND SQUASH SALAD
page 195

JANUARY

PILES OF DELICATELY FLAVORED PANCAKES ARE A SUREFIRE WAY TO START THE DAY OFF RIGHT. NO MATTER WHAT YOUR TASTES—SAVORY OR SWEET— YOU'LL FIND A NEW FAVORITE FLAPJACK!

SPICED EGGNOG PANCAKES
page 12

Top of the Morning

Plus

PUMPKIN PANCAKES
page 16

SALMON WITH WILTED GREENS
page 21

TORTELLINI STIR-FRY
page 23

TOP

of the morning

PUMPKIN

NUTTY SOUR CREAM

ORANGE BUTTERMILK

SPICED EGGNOG

CHOCOLATE

PEANUT BUTTER

PARMESAN-CORNMEAL

Turn a stack of humble hotcakes into the high-rise headliner of the breakfast table. Your family will flip.

BY **RICHARD SWEARINGER** PHOTOGRAPHS BY **COLLEEN DUFFLEY** FOOD STYLING BY **SUSAN BROWN DRAUDT** PROP STYLING BY **KAREN JOHNSON**

PANCAKES ARE A SIMPLE SOLUTION FOR AN EARLY-MORNING SCHEDULE. THE BATTER CAN BE WHIPPED UP IN JUST 15 MINUTES. AND GOOD NEWS FOR SLOW RISERS: ONCE PANCAKES ARE COOKED, THEY CAN BE KEPT WARM IN THE OVEN FOR UP TO HALF AN HOUR.

MAKING SHAPES

Coat a 3- to 4-inch pancake ring or metal cookie cutter* with nonstick cooking spray. Preheat on griddle 2 minutes. Fill ring about one-third full. Cook until sides start to pull away from ring, about 2 minutes. Lift off ring with handle or lift cookie cutter with tongs, using table knife to ease pancake from ring. Flip and continue to cook—without ring— as directed.

* Make sure cutter is riveted rather than soldered; solder can melt on griddle.

SPICED EGGNOG PANCAKES

Half a carton of eggnog adds richness to these nutmeg-perfumed pancakes. For a tasty topping, stir together orange marmalade, pineapple, and ginger (see "Syrups," page 19).

PREP: 20 minutes **COOK:** 2 minutes per batch

INGREDIENTS

2	cups all-purpose flour
1	Tbsp. baking powder
1/2	tsp. salt
1/4	tsp. ground nutmeg
2	eggs, lightly beaten
2	cups dairy or canned eggnog
1/4	cup cooking oil

PREPARATION

1. In a large bowl combine flour, baking powder, salt, and nutmeg. In a second bowl combine eggs, eggnog, and oil. Stir eggnog mixture into flour mixture until slightly lumpy.

2. Heat a lightly greased griddle or heavy skillet over medium heat. For each pancake pour 1/4 cup batter onto griddle. Cook until golden; turn when tops are bubbly and edges are slightly dry (1 to 2 minutes per side). Makes 16 pancakes.

EACH PANCAKE: *140 cal., 7 g fat (2 g sat. fat), 45 mg chol., 167 mg sodium, 16 g carbo., 0 g fiber, 4 g pro. Daily Values: 2% vit. A, 1% vit. C, 11% calcium, 6% iron.*

SPICED EGGNOG PANCAKES

PARMESAN-CORNMEAL PANCAKES

PARMESAN-CORNMEAL PANCAKES

These savory hotcakes have the crunch of cornmeal and the nutty flavor of Parmesan. Although great at breakfast, try them at dinner with a topping of sour cream and herbs.

PREP: 15 minutes **COOK:** 2 minutes per batch

INGREDIENTS

1	cup all-purpose flour
¾	cup yellow cornmeal
⅓	cup grated Parmesan cheese
1	Tbsp. sugar (optional)
1	tsp. baking soda
½	tsp. salt
1¾	cups buttermilk
2	eggs, lightly beaten
2	Tbsp. cooking oil
⅓	cup chopped green onion

PREPARATION

1. In a bowl combine flour, cornmeal, Parmesan cheese, sugar (if desired), baking soda, and salt. In a second bowl combine buttermilk, eggs, oil, and green onion. Stir buttermilk mixture into flour mixture until slightly lumpy.

2. Heat a lightly greased griddle or heavy skillet over medium heat. For each pancake pour ¼ cup batter onto griddle. Cook until golden; turn when tops are bubbly and edges are slightly dry (1 to 2 minutes per side). Makes 16 pancakes.

EACH PANCAKE: *92 cal., 3 g fat (1 g sat. fat), 29 mg chol., 216 mg sodium, 12 g carbo., 1 g fiber, 4 g pro. Daily Values: 2% vit. A, 1% vit. C, 6% calcium, 4% iron.*

CHOCOLATE PANCAKES

Ultradecadent and oozing with chocolaty flavor, these flapjacks are good enough for dessert! For a special treat, top the stack with a small scoop of vanilla ice cream.

PREP: 15 minutes **COOK:** 4 minutes per batch

INGREDIENTS

1⅔	cups all-purpose flour
⅓	cup unsweetened cocoa powder
¼	cup sugar
1	tsp. baking soda
¼	tsp. salt
2¼	cups buttermilk
1	egg, lightly beaten
3	Tbsp. cooking oil

PREPARATION

1. In a large bowl combine flour, cocoa powder, sugar, baking soda, and salt. In a second bowl combine buttermilk, egg, and oil. Stir buttermilk mixture into flour mixture until slightly lumpy.

2. Heat a lightly greased griddle or heavy skillet over medium heat. Reduce heat to medium-low.* For each pancake pour ¼ cup batter onto griddle. Cook until lightly browned; turn when tops are bubbly and edges are slightly dry (about 2 to 3 minutes per side). Makes 16 pancakes.

*****NOTE:** Because of the chocolate in these pancakes, they need to cook at a lower temperature.

EACH PANCAKE: *104 cal., 4 g fat (1 g sat. fat), 15 mg chol., 156 mg sodium, 16 g carbo., 1 g fiber, 3 g pro. Daily Values: 1% vit. C, 5% calcium, 5% iron.*

NUTTY SOUR CREAM PANCAKES

Sour cream adds tenderness and tang to the cakes, while walnuts add flavorful crunch.

PREP: 15 minutes **COOK:** 2 minutes per batch

INGREDIENTS

2¼ cups all-purpose flour
¾ cup finely chopped toasted walnuts*
¼ cup packed brown sugar
1 Tbsp. baking powder
½ tsp. salt
1¼ cups milk
2 eggs, lightly beaten
1 8-oz. carton dairy sour cream
2 Tbsp. cooking oil

PREPARATION

1. In a large bowl combine flour, walnuts, brown sugar, baking powder, and salt. In a second bowl combine milk, eggs, sour cream, and oil. Stir milk mixture into flour mixture until slightly lumpy.
2. Heat a lightly greased griddle or heavy skillet over medium heat. For each pancake pour ¼ cup batter onto griddle. Cook until golden; turn when tops are bubbly and edges are slightly dry (1 to 2 minutes per side). Makes 16 pancakes.
*TEST KITCHEN TIP: You can substitute coarsely chopped toasted pecans, almonds, or hazelnuts for the walnuts.

EACH PANCAKE: *173 cal., 9 g fat (3 g sat. fat), 34 mg chol., 144 mg sodium, 18 g carbo., 1 g fiber, 4 g pro. Daily Values: 3% vit. A, 7% calcium, 6% iron.*

PUMPKIN PANCAKES

KID FRIENDLY

Pumpkin added to flapjack batter makes it extra rich—and good for you. Crown it with Caramel-Coconut Topper (page 19) and you'll feel like you're eating pumpkin pie for breakfast!

PREP: 15 minutes **COOK:** 2 minutes per batch

INGREDIENTS

2 cups all-purpose flour
3 Tbsp. packed brown sugar
1 Tbsp. baking powder
½ tsp. salt
1¾ cups milk
3 eggs, lightly beaten
¾ cup canned pumpkin
¼ cup cooking oil

PREPARATION

1. In a large bowl combine flour, brown sugar, baking powder, and salt. In a second bowl combine milk, eggs, pumpkin, and oil. Stir milk mixture into flour mixture until slightly lumpy.
2. Heat a lightly greased griddle or heavy skillet over medium heat. For each pancake pour ¼ cup batter onto griddle. Cook until golden; turn when tops are bubbly and edges are slightly dry (1 to 2 minutes per side). Makes 16 pancakes.

EACH PANCAKE: *128 cal., 5 g fat (1 g sat. fat), 42 mg chol., 167 mg sodium, 17 g carbo., 1 g fiber, 4 g pro. Daily Values: 38% vit. A, 1% vit. C, 11% calcium, 7% iron.*

TO KEEP PANCAKES WARM
Preheat oven to 200°F.
As pancakes come off
the griddle, transfer to an
ovenproof dish, cover lightly
with foil, and keep in the oven
for up to 30 minutes.

SALMON WITH WILTED GREENS

PREP: 15 minutes **BROIL:** 6 minutes

INGREDIENTS

1   lb. fresh or frozen salmon fillets (thawed)
½   cup plus 1 Tbsp. bottled Asian salad dressing, such as sesame ginger
6   cups torn mixed salad greens
1   medium orange, peeled and sectioned

PREPARATION

1. Preheat broiler. Rinse salmon; pat dry. Cut into 4 pieces. Broil salmon on the greased unheated rack of a broiler pan 4 inches from the heat for 6 to 9 minutes or until salmon begins to flake easily. Halfway through broiling brush with 1 tablespoon of the dressing. Cover; keep warm.
2. In a salad bowl combine greens and orange sections. In a large skillet bring remaining ½ cup dressing to boiling. Boil gently, uncovered, for 1 minute. Remove from heat. Pour over greens; toss.
3. Divide greens among 4 serving plates. Top with salmon. Serve immediately. Makes 4 servings.

EACH SERVING: *397 cal., 25 g fat (5 g sat. fat), 67 mg chol., 623 mg sodium, 20 g carbo., 3 g fiber, 24 g pro. Daily Values: 12% vit. A, 69% vit. C, 6% calcium, 5% iron.*

BEEF AND CABBAGE WRAPS

START TO FINISH: 20 minutes

INGREDIENTS

8   8-inch flour tortillas
12   oz. lean ground beef
½   cup chopped onion (1 medium)
1   cup frozen whole kernel corn
½   to ⅔ cup bottled barbecue sauce
2   cups packaged shredded cabbage with carrot (coleslaw mix)

PREPARATION

1. Preheat oven to 350°F. Wrap tortillas tightly in foil; place on baking sheet. Heat in oven for 10 minutes or until heated through.
2. Meanwhile, in a large skillet cook beef and onion until beef is brown and onion is tender. Drain. Stir in corn and ⅓ cup of the barbecue sauce. Cook and stir until heated through.
3. To serve, spread one side of each tortilla with some of the remaining barbecue sauce. Spoon about ½ cup filling onto each tortilla. Add shredded cabbage mix. Roll to make wraps. Makes 4 servings.

EACH SERVING: *391 cal., 14 g fat (4 g sat. fat), 54 mg chol., 535 mg sodium, 46 g carbo., 3 g fiber, 21 g pro. Daily Values: 12% vit. A, 30% vit. C, 9% calcium, 21% iron.*

BEEF AND CABBAGE WRAPS

PINEAPPLE PORK CHILI

JAMAICAN PORK STIR-FRY

START TO FINISH: 20 minutes

INGREDIENTS

1   Tbsp. cooking oil
1   16-oz. pkg. frozen stir-fry vegetables (yellow, green, and red sweet peppers and onions)
12   oz. pork strips for stir-frying
2   to 3 tsp. Jamaican jerk seasoning
½   cup bottled plum sauce
     Soy sauce (optional)
     Peanuts (optional)
2   cups hot cooked rice or pasta

PREPARATION

1. In a wok or large skillet heat oil over medium-high heat. Add frozen vegetables; cook and stir for 5 to 7 minutes or until vegetables are crisp-tender. Remove from wok.
2. Toss pork with jerk seasoning; add to wok. Add more oil if necessary. Cook and stir for 2 to 5 minutes or until pork is no longer pink.
3. Add plum sauce to wok; return vegetables. Toss gently to coat; heat through. If desired, season with soy sauce and sprinkle with peanuts. Serve over rice. Makes 4 servings.

EACH SERVING: *357 cal., 9 g fat (2 g sat. fat), 54 mg chol., 405 mg sodium, 45 g carbo., 2 g fiber, 22 g pro. Daily Values: 14% vit. A, 68% vit. C, 2% calcium, 15% iron.*

JAMAICAN PORK STIR-FRY

PINEAPPLE PORK CHILI

START TO FINISH: 20 minutes

INGREDIENTS

1   lb. ground pork or beef
1   16-oz. jar pineapple salsa
1   15-oz. can red kidney beans, rinsed and drained
1   8-oz. can tomato sauce
1   Tbsp. chili powder
     Pineapple slices (optional)

PREPARATION

1. In a 3-quart saucepan brown pork; drain. Stir in salsa, beans, tomato sauce, and chili powder. Bring to boiling; reduce heat. Simmer, uncovered, for 10 minutes. If desired, serve with pineapple slices. Makes 4 servings.

EACH SERVING: *356 cal., 9 g fat (4 g sat. fat), 53 mg chol., 1,026 mg sodium, 47 g carbo., 5 g fiber, 23 g pro. Daily Values: 26% vit. A, 27% vit. C, 6% calcium, 23% iron.*

FAST! **KID FRIENDLY**

TORTELLINI STIR-FRY

START TO FINISH: 20 minutes

INGREDIENTS

1   9-oz. pkg. refrigerated cheese-filled tortellini
1   16-oz. pkg. fresh cut or frozen stir-fry vegetables, such as broccoli, pea pods, carrots, and celery*
1   Tbsp. cooking oil
¾   cup peanut stir-fry sauce*
¼   cup chopped dry-roasted cashews

PREPARATION

1. Cook tortellini according to package directions. Drain and set aside.
2. In a wok or large skillet stir-fry fresh vegetables in hot oil over medium-high heat for 3 to 5 minutes (7 to 8 minutes for frozen vegetables) or until crisp-tender. Add pasta and stir-fry sauce; toss gently to coat. Heat through. Sprinkle with cashews; serve immediately. Makes 4 servings.

*TEST KITCHEN TIP: Vary this recipe each time you make it by choosing a different vegetable blend and different sauce.

EACH SERVING: *400 cal., 16 g fat (3 g sat. fat), 30 mg chol., 1,256 mg sodium, 48 g carbo., 4 g fiber, 18 g pro. Daily Values: 30% vit. A, 42% vit. C, 13% calcium, 14% iron.*

TORTELLINI STIR-FRY

Snack of Champions

Here's a game plan for munchies that are easy to handle while your eyes are on the ball. The lineup includes these fish nachos and a no-meat version on page 25.

BY **STEPHEN EXEL** PHOTOGRAPHS BY **GREG SCHEIDEMANN** FOOD STYLING BY **JILL LUST**

Use 5-inch **tostada shells** for sturdier, more manageable nachos.

Add **avocado** slices for classic guacamole flavor. You won't miss the sugar, fat, and sodium of prepared dip.

Melt **pepper Jack cheese** on the tostadas before adding toppings to help keep the shells from getting soggy.

Sprinkle sliced **radishes** for color and crunch.

Gently mash canned **black beans** for creamy, smooth texture. (Mashed beans also help secure the toppings.) For extra creaminess, stir in shredded pepper Jack cheese. Bake the cheese-and-bean-topped shells in a 475°F oven for 4 to 5 minutes before assembling.

Finish nachos with a tangy squeeze of **lime** to add snap.

For a bit of heat, saute lightly flavored **tilapia** with thin slivers of jalapeño. This fish is lower in fat than ground beef.

Before serving, top with your favorite **crumbled cheese**. Try Greek feta cheese or Mexican cotija cheese, a widely available semisoft cheese that crumbles well and is less salty than shredded cheeses.

MEDITERRANEAN NACHOS

PREP: 15 minutes **BAKE:** 6 minutes

INGREDIENTS

6	cups tortilla chips
1	7-oz. container roasted red pepper hummus
½	cup dried tomato pesto
1	12-oz. jar marinated artichoke salad, drained and coarsely chopped
4	oz. basil-and-tomato-flavored feta cheese
2	Tbsp. minced shallot
	Crushed red pepper

PREPARATION

1. Preheat oven to 475°F. Line a 15×10×1-inch baking pan with nonstick foil. Arrange chips in baking pan.

2. Dollop hummus over chips. Top with spoonfuls of pesto and artichoke salad. Sprinkle with cheese, shallot, and red pepper. Bake for 6 to 8 minutes or until the cheese is softened. Makes 6 servings.

EACH SERVING: *371 cal., 25 g fat (5 g sat. fat), 18 mg chol., 866 mg sodium, 34 g carbo., 4 g fiber, 8 g pro. Daily Values: 6% vit. A, 25% vit. C, 18% calcium, 9% iron.*

MORE NACHO KNOW-HOW

This easy-prep, short-bake recipe adds Mediterranean flair to game-time snacking.

MEDITERRANEAN NACHOS

FEBRUARY

BRING THE ROMANTIC SPARKLE BACK TO VALENTINE'S DAY WITH A SPECIAL DINNER FOR TWO (COOKED BY THE TWO OF YOU!).

SWEET-AND-FIERY POLENTA FRIES
page 34

A Valentine's Dinner

EASY MIXED GRILL
page 33

PUMPKIN-BEAN SOUP
page 37

GRAPEFRUIT-WATERCRESS SUPPER SALAD
page 45

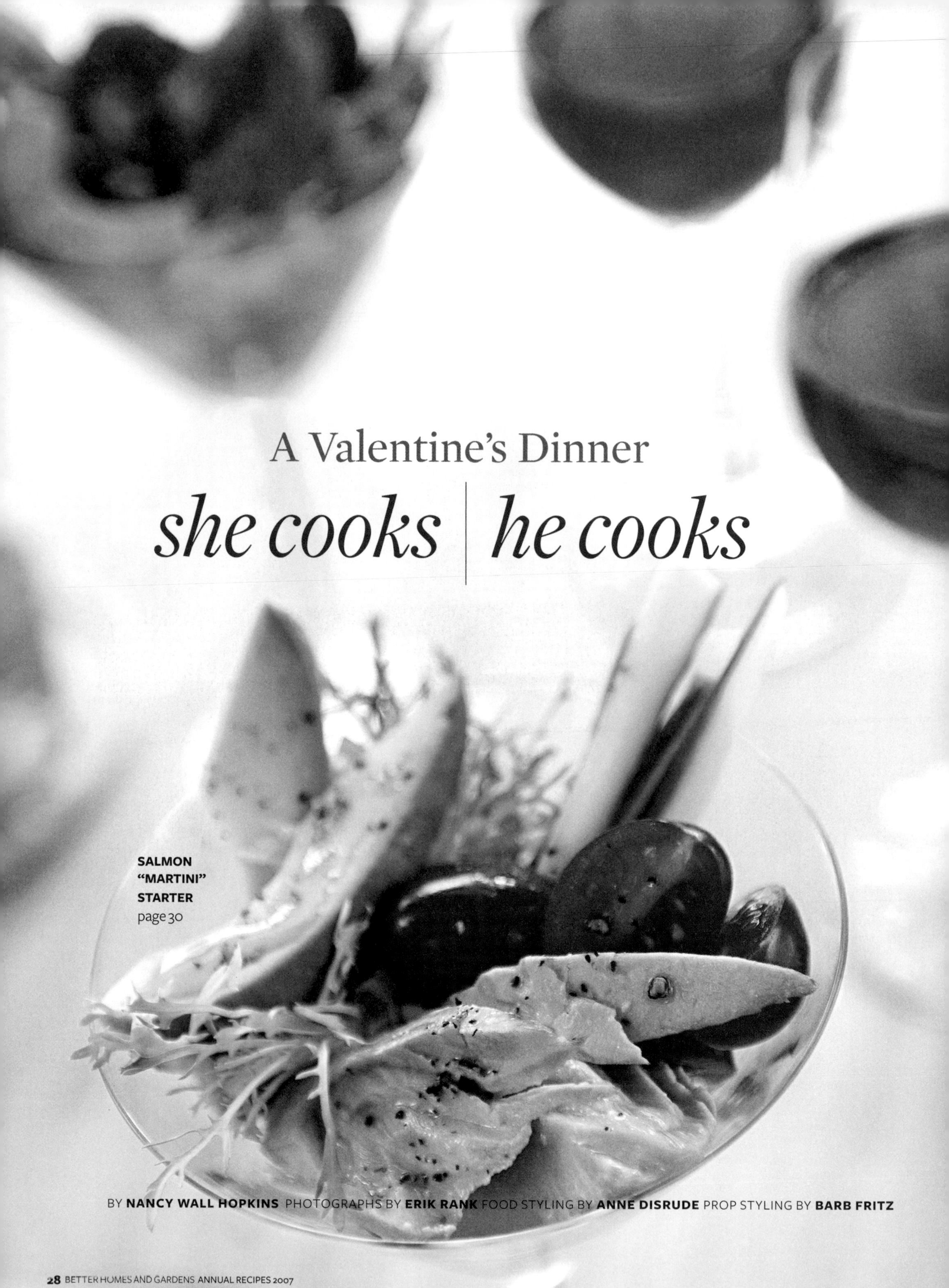

A Valentine's Dinner

she cooks | he cooks

SALMON "MARTINI" STARTER
page 30

BY **NANCY WALL HOPKINS** PHOTOGRAPHS BY **ERIK RANK** FOOD STYLING BY **ANNE DISRUDE** PROP STYLING BY **BARB FRITZ**

CAN A FIERY FOOD WRITER (SHE) AND A COOL-AND-CALM
CHEF (HE) CREATE A DELICIOUS DINNER TOGETHER?
IT'S ALL IN THE GIVE-AND-TAKE. NEWLYWEDS MARGE PERRY
AND DAVID BONOM SHARE SMART TIPS, A FOOLPROOF
MENU—AND A GENEROUS SERVING OF FUN.
COOKING TOGETHER NEVER TASTED SO GOOD.

FAST!

SALMON "MARTINI" STARTER

The curly green in this recipe is frisée. Any green, such as escarole or curly endive, can be substituted.

PREP: 20 minutes **BAKE:** 10 minutes

INGREDIENTS
	Nonstick cooking spray
4	oz. salmon fillet, ¾ to 1 inch thick
½	of a medium avocado, seeded, peeled, and sliced
¼	of a small cucumber, halved, seeded, and cut into spears
½	cup grape or cherry tomatoes, halved
½	cup frisée, escarole, or lettuce leaves
2	Tbsp. fresh lemon juice
2	tsp. olive oil
	Freshly ground black pepper

PREPARATION

1. Preheat oven to 425°F. Lightly coat a shallow baking pan with cooking spray.

2. Sprinkle salmon with *salt* and *ground black pepper*. Bake for 10 to 12 minutes or until fish flakes easily when tested with a fork. Remove from oven; cool in pan 10 minutes. Remove skin from salmon; discard. Break salmon into large chunks. Using a metal spatula, transfer salmon to plate. Chill for 30 minutes.

3. In martini glasses or small bowls arrange salmon, avocado, cucumber, tomatoes, and frisée. Combine lemon juice and olive oil; drizzle over salmon mixture. Season to taste with pepper. Cover; chill until serving time. Makes 2 servings.

EACH SERVING: *198 cal., 13 g fat (2 g sat. fat), 30 mg chol., 50 mg sodium, 9 g carbo., 4 g fiber, 13 g pro. Daily Values: 31% vit. A, 35% vit. C, 3% calcium, 6% iron.*

FAST!

INSIDE-OUT BLTS

PREP: 15 minutes **BAKE:** 10 minutes

INGREDIENTS
3	slices bacon
⅓	cup chopped romaine lettuce
⅓	cup coarse soft bread crumbs
2	Tbsp. grated Parmesan cheese
2	tsp. olive oil
2	medium plum tomatoes
⅛	tsp. freshly ground black pepper
2	tsp. mayonnaise
	Cherry tomatoes, halved (optional)

PREPARATION

1. Preheat oven to 400°F. In a large skillet cook bacon over medium heat until crisp. Drain on paper towels; chop.

2. In a medium bowl combine bacon, lettuce, crumbs, cheese, and olive oil; mix well. Set aside. Halve plum tomatoes lengthwise. Scoop out insides, leaving ¼- to ½-inch shells. Sprinkle inside of each tomato shell with pepper. Brush with some of the mayonnaise. Mound bacon mixture in tomato shells; transfer to a baking pan.

3. Bake stuffed tomatoes, uncovered, for 10 to 12 minutes or until tomatoes start to wilt. If desired, serve with cherry tomatoes. Makes 2 servings (2 halves each).

EACH HALF: *98 cal., 8 g fat (2 g sat. fat), 10 mg chol., 217 mg sodium, 10 g carbo., 1 g fiber, 4 g pro. Daily Values: 13% vit. A, 11% vit. C, 4% calcium, 2% iron.*

SALMON "MARTINI" STARTER

Marge and David, professional cooking teachers and recipe developers in New Jersey, like to serve this fresh and light starter in their seldom-used martini glasses.

INSIDE-OUT BLTS
Bacon is a splurge for Marge; David would add it to every dish he makes. This tempting side dish is the compromise. Plum tomato halves brim with a savory bacon, lettuce, and cheese filling.

SWEET-AND-FIERY POLENTA FRIES

Sugar and cumin provide the sweet; chili powder and cayenne add heat. Sprinkle the combo on fries cut from ready-made polenta.

FAST!

SWEET-AND-FIERY POLENTA FRIES

START TO FINISH: 22 minutes

INGREDIENTS

1	tsp. sugar
¼	tsp. salt
¼	tsp. ground cumin
¼	tsp. chili powder
	Dash cayenne pepper
½	of a 16-oz. tube refrigerated cooked polenta (cut crosswise)
2	Tbsp. all-purpose flour
¼	cup canola oil
2	Tbsp. finely chopped red sweet pepper
1	Tbsp. chopped fresh basil or fresh Italian (flat-leaf) parsley

PREPARATION

1. In a large bowl combine sugar, salt, cumin, chili powder, and cayenne pepper; set aside.

2. Cut polenta lengthwise into 6 thin slices; cut each slice lengthwise into 4 strips. In a medium bowl toss polenta strips with flour to coat.

3. In a large skillet heat oil over medium-high heat. Shake excess flour off polenta strips; add strips to hot oil. Cook strips, turning occasionally, for 7 to 8 minutes or until golden. Drain on paper towels. Place fries in bowl with sugar mixture; toss to coat. Sprinkle with sweet pepper and basil. Serve immediately or keep warm on a baking sheet in a 325°F oven for up to 20 minutes. Makes 2 to 4 servings.

TEST KITCHEN TIP: To reheat any leftovers, place fries in a single layer on a foil-lined baking sheet. Bake, uncovered, in a 350°F oven for 8 to 10 minutes or until hot.

EACH SERVING (6 FRIES): *160 cal., 10 g fat (1 g sat. fat), 0 mg chol., 367 mg sodium, 15 g carbo., 2 g fiber, 2 g pro. Daily Values: 5% vit. A, 15% vit. C, 1% iron.*

FAST!

CHOCOLATE PILLOWS

PREP: 20 minutes **COOK:** 1 minute each

INGREDIENTS

½   cup port or red Zinfandel*
1   Tbsp. sugar
¼   cup dried tart cherries
1   Tbsp. butter
2   cups canola oil or cooking oil
12   wonton wrappers
1   egg, beaten
1   3-oz. bar bittersweet chocolate, cut into 6 pieces
     Sugar
     Vanilla ice cream
     Grated bittersweet chocolate

PREPARATION

1. For cherry sauce, in a small saucepan heat port to boiling; reduce heat. Boil gently, uncovered, for 3 to 4 minutes or until reduced to ⅓ cup. Add sugar; cook and stir 1 minute more. Add cherries; cook for 2 minutes more, stirring occasionally. Remove from heat. Whisk in butter; keep warm.

2. Meanwhile, heat oil in a 2-quart saucepan over medium heat until temperature reaches 350°F. While oil heats, brush edges of 1 wonton wrapper with some of the beaten egg. Place 1 piece of chocolate in the center and top with another wrapper to form pillow. Press edges to seal. Repeat with remaining wrappers, beaten egg, and chocolate.

3. Cook filled pillows, 1 at a time, in hot oil for 1 minute or until golden, turning frequently. Adjust heat as needed to maintain oil temperature. Remove with a slotted spoon; drain on paper towels. Cool slightly; sprinkle with sugar.

4. Serve pillows with cherry sauce and ice cream. Sprinkle ice cream with grated chocolate. Cover and refrigerate any remaining pillows up to 24 hours. Makes 6 pillows.

***TEST KITCHEN TIP:** If using Zinfandel, increase sugar in sauce to 2 tablespoons.

EACH PILLOW: *218 cal., 9 g fat (5 g sat. fat), 42 mg chol., 120 mg sodium, 27 g carbo., 2 g fiber, 4 g pro. Daily Values: 5% vit. A, 2% calcium, 9% iron.*

CHOCOLATE PILLOWS
What's not to love about this dessert? It's pantry friendly, supereasy, and chocolaty delicious!

BUFFALO CHICKEN PIZZA

TUNA-POTATO CAKES

START TO FINISH: 18 minutes

INGREDIENTS

1 cup packaged refrigerated mashed potatoes with garlic
1 12-oz. can tuna (water pack), drained and broken into chunks
⅓ cup seasoned fine dry bread crumbs
½ cup finely chopped celery
¼ tsp. ground black pepper
2 Tbsp. cooking oil
¼ cup tartar sauce

PREPARATION

1. In a bowl combine potatoes, tuna, bread crumbs, celery, and pepper.
2. In skillet heat oil over medium heat. Drop about ⅓ cup potato mixture into hot oil; flatten to ½-inch patty. Cook for 4 minutes or until browned. Carefully turn; cook for 4 minutes more. Repeat with remaining mixture. Serve with tartar sauce. Makes 4 servings.

EACH SERVING (2 CAKES): *267 cal., 14 g fat (2 g sat. fat), 22 mg chol., 621 mg sodium, 16 g carbo., 1 g fiber, 19 g pro. Daily Values: 2% vit. A, 16% vit. C, 3% calcium, 8% iron.*

BUFFALO CHICKEN PIZZA

START TO FINISH: 20 minutes

INGREDIENTS

4 pita bread rounds
¼ cup bottled blue cheese salad dressing
1 9-oz. pkg. refrigerated Southwest-flavor cooked chicken breast strips
¾ cup thinly sliced celery
   Blue cheese crumbles (optional)
   Bottled hot pepper sauce (optional)

PREPARATION

1. Preheat oven to 450°F. Place pita rounds on a baking sheet. Brush with blue cheese dressing. Scatter chicken strips and celery over dressing. Bake, uncovered, for 10 minutes or until heated through and pitas are crisp.
2. Transfer to plates. If desired, sprinkle with crumbled blue cheese and pass hot pepper sauce. Makes 4 servings.

EACH SERVING: *327 cal., 11 g fat (2 g sat. fat), 44 mg chol., 1,084 mg sodium, 36 g carbo., 2 g fiber, 20 g pro. Daily Values: 3% vit. A, 2% vit. C, 7% calcium, 12% iron.*

TUNA-POTATO CAKES

Fast-Fix Dinners

Delicious recipes for busy families.

BY **NANCY WALL HOPKINS**
PHOTOGRAPHS BY **ANDY LYONS**
FOOD STYLING BY **JILL LUST**

READY IN
20
MINUTES

MEAT LOAF OPEN-FACERS

FAST!

CHOCOLATE PILLOWS

PREP: 20 minutes **COOK:** 1 minute each

INGREDIENTS

1/2   cup port or red Zinfandel*
1   Tbsp. sugar
1/4   cup dried tart cherries
1   Tbsp. butter
2   cups canola oil or cooking oil
12   wonton wrappers
1   egg, beaten
1   3-oz. bar bittersweet chocolate, cut into 6 pieces
    Sugar
    Vanilla ice cream
    Grated bittersweet chocolate

PREPARATION

1. For cherry sauce, in a small saucepan heat port to boiling; reduce heat. Boil gently, uncovered, for 3 to 4 minutes or until reduced to 1/3 cup. Add sugar; cook and stir 1 minute more. Add cherries; cook for 2 minutes more, stirring occasionally. Remove from heat. Whisk in butter; keep warm.

2. Meanwhile, heat oil in a 2-quart saucepan over medium heat until temperature reaches 350°F. While oil heats, brush edges of 1 wonton wrapper with some of the beaten egg. Place 1 piece of chocolate in the center and top with another wrapper to form pillow. Press edges to seal. Repeat with remaining wrappers, beaten egg, and chocolate.

3. Cook filled pillows, 1 at a time, in hot oil for 1 minute or until golden, turning frequently. Adjust heat as needed to maintain oil temperature. Remove with a slotted spoon; drain on paper towels. Cool slightly; sprinkle with sugar.

4. Serve pillows with cherry sauce and ice cream. Sprinkle ice cream with grated chocolate. Cover and refrigerate any remaining pillows up to 24 hours. Makes 6 pillows.

*TEST KITCHEN TIP: If using Zinfandel, increase sugar in sauce to 2 tablespoons.

EACH PILLOW: *218 cal., 9 g fat (5 g sat. fat), 42 mg chol., 120 mg sodium, 27 g carbo., 2 g fiber, 4 g pro. Daily Values: 5% vit. A, 2% calcium, 9% iron.*

CHOCOLATE PILLOWS
What's not to love about this dessert? It's pantry friendly, supereasy, and chocolaty delicious!

BUFFALO CHICKEN PIZZA

FAST! KID FRIENDLY

TUNA-POTATO CAKES

START TO FINISH: 18 minutes

INGREDIENTS

1   cup packaged refrigerated mashed potatoes with garlic
1   12-oz. can tuna (water pack), drained and broken into chunks
⅓   cup seasoned fine dry bread crumbs
½   cup finely chopped celery
¼   tsp. ground black pepper
2   Tbsp. cooking oil
¼   cup tartar sauce

PREPARATION

1. In a bowl combine potatoes, tuna, bread crumbs, celery, and pepper.

2. In skillet heat oil over medium heat. Drop about ⅓ cup potato mixture into hot oil; flatten to ½-inch patty. Cook for 4 minutes or until browned. Carefully turn; cook for 4 minutes more. Repeat with remaining mixture. Serve with tartar sauce. Makes 4 servings.

EACH SERVING (2 CAKES): *267 cal., 14 g fat (2 g sat. fat), 22 mg chol., 621 mg sodium, 16 g carbo., 1 g fiber, 19 g pro. Daily Values: 2% vit. A, 16% vit. C, 3% calcium, 8% iron.*

TUNA-POTATO CAKES

FAST! LOW FAT

BUFFALO CHICKEN PIZZA

START TO FINISH: 20 minutes

INGREDIENTS

4   pita bread rounds
¼   cup bottled blue cheese salad dressing
1   9-oz. pkg. refrigerated Southwest-flavor cooked chicken breast strips
¾   cup thinly sliced celery
    Blue cheese crumbles (optional)
    Bottled hot pepper sauce (optional)

PREPARATION

1. Preheat oven to 450°F. Place pita rounds on a baking sheet. Brush with blue cheese dressing. Scatter chicken strips and celery over dressing. Bake, uncovered, for 10 minutes or until heated through and pitas are crisp.

2. Transfer to plates. If desired, sprinkle with crumbled blue cheese and pass hot pepper sauce. Makes 4 servings.

EACH SERVING: *327 cal., 11 g fat (2 g sat. fat), 44 mg chol., 1,084 mg sodium, 36 g carbo., 2 g fiber, 20 g pro. Daily Values: 3% vit. A, 2% vit. C, 7% calcium, 12% iron.*

FAST!

MEAT LOAF OPEN-FACERS

START TO FINISH: 18 minutes

INGREDIENTS

4	½-inch slices eggplant
2	Tbsp. olive oil
	Salt and ground black pepper
1	17-oz. pkg. refrigerated meat loaf with tomato sauce
½	cup no-salt-added tomato sauce
4	1-inch diagonal slices Italian bread, toasted
¼	cup finely shredded Parmesan cheese (optional)

PREPARATION

1. Preheat broiler. Brush both sides of eggplant with oil. Sprinkle with salt and pepper. Place eggplant slices on the unheated rack of a broiler pan. Broil 3 to 4 inches from the heat for 2 to 3 minutes per side or until browned.

2. Meanwhile, slice meat loaf; place in a large skillet. Pour the ½ cup tomato sauce over meat. Cook over medium-high heat for 6 minutes or until heated through.

3. Place meat loaf slices on toast; top with eggplant, any remaining sauce in skillet, and, if desired, Parmesan cheese. Makes 4 servings.

EACH SERVING: *327 cal., 16 g fat (5 g sat. fat), 64 mg chol., 707 mg sodium, 21 g carbo., 2 g fiber, 27 g pro. Daily Values: 2% vit. A, 7% vit. C, 3% calcium, 15% iron.*

FAST!

PUMPKIN-BEAN SOUP

START TO FINISH: 15 minutes

INGREDIENTS

1	15-oz. can pumpkin
1	14-oz. can unsweetened coconut milk
1	15-oz. can cannellini beans, rinsed and drained
1	14-oz. can vegetable broth
1	tsp. dried leaf sage, crushed
	Salt and ground black pepper
	Cracked black peppercorns (optional)
	Fresh lime slices (optional)

PREPARATION

1. In a medium saucepan combine pumpkin, unsweetened coconut milk, beans, broth, and sage. Heat through.

2. Season to taste with salt and pepper. If desired, sprinkle with black peppercorns and drizzle with lime. Makes 4 servings.

EACH SERVING: *285 cal., 19 g fat (17 g sat. fat), 0 mg chol., 729 mg sodium, 28 g carbo., 8 g fiber, 9 g pro. Daily Values: 335% vit. A, 7% vit. C, 6% calcium, 21% iron.*

PUMPKIN-BEAN SOUP

FAST!

MAPLE PORK AND APPLES

START TO FINISH: 20 minutes

INGREDIENTS

4	pork loin chops, cut ½ inch thick (about 1¾ lb.)
	Salt and ground black pepper
2	Tbsp. butter
12	baby carrots with tops, halved lengthwise
1	medium apple, sliced and seeds removed
⅓	cup maple syrup

PREPARATION

1. Sprinkle chops with salt and pepper. In a large skillet melt butter over medium heat; add chops. Brown for 2 minutes, turning once. Reduce heat to medium-low. Add carrots, apple, and maple syrup. Cover; simmer for 8 minutes or until desired doneness.

2. Using a slotted spoon, transfer chops, carrots, and apple to a platter; bring the syrup mixture to boiling. Boil gently, uncovered, for 1 to 2 minutes or until mixture is thickened. Pour over chops. Makes 4 servings.

EACH SERVING: *451 cal., 19 g fat (6 g sat. fat), 124 mg chol., 447 mg sodium, 25 g carbo., 1 g fiber, 44 g pro. Daily Values: 87% vit. A, 8% vit. C, 4% calcium, 12% iron.*

MAPLE PORK AND APPLES

Double-Duty Dinners

These slow cooker recipes stretch into return-reward dishes. One hearty batch makes two tasty winter meals.

CREAMY BASIL CHICKEN

BY STEPHEN EXEL PHOTOGRAPHS BY ANDY LYONS FOOD STYLING BY JILL LUST

CREAMY BASIL CHICKEN

PREP: 25 minutes
COOK: 6 hours (low) + 30 minutes (high) or 3½ hours (high)

INGREDIENTS

2	cups sliced mushrooms
2	medium red and/or yellow sweet peppers, cut into strips
1	large onion, sliced
4	oz. cooked bacon, chopped
8	cloves garlic, minced
3	Tbsp. quick-cooking tapioca, crushed
8	skinless, boneless chicken breast halves (2½ to 3 lb.)
1	cup chicken broth
¼	cup dry white wine or vermouth
1	lb. fresh asparagus spears
⅓	cup whipping cream
½	cup snipped fresh basil
2	cups hot cooked orzo pasta
2	Tbsp. snipped fresh basil
2	Tbsp. grated Parmesan cheese

PREPARATION

1. In a 5- or 6-quart slow cooker stir together mushrooms, sweet pepper, onion, bacon, and garlic. Sprinkle with tapioca. Place chicken on top of mixture in cooker. Pour broth and wine over all.
2. Cover; cook on low-heat setting for 6 to 7 hours or on high-heat setting for 3 to 3½ hours.
3. Meanwhile, snap off and discard woody bases from asparagus. Cut into 2- to 3-inch lengths. If using low-heat setting, turn to high-heat setting. Stir in asparagus, cream, and the ½ cup fresh basil. Cover; cook for 30 minutes more.
4. Reserve 4 chicken breast halves to prepare Chicken and Wild Rice Chowder (right); store as directed below.* Serve remaining chicken, vegetables, and sauce with orzo. Sprinkle with the 2 tablespoons fresh basil and the Parmesan cheese. Makes 4 servings plus additional chicken for Chicken and Wild Rice Chowder (right).
*TEST KITCHEN TIP: To store chicken breast halves, wrap tightly and refrigerate for up to 3 days.

EACH SERVING: *556 cal., 21 g fat (9 g sat. fat), 132 mg chol., 892 mg sodium, 43 g carbo., 5 g fiber, 47 g pro. Daily Values: 62% vit. A, 177% vit. C, 12% calcium, 26% iron.*

CHICKEN AND WILD RICE CHOWDER

PREP: 20 minutes COOK: 25 minutes

INGREDIENTS

1	cup sliced carrot (2 medium)
1	cup sliced celery (2 stalks)
1	cup quartered mushrooms
3	Tbsp. butter
3	Tbsp. all-purpose flour
2	14-oz. cans chicken broth
4	chicken breast halves from Creamy Basil Chicken, chopped (left)
¾	cup cooked wild rice
¼	tsp. ground black pepper
1½	cups half-and-half

PREPARATION

1. In a large saucepan cook carrot, celery, and mushrooms in hot butter over medium heat until tender. Stir in flour. Add broth, chicken, wild rice, and pepper. Cook and stir until mixture is bubbly and slightly thickened. Stir in half-and-half; heat through. Makes 4 servings.

EACH SERVING (2 CUPS): *445 cal., 22 g fat (13 g sat. fat), 140 mg chol., 1,019 mg sodium, 21 g carbo., 2 g fiber, 40 g pro. Daily Values: 113% vit. A, 6% vit. C, 14% calcium, 10% iron.*

CHICKEN AND WILD RICE CHOWDER

SPICY BEEF SLOPPY JOES

LOW FAT · **KID FRIENDLY**

SPICY BEEF SLOPPY JOES

PREP: 20 minutes **COOK:** 8 hours (low) or 4 hours (high)

INGREDIENTS

2	lb. lean ground beef
2	16-oz. jars salsa
3	cups sliced fresh mushrooms (8 oz.)
1½	cups shredded carrot (3 medium)
1½	cups finely chopped red and/or green sweet pepper
⅓	cup tomato paste
2	tsp. dried basil, crushed
1	tsp. dried oregano, crushed
½	tsp. salt
¼	tsp. cayenne pepper
4	cloves garlic, minced
6	kaiser rolls, split and toasted

PREPARATION

1. In a large skillet cook beef over medium heat until brown, stirring to break meat into pieces. Drain fat. In a 5- or 6-quart slow cooker stir together beef and remaining ingredients (except rolls).

2. Cover; cook on low-heat setting for 8 to 10 hours or on high-heat setting for 4 to 5 hours.

3. Reserve 5 cups of the meat mixture for Spicy Beef Taco Salad (page 43); cover tightly, refrigerate. Serve remaining meat mixture on toasted kaiser rolls. Makes 6 servings plus additional meat mixture for Spicy Beef Taco Salad (page 43).

EACH SERVING: *294 cal., 8 g fat (3 g sat. fat), 36 mg chol., 756 mg sodium, 37 g carbo., 3 g fiber, 18 g pro. Daily Values: 37% vit. A, 42% vit. C, 8% calcium, 20% iron.*

SPICY BEEF TACO SALAD

PREP: 20 minutes   COOK: 10 minutes

INGREDIENTS

5   cups reserved meat mixture from Spicy Beef Sloppy Joes (page 42)
1   15-oz. can black beans, rinsed and drained
1   2.25-oz. can sliced, pitted ripe olives, drained
1   tsp. taco seasoning
1   head iceberg lettuce, cut into 6 thick slices
1   cup shredded cheddar cheese (4 oz.)
1   cup chopped tomato (2 medium)
⅓   cup dairy sour cream
    Assorted tortilla chips

PREPARATION

1. In a large saucepan stir together meat mixture from Spicy Beef Sloppy Joes, beans, olives, and seasoning. Heat to boiling; reduce heat. Simmer, covered, for 10 minutes.

2. To serve, place lettuce slices on serving plates. Add meat mixture. Top with cheese, tomato, and sour cream. Add tortilla chips. Makes 6 servings.

EACH SERVING: *495 cal., 26 g fat (10 g sat. fat), 84 mg chol., 1,181 mg sodium, 41 g carbo., 9 g fiber, 32 g pro. Daily Values: 81% vit. A, 81% vit. C, 25% calcium, 29% iron.*

SPICY BEEF TACO SALAD

Sweet on Sour

Grapefruit's grown-up flavor refreshes beyond breakfast—no matter which variety you choose. And it's good for you any time of day. A plain grapefruit half has 40 calories and half of your daily vitamin C. It also provides cancer fighters lycopene and beta-carotene. **Precaution:** Grapefruit can react with many medications, so check with your pharmacist.

BY **RICHARD SWEARINGER** PHOTOGRAPHS BY **ANDY LYONS** FOOD STYLING BY **JILL LUST**

WHAT'S NEW

This small green fruit, the cocktail grapefruit—a cross between a pummelo and a mandarin—is sweeter and less acidic than its grapefruit cousin. Find it in grocery stores or go to melissas.com.

Quick Tricks: From Drinks to Desserts

1. Sprinkle grapefruit halves with allspice and sugar; broil 5 minutes.

2. Mix equal parts grapefruit juice, cranberry juice, and club soda for a refreshing drink.

3. Substitute grapefruit peel for orange peel in dessert recipes.

4. Mix together the sections from 2 grapefruit with a banana, a 6-ounce carton of vanilla yogurt, ice cubes, and drizzle of honey for a tangy smoothie.

GRAPEFRUIT-WATERCRESS SUPPER SALAD

START TO FINISH: 25 minutes

INGREDIENTS

3   medium pink and/or white grapefruit
¼   cup grapefruit juice or orange juice
3   Tbsp. olive oil
1   Tbsp. snipped fresh mint or 1 tsp. dried mint, crushed
½   tsp. freshly ground black pepper
¼   tsp. salt
4   cups watercress, tough stems removed
½   cup coarsely snipped fresh cilantro
2   medium avocados, halved, seeded, peeled, and cut into 1- to 2-inch pieces

PREPARATION

1. Halve 2 of the grapefruit. With a grapefruit knife or other small knife cut between fruit segments and around outer edge; gently loosen fruit from each shell. Peel and section remaining grapefruit over a small bowl to catch juice; set aside sections. Measure juice in bowl; add enough grapefruit juice to equal ¼ cup.
2. For dressing, whisk together grapefruit juice, oil, mint, pepper, and salt.
3. Place grapefruit halves in shallow serving bowls. Layer each half with watercress, cilantro, and avocado. Top with reserved grapefruit sections. Drizzle with dressing. Makes 4 servings.

EACH SERVING: *316 cal., 24 g fat (3 g sat. fat), 0 mg chol., 172 mg sodium, 28 g carbo., 9 g fiber, 4 g pro. Daily Values: 89% vit. A, 138% vit. C, 10% calcium, 6% iron.*

GRAPEFRUIT-WATERCRESS SUPPER SALAD

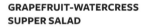

BUILD A BETTER DISH

Easy Pizzeria Flavor

Use these tips for a saucy, cheesy, gooey stovetop pizza that cooks in just 8 minutes.

BY **STEPHEN EXEL**   PHOTOGRAPH BY **ANDY LYONS**   FOOD STYLING BY **JILL LUST**

Start with a pizza crust mix. Add a **fresh chopped herb** to the mix for subtle spice. Instead of baking the pizza, use an oiled **grill pan** to cook the crust and topped pizza. The ridges allow air to circulate so the crust cooks evenly.

Spread your favorite purchased **marinara sauce** (about ½ cup) over the cooked crust, then layer with the other ingredients.

Overlap slices of fresh **mozzarella cheese** on top of the sauce. Fresh cheese melts well and tastes both slightly salty and sweet. If you can't get fresh, choose shredded.

Scatter one **chopped tomato** over the cheese for juiciness. Cooked **Canadian bacon** strips (about ½ cup) add hearty taste.

Drizzle **olive oil** mixed with a few drops of **olive brine** and flecks of **cracked pepper** over the top for a pizzeria flourish.

For a briny snap, toss on ¼ cup chopped **green olives**.

Sprinkle crumbled fresh **Parmesan cheese** for pockets of salty flavor. To thoroughly melt the cheese, cover the grill pan with a baking sheet.

TEST KITCHEN TIP: We tested a range of ready-made pizza crusts and found easy-prep **pizza crust mix** to be best for stovetop pizzas. Prepare as directed, then brush dough with olive oil. Cook crust on grill pan for 3 minutes per side, flipping halfway through cooking. Top pizza; cook 1 to 2 minutes more to heat ingredients.

1

RED DELICIOUS
Melted red or pink
confectioners' coating

2

SUGAR AND CREAM DREAM
Sour cream, brown sugar

3

CHOCOLATE AND NUTS
Melted milk chocolate, salted
cashews or mixed nuts

Dipped Strawberries
Cool ways to top a fresh heart-shape treat

4

PERFECT PAIRING
White chocolate on one side,
dark chocolate on the other

5

A.M. PLEASER
Strawberry yogurt and granola
or cereal with dried fruits

6

LEMON SUPREME
Velvety lemon curd, freshly
shredded lemon peel

7

PEPPERY FINALE
Honey, cracked black pepper

8

MOJITO BERRY
Honey, lime juice, coarse sugar,
snipped fresh mint leaves

9

TAFFY BERRY
Melted caramels or a rich
caramel ice cream topping

10

ISLAND DELIGHT
Buttery vanilla frosting, crunchy
toasted coconut

BHG BASICS
For best dipping results,
strawberries must be
completely dry. Use a
paper towel to gently
blot berries until
there's no excess
moisture.

BY **NANCY WALL HOPKINS** PHOTOGRAPHS BY **ANDY LYONS** FOOD STYLING BY **JILL LUST**

MARCH

EXPERIENCE DINNER THE OLD-FASHIONED WAY—WITH A HEARTY HELPING OF MEAT AND POTATOES. THESE FRESH FLAVOR COMBOS START SPRING OFF RIGHT.

MARINATED FLANK STEAK
page 52

Meet & Potatoes

SIRLOIN STROGANOFF
page 56

STOVETOP SHORT RIBS
page 55

MOCHA TWISTS
page 67

BY **RICHARD SWEARINGER** PHOTOGRAPHS BY **IAIN BAGWELL**
FOOD STYLING BY **SUSAN BROWN DRAUDT** PROP STYLING BY **KAREN JOHNSON**

Meat
& Potatoes

Fresh for spring: beef combos you love with bold flavors,
bright looks, easy techniques, and timesaving ingredients.

BEEF AND SWEET POTATO PAN ROAST

This one-pan dinner, left, uses beef shoulder petite tenders, a new lean roast notable for its full flavor, tenderness, and bargain price.

Fresh difference

Tossed in the pan during the last minutes of roasting, sweet cherry tomatoes become meltingly delicious. A dusting of fresh parsley, garlic, and orange peel adds a fragrant finish.

TEST KITCHEN TIP:
To substitute beef tenderloins for shoulder petite tenders, prepare potatoes and meat as at right, except do not roast potatoes before adding beef. Place browned tenderloin in center of greased roasting pan. Place potato wedges around pan edges. Roast, uncovered, 30 to 35 minutes for medium rare (140°F) or 40 to 45 minutes for medium (155°F). Let stand for 5 minutes before carving beef.

BEEF AND SWEET POTATO PAN ROAST

You'll love the mix of orange and white sweet potatoes in this quick-roast meal.

PREP: 25 minutes ROAST: 30 minutes STAND: 5 minutes

INGREDIENTS

1	Tbsp. dried Italian seasoning
1	Tbsp. bottled roasted minced garlic
1	tsp. salt
½	tsp. crushed red pepper
3	Tbsp. olive oil
2	lb. medium orange and/or white sweet potatoes, cut into 1-inch wedges
4	6- to 8-oz. beef shoulder petite tenders or 1½ to 2 lb. beef tenderloin
1	cup cherry tomatoes
1	recipe Chopped Parsley Topping

PREPARATION

1. Preheat oven to 425°F. In a bowl combine Italian seasoning, garlic, salt, and crushed red pepper. Stir in olive oil. Divide seasoning mixture between two large resealable plastic bags. Place sweet potatoes in one bag; shake to coat potatoes. Spread potatoes in a single layer on a greased shallow roasting pan. Roast, uncovered, for 15 minutes.

2. Meanwhile, place beef tenders in remaining bag. Shake to coat. In a large skillet brown beef tenders over medium-high heat, turning to brown evenly. Stir sweet potatoes in roasting pan and push to edges of pan. Place beef tenders in center of pan. Roast, uncovered, for 5 minutes. Add tomatoes; roast for 10 to 15 minutes more or until an instant-read thermometer inserted in center of thickest part of tenders registers 145°F for medium rare or 160°F for medium. Let stand for 10 minutes before carving. Serve with Chopped Parsley Topping. Makes 8 servings.

CHOPPED PARSLEY TOPPING: Stir together ¼ cup snipped fresh parsley; 2 teaspoons finely shredded orange peel; 2 cloves garlic, minced; and ⅛ teaspoon salt.

EACH SERVING: *362 cal., 14 g fat (3 g sat. fat), 65 mg chol., 587 mg sodium, 32 g carbo., 5 g fiber, 26 g pro. Daily Values: 434% vit. A, 16% vit. C, 7% calcium, 21% iron.*

FAST! **LOW FAT**

BUTTERMILK MASHED POTATOES

PREP: 10 minutes **COOK:** 20 minutes

INGREDIENTS
2   lb. russet and/or yellow potatoes, such as Yukon gold
¾   cup buttermilk
1   Tbsp. butter
½   tsp. salt
¼   tsp. ground black pepper

PREPARATION
1. Peel and quarter potatoes. Cook, covered, in boiling salted water for 20 to 25 minutes or until tender; drain.
2. Meanwhile, in a small saucepan combine buttermilk, butter, salt, and pepper. Heat over low heat until just warm, stirring frequently (do not boil).
3. Transfer potatoes to a mixing bowl; mash with potato masher or beat with mixer on low speed. Slowly add buttermilk mixture, mashing until smooth. Makes 6 servings.

EACH SERVING: *149 cal., 2 g fat (1 g sat. fat), 6 mg chol., 247 mg sodium, 29 g carbo., 2 g fiber, 4 g pro. Daily Values: 1% vit. A, 50% vit. C, 6% calcium, 7% iron.*

CHUNKY KETCHUP

PREP: 5 minutes **COOK:** 35 minutes

INGREDIENTS
2   28-oz. cans diced tomatoes, drained
½   cup red wine vinegar
¼   cup bourbon or apple cider
¼   cup olive oil
4   cloves garlic, minced
2   tsp. dried oregano, crushed
½   tsp. cracked black pepper

PREPARATION
1. In a large saucepan combine tomatoes, vinegar, bourbon, olive oil, garlic, oregano, and pepper. Bring to boiling; reduce heat. Simmer, uncovered, for 35 minutes or until juices are nearly evaporated. Cool to room temperature.
2. Cover tightly and chill any leftovers for up to 3 days. Makes 4 cups (thirty-two 2-tablespoon servings).

EACH SERVING: *30 cal., 2 g fat (0 g sat. fat), 0 mg chol., 99 mg sodium, 3 g carbo., 1 g fiber, 0 g pro. Daily Values: 4% vit. A, 6% vit. C, 1% calcium, 1% iron.*

MARINATED FLANK STEAK

PREP: 15 minutes **MARINATE:** 6 hours **GRILL:** 23 minutes

INGREDIENTS
1   recipe Chunky Ketchup (below left)
1   1½-lb. beef flank steak
1   recipe Buttermilk Mashed Potatoes (left)

PREPARATION
1. Prepare Chunky Ketchup.
2. Trim fat from steak. Score steak on both sides by making shallow cuts at 1-inch intervals in a diamond pattern. Place steak in a resealable plastic bag set in a shallow dish.
3. Add 1 cup of the Chunky Ketchup to the plastic bag with meat. Seal; marinate in the refrigerator for 6 to 24 hours, turning bag occasionally. Drain steak; discard ketchup.
4. For a charcoal grill, arrange medium-hot coals around drip pan. Test for medium heat above pan. Place steak on grill rack over drip pan. Cover; grill for 23 to 28 minutes for medium (160°F), turning halfway through grilling. (For a gas grill, preheat grill. Reduce heat to medium. Adjust for indirect cooking. Grill as above.) Cover and keep warm.
5. Heat 1 cup of the remaining Chunky Ketchup to serve with steak (or serve cold). Thinly slice steak diagonally across the grain. Serve steak with Buttermilk Mashed Potatoes. Makes 6 servings.

EACH SERVING: *340 cal., 17 g fat (5 g sat. fat), 46 mg chol., 596 mg sodium, 14 g carbo., 5 g fiber, 27 g pro. Daily Values: 22% vit. A, 33% vit. C, 6% calcium, 17% iron.*

MARINATED FLANK STEAK

Flank steak is such a flavorful and convenient cut that the sauce can be supersimple: This favorite comes to life with just a splash of bourbon.

Fresh difference Yukon gold and russet potatoes taste their best when mashed together, chunky fashion, with just a bit of buttermilk. On top? Butter accented with Italian seasoning and snipped green onions.

STEAK 'N' BAKE

STEAK 'N' BAKE

This recipe stars a baked potato stuffed with classic steakhouse flavors.

PREP: 20 minutes BROIL: 16 minutes

INGREDIENTS

4   medium baking potatoes
12   to 16 oz. boneless beef sirloin steak, cut 1 inch thick
2   cups fresh baby spinach
¾   cup bottled blue cheese salad dressing
1   small red onion, cut into thin wedges

PREPARATION

1. Wash potatoes; pierce with a fork. Arrange potatoes on a microwave-safe plate in spoke formation, leaving 1 inch between each potato. Microwave, uncovered, on 100% power (high) for 14 to 18 minutes or until tender. (Or bake potatoes in a 425°F oven for 40 to 60 minutes.) Let stand 5 minutes.
2. Meanwhile, preheat broiler. Trim fat from steak. Place meat on the unheated rack of a broiler pan. Broil 3 to 4 inches from the heat for 16 to 18 minutes for medium rare (145°F) or 19 to 21 minutes for medium (160°F), turning once halfway through broiling. Transfer meat to a cutting board; let stand 5 minutes. Or, to grill, prepare steak as above. For a charcoal grill, grill on rack of uncovered grill directly over medium coals 18 to 22 minutes for medium (160°F), turning once. (For a gas grill, preheat grill. Reduce heat to medium. Place meat on grill rack over heat. Cover; grill as above.)
3. To serve, roll each potato gently under your hand. Cut an "X" in top of potato. Press in and up on ends of potato. Cut steak into bite-size strips. Top potatoes with beef strips and spinach; drizzle with dressing. Top with onion wedges. Makes 4 servings.

EACH SERVING: *580 cal., 35 g fat (9 g sat. fat), 65 mg chol., 577 mg sodium, 35 g carbo., 4 g fiber, 32 g pro. Daily Values: 30% vit. A, 66% vit. C, 9% calcium, 28% iron.*

STOVETOP SHORT RIBS

Rich broth and falling-off-the-bone tender meat make this dish a delicious winner.

PREP: 30 minutes COOK: 2¼ hours

INGREDIENTS

4   to 5 lb. bone-in beef short ribs, 3 lb. boneless beef short ribs, or one 3-lb. beef chuck roast
2   Tbsp. olive oil or cooking oil
3   large white or red onions, sliced into ½-inch rings
1   14-oz. can beef broth
1   cup dry red wine or beef broth
2   lb. small Yukon gold potatoes
1   lb. small carrots, peeled
¼   cup water
2   Tbsp. all-purpose flour

PREPARATION

1. Trim fat from meat; sprinkle with *salt* and *ground black pepper*. In a 6- to 8-quart Dutch oven brown beef in hot oil over medium heat. Drain off fat; discard. Add onions, broth, and wine.
2. Bring broth mixture to boiling; reduce heat. Simmer, covered, for 1 hour. Add whole potatoes. Return to boiling; reduce heat. Simmer, covered, for 45 minutes. Add carrots. Cover; cook for 30 minutes more or until meat and vegetables are tender, spooning juices over meat and vegetables twice during cooking.
3. Using a slotted spoon, transfer meat and vegetables to a serving platter. Skim fat from juices. If necessary, add *water* to juices to equal 1½ cups. Return juices to pan. In a screw-top jar combine the ¼ cup water and the flour. Cover; shake to combine. Add to juices in pan. Cook and stir over medium heat until thickened; cook and stir for 1 minute more. Season with *salt* and *ground black pepper*. Spoon over meat and vegetables. Makes 6 servings.

EACH SERVING: *660 cal., 28 g fat (10 g sat. fat), 133 mg chol., 652 mg sodium, 45 g carbo., 7 g fiber, 49 g pro. Daily Values: 254% vit. A, 66% vit. C, 8% calcium, 38% iron.*

STOVETOP SHORT RIBS

SPICY MEAT LOAF

Looking for the "potato" in this sandwich? Surprise! It's in the moist potato bread.

PREP: 20 minutes **BAKE:** 1 hour **STAND:** 15 minutes

INGREDIENTS

2	eggs, beaten
2/3	cup seasoned fine dry bread crumbs
1	large onion, finely chopped (1 cup)
2	medium tomatoes, seeded and chopped (1 1/3 cups)
1/2	cup raisins
1/2	tsp. salt
1/4	tsp. ground cloves
1/8	tsp. ground black pepper
1 1/2	lb. lean ground beef or 12 oz. *each* lean ground beef and lean ground pork
1/3	cup ketchup
3	Tbsp. packed brown sugar
1/3	cup mayonnaise or salad dressing
1	Tbsp. prepared horseradish
12	slices potato bread

PREPARATION

1. Preheat oven to 350°F. In a medium bowl combine eggs, bread crumbs, onion, tomato, raisins, salt, cloves, and pepper. Add meat; mix well. Lightly pat meat mixture into a 9×5×3-inch loaf pan.
2. Bake for 1 to 1 1/4 hours or until internal temperature registers 160°F. Spoon off fat. In a bowl combine ketchup and brown sugar; spread over meat. Bake 5 minutes more. Let stand 15 minutes. Using two spatulas, lift meat loaf from pan to a cutting board. Cut into 12 slices.
3. Stir together mayonnaise and horseradish. Spread mayonnaise mixture on potato bread. Top bread with 2 meat loaf slices and a bread slice. Makes 6 servings.

EACH SERVING: *576 cal., 24 g fat (7 g sat. fat), 146 mg chol., 1,171 mg sodium, 60 g carbo., 3 g fiber, 29 g pro. Daily Values: 11% vit. A, 17% vit. C, 13% calcium, 28% iron.*

SIRLOIN STROGANOFF

To easily slice beef into thin strips, partially freeze it beforehand.

PREP: 20 minutes **COOK:** 20 minutes

INGREDIENTS

1	20-oz. pkg. refrigerated red potato wedges
1	large onion, chopped (1 cup)
3	cloves garlic, minced
2	Tbsp. butter
12	to 16 oz. boneless beef sirloin steak, thinly sliced into bite-size strips
4	small apples, halved and, if desired, cored (or 2 large apples, quartered)
1	cup apple juice
1	8-oz. carton dairy sour cream
1/4	tsp. salt
1/4	tsp. ground black pepper

PREPARATION

1. In an extra-large skillet cook potato wedges, onion, and garlic in hot butter over medium-high heat for 8 minutes or until nearly tender. Stir in meat. Cook and stir for 3 minutes more or until meat is desired doneness; transfer meat and potatoes to a serving plate. Cover; keep warm.
2. In same skillet cook apples, cut sides down, in drippings for 2 minutes or until browned. Stir in apple juice. Bring to boiling; reduce heat. Simmer, covered, for 6 to 8 minutes or until tender; remove from skillet with a slotted spoon to plate with meat and potatoes. Cover; keep warm.
3. Remove skillet from heat. For sauce, whisk sour cream, salt, and pepper into juices in skillet until smooth. Spoon sauce over steak, potatoes, and apples. Makes 4 servings.

EACH SERVING: *538 cal., 25 g fat (14 g sat. fat), 82 mg chol., 359 mg sodium, 51 g carbo., 5 g fiber, 22 g pro. Daily Values: 12% vit. A, 30% vit. C, 10% calcium, 15% iron.*

SPICY MEAT LOAF

Who says sandwiches are only for the second night of meat loaf? You'll want to serve this clove-spiced meat loaf warm from the oven between thick slices of potato bread.

Fresh difference

Chopped tomatoes and succulent raisins add juicy goodness— making for an extra-moist loaf.

SIRLOIN STROGANOFF
This skillet supper goes together in three easy steps. Reduce prep time by using refrigerated cut potatoes from the supermarket.

Fresh difference
Small apples are pan-sizzled until they're browned and caramelized, sealing in their fresh, unexpected flavor.

STEAK AND POTATO PIZZA

PREP: 20 minutes **BAKE:** 18 minutes

INGREDIENTS

2   medium potatoes, scrubbed and cut into 1-inch pieces
1   cup water
12   oz. beef ribeye steak, trimmed of fat and cut into 1-inch pieces
4   to 6 cloves garlic, minced
1   Tbsp. olive oil
1   13.8-oz. pkg. refrigerated pizza dough
1   8-oz. pkg. shredded pizza cheese
2   to 3 tsp. snipped fresh rosemary or 1 tsp. dried rosemary, crushed
⅓   cup small slivers red onion
      Cracked black pepper (optional)
      Kosher salt (optional)
      Olive oil (optional)

PREPARATION

1. Preheat oven to 425°F. In a large skillet combine potatoes and water. Bring to boiling; reduce heat. Simmer, covered, for 10 minutes or until tender; drain. Set aside. Wipe skillet. In same skillet cook steak and garlic in hot oil over medium-high heat for 4 to 5 minutes or until steak pieces are browned on outside; stir occasionally. Remove from heat; set aside.

2. Unroll pizza dough onto greased large baking sheet; press into 16×11-inch oval. Build up edges. Bake for 8 to 10 minutes or until golden; sprinkle with 1½ cups of the cheese. Add potatoes and beef. Add remaining cheese and rosemary.

3. Bake for 10 to 12 minutes or until cheese is melted. Sprinkle with onion. If desired, sprinkle with pepper and salt and drizzle with olive oil. Makes 4 servings.

EACH SERVING: *647 cal., 25 g fat (12 g sat. fat), 81 mg chol., 982 mg sodium, 60 g carbo., 3 g fiber, 43 g pro. Daily Values: 12% vit. A, 23% vit. C, 43% calcium, 23% iron.*

STEAK AND POTATO PIZZA
Assemble dinner in 20 minutes with quick-cooking ribeye steak and refrigerated pizza dough.
Fresh difference
The cheese goes on the bottom. On top, red onion pieces, cracked black pepper, a drizzle of olive oil, and a sprinkle of sea salt add zip.

Home for Dinner

These "eating out" favorites couldn't be simpler—or faster.

BY **NANCY WALL HOPKINS**
PHOTOGRAPHS BY **ANDY LYONS**
FOOD STYLING BY **JILL LUST**

READY IN
20
MINUTES

MEXICAN BEEF AND TORTILLAS

MEXICAN BEEF AND TORTILLAS

START TO FINISH: 20 minutes

INGREDIENTS

8 6-inch corn tortillas
1 17-oz. pkg. refrigerated beef pot roast with juices
1 14.5-oz. can diced tomatoes and green chiles, undrained
1 green sweet pepper, cut into strips
1 lime, cut into wedges
   Dairy sour cream (optional)
   Fresh cilantro sprigs (optional)

PREPARATION

1. Wrap tortillas in microwave-safe paper towels. Microwave on 100% power (high) for 45 to 60 seconds or until warm. Cover and set aside.
2. Microwave beef according to package directions. Meanwhile, place undrained tomatoes in a small saucepan; heat through.
3. Remove meat, reserving juices. Cut into slices. Serve on warmed tortillas with tomatoes and green pepper strips. Pass lime wedges and, if desired, sour cream and cilantro. Drizzle with reserved juices. Makes 4 servings.

EACH SERVING: *319 cal., 10 g fat (5 g sat. fat), 64 mg chol., 857 mg sodium, 34 g carbo., 5 g fiber, 19 g pro. Daily Values: 15% vit. A, 68% vit C, 7% calcium, 19% iron.*

CORN CHOWDER

START TO FINISH: 20 minutes

INGREDIENTS

1 8-oz. tub cream cheese with chives and onions
1 14.75-oz. can cream-style corn
2 cups milk
8 oz. smoked turkey breast, chopped
1 cup frozen peas
   Ground black pepper

PREPARATION

1. In a medium saucepan heat cream cheese over medium heat to soften; blend in corn and milk. Add turkey and peas; heat through. Season to taste with pepper. Makes 4 (1/2-cup) servings.

EACH SERVING: *397 cal., 23 g fat (15 g sat. fat), 88 mg chol., 1,159 mg sodium, 27 g carbo., 3 g fiber, 19 g pro. Daily Values: 34% vit. A, 15% vit. C, 23% calcium, 8% iron.*

CORN CHOWDER

FAST!

SHRIMP AVOCADO HOAGIES

START TO FINISH: 20 minutes

INGREDIENTS

1   10- to 12-oz. pkg. frozen peeled cooked shrimp, thawed
     and chopped
2   large avocados, seeded, peeled, and chopped
½   cup packaged shredded carrot
⅓   cup bottled coleslaw salad dressing
4   hoagie buns
     Lemon wedges (optional)

PREPARATION

1. In a large mixing bowl combine shrimp, avocado, carrot, and salad dressing.
2. Halve hoagie buns. Using a spoon, slightly hollow bottoms and tops of hoagie buns, leaving ½-inch shells. Discard excess bread. Toast buns.
3. Spoon shrimp mixture into hoagie buns. If desired, serve with lemon wedges. Makes 4 servings.

EACH SERVING: *560 cal., 24 g fat (4 g sat. fat), 144 mg chol., 825 mg sodium, 63 g carbo., 8 g fiber, 25 g pro. Daily Values: 52% vit. A, 16% vit. C, 13% calcium, 26% iron.*

SHRIMP AVOCADO HOAGIES

TILAPIA WITH GRAPE CHUTNEY

VEGETABLE CURRY

START TO FINISH: 20 minutes

INGREDIENTS

1   16-oz. pkg. frozen baby lima beans
½   cup water
1   15-oz. can tomato sauce with garlic and onion
1½ tsp. curry powder
2   8.8-oz. pouches cooked Spanish-style rice
¼   cup sliced green onion or snipped fresh cilantro
    Olive oil (optional)

PREPARATION

1. In a medium saucepan combine beans and water. Bring to boiling; reduce heat. Simmer, covered, for 5 minutes. Stir in tomato sauce and curry powder; return to boiling. Reduce heat. Simmer, covered, for 3 minutes.
2. Meanwhile, heat rice according to package directions. Spoon rice onto one side of 4 dinner plates; spoon bean mixture alongside rice. Sprinkle with onion. If desired, drizzle with oil. Makes 4 servings.

EACH SERVING: *385 cal., 3 g fat (0 g sat. fat), 0 mg chol., 939 mg sodium, 72 g carbo., 9 g fiber, 14 g pro. Daily Values: 14% vit. A, 27% vit. C, 8% calcium, 24% iron.*

TILAPIA WITH GRAPE CHUTNEY

START TO FINISH: 20 minutes

INGREDIENTS

4   4-oz. fresh or frozen skinless tilapia or sole fillets
    Salt and ground black pepper
2   Tbsp. cooking oil
1   cup seedless green grapes
½   cup tropical blend mixed dried fruit bits
⅓   cup sliced green onion
⅓   cup apricot spreadable fruit
    Cooked brown rice (optional)

PREPARATION

1. Thaw fish, if frozen. Rinse fish; pat dry with paper towels. Season with salt and pepper.
2. In a 12-inch skillet heat oil over medium-high heat; add fish. Cook for 3 to 4 minutes or until fish flakes easily when tested with a fork, turning once. Meanwhile, halve grapes.
3. Transfer fish to platter; keep warm. For grape mixture, add grapes, fruit bits, onion, and spreadable fruit to skillet; cook and stir for 2 minutes. Season to taste with salt and pepper. Serve grape mixture over fish. If desired, serve with rice. Makes 4 servings.

EACH SERVING: *305 cal., 9 g fat (1 g sat. fat), 57 mg chol., 208 mg sodium, 37 g carbo., 2 g fiber, 24 g pro. Daily Values: 10% vit. A, 10% vit. C, 3% calcium, 8% iron.*

VEGETABLE CURRY

Heartfelt Suppers

When it comes to matters of the heart, these recipes can keep yours in good shape.

BY **STEPHEN EXEL** PHOTOGRAPHS BY **ANDY LYONS** FOOD STYLING BY **JILL LUST**
RECIPES BY **LAURA MARZEN, R.D.**

SALMON WITH RED CABBAGE

FAST!

SALMON WITH RED CABBAGE

Salmon contains omega-3 fatty acids; red cabbage is rich in antioxidants. Both are important heart disease preventives.

PREP: 10 minutes **BROIL:** 4 to 6 minutes per ½-inch thickness

INGREDIENTS
4	5-oz. fresh or frozen skinless salmon fillets
¼	cup balsamic vinegar
¼	tsp. kosher or sea salt or ⅛ tsp. salt
¼	tsp. ground black pepper
¼	cup prepared basil pesto
6	cups coarsely shredded red cabbage
2	green onions, bias-sliced

PREPARATION
1. Thaw salmon, if frozen. Preheat broiler. Rinse salmon; pat dry with paper towels. Place salmon on the greased unheated rack of a broiler pan. Measure thickness of the salmon. Brush salmon with 1 tablespoon of the vinegar; sprinkle salmon with salt and pepper. Broil salmon 4 to 5 inches from the heat for 4 to 6 minutes per ½-inch thickness or until the salmon flakes easily with a fork.
2. Meanwhile, in a bowl whisk together the remaining vinegar and pesto until combined. Remove 2 tablespoons pesto mixture. Add cabbage to pesto mixture in bowl; toss to coat.
3. To serve, divide cabbage mixture among 4 plates; top with salmon. Drizzle with reserved pesto mixture. Sprinkle with green onion slices. Makes 4 servings.

EACH SERVING: *327 cal., 16 g fat (3 g sat. fat), 83 mg chol., 354 mg sodium, 14 g carbo., 3 g fiber, 31 g pro. Daily Values: 27% vit. A, 100% vit. C, 12% calcium, 12% iron.*

FAST! **LOW FAT**

SOUTHWEST PORK SALSA STEW

Edamame (sweet soybeans) are full of fiber, which lowers cholesterol levels. Tomato paste contains high amounts of the heart-healthy phytochemical lycopene.

START TO FINISH: 25 minutes

INGREDIENTS

	Nonstick cooking spray
12	oz. boneless pork loin or sirloin, trimmed of fat and cut into bite-size strips
1	14-oz. can reduced-sodium chicken broth
1	6-oz. can no-salt-added tomato paste
½	cup bottled cilantro-flavor salsa or basic salsa
½	tsp. ground cumin
1	medium zucchini, halved lengthwise and thinly sliced (2 cups)
1	cup frozen sweet soybeans (edamame) or baby lima beans
1	small mango, pitted, peeled, and chopped (about ½ cup)

PREPARATION

1. Lightly coat a large saucepan with cooking spray. Preheat over medium-high heat. Add pork to hot pan; cook and stir for 2 minutes or until browned.

2. Add broth, tomato paste, salsa, and cumin; stir until combined. Stir in zucchini and soybeans. Bring to boiling; reduce heat. Simmer, covered, for 10 minutes or until vegetables are tender. Top with mango. Makes 4 servings.

EACH SERVING: *243 cal., 7 g fat (2 g sat. fat), 47 mg chol., 594 mg sodium, 19 g carbo., 6 g fiber, 26 g pro. Daily Values: 31% vit. A, 19% vit. C, 8% calcium, 17% iron.*

TEST KITCHEN TIP: In place of cilantro-flavor salsa, use basic salsa and stir in 2 tablespoons snipped fresh cilantro. In place of fresh mango, use refrigerated mango slices, rinsed, drained, and chopped; or use frozen chopped mango, thawed.

FAST! **LOW FAT**

CHICKEN WITH PRETZELS AND COUSCOUS

Peanuts have a hefty amount of vitamin E and omega-3 fats, which help keep LDL (bad) cholesterol low.

PREP: 15 minutes **BAKE:** 10 minutes

INGREDIENTS

1	cup pretzel sticks
⅔	cup unsalted peanuts
¼	to ½ tsp. crushed red pepper (optional)
½	cup refrigerated or frozen egg product, thawed
1	14- to 16-oz. pkg. chicken breast tenderloins
½	cup reduced-sodium chicken broth
1	16-oz. pkg. frozen sweet peppers and onion stir-fry vegetables
½	cup uncooked couscous
2	Tbsp. seasoned rice vinegar
1	Tbsp. canola oil
1	recipe Dipping Sauce

PREPARATION

1. Preheat oven to 425°F. Line a 15×10×1-inch baking pan with foil; coat with *nonstick cooking spray*; set pan aside. Place pretzels, ½ cup of the peanuts, and, if desired, red pepper in a food processor. Cover; process until coarsely ground. Transfer to a resealable plastic bag.

2. Place egg product in a shallow dish. Dip chicken tenderloins into egg product. Allowing excess egg product to drip off, transfer tenderloins, half at a time, to bag with pretzel mixture. Seal bag; turn to coat chicken pieces. Arrange chicken in prepared pan. Bake chicken for 10 to 15 minutes or until no longer pink (170°F).

3. Meanwhile, in a saucepan combine broth and stir-fry vegetables. Bring to boiling. Stir in couscous; remove from heat. Cover; let stand for 5 minutes. Chop remaining peanuts. Stir peanuts, rice vinegar, and oil into couscous mixture. Serve couscous mixture with chicken and Dipping Sauce. Makes 4 servings.

DIPPING SAUCE: In a bowl combine ⅓ cup plain yogurt, 2 tablespoons yellow mustard, and 2 teaspoons honey.

EACH SERVING: *335 cal., 12 g fat (2 g sat. fat), 39 mg chol., 369 mg sodium, 31 g carbo., 4 g fiber, 26 g pro. Daily Values: 14% vit. A, 46% vit. C, 5% calcium, 12% iron.*

CHICKEN WITH PRETZELS AND COUSCOUS

Cookie Break

Crisp, casual nibbles for grown-up taste buds

BY **RICHARD SWEARINGER**
PHOTOGRAPHS BY **ANDY LYONS**
FOOD STYLING BY **JILL LUST**

MOCHA TWISTS

MOCHA TWISTS

PREP: 15 minutes BAKE: 8 minutes per batch

INGREDIENTS

1   cup butter, softened
⅔   cup sugar
3   Tbsp. unsweetened cocoa powder
1   tsp. instant coffee crystals
¾   tsp. baking powder
¼   tsp. salt
1   egg
1   tsp. vanilla
2¼ cups all-purpose flour
1   recipe Cocoa Glaze

PREPARATION

1. In a large mixing bowl beat butter with mixer on medium to high speed for 30 seconds. Add sugar, cocoa powder, coffee crystals, baking powder, and salt; beat until combined. Beat in egg and vanilla. Beat in as much flour as you can with mixer. Using a wooden spoon, stir in remaining flour. Divide dough in half; wrap. Chill dough for 1 to 2 hours or until easy to handle.
2. Preheat oven to 375°F. Divide each dough half into 24 pieces. On a lightly floured surface, roll each dough piece into a 6-inch rope. Twist 2 ropes together; pinch ends to seal. Place ropes 2 inches apart on ungreased cookie sheets. Bake about 8 minutes or until edges are firm. Cool on cookie sheets for 5 minutes. Transfer to wire racks; cool completely.
3. Dip one end of each twist in Cocoa Glaze, allowing excess to drip off. Place on waxed paper until set. Makes 24 twists.
COCOA GLAZE: In a bowl combine 2 cups powdered sugar, 1 tablespoon unsweetened cocoa powder, and enough milk (about 3 tablespoons) to make glazing consistency. Makes ¾ cup.

EACH TWIST: *180 cal., 8 g fat (5 g sat. fat), 29 mg chol., 90 mg sodium, 25 g carbo., 0 g fiber, 2 g pro. Daily Values: 5% vit. A, 2% calcium, 4% iron.*

APRICOT-SAGE COOKIES

PREP: 30 minutes BAKE: 10 minutes per batch

INGREDIENTS

1¾ cups all-purpose flour
⅓   cup sugar
¼   cup yellow cornmeal
½   cup butter
2   Tbsp. snipped fresh sage or 2 tsp. dried sage
3   Tbsp. milk
     Apricot spreadable fruit

PREPARATION

1. Preheat oven to 375°F. In a bowl stir together flour, sugar, and cornmeal. Using a pastry blender, cut in butter until mixture resembles fine crumbs. Stir in sage. Add milk. Stir with a fork to combine; form into a ball. Knead until smooth; divide in half.
2. On a lightly floured surface, roll half of the dough at a time to ¼-inch thickness. Using a 2-inch round cookie cutter, cut out the dough.
3. Place cutouts 1 inch apart on ungreased cookie sheet. Bake about 10 minutes or until edges are firm and bottoms are very lightly browned. Transfer cookies to a wire rack. Cool.
4. Spread bottoms of half of the cookies with spreadable fruit. Top with remaining cookies. Makes 20 sandwich cookies.
TO STORE: Place in layers separated by waxed paper in an airtight container; cover. Store at room temperature for up to 3 days. Or freeze unfilled cookies up to 3 months. Thaw cookies; fill with spreadable fruit.

EACH COOKIE: *123 cal., 5 g fat (3 g sat. fat), 12 mg chol., 35 mg sodium, 19 g carbo., 0 g fiber, 1 g pro. Daily Values: 4% vit. A, 1% calcium, 3% iron.*

APRICOT-SAGE COOKIES

PEANUT MUNCHIES

PEANUT MUNCHIES

PREP: 35 minutes BAKE: 8 minutes per batch

INGREDIENTS

1½   cups all-purpose flour
½   cup unsweetened cocoa powder
½   tsp. baking soda
½   cup butter, softened
½   cup granulated sugar
½   cup packed brown sugar
¾   cup peanut butter
1   egg
1   Tbsp. milk
1   tsp. vanilla
¾   cup powdered sugar
2   Tbsp. granulated sugar

PREPARATION

1. In a medium bowl stir together flour, cocoa powder, and baking soda; set aside.

2. In a large mixing bowl combine butter, the ½ cup granulated sugar, the brown sugar, and ¼ cup of the peanut butter; beat with a mixer until combined. Add egg, milk, and vanilla; beat well. Beat in as much of the flour mixture as you can with the mixer. Using a wooden spoon, stir in any remaining flour mixture. Shape dough into 32 balls, each about 1¼ inches in diameter. Set aside.

3. For filling, in a bowl combine powdered sugar and the remaining ½ cup peanut butter. Beat with a mixer until smooth; knead by hand if necessary. Shape into 32 balls.

4. Preheat oven to 350°F. On work surface, flatten a chocolate dough ball; top with peanut butter ball. Shape flattened dough over peanut butter ball, completely covering peanut butter ball; reshape into ball. Repeat with remaining balls.

5. Place balls 2 inches apart on cookie sheet. Flatten with bottom of glass dipped in the 2 tablespoons granulated sugar. Bake about 8 minutes. Let stand for 1 minute. Transfer to wire racks; cool. Makes 32 cookies.

EACH COOKIE: *127 cal., 6 g fat (3 g sat. fat), 14 mg chol., 72 mg sodium, 16 g carbo., 1 g fiber, 3 g pro. Daily Values: 2% vit. A, 1% calcium, 2% iron.*

GINGER SQUARES

PREP: 25 minutes   FREEZE: 30 minutes   BAKE: 8 minutes per batch

INGREDIENTS

1/3   cup molasses
1/3   cup butter
2   cups all-purpose flour
1/3   cup packed brown sugar
1½   tsp. ground ginger
½   tsp. baking soda
½   tsp. ground cinnamon
¼   tsp. salt
¼   tsp. ground black pepper (optional)
⅛   tsp. ground cloves
1   egg, lightly beaten
      Powdered sugar (optional)

PREPARATION

1. In a saucepan combine molasses and butter. Cook and stir over low heat until butter is melted; remove from heat. Pour into a large bowl; cool to room temperature.
2. In a second bowl stir together flour, brown sugar, ginger, baking soda, cinnamon, salt, pepper (if desired), and cloves. Set aside.
3. Stir egg into cooled molasses mixture. Stir in flour mixture until combined. Divide dough in half. On waxed paper, shape each dough half into a 1½-inch-thick square log, about 5½ inches long. Wrap; chill in freezer about 30 minutes or until dough is firm enough to slice.
4. Preheat oven to 375°F. Slice logs into ⅛-inch slices, reshaping logs as necessary. Place 1 inch apart on ungreased cookie sheets. Prick each slice several times with a fork. Bake for 8 to 10 minutes or until edges are firm and lightly browned. Transfer to wire racks; cool completely. If desired, sprinkle with powdered sugar. Makes about 48 cookies.

EACH COOKIE: *44 cal., 1 g fat (1 g sat. fat), 8 mg chol., 37 mg sodium, 7 g carbo., 0 g fiber, 1 g pro. Daily Values: 1% vit. A, 1% calcium, 2% iron.*

GINGER SQUARES

Snap to It!

Inside the edible pods of **sugar snap peas** hide tender buttons of sweet flavor. Snatch up these crunchy delicate treats in spring when they're freshest and most affordable. Try them steamed, sauteed, stir-fried, or raw. They're a healthful choice: One-half cup of pea pods has only 35 calories and is loaded with iron and vitamins A and C. Choose crisp, plump, bright green pods that are tightly closed. Store pods for 4 to 7 days in a perforated bag in the refrigerator.

FAST! **LOW FAT**

LEMONY SUGAR SNAP PEA STIR-FRY

Don't confuse sugar snap peas with their cousin—flat, less mature snow peas—although they can be used interchangeably.

START TO FINISH: 20 minutes

INGREDIENTS

1	to 2 Tbsp. olive oil
¼	lemon, cut into thin slices
2½	cups sugar snap peas
1	leek, sliced
1	Tbsp. snipped fresh dill (optional)
	Salt and ground black pepper

PREPARATION

1. In a large skillet heat oil over medium-high heat. Add lemon slices; cook 4 minutes, turning once. Remove lemon; set aside. Add pea pods and leek to skillet; stir-fry for 3 to 4 minutes or until pea pods are crisp-tender. Stir in reserved lemon slices and, if desired, dill. Season to taste with salt and pepper. Makes 4 servings.

EACH SERVING: *73 cal., 3 g fat (0 g sat. fat), 0 mg chol., 87 mg sodium, 10 g carbo., 3 g fiber, 2 g pro. Daily Values: 9% vit. A, 21% vit. C, 6% calcium, 5% iron.*

TEST KITCHEN TIP

To flash-cool cooked sugar snap pea pods, immerse them in ice water immediately after draining.

Snappy Ways to Serve Sugar Snap Peas

1. Toss cooked pods, chopped tomato, snipped parsley, and olive oil with cooked pasta. Sprinkle with salt, black pepper, and Parmesan cheese.

2. Stir chopped raw pea pods and crushed garlic into spinach dip.

3. Sprinkle steamed pods with crumbled blue cheese and a dash of crushed red pepper.

4. Toss chilled cooked pods, cucumber slices, and slivered sweet onion with ranch dressing.

BY **STEPHEN EXEL**
PHOTOGRAPHS BY **ANDY LYONS**
FOOD STYLING BY **JILL LUST**

1
FRUIT AND CHEESE
White cheddar cheese, sliced fresh pear

2
BRUNCH STARTER
Sliced cucumber, smoked salmon, sour cream, chives

3
GARDEN SNACK
Herbed cheese spread, fresh basil, cherry tomatoes

One-Bite Wonders
Delicious ideas for dressing up everyday snack crackers

4
BREAKFAST TO GO
Cooked bacon, hard-cooked egg wedge, ground black pepper

5
KID PLEASER
Peanut butter, banana slices, fudge sauce

6
MEDITERRANEAN TREAT
Mixed olive tapenade, capers, fresh parsley, chopped pimiento

7
COMPANY COMING
Horseradish spread, blue cheese, roast beef slices, fresh dill

8
DELI SPECIAL
Honey mustard, smoked turkey, fruit preserves

9
MEXICAN SPICE
Black bean spread, avocado slices, fresh tomato salsa

10
SWEET SURPRISE
Vanilla frosting, fresh raspberry, shaved milk chocolate

BHG BASICS

A small dab of butter spread on each cracker adds flavor—and helps hold toppers in place.

BY **NANCY WALL HOPKINS** PHOTOGRAPHS BY **ANDY LYONS** FOOD STYLING BY **JILL LUST**

APRIL

SPRING IS BACK—AND SO IS
GREEN! PLUNDER THE MARKETS'
FRESHEST INGREDIENTS FOR
THESE BEST-OF-SEASON DISHES.

**BAKED MEDITERRANEAN COD
AND ASPARAGUS**
page 76

Spring Greens

CHICKEN-CHERVIL SAUTE
page 79

TRIPLE-MANGO CHICKEN
page 87

MARKETS ABOUND WITH APRIL'S MOST SCRUMPTIOUS COLOR. TIME TO COOK UP SOME…

spring greens

This bouquet of seasonal offerings includes baby bok choy, dill, basil, asparagus, chervil, and Italian (flat-leaf) parsley—ingredients called for in the recipes that follow. Check out our buying guide on page 75.

BY **STEPHEN EXEL** PHOTOGRAPHS BY **IAIN BAGWELL** FOOD STYLING BY **SUSAN BROWN DRAUDT** PROP STYLING BY **KAREN JOHNSON**

KNOW YOUR GREENS Key ingredients for a green spring meal

1. KEY LIMES Small, round limes native to Florida. Aromatic and juicy. Store at room temperature until ripe, then refrigerate for up to 2 weeks.

2. PUNGENT HERBS Full-flavor herbs such as mint, rosemary, sage, and oregano. Refrigerate standing in water and covered with a plastic bag.

3. BABY BOK CHOY Crisp, juicy baby bok choy can be stir-fried, steamed, or braised. Look for crisp stalks and bright green leaves.

4. BROCCOLINI A cross between broccoli and Chinese kale. Steam or saute. Look for bright green stalks and closed buds.

5. OLIVE OIL Green-hued extra virgin olive oil is pressed from young ripened olives. Fruitier and less acidic than yellow olive oil.

6. GREEN APPLES Most green apples are "all-purpose." Granny Smiths are tart and supercrisp. Choose fruit with smooth, unblemished skin.

7. FENNEL A sweet vegetable with a white bulb, celerylike stalks, and feathery leaves. The bulb and fronds are edible. Select fennel with firm, fragrant, rounded bulbs.

8. GREEN GRAPES Olive shape, light, sweet, seedless. Refrigerate in a plastic bag; wash thoroughly before eating.

9. SUGAR SNAP PEAS Eat sugar snap peas raw or slightly steamed or sauteed to retain their crispness and flavor. Refrigerate in a plastic bag for up to 3 days

10. CUCUMBER Choose cucumbers with smooth, bright skin. Refrigerate in a plastic bag for up to 10 days; wash before using.

11. ASPARAGUS The tenderest asparagus makes its appearance in spring. Choose straight, firm stalks with purple-tinged tips. Store upright in 1 inch of water.

12. AROMATIC HERBS Delicate herbs such as tarragon, thyme, and chervil. Refrigerate standing in water, covered with a plastic bag.

FAST! **LOW FAT**

SPRING WALDORF SALAD

START TO FINISH: 20 minutes

INGREDIENTS

2   medium Granny Smith apples, cored and cut into wedges
1   Tbsp. lemon juice
1   head Boston lettuce, separated into leaves
2   heads green and/or red Belgian endive, separated into leaves
¾   cup seedless green grapes, halved
¼   cup Marcona almonds or blanched whole almonds, toasted
1   recipe Lemon Dressing

PREPARATION

1. In a medium bowl toss apples with lemon juice. On salad plates arrange Boston lettuce, endive, apple wedges, grapes, and almonds. Spoon on Lemon Dressing. Makes 6 side-dish servings.
LEMON DRESSING: In a small bowl stir together one 6-ounce container lemon low-fat yogurt, 1 tablespoon cider vinegar, ¼ teaspoon salt, 1 tablespoon snipped fresh dill or ¼ teaspoon dried dill, and ¼ teaspoon ground black pepper until well combined. Makes ⅔ cup.

EACH SERVING: 112 cal., 4 g fat (0 g sat. fat), 1 mg chol., 120 mg sodium, 19 g carbo., 2 g fiber, 4 g pro. Daily Values: 32% vit. A, 15% vit. C, 8% calcium, 6% iron.

SPRING WALDORF SALAD

FAST! **LOW FAT**

BAKED MEDITERRANEAN COD AND ASPARAGUS

PREP: 15 minutes   **BAKE:** 12 minutes

INGREDIENTS

2   Tbsp. olive oil
4   cod fillets, skinned (1½ lb.)
1   lb. fresh asparagus spears, trimmed
1   recipe Olive Relish (below)

PREPARATION

1. Preheat oven to 475°F. Lightly coat a 15×10×1-inch baking pan with some of the olive oil. On one side of pan arrange cod fillets, turning under any thin portions. Brush fish with 1 teaspoon of the remaining olive oil. Sprinkle with *salt* and *ground black pepper*. Bake for 5 minutes. Place asparagus in opposite side of pan; brush with remaining olive oil; sprinkle with *salt* and *ground black pepper*.
2. Bake 7 to 10 minutes more or until cod flakes easily when tested with a fork. Serve fish with Olive Relish and asparagus. Makes 4 servings.

EACH SERVING (WITH OLIVE RELISH): 258 cal., 12 g fat (2 g sat. fat), 73 mg chol., 720 mg sodium, 6 g carbo., 3 g fiber, 32 g pro. Daily Values: 21% vit. A, 27% vit. C, 7% calcium, 14% iron.

FAST!

OLIVE RELISH

START TO FINISH: 15 minutes

INGREDIENTS

¾   cup whole pimiento-stuffed green olives, coarsely chopped
⅓   cup chopped onion
¼   cup snipped fresh Italian (flat-leaf) parsley
2   Tbsp. capers, drained
1   small fresh jalapeño chile pepper, seeded and chopped*
1   Tbsp. white wine vinegar
    Ground black pepper

PREPARATION

1. In a bowl combine all ingredients, except black pepper. Season to taste with black pepper. Serve with Baked Mediterranean Cod and Asparagus (recipe, above). Makes 4 (⅓-cup) servings.

*NOTE: Because hot chile peppers, such as jalapeños, contain volatile oils that can burn your skin and eyes, avoid direct contact with chiles as much as possible. When working with chile peppers, wear plastic or rubber gloves. If your bare hands do touch the chile peppers, wash your hands well with soap and water.

EACH SERVING: 46 cal., 4 g fat (1 g sat. fat), 0 mg chol., 500 mg sodium, 3 g carbo., 1 g fiber, 1 g pro. Daily Values: 10% vit. A, 17% vit. C, 2% calcium, 3% iron.

Baked Mediterranean Cod and Asparagus

Team this lean, firm saltwater white fish with tender asparagus spears and top with a tangy chopped green olive and caper relish. The cod and asparagus cook together in only 12 minutes.

Spring is the green light to try fresh produce with bright flavors.

CHICKEN-CHERVIL SAUTE AND SPINACH PASTA

Think homemade pasta is a chore? Think again. These gnocchi-like pasta balls come together in about 5 minutes in the food processor. Add them to chicken and mushrooms cooked in a flavorful broth accented with chervil, a close cousin to parsley with a subtle anise flavor.

CHICKEN-CHERVIL SAUTE

PREP: 15 minutes **MARINATE:** 30 minutes **COOK:** 17 minutes

INGREDIENTS

6	medium skinless, boneless chicken breast halves (about 1¾ lb.)
½	cup Italian oil-and-vinegar dressing
1	tsp. green peppercorns, coarsely crushed (optional)
2	to 3 Tbsp. olive oil
8	oz. baby portobello mushrooms, coarsely chopped
2¼	cups chicken broth
¼	cup torn fresh chervil or fresh Italian (flat-leaf) parsley
1	recipe Spinach Pasta (right)

PREPARATION

1. Place chicken in a resealable plastic bag; add dressing. Seal bag. Turn to coat. Marinate in the refrigerator for 30 minutes.
2. Start water for pasta (Spinach Pasta, Step 3, right). Remove chicken from bag; reserve marinade. If desired, sprinkle chicken with green peppercorns. In a large skillet cook chicken in hot oil over medium heat for 12 to 15 minutes or until chicken is no longer pink (170°F), turning once. Remove chicken; cover and keep warm. Add mushrooms to skillet; cook for 5 minutes. Add broth and reserved marinade to skillet. Bring to boiling. Stir in half of the chervil. Remove from heat; cover and keep warm. Cook Spinach Pasta (Step 3, right).
3. To serve, place broth and Spinach Pasta in a serving bowl; top with chicken and mushrooms. Sprinkle with remaining chervil. Makes 6 servings.

EACH SERVING (WITH SPINACH PASTA): *547 cal., 24 g total fat (4 g sat. fat), 148 mg chol., 698 mg sodium, 42 g carbo., 3 g fiber, 40 g pro. Daily Values: 77% vit. A, 26% vit. C, 7% calcium, 28% iron.*

SPINACH PASTA

PREP: 40 minutes **STAND:** 20 minutes **COOK:** 2 minutes

INGREDIENTS

8	oz. fresh spinach, washed and destemmed
2⅓	cups all-purpose flour
2	large eggs, lightly beaten
½	tsp. salt
2	Tbsp. olive oil
1	to 3 Tbsp. water

PREPARATION

1. In a 6-quart Dutch oven bring ½ inch of water to boiling. Add spinach; cover. Cook for 3 minutes. Drain; squeeze dry. Place in a food processor; puree. Add flour, eggs, and salt. Process until mixture forms fine crumbs. With processor running slowly pour 1 tablespoon of the oil and enough of the water through feed tube to form a dough ball. Transfer to a lightly floured surface. Cover; let rest 3 minutes. Divide into 4 portions.
2. On a floured work surface roll dough into ½-inch-wide logs. Slice into 1-inch pieces. Roll each piece into a ball. Slightly press balls over fork tines to make grooves on one side. Cover; let stand 20 minutes.
3. In a 6-quart pot bring 3 quarts salted water and the remaining 1 tablespoon olive oil to boiling. Add pasta. Reduce heat slightly. Boil, uncovered, for 2 to 3 minutes or until pasta floats to top, stirring occasionally. Drain. Serve with Chicken-Chervil Saute (left). Makes 6 servings.

EACH SERVING PASTA: *250 cal., 7 g total fat (1 g sat. fat), 71 mg chol., 248 mg sodium, 39 g carbo., 2 g fiber, 8 g pro. Daily Values: 73% vit. A, 18% vit. C, 5% calcium, 20% iron.*

LOW FAT

HEARTY GARLIC AND SNAP PEA SOUP

PREP: 30 minutes COOK: 19 minutes

INGREDIENTS

4	cloves garlic or 1 to 2 bulbs spring garlic, chopped
2	Tbsp. olive oil
¼	cup chopped onion
1	lb. Yukon gold potatoes, quartered
2	14-oz. cans reduced-sodium chicken broth
1¾	cups water
1	medium fennel bulb, thinly slivered (fronds reserved)
1½	cups sugar snap peas, trimmed
½	tsp. salt
¼	tsp. ground black pepper
1	Tbsp. reserved snipped fresh fennel fronds
	Plain yogurt (optional)
	Olive oil (optional)

PREPARATION

1. In a large saucepan cook garlic in 2 tablespoons hot oil over medium heat for 1 minute. Add onion and cook until tender. Add potatoes, chicken broth, and water. Bring to boiling; reduce heat. Cook, covered, for 15 to 18 minutes or until potatoes are tender. Cool soup slightly.

2. Using a food processor or blender, puree soup in batches until smooth. Return to saucepan. Add fennel and peas. Bring to boiling; reduce heat. Simmer, uncovered, for 3 minutes.

3. Stir in salt and pepper. Top with fennel fronds. If desired, spoon on yogurt and drizzle with olive oil. Makes 8 side-dish servings or 4 main-dish servings.

EACH SERVING: *101 cal., 3 g fat (0 g sat. fat), 0 mg chol., 403 mg sodium, 15 g carbo., 3 g fiber, 3 g pro. Daily Values: 1% vit. A, 28% vit. C, 4% calcium, 5% iron.*

PISTACHIO-CHIVE CRISPS

PREP: 30 minutes BAKE: 20 minutes

INGREDIENTS

1	cup all-purpose flour
⅓	cup snipped fresh chives
½	tsp. salt
⅛	tsp. ground black pepper
3	Tbsp. water
3	Tbsp. olive oil
2	Tbsp. chopped pistachios or almonds
2	Tbsp. grated Parmesan cheese
1	recipe Caper Mustard

PREPARATION

1. Preheat oven to 325°F. In a medium bowl combine flour, chives, salt, and pepper. In another bowl combine water and oil. Drizzle oil mixture into flour mixture, stirring constantly (dough will appear dry but will come together when gently worked with hands). Form dough into a ball.

2. On a lightly floured surface roll dough into a 12×7½-inch rectangle. Prick all over with a fork. Sprinkle with pistachios and cheese; press in nuts. Using a pizza cutter, cut dough into 3×1½-inch rectangles. Transfer to a large ungreased baking sheet.

3. Bake for 20 to 23 minutes or until crisps begin to brown. Transfer the crisps to wire racks; cool. Serve crisps with Caper Mustard. Makes 20 crisps.

CAPER MUSTARD: In a small bowl combine 1 tablespoon Dijon-style mustard; 1 tablespoon capers, drained; and 1 tablespoon snipped chives.

EACH CRISP: *51 cal., 3 g total fat (1 g sat. fat), 1 mg chol., 151 mg sodium, 5 g carbo., 0 g fiber, 1 g pro. Daily Values: 1% vit. A, 1% vit. C, 1% calcium, 2% iron.*

HEARTY GARLIC AND SNAP PEA SOUP

A hint of spring garlic, crunchy-sweet sugar snap peas, and fennel combine in this potato-based soup. Mild-flavor spring garlic, or green garlic, resembles a green onion and is in markets in April and May.

Pistachio-Chive Crisps

Snips of chives are scattered through these easy-to-make pistachio-laden crackers. Alongside serve tart green apple slices and pungent Dijon mustard with capers and herbs.

FAST!

SHARP AND SWEET GREEN SALAD

START TO FINISH: 20 minutes

INGREDIENTS

1   recipe Lime-Pepper Dressing
4   cups torn butterhead (Boston or Bibb) lettuce
1   cup fresh watercress sprigs
¾   cup fresh cilantro sprigs
1   small or ½ of a large cucumber, cut into bite-size sticks
1   to 2 baby bok choy, separated into leaves, or 2 stalks bok choy, cut into bite-size sticks
2   kiwifruits, peeled, halved, and sliced, or 1 cup sliced fresh strawberries (optional)

PREPARATION

1. Prepare Lime-Pepper Dressing; set aside. Rinse lettuce, watercress, and cilantro in cold water; pat dry with paper towels.
2. In a large bowl combine rinsed greens, cucumber, bok choy, and, if desired, kiwi. Drizzle with Lime-Pepper Dressing; toss to coat. Serve immediately. Makes 6 side-dish servings.
LIME-PEPPER DRESSING: In a screw-top jar combine ⅓ cup rice vinegar; half of a fresh Anaheim (¼ cup) or 1 jalapeño chile pepper, seeded and finely chopped (see Note, page 76); 3 tablespoons olive oil; and 1 teaspoon finely shredded lime peel. Add ½ teaspoon sugar, ¼ teaspoon salt, and ¼ teaspoon freshly ground black pepper. Cover; shake well. Refrigerate until ready to use. Stir in 1 to 2 tablespoons chopped fresh herb (cilantro, basil, mint, or parsley) before serving.

EACH SERVING: 104 cal., 7 g fat (1 g sat. fat), 0 mg chol., 200 mg sodium, 8 g carbo., 3 g fiber, 3 g pro. Daily Values: 170% vit. A, 146% vit. C, 18% calcium, 12% iron.

SHARP AND SWEET GREEN SALAD

Here's one big, delicious salad straight from the garden: butterhead lettuce, crunchy cucumbers, peppery watercress, baby bok choy, and—the surprise—sweet kiwi, drizzled with tart Lime-Pepper Dressing.

MINTY ROASTED LAMB CHOPS

A spring tradition, these lamb chops are freshened with a garlicky mint rub. In place of mashed potatoes, serve peas pureed with tarragon.

MINTY ROASTED LAMB CHOPS

PREP: 20 minutes **ROAST:** 17 minutes

INGREDIENTS

½	cup snipped fresh mint leaves
2	Tbsp. finely shredded lemon peel
2	cloves garlic, minced
1	tsp. sea salt or kosher salt
½	tsp. freshly ground black pepper
8	lamb rib or loin chops, cut 1 inch thick
2	Tbsp. olive oil
1	10-oz. pkg. frozen peas
¼	cup milk, half-and-half, or light cream
¼	tsp. sea salt or kosher salt
2	Tbsp. coarsely snipped fresh tarragon
	Melted butter (optional)
	Fresh herb sprigs (optional)
4	slices hearty bread, toasted (optional)

PREPARATION

1. Preheat oven to 450°F. In a bowl combine mint, lemon peel, garlic, the 1 teaspoon salt, and the pepper. Place chops on rack in shallow roasting pan. Brush both sides of chops with olive oil. Press mint mixture onto both sides of chops. Roast, uncovered, for 17 to 20 minutes or until desired doneness (145°F for medium rare or 160°F for medium).

2. Meanwhile, cook peas according to package directions. Drain. Place in food processor or blender. Add milk and ¼ teaspoon salt. Cover and process or blend until nearly smooth. Transfer to a bowl; stir in tarragon. If desired, drizzle peas with melted butter and top with fresh herb sprigs. Place chops on bread slices (if desired) alongside peas. Makes 4 servings.

EACH SERVING: *377 cal., 17 g fat (5 g sat. fat), 122 mg chol., 811 mg sodium, 12 g carbo., 3 g fiber, 43 g pro. Daily Values: 33% vit. A, 44% vit. C, 7% calcium, 38% iron.*

Spring Dinners

Fresh ingredients make these fast suppers shine.

BY **NANCY WALL HOPKINS**
PHOTOGRAPHS BY **ANDY LYONS**
FOOD STYLING BY **JILL LUST**
RECIPES BY **MARYELLYN KRANTZ**

READY IN
20
MINUTES

**SALMON WITH
MATZO CRUST**

SALMON WITH MATZO CRUST

START TO FINISH: 20 minutes

INGREDIENTS

1½	6-inch squares matzo (1½ oz.), broken up
2	Tbsp. snipped fresh dill or 1½ tsp. dried dillweed
½	tsp. salt
¼	tsp. ground black pepper
3	Tbsp. olive or cooking oil
4	4- to 5-oz. skinless salmon fillets, 1 inch thick
	Lemon wedges (optional)
	Fresh dill sprigs (optional)
	Steamed green beans (optional)

PREPARATION

1. Preheat oven to 450°F. In a blender or food processor combine matzo, dill, salt, and pepper. Cover; blend or process until mixture forms coarse crumbs. Transfer to a sheet of waxed paper or a shallow container.
2. Brush a shallow baking pan with oil. Brush fish with oil. Roll fish in matzo mixture; place in prepared pan. Drizzle with remaining oil.
3. Bake, uncovered, for 10 to 12 minutes or until fish flakes easily when tested with a fork. If desired, serve with lemon wedges, fresh dill sprigs, and steamed green beans. Makes 4 servings.

EACH SERVING: *340 cal, 23 g fat (4 g sat. fat), 67 mg chol., 358 mg sodium, 9 g carbo., 0 g fiber, 24 g pro. Daily Values: 1% vit. A, 7% vit. C, 2% calcium, 5% iron.*

FAST NIÇOISE SALAD

START TO FINISH: 20 minutes

INGREDIENTS

1	Tbsp. butter
2	cups refrigerated red potato wedges
6	cups packaged mixed salad greens
2	5-oz. pouches or cans lemon-pepper chunk light tuna
1	cup cherry tomatoes, halved
⅓	to ½ cup bottled roasted garlic vinaigrette salad dressing

PREPARATION

1. Melt 1 tablespoon butter over medium heat in a large skillet. Add potato wedges. Cover and cook about 15 minutes or until golden, stirring occasionally.
2. Meanwhile, place greens on 4 plates. Top with potatoes, tuna, and tomatoes. Drizzle with vinaigrette. Season with *salt* and *ground black pepper*. Makes 4 servings.

EACH SERVING: *269 cal., 11 g fat (1 g sat. fat), 31 mg chol., 426 mg sodium, 15 g carbo., 4 g fiber, 26 g pro. Daily Values: 16% vit. A, 17% vit. C, 2% calcium, 5% iron.*

FAST NIÇOISE SALAD

FAST!

HERBED STEAKS WITH HORSERADISH

START TO FINISH: 20 minutes

INGREDIENTS

2	12- to 14-oz. beef top loin steaks, cut 1 inch thick
2	Tbsp. prepared horseradish
1	Tbsp. Dijon-style mustard
2	tsp. snipped fresh Italian (flat-leaf) parsley
1	tsp. snipped fresh thyme
	Broiled cherry tomatoes (optional)
	Broiled sweet pepper strips (optional)
	Herbed mayonnaise (optional)

PREPARATION

1. Preheat broiler. Season steaks with *salt* and *ground black pepper*. Place on the unheated rack of a broiler pan. Broil 4 inches from the heat for 7 minutes. Meanwhile, combine horseradish, mustard, parsley, and thyme.

2. Turn steaks. Broil for 8 to 9 minutes more for medium. The last 1 minute of broiling, spread with horseradish mixture. If desired, serve with tomatoes, peppers, and mayonnaise. Makes 4 servings.

EACH SERVING: *284 cal., 15 g fat (6 g sat. fat), 84 mg chol., 351 mg sodium, 1 g carbo., 0 g fiber, 33 g pro. Daily Values: 1% vit. A, 5% vit. C, 3% calcium, 19% iron.*

HERBED STEAKS WITH HORSERADISH

TRIPLE-MANGO CHICKEN

VEGGIE-CHEESE SANDWICHES

START TO FINISH: 20 minutes

INGREDIENTS

- 8 ½-inch slices country French white bread
- 4 tsp. olive oil
- 2 Tbsp. honey mustard
- 4 oz. sliced cheddar cheese
- ½ cup thinly sliced cucumber
- ½ cup fresh spinach leaves
- ¼ cup thinly sliced red onion

PREPARATION

1. Brush one side of each bread slice with oil; spread other side with mustard. Top mustard side of 4 slices with cheese, cucumber, spinach, and onion. Top vegetables with remaining bread slices, mustard side down.

2. Preheat indoor electric grill. Place sandwiches on grill. If using covered grill, close lid. Grill sandwiches until bread is golden. For covered grill, allow 3 to 5 minutes. For uncovered grill, allow 6 to 8 minutes, turning once halfway through grilling. Serve immediately. Makes 4 servings.

EACH SERVING: *194 cal., 7 g fat (1 g sat. fat), 0 mg chol., 244 mg sodium, 22 g carbo., 1 g fiber, 10 g pro. Daily Values: 8% vit. A, 3% vit. C, 29% calcium, 15% iron.*

TRIPLE-MANGO CHICKEN

START TO FINISH: 20 minutes

INGREDIENTS

- 1 Tbsp. olive oil
- 4 small skinless, boneless chicken breast halves
- 1 mango, seeded, peeled, and cubed
- ½ cup mango-blend fruit drink
- ¼ cup mango chutney
- 2 medium zucchini, thinly sliced lengthwise
  Salt
  Crushed red pepper

PREPARATION

1. In a very large skillet heat oil over medium-high heat; reduce to medium. Add chicken. Cook for 6 minutes; turn. Add mango cubes, mango drink, and chutney. Cook for 4 to 6 minutes more or until chicken is no longer pink (170°F), stirring occasionally.

2. Meanwhile, place zucchini and ¼ cup water in a microwave-safe 2-quart square dish. Cover with vented plastic wrap. Microwave on 100% power (high) for 2 to 3 minutes, stirring once; drain. Place chicken on top of zucchini. Season with salt and crushed red pepper. Makes 4 servings.

EACH SERVING: *274 cal., 9 g fat (1 g sat. fat), 66 mg chol., 277 mg sodium, 22 g carbo., 2 g fiber, 28 g pro. Daily Values: 16% vit. A, 59% vit. C, 4% calcium, 8% iron.*

VEGGIE-CHEESE SANDWICHES

Primo Pasta

When it's made from whole grains, pasta has a rustic taste and firm texture. And these four delicious recipes help meet daily requirements for important nutrients.

BY **STEPHEN EXEL**

PHOTOGRAPHS BY **ANDY LYONS**

FOOD STYLING BY **JILL LUST**

RECIPES BY **LAURA MARZEN, R.D.**

PASTA SALAD WITH ORANGE DRESSING

LOW FAT

PASTA SALAD WITH ORANGE DRESSING

This recipe provides nearly 25 percent of daily iron needs. Vitamin C in the dressing helps your body absorb the iron.

PREP: 30 minutes **CHILL:** 2 hours

INGREDIENTS

6	oz. dried whole grain pasta, such as penne or bow tie (1½ cups)
1	15-oz. can black beans, rinsed and drained
1	cup chopped cooked chicken
½	of a large green sweet pepper, seeded and cut into bite-size strips
½	cup thin wedges of red onion
1	orange
1	8-oz. carton light dairy sour cream
¼	tsp. salt
¼	tsp. ground black pepper
	Milk
1½	cups lightly packed arugula leaves, coarsely shredded
3	Tbsp. snipped fresh cilantro

PREPARATION

1. Cook pasta according to package directions; drain. Rinse with cold water; drain again. Transfer to a large bowl. Add black beans, chicken, sweet pepper, and red onion; set aside.

2. Finely shred enough peel from the orange to get 1½ teaspoons. Place shredded peel in a small bowl; stir in sour cream, salt, and pepper. Juice orange. Add 3 tablespoons of the orange juice to sour cream mixture.

3. Add sour cream mixture to pasta mixture; toss to coat. Cover; refrigerate for 2 to 24 hours. Before serving, stir in enough milk (1 to 2 tablespoons) until salad reaches desired consistency. Stir in arugula and cilantro. Makes 4 servings.

EACH SERVING: *390 cal., 10 g fat (5 g sat. fat), 51 mg chol., 624 mg sodium, 57 g carbo., 9 g fiber, 23 g pro. Daily Values: 15% vit. A, 64% vit. C, 17% calcium, 24% iron.*

ASIAN NOODLE SLAW

Soba noodles, made from buckwheat, have a nutty flavor.
Find them in specialty or Asian markets.

START TO FINISH: 25 minutes

INGREDIENTS

6	oz. multigrain spaghetti or soba (buckwheat) noodles
⅓	cup peanut sauce
⅓	cup carrot juice
1	Tbsp. finely chopped, peeled fresh ginger
1	Tbsp. canola oil
1	16-oz. pkg. shredded broccoli (broccoli slaw mix)
¾	cup shredded carrot

PREPARATION

1. Cook pasta according to package directions; drain. Return to pan. Using kitchen scissors, snip pasta into small pieces. Cover; keep warm. In a small bowl whisk together peanut sauce and carrot juice; set aside.

2. In a wok or large nonstick skillet stir-fry ginger in hot oil over medium-high heat for 15 seconds. Add broccoli slaw and carrot. Cook for 1 minute, stirring constantly.

3. Add peanut sauce mixture to wok or skillet. Stir to coat vegetables. Cook and stir for 2 minutes more. Add pasta. Using tongs, toss to coat. Serve warm. Makes 4 servings.

BEEFY ASIAN NOODLE TOSS: Partially freeze 12 ounces boneless beef sirloin steak. Thinly slice beef across the grain into bite-size strips. Prepare stir-fry as above through Step 2. Remove vegetables from wok. Add beef strips to hot wok. Cook and stir for 2 to 3 minutes or until beef is brown. Continue as directed in Step 3, adding vegetables to wok with peanut sauce mixture.

EACH SERVING (WITHOUT BEEF): *285 cal., 7 g fat (1 g sat. fat),*
0 mg chol., 318 mg sodium, 45 g carbo., 7 g fiber, 12 g pro.
Daily Values: 219% vit. A, 166% vit. C, 9% calcium, 14% iron.

ASIAN NOODLE SLAW

CHICKEN CAESAR LASAGNA

CHICKEN CAESAR LASAGNA

Serve this recipe when you crave classic comfort food but want more nutrients and fiber than refined wheat pasta contains.

PREP: 35 minutes **BAKE:** 50 minutes **STAND:** 15 minutes

INGREDIENTS

9 dried whole wheat lasagna noodles
2 10-oz. containers refrigerated light Alfredo sauce
3 Tbsp. lemon juice
½ tsp. cracked black pepper
3 cups chopped cooked chicken breast*
1 10-oz. pkg. frozen chopped spinach, thawed and well drained
1 cup bottled roasted red sweet peppers, drained and chopped
   Nonstick cooking spray
¾ cup shredded Italian blend cheese

PREPARATION

1. Preheat oven to 325°F. Cook noodles according to package directions; drain. Rinse with cold water; drain again. Meanwhile, in a bowl combine Alfredo sauce, lemon juice, and black pepper. Stir in chicken, spinach, and red peppers.

2. Lightly coat a 3-quart rectangular baking dish with cooking spray. Arrange 3 noodles in bottom of dish. Top with one-third of the chicken mixture. Repeat layers twice. Cover; bake for 45 to 55 minutes or until heated through. Uncover; sprinkle with cheese. Bake, uncovered, for 5 minutes more or until cheese is melted. Let stand 15 minutes before serving. Makes 9 servings.

*NOTE: For chopped cooked chicken, season 2 pounds raw skinless, boneless chicken breast halves with ¼ teaspoon salt and ⅛ teaspoon ground black pepper. Heat 1 tablespoon olive oil in a large skillet over medium-high heat. Reduce heat to medium. Add chicken. Cook, uncovered, for 8 to 12 minutes or until no longer pink (170°F), turning once halfway through cooking. Cool chicken slightly before chopping.

EACH SERVING: *268 cal., 10 g fat (6 g sat. fat), 68 mg chol., 557 mg sodium, 20 g carbo., 2 g fiber, 24 g pro. Daily Values: 49% vit. A, 83% vit. C, 21% calcium, 8% iron.*

ORZO RISOTTO WITH ROASTED VEGETABLES

Whole grain orzo is full of flavor yet low in fat.

START TO FINISH: 45 minutes

INGREDIENTS

Nonstick cooking spray
½   of a 2-lb. butternut squash, peeled, seeded, and cut into ¾- to 1-inch cubes
⅛   tsp. ground black pepper
8   oz. button or cremini mushrooms, halved (3 cups)
1   large onion, cut into thin wedges
1   Tbsp. snipped fresh rosemary or oregano or 1 tsp. dried rosemary or oregano, crushed
1   Tbsp. olive oil
2   14-oz. cans reduced-sodium chicken broth
8   oz. whole grain orzo (1⅓ cups)
2   cloves garlic, minced
¼   cup chopped walnuts, toasted
¼   cup crumbled feta cheese (optional)

PREPARATION

1. Preheat oven to 425°F. Coat a 15×10×1-inch baking pan with cooking spray. Place squash pieces in pan. Sprinkle with pepper. Cover; bake for 10 minutes. Uncover; add mushrooms, onion, rosemary, and oil; toss. Roast, uncovered, for 15 to 20 minutes or until vegetables are tender and lightly browned; stir once or twice.
2. Meanwhile, in a saucepan bring broth to boiling; reduce heat. Cover; keep broth simmering. Coat a skillet with cooking spray. Heat over medium heat. Add orzo and garlic. Cook for 2 to 3 minutes or until orzo is lightly browned, stirring frequently. Remove from heat.
3. Add ½ cup of the hot broth to orzo mixture. Return to heat. Cook, stirring frequently, over medium heat until liquid is absorbed. Continue adding broth to orzo mixture, ½ cup at a time, stirring frequently and cooking until liquid is absorbed before adding more. Cook and stir until orzo is tender and creamy (about 15 minutes).
4. Add roasted vegetables and walnuts to orzo mixture; stir gently to combine. If desired, sprinkle each serving with feta cheese. Makes 4 servings.

EACH SERVING: *385 cal., 9 g fat (1 g sat. fat), 0 mg chol., 471 mg sodium, 64 g carbo., 6 g fiber, 15 g pro. Daily Values: 241% vit. A, 48% vit. C, 10% calcium, 22% iron.*

ORZO RISOTTO WITH ROASTED VEGETABLES

BY **STEPHEN EXEL**
PHOTOGRAPHS BY **ANDY LYONS**
FOOD STYLING BY **JILL LUST**

What a Ham!

Tasty glaze and robust flavor
make this perennial spring
favorite a welcome sight on
the dinner table.

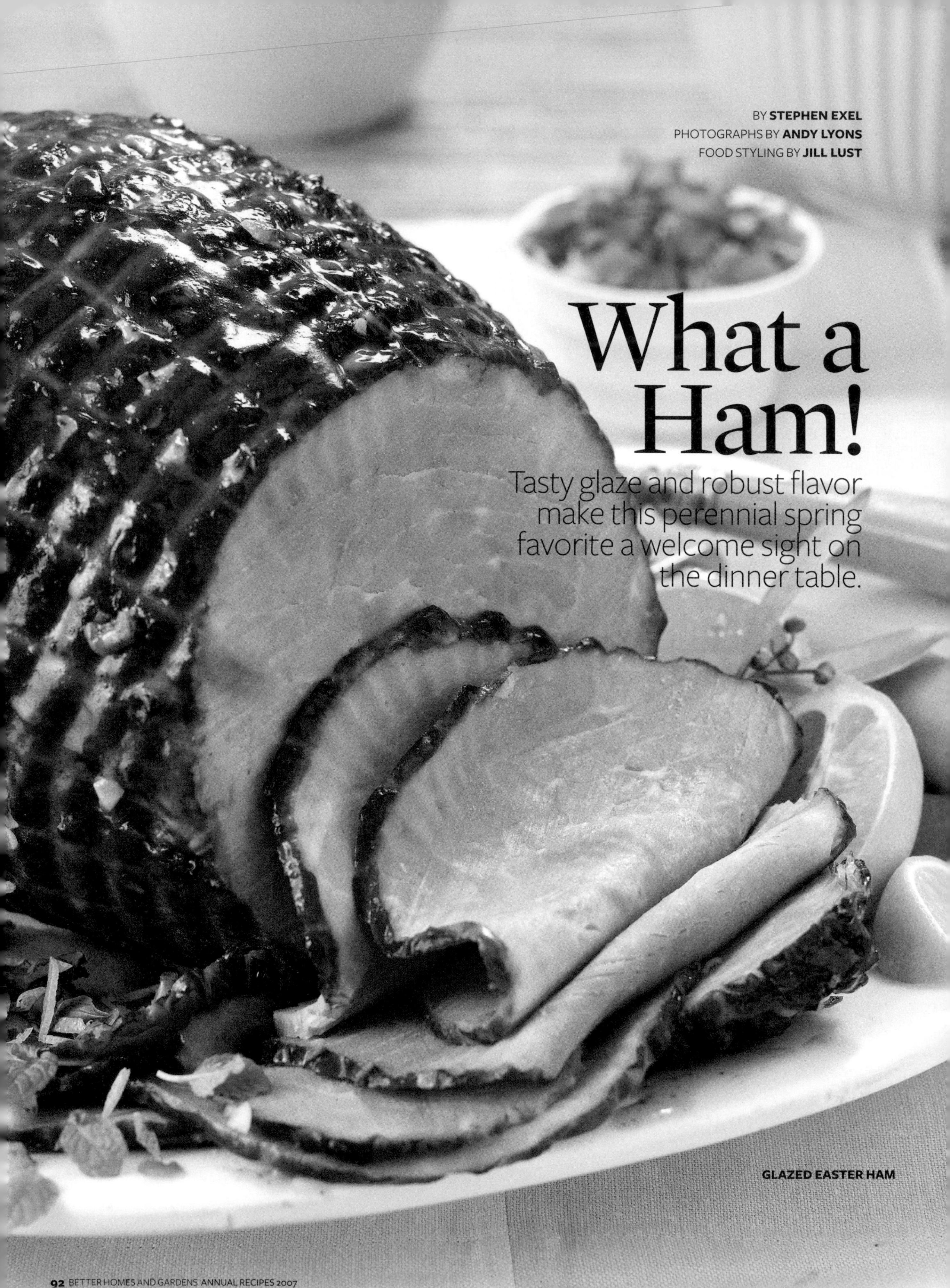

GLAZED EASTER HAM

GLAZED EASTER HAM

PREP: 15 minutes **BAKE:** 2¼ hours

INGREDIENTS

1   8- to 10-lb. cooked boneless ham
1   recipe desired holiday glaze (see "Glorious Holiday Glazes," page 94)
1   recipe Mint and Lemon Sprinkle (optional)

PREPARATION

1. Preheat oven to 325°F. Place ham on rack in roasting pan. Insert an oven-going meat thermometer into center. Bake, uncovered, for 2¼ to 2¾ hours or until thermometer registers 140°F. Brush ham with desired holiday glaze during the last 20 to 30 minutes of baking.
2. If desired, serve with Mint and Lemon Sprinkle. Makes 16 to 20 (3-ounce) servings plus leftovers.

MINT AND LEMON SPRINKLE: Combine ½ cup snipped fresh mint; 1 tablespoon shredded lemon peel; and 2 cloves garlic, minced.

EACH SERVING: *153 cal., 8 g fat (3 g sat. fat), 51 mg chol., 1,146 mg sodium, 6 g carbo., 1 g fiber, 14 g pro. Daily Values: 26% vit. C, 2% calcium, 6% iron.*

HAM BALLS IN BARBECUE SAUCE

Buy ground ham in the supermarket or use leftover ham that has been finely diced or ground in a food processor.

PREP: 20 minutes **BAKE:** 45 minutes

INGREDIENTS

2   eggs, beaten
1½   cups bread crumbs (2 slices)
½   cup finely chopped onion (1 medium)
2   Tbsp. milk
1   tsp. dry mustard
¼   tsp. ground black pepper
12   oz. ground cooked ham
12   oz. ground pork or ground beef
1   cup purchased barbecue sauce

PREPARATION

1. Preheat oven to 350°F. In a large bowl combine eggs, bread crumbs, onion, milk, dry mustard, and pepper. Add ground ham and pork; mix well. Using about ⅓ cup mixture for each, shape into 12 balls. Place ham balls in a lightly greased 2-quart rectangular baking dish. Pour barbecue sauce over ham balls.
2. Bake, uncovered, for 45 minutes or until an instant-read thermometer inserted into balls registers 160°F. Makes 6 servings.

EACH SERVING: *330 cal., 19 g fat (7 g sat. fat), 144 mg chol., 1,193 mg sodium, 15 g carbo., 2 g fiber, 24 g pro. Daily Values: 2% vit. A, 10% vit. C, 10% calcium, 15% iron.*

HAM BALLS IN BARBECUE SAUCE

GLORIOUS HOLIDAY GLAZES

LEMON-MUSTARD GLAZE: In a small bowl stir together ½ cup lemon curd; ¼ cup Dijon-style mustard; and 4 cloves garlic, minced. Makes ¾ cup glaze.

STOUT GLAZE: In a small saucepan combine ½ cup Irish stout or apple cider and ¼ cup *each* honey and butter. Bring to boiling; reduce heat. Simmer, uncovered, for 10 minutes. Makes ¾ cup glaze.

APRICOT-CHERRY GLAZE: In a small bowl stir together ½ cup *each* apricot preserves and cherry preserves and 1 tablespoon lemon juice. Makes 1 cup glaze.

PEACH-PINEAPPLE GLAZE: In a saucepan combine one 8-oz. can crushed pineapple, undrained; ½ cup peach preserves; 2 tablespoons cider vinegar; and ½ teaspoon ground ginger. Cook and stir over medium heat until heated through. Makes 1¼ cups glaze.

HAM-ASPARAGUS STRATA

HAM-ASPARAGUS STRATA

PREP: 25 minutes **CHILL:** 2 hours
BAKE: 1 hour **STAND:** 10 minutes

INGREDIENTS

4	English muffins, torn or cut into bite-size pieces (4 cups)
2	cups cubed cooked ham (10 oz.)
2	cups cut-up cooked fresh asparagus or broccoli
4	oz. shredded Swiss cheese
4	eggs, beaten
¼	cup dairy sour cream
1¼	cups milk
2	Tbsp. finely chopped onion
1	Tbsp. Dijon-style mustard
⅛	teaspoon ground black pepper

PREPARATION

1. In a greased 2-quart square baking dish spread half of the muffin pieces. Top with ham, asparagus, and cheese. Top with remaining muffin pieces.

2. In a bowl whisk together eggs and sour cream. Stir in milk, onion, mustard, and pepper. Pour over layers in dish. Cover; chill for 2 to 24 hours.

3. Preheat oven to 325°F. Bake, uncovered, for 60 to 65 minutes or until internal temperature registers 170°F on an instant-read thermometer. Let stand 10 minutes. Makes 6 servings.

EACH SERVING: 349 cal., 16 g fat (7 g sat. fat), 193 mg chol., 1,224 mg sodium, 25 g carbo., 2 g fiber, 26 g pro. Daily Values: 20% vit. A, 26% vit. C, 32% calcium, 15% iron.

HAM IT UP

Check the label. Almost all hams come fully cooked and are ready to eat or heat to 140°F. Uncooked hams should be heated to 160°F. For details, see TheOtherWhiteMeat.com.

SPIRAL
This convenient ham is presliced around the bone, so every cut can be easily removed.

BONELESS
Available sliced, whole, or halved, this ham will keep for several weeks refrigerated in its original packaging. Count on 4 to 5 servings per pound.

BONE-IN
Bone-in hams are available in a variety of shapes, like whole or as a shank or butt half. Plan on 2 to 3 servings per pound.

COUNTRY
These hams are dry salt-cured, may or may not be smoked, and are usually aged. Follow package directions to prepare. Serve thinly sliced.

Ring in Spring

Since 1950 the swoops and curves of the Bundt pan have turned bowls of batter into eye-catching cakes. Here's a dessert that salutes spring using the classic fluted pan.

BY **RICHARD SWEARINGER**
PHOTOGRAPH BY **ANDY LYONS**
FOOD STYLING BY **LYNN BLANCHARD**

ALMOND POUND CAKE

ALMOND POUND CAKE

PREP: 40 minutes **BAKE:** 1¼ hours
COOL: 2¼ hours

INGREDIENTS

1	cup butter
1	8-oz. pkg. cream cheese
6	eggs
3	cups all-purpose flour
1	tsp. baking powder
¼	tsp. salt
2¼	cups sugar
1	tsp. almond extract
1	recipe Almond Glaze

PREPARATION

1. Allow butter, cream cheese, and eggs to stand at room temperature for 30 minutes. Meanwhile, grease and lightly flour a 10-inch fluted tube pan; set aside. Combine flour, baking powder, and salt. Set aside. Preheat oven to 325°F.

2. In a large mixing bowl beat butter and cream cheese with an electric mixer on medium to high speed about 30 seconds or until softened. Gradually add sugar, 2 tablespoons at a time, beating on medium speed about 5 minutes or until very light and fluffy. Add almond extract. Add eggs, 1 at a time, beating on low to medium speed for 1 minute after each addition and scraping bowl frequently. Gradually add flour mixture, beating on low speed just until combined. Spoon batter into prepared pan.

3. Bake about 1¼ hours or until a wooden toothpick inserted near center of cake comes out clean. Cool in pan on a wire rack for 15 minutes. Remove from pan. Cool thoroughly on wire rack about 2 hours. Top cake with Almond Glaze. Let stand 30 minutes to allow glaze to set. Makes 16 servings.

ALMOND GLAZE: In a small mixing bowl beat together 1½ cups sifted powdered sugar, 3 ounces softened cream cheese, ½ teaspoon almond extract, and enough milk (1 to 2 tablespoons) for mixture to reach glazing consistency.

EACH SERVING: 430 cal., 20 g total fat (12 g sat. fat), 131 mg chol., 226 mg sodium, 56 g carbo., 1 g fiber, 6 g pro. Daily Values: 14% vit. A, 6% calcium, 9% iron.

Shoots That Score

Asparagus has a sweet, grassy flavor and high nutrient content (spears are loaded with vitamin C and folate), which make it a welcome spring arrival. Look for spears that are crisp, straight, and firm with tightly closed buds.

FAST! **LOW FAT**

GARLIC-ROASTED ASPARAGUS

PREP: 15 minutes **ROAST:** 10 minutes

INGREDIENTS

1½	lb. fresh asparagus spears
2	to 3 cloves garlic, thinly sliced
2	to 3 Tbsp. olive oil
¼	tsp. salt
¼	tsp. ground black pepper

PREPARATION

1. Preheat oven to 450°F. Snap off and discard woody bases from asparagus. Place asparagus and garlic in a 15×10×1-inch baking pan. Drizzle with oil and sprinkle with salt and pepper. Toss to coat.
2. Roast for 10 to 15 minutes or until asparagus is crisp-tender, stirring once halfway through roasting. Makes 6 servings.

EACH SERVING: 64 cal., 5 g fat (1 g sat. fat), 0 mg chol., 99 mg sodium, 5 g carbo., 2 g fiber, 3 g pro. Daily Values: 17% vit. A, 11% vit. C, 3% calcium, 14% iron.

TEST KITCHEN TIP Asparagus spears range from pencil thin to nearly half an inch in diameter. Which is best? Thicker tends to be more tender, but size depends on the time of year and age of plant. You'll find what is available to your grocer. Fortunately all are equally tasty.

More ways to enjoy asparagus

1. For a spicy, icy salad, gently toss together 1 pound steamed asparagus, cut into 3-inch pieces, and sections from 3 peeled oranges. Sprinkle with ¼ teaspoon crushed red pepper and refrigerate for up to 1 hour.

2. For an Asian stir-fry, in a large skillet over medium heat cook 1 pound asparagus, cut into bite-size pieces, in hot oil until the color changes to bright green. Sprinkle lightly with ground ginger. Add 1 teaspoon reduced-sodium soy sauce, 1 teaspoon sugar, and 1 tablespoon white wine. Cook and stir until liquid is syrupy, 2 to 3 minutes.

3. Steam whole asparagus spears, then smother with a handful of chopped green onion and a drizzle of honey. Sprinkle with salt. Cover; cook 1 minute more. Serve immediately

4. Substitute chilled cooked asparagus for the cucumbers in a Greek salad.

5. For spicy food lovers: In a large skillet cook asparagus in hot oil over medium heat until it begins to brown. Remove from heat; sprinkle with ½ teaspoon coarsely ground black pepper (avoid inhaling pepper fumes from skillet).

BY **RICHARD SWEARINGER**
PHOTOGRAPHS BY **ANDY LYONS**
FOOD STYLING BY **JILL LUST**

1

Yellow mustard, mayonnaise, parsley, paprika

2

Confetti of finely chopped sweet peppers, ranch dressing

3

Bacon pieces, snipped basil, sliced cherry tomatoes

Deviled Eggs

It's not always easy to improve on a classic, but have some fun trying. Add these tasty tidbits to your favorite egg-yolk filling.

4

Sour cream, slivers of smoked salmon, snipped chives

5

Flaked tuna, pickle relish, fresh lemon juice, lemon slice

6

Cooked diced potatoes, mayonnaise, chopped onion, radish slices

7

Fresh asparagus, Canadian bacon, hollandaise sauce

8

Herbed cream cheese, sliced apples, toasted walnuts

9

Cucumber slices, cooked shrimp, lemon thyme

10

Mexican sour cream dip, chopped chiles, olives, cilantro

BHG BASICS

Peeling is a cinch. Let hard-cooked eggs stand in ice water until cool enough to handle, then roll between the palms of your hands to crack the shell; remove.

BY **NANCY WALL HOPKINS** PHOTOGRAPHS BY **ANDY LYONS** FOOD STYLING BY **JILL LUST**

MAY

BRING A BIT OF THE BEST TO ALL OF THE
PICNICS, POTLUCKS, AND PARTIES YOU ATTEND!

**PULLED PORK AND PEACH SANDWICHES
WITH MACARONI SALAD**

page 104

Pride of the Potluck

Plus

Everyday Easy—

Ten to Try—

What's Cooking—

SHRIMP QUESADILLAS
page 112

LAMB CHOPS WITH TOMATOES
page 113

CARAMELIZED CARROTS
page 115

pride of the potluck

CONTRIBUTE YOUR "FARE" SHARE TO THE BUFFET TABLE WITH ONE OF THESE FAVORITES MADE FRESHER, EASIER, AND MORE FLAVORFUL THAN EVER.

BY **RICHARD SWEARINGER** AND **STEPHEN EXEL**

PHOTOGRAPHS BY **JENNIFER LEVY** FOOD STYLING BY **POUKÉ** PROP STYLING BY **SUE MITCHELL**

Potluck Chicken Tetrazzini

Not only is this dish loaded with fresh asparagus, sweet peppers, and mushrooms, but lemon peel gives the from-scratch sauce a unique accent. And it takes less than an hour to prepare.

These dishes ride to the party with poise and stay wilt-free until the last morsel is gone.

Baked Butter Beans with Mustard

With smoky bacon and a hint of rosemary, a combo of butter beans and Great Northerns makes a rich side dish.

BAKED BUTTER BEANS WITH MUSTARD

PREP: 25 minutes **BAKE:** 45 minutes

INGREDIENTS

8	slices bacon
1	large onion, chopped (1 cup)
4	16-oz. cans butter beans and/or Great Northern beans, rinsed and drained
1	8-oz. container dairy sour cream
½	cup chicken or vegetable broth
1	Tbsp. all-purpose flour
1	Tbsp. snipped fresh rosemary
1	Tbsp. Dijon-style mustard
¼	tsp. freshly ground black pepper
2	Tbsp. chopped Italian (flat-leaf) parsley
2	tsp. finely shredded lemon peel

PREPARATION

1. Preheat oven to 325°F. In a large skillet cook bacon over medium heat until crisp. Remove; drain on paper towels. Crumble; set aside. Drain skillet of all but 1 tablespoon drippings. Cook onion in drippings over medium heat until tender. Transfer to a large bowl. Add beans and all but 2 tablespoons of the bacon; set aside.
2. In another bowl whisk together sour cream, broth, flour, rosemary, mustard, and pepper. Stir into bean mixture. Transfer to a 2-quart casserole. Bake, covered, for 45 minutes, stirring once halfway through baking.
3. In a bowl combine remaining bacon, the parsley, and lemon peel; sprinkle over beans just before serving. Makes 10 (¾-cup) servings.

EACH SERVING: *247 cal., 10 g fat (5 g sat. fat), 20 mg chol., 892 mg sodium, 26 g carbo., 6 g fiber, 12 g pro. Daily Values: 4% vit. A, 5% vit. C, 9% calcium, 13% iron.*

LOW FAT

POTLUCK CHICKEN TETRAZZINI

The original dish was created in 1908 in San Francisco in honor of opera star Luisa Tetrazzini.

PREP: 30 minutes **BAKE:** 15 minutes **STAND:** 5 minutes

INGREDIENTS

1	purchased roasted chicken
8	oz. dried spaghetti or linguine, broken in half
12	oz. fresh asparagus spears, trimmed and cut into 1-inch pieces
8	oz. small whole fresh mushrooms
3	red and/or yellow sweet peppers, seeded and cut into 1-inch pieces
2	Tbsp. butter
¼	cup all-purpose flour
⅛	tsp. ground black pepper
1	14-oz. can chicken broth
¾	cup milk
½	cup shredded Swiss cheese (2 oz.)
1	Tbsp. finely shredded lemon peel
2	slices sourdough bread, cut into cubes
1	Tbsp. olive oil
2	Tbsp. snipped fresh parsley

PREPARATION

1. Preheat oven to 350°F. Remove meat from chicken; discard bones. Cut chicken pieces into chunks to equal 3 cups. Save remaining chicken for another use.
2. In a Dutch oven cook spaghetti according to package directions. Add asparagus the last 1 minute of cooking. Drain. Return to pan.
3. Meanwhile, in a large skillet cook mushrooms and sweet pepper in hot butter over medium heat for 8 to 10 minutes or until mushrooms are tender, stirring occasionally. Stir in flour and black pepper until well combined. Add broth and milk all at once. Cook and stir until thickened and bubbly.
4. Add mushroom mixture, chicken pieces, Swiss cheese, and half of the lemon peel to pasta mixture in Dutch oven. Toss gently to coat. Spoon pasta mixture into a 3-quart rectangular baking dish.
5. In a medium bowl toss together bread cubes, olive oil, and the remaining lemon peel. Spread bread cube mixture over pasta mixture. Bake, uncovered, for 15 minutes or until heated through. Let stand for 5 minutes before serving. Sprinkle with parsley before serving. Makes 10 (1-cup) servings.

EACH SERVING: *282 cal., 10 g fat (4 g sat. fat), 48 mg chol., 258 mg sodium, 28 g carbo., 2 g fiber, 20 g pro. Daily Values: 10% vit. A, 176% vit. C, 9% calcium, 13% iron.*

POTLUCK CHICKEN TETRAZZINI

PULLED PORK AND PEACH SANDWICHES

PREP: 15 minutes **COOK:** 8 hours (low) or 4 hours (high)

INGREDIENTS

1	3- to 4-lb. boneless pork shoulder roast
3	medium onions, cut into wedges
½	tsp. salt
½	tsp. ground black pepper
6	cloves garlic, minced
2	12- to 16-oz. pkg. frozen peaches
1	cup ginger ale
1	28-oz. can diced tomatoes with basil, garlic, and oregano, drained
20	hamburger buns, split
	Lettuce leaves (optional)
	Sliced peaches (optional)

PREPARATION

1. Trim fat from meat. If necessary, cut meat to fit a 5- to 6-quart slow cooker. Place onion in cooker. Transfer meat to cooker. Sprinkle with salt and pepper. Add garlic, peaches, and ginger ale.
2. Cover. Cook on low-heat setting for 8 to 10 hours or on high-heat setting for 4 to 5 hours.
3. Remove meat to cutting board, reserving remaining mixture in cooker. Using two forks, pull meat apart into bite-size pieces. Return meat to cooker. Add drained tomatoes. Stir to combine. Keep warm on warm setting, if available, or low setting.
4. If desired, line buns with lettuce leaves. Use a slotted spoon to spoon meat mixture onto buns. If desired, top with additional sliced peaches. Makes 20 (½-cup, plus bun) servings.

EACH SERVING: *339 cal., 14 g fat (5 g sat. fat), 48 mg chol., 517 mg sodium, 36 g carbo., 2 g fiber, 17 g pro. Daily Values: 7% vit. A, 61% vit. C, 10% calcium, 16% iron.*

FAST!

MACARONI SALAD

START TO FINISH: 25 minutes

INGREDIENTS

8	oz. dried elbow macaroni (2 cups)
½	lb. green beans, trimmed and cut into 1-inch pieces (2 cups)
¼	cup lemon juice
1	Tbsp. Dijon-style mustard
1	tsp. kosher salt
¼	tsp. freshly ground black pepper
⅓	cup olive oil
⅓	cup plain yogurt or dairy sour cream
5	oz. cheddar cheese, cubed (1¼ cups)
1	cup fresh spinach leaves
1	large tomato, seeded and chopped (1 cup)
½	cup chopped green onion
1	Tbsp. snipped fresh tarragon or ½ tsp. dried tarragon, crumbled

PREPARATION

1. Cook macaroni according to package directions. Add green beans during the last 5 minutes of cooking. Drain. Rinse with cold water; drain well.
2. For dressing, in a medium bowl whisk together lemon juice, mustard, salt, and pepper. Whisk in olive oil until thickened. Whisk in yogurt.
3. Add cheese, spinach, tomato, green onion, and tarragon to macaroni mixture. Add dressing; toss. Serve immediately or cover and refrigerate for 2 to 24 hours. Makes 20 (½-cup) servings.

EACH SERVING: *150 cal., 8 g fat (3 g sat. fat), 10 mg chol., 220 mg sodium, 14 g carbo., 1 g fiber, 5 g pro. Daily Values: 11% vit. A, 12% vit. C, 9% calcium, 5% iron.*

Pulled Pork and Peach Sandwiches

Slow cookers are convenient for any potluck gathering—perfect for keeping big-batch recipes hot. This pulled pork recipe provides hearty sandwiches for more than a dozen partygoers.

Macaroni Salad

For a colorful spin on the classic, add tomato, green beans, chunks of cheddar cheese, and spinach to elbow macaroni. Lemon juice, mustard, and yogurt give the dressing tang.

Roasted Squash and Pepper Tart

After the vegetables caramelize in the oven, a drizzle of balsamic vinegar makes them extra sweet. A little more baking crisps the puff pastry crust; then it's an easy flip to a serving board.

ROASTED SQUASH AND PEPPER TART

PREP: 25 minutes BAKE: 35 minutes COOL: 5 minutes

INGREDIENTS

Nonstick cooking spray
3 cups cut-up squash, such as pattypan, yellow summer squash, or zucchini
2 red and/or yellow sweet peppers, cut into wide strips
1 large sweet onion and/or fennel bulb, cut into wedges
2 Tbsp. olive oil
Salt and freshly ground black pepper
2 oz. Parmesan cheese
½ of a 17.3-oz. pkg. frozen puff pastry sheets (1 sheet), thawed
½ cup halved cherry tomatoes
2 Tbsp. balsamic vinegar
3 tsp. snipped fresh thyme
1 cup purchased refrigerated creamy Parmesan dressing
¼ cup finely chopped sweet onion

PREPARATION

1. Preheat oven to 450°F. Coat the sides and bottom of a 13×9×2-inch baking pan with cooking spray. Spread squash, sweet pepper, and onion wedges in pan. Toss with olive oil; sprinkle with salt and black pepper. Roast, uncovered, for 20 to 25 minutes or until tender, stirring once.
2. Meanwhile, using a vegetable peeler, cut Parmesan cheese into thin strips. Set aside. On a lightly floured surface, roll puff pastry into a 13×9-inch rectangle. Remove baking pan from oven. Add tomatoes to pan. Toss vegetables with balsamic vinegar and half of the Parmesan cheese. Spread vegetable mixture evenly in pan. Lay pastry over vegetables, tucking in edges. Return pan to oven; bake for 15 minutes or until pastry is puffed and golden.
3. Remove pan from oven; cool for 5 minutes. Invert a 15×10×1-inch baking pan over pan with pastry. Carefully invert pans together; remove 13×9-inch pan. Transfer any vegetables that stick to finished tart. Sprinkle tart evenly with remaining cheese and 2 teaspoons of the thyme. In a small bowl stir together dressing, chopped onion, and remaining 1 teaspoon thyme. Cut into squares. Serve tart warm or at room temperature with dressing. Makes 12 servings.

EACH SERVING: *277 cal., 23 g fat (3 g sat. fat), 7 mg chol., 256 mg sodium, 15 g carbo., 2 g fiber, 4 g pro. Daily Values: 12% vit. A, 101% vit. C, 8% calcium, 3% iron.*

FAST!

BROCCOLI-RAISIN-CAULIFLOWER SALAD

START TO FINISH: 30 minutes

INGREDIENTS

6 cups broccoli florets
3 cups cauliflower florets
½ cup golden raisins
⅓ cup walnut pieces, toasted
¼ cup olive oil or canola oil
¼ cup cider vinegar
1 tsp. salt
1 tsp. honey or sugar
½ tsp. dried basil, crushed
½ tsp. ground black pepper
¼ tsp. crushed red pepper (optional)

PREPARATION

1. In a large saucepan bring 2 inches of water to boiling. Add broccoli; return to boiling. Cook, covered, for 2 minutes or until broccoli is crisp-tender and bright green; drain. Rinse with cold water; drain well.
2. In same saucepan cook cauliflower in water using same method as in Step 1.
3. In a 2- to 2½-quart bowl layer half each of the broccoli, cauliflower, raisins, and walnuts. Repeat layers. Cover and chill. For dressing, in a screw-top jar combine oil, vinegar, salt, honey, basil, black pepper, and, if desired, red pepper. Cover tightly and shake well. Add dressing just before serving; toss to coat. Makes 10 (⅔-cup) servings.

EACH SERVING: *128 cal., 8 g fat (1 g sat. fat), 0 mg chol., 261 mg sodium, 13 g carbo., 3 g fiber, 3 g pro. Daily Values: 7% vit. A, 105% vit. C, 4% calcium, 5% iron.*

BROCCOLI-RAISIN-CAULIFLOWER SALAD

Broccoli-Raisin-Cauliflower Salad

Broccoli salad is always a popular bring-along. Add cauliflower for a little dazzle and bump up the flavor with a new sweet-spicy honey-and-cider vinegar dressing.

BEST-EVER CARROT CAKE

The carrots should be finely chopped or they may sink to the bottom of the pan during baking.

PREP: 50 minutes **BAKE:** 50 minutes **COOL:** 10 minutes

INGREDIENTS

4	eggs
¾	cup butter
½	of an 8-oz. pkg. cream cheese
2½	cups all-purpose flour
1	Tbsp. baking powder
1	Tbsp. finely shredded lemon peel
½	tsp. salt
1	lb. carrots, cut up
1	cup pecans, toasted
1½	cups sugar
1	8-oz. can crushed pineapple (juice pack), drained
1	recipe Cream Cheese Frosting (right)
	Fresh pineapple slices, drained

PREPARATION

1. Allow eggs, butter, and cream cheese to stand at room temperature for 30 minutes. Meanwhile, grease the bottoms and 1 inch up the sides of two 8×4×2-inch loaf pans. Set pans aside.
2. Preheat oven to 350°F. In a large bowl stir together flour, baking powder, lemon peel, and salt; set aside.
3. In a food processor* cover and process carrots with on-off turns until finely chopped. Add pecans and ½ cup of the sugar; process until pecans are finely chopped.
4. In a very large mixing bowl beat butter and cream cheese for 30 seconds; beat in the remaining 1 cup sugar until fluffy. Beat in eggs, 1 at a time, until combined. Stir carrot mixture and drained crushed pineapple into sugar-butter mixture until combined. Stir in flour mixture. Divide batter evenly among prepared pans.
5. Bake for 50 to 55 minutes or until a wooden toothpick inserted near centers comes out clean. Cool loaves in pans on wire rack for 10 minutes. Remove from pans; cool completely.
6. Frost with Cream Cheese Frosting. Serve immediately or cover and store in refrigerator up to 3 days. Just before serving, top with pineapple slices. Makes 2 loaves (twenty 1-slice servings).
*NOTE: If you do not have a food processor, finely shred the carrots and finely chop the pecans. Prepare as directed above, except add the sugar all at once, stir in the shredded carrot with the crushed pineapple, and stir in the pecans with the flour mixture.

EACH SLICE (WITH CREAM CHEESE FROSTING): *470 cal., 23 g fat (11 g sat. fat), 99 mg chol., 340 mg sodium, 63 g carbo., 2 g fiber, 6 g pro. Daily Values: 108% vit. A, 8% vit. C, 10% calcium, 10% iron.*

Best-Ever Carrot Cake

Less sweet than the traditional version, this lemony dessert is studded with pineapple chunks and pecans. Made with less fat than the traditional cake, it also has about a third fewer calories.

CREAM CHEESE FROSTING

PREP: 15 minutes

INGREDIENTS

4	oz. cream cheese, softened
¼	cup butter, softened
1	tsp. vanilla
2¾	to 3 cups powdered sugar

PREPARATION

1. In a large mixing bowl combine softened cream cheese, butter, and vanilla. Beat with an electric mixer on medium speed until light and fluffy. Gradually beat in enough powdered sugar to reach spreading consistency.

Best-Ever
Carrot Cake
*From Nancy's Mom

STRAWBERRY-RHUBARB BARS

4. Meanwhile, for filling, in a medium saucepan combine rhubarb, ⅓ cup sugar, the water, and ginger. Cook and stir over medium heat for 8 to 10 minutes or until filling is thickened and bubbly. Stir in strawberries. Remove ½ cup filling; cover and set aside. Carefully spoon remaining filling over hot baked crust. Sprinkle with reserved oat mixture, pressing lightly into rhubarb filling.
5. Bake for 30 to 35 minutes more or until top is golden and filling is bubbly. Cool in pan on wire rack. Lift from pan using foil. Carefully pull foil away from sides. Cut into bars. Top each bar with a spoonful of reserved filling. Drizzle with Ginger Icing just before serving. Makes 16 bars.
To store: Transfer cut bars to covered storage container. Refrigerate up to 2 days or freeze up to 3 months. Thaw at room temperature to serve.

EACH BAR (WITH GINGER ICING): *221 cal., 10 g fat (5 g sat. fat), 24 mg chol., 70 mg sodium, 32 g carbo., 1 g fiber, 2 g pro. Daily Values: 7% vit. A, 3% vit. C, 2% calcium, 5% iron.*

GINGER ICING

PREP: 5 minutes

INGREDIENTS
¼ cup sifted powdered sugar
¼ tsp. ground ginger
3 to 4 tsp. orange juice

PREPARATION

1. In a small bowl stir together powdered sugar, ginger, and enough orange juice to reach drizzling consistency. Use with Strawberry-Rhubarb Bars (left). Makes ¼ cup icing.

STRAWBERRY-RHUBARB BARS

PREP: 25 minutes BAKE: 50 minutes

INGREDIENTS
Nonstick cooking spray
1½ cups quick-cooking rolled oats
1 cup all-purpose flour
¾ cup sugar
¾ cup butter
1½ cups chopped fresh or frozen rhubarb, thawed
⅓ cup sugar
¼ cup water
½ tsp. ground ginger
2 cups chopped fresh strawberries
1 recipe Ginger Icing (right)

PREPARATION

1. Preheat oven to 350°F. Line an 8×8×2-inch baking pan with foil, allowing foil to extend over edges of pan. Coat foil with cooking spray; set aside.
2. In a large bowl stir together oats, flour, and ¾ cup sugar. Using a pastry blender, cut in butter until mixture resembles coarse crumbs (use fingers, if necessary, to break up mixture). Remove 1½ cups oat mixture; set aside.
3. Press remaining oat mixture evenly into bottom of pan. Bake for 20 minutes.

Impromptu Drinks

Beverages look special when served in pitchers brimming with fresh fruit: Slices of honeydew, lime, and grapefruit accent rosé wine; fresh mint leaves garnish lemonade; and fresh raspberries bob merrily in iced green tea.

RAVIOLI WITH SPINACH PESTO

READY IN
20
MINUTES

BY **NANCY WALL HOPKINS**
PHOTOGRAPHS BY **ANDY LYONS**
FOOD STYLING BY **JILL LUST**
RECIPES BY **MARYELLYN KRANTZ**

Carefree Suppers
Spring-fresh flavors, superfast assembly. Dinner is served.

FAST! **LOW FAT**

RAVIOLI WITH SPINACH PESTO

START TO FINISH: 20 minutes

INGREDIENTS

1   9-oz. pkg. refrigerated four-cheese ravioli or tortellini
12   oz. baby pattypan squash, halved, or yellow summer squash, halved lengthwise and sliced ½ inch thick
3½   cups fresh baby spinach
½   cup torn fresh basil
¼   cup bottled Caesar Parmesan vinaigrette salad dressing
2   Tbsp. water
     Shredded Parmesan cheese (optional)

PREPARATION

1. Cook ravioli according to package directions, adding squash the last 2 minutes of cooking. Drain.
2. Meanwhile, for pesto, in a blender combine spinach, basil, salad dressing, and water. Cover and process until smooth, stopping to scrape down blender sides as needed.
3. Toss ravioli mixture with pesto. If desired, sprinkle with cheese. Makes 4 servings.

EACH SERVING: *218 cal., 6 g fat (2 g sat. fat), 27 mg chol., 525 mg sodium, 31 g carbo., 3 g fiber, 11 g pro. Daily Values: 58% vit. A, 38% vit. C, 13% calcium, 12% iron.*

FAST!

QUICK CHICKEN PANZANELLA

START TO FINISH: 20 minutes

INGREDIENTS

1   14.5-oz. can diced tomatoes with green pepper, celery, and onions, undrained
3   Tbsp. olive oil
1   2- to 2¼-lb. whole roasted chicken
4   cups cubed Italian bread
2   medium cucumbers, halved lengthwise and sliced
1   cup torn fresh basil or spinach

PREPARATION

1. Spoon off 2 tablespoons of tomato liquid. Combine with 1 tablespoon of the olive oil, dash *salt*, and *ground black pepper*; set aside. Remove meat from roasted chicken. Cut into pieces.
2. In a large skillet stir bread cubes in remaining 2 tablespoons oil over medium heat for 5 minutes or until golden; remove. Add remaining undrained tomatoes to bread cubes; toss. Divide on 4 plates. Add cucumbers, chicken, and basil. Pass tomato-oil mixture. Makes 4 servings.

EACH SERVING: *596 cal., 27 g fat (6 g sat. fat), 92 mg chol., 824 mg sodium, 50 g carbo., 4 g fiber, 37 g pro. Daily Values: 21% vit. A, 17% vit. C, 15% calcium, 27% iron.*

QUICK CHICKEN PANZANELLA

FAST!

SHRIMP QUESADILLAS

START TO FINISH: 20 minutes

INGREDIENTS

4	8-inch vegetable tortillas
	Nonstick cooking spray
½	of a 7-oz. carton garlic or spicy three-pepper hummus (⅓ cup)
6	oz. peeled, deveined cooked medium shrimp
1	6-oz. jar marinated artichoke hearts or half of a 16-oz. jar pickled mixed vegetables, drained and coarsely chopped
1	4-oz. pkg. crumbled feta cheese

PREPARATION

1. Coat one side of each tortilla with cooking spray. Place tortillas, sprayed sides down, on work surface; spread with hummus. Top half of each tortilla with shrimp, artichokes, and cheese. Fold tortillas in half, pressing gently.

2. Heat a large nonstick skillet or griddle over medium heat for 1 minute. Cook quesadillas, 2 at a time, for 4 to 6 minutes or until browned and heated through, turning once. Makes 4 servings.

EACH SERVING: *430 cal., 20 g fat (7 g sat. fat), 108 mg chol., 1,099 mg sodium, 42 g carbo., 4 g fiber, 21 g pro. Daily Values: 4% vit. A, 9% vit. C, 29% calcium, 14% iron.*

SHRIMP QUESADILLAS

LAMB CHOPS WITH TOMATOES

CHICKEN AND LEMON-BROCCOLI ALFREDO

START TO FINISH: 20 minutes

INGREDIENTS

4	small skinless, boneless chicken breast halves
	Salt and ground black pepper
8	oz. mushrooms, halved
1	Tbsp. olive oil or cooking oil
1	lemon
3	cups fresh broccoli florets
1	10-oz. container refrigerated light Alfredo pasta sauce

PREPARATION

1. Season chicken with salt and pepper. In a large skillet brown chicken and mushrooms in hot oil for 4 minutes, turning chicken halfway through cooking.
2. Meanwhile, shred 2 teaspoons lemon peel; set aside. Slice lemon. Add lemon slices and broccoli to skillet. Cover; cook for 8 minutes or until chicken is done (170°F on an instant-read thermometer).
3. Place chicken and vegetables on 4 plates. Add Alfredo sauce to skillet; heat through. Serve with chicken. Add lemon peel and season with pepper. Makes 4 servings.

EACH SERVING: 295 cal., 12 g fat (5 g sat. fat), 91 mg chol., 705 mg sodium, 16 g carbo., 4 g fiber, 35 g pro. Daily Values: 12% vit. A, 140% vit. C, 19% calcium, 10% iron.

LAMB CHOPS WITH TOMATOES

START TO FINISH: 20 minutes

INGREDIENTS

8	1-inch lamb loin chops
	Salt and ground black pepper
1	8.8-oz. pouch cooked long grain rice
4	medium plum tomatoes, cut up
4	green onions, cut into 1-inch pieces
1	Tbsp. snipped fresh oregano
1	Tbsp. balsamic vinegar

PREPARATION

1. Season chops with salt and pepper. Grill over medium coals for 12 to 14 minutes for medium rare (145°F), turning once halfway through grilling.
2. Meanwhile, microwave rice according to package directions. In a food processor combine tomatoes, green onion, and oregano; process with on/off turns until coarsely chopped. Transfer to a bowl; stir in vinegar. Season with salt and pepper. Arrange chops on rice; top with tomato mixture. Makes 4 servings.

EACH SERVING: 273 cal., 7 g fat (2 g sat. fat), 70 mg chol., 153 mg sodium, 26 g carbo., 3 g fiber, 25 g pro. Daily Values: 22% vit. A, 29% vit. C, 4% calcium, 15% iron.

CHICKEN AND LEMON-BROCCOLI ALFREDO

Natural Goodness

A squeeze of this, a splash of that—and spring's freshest produce is served up as colorful, flavorful side dishes.

BY **RICHARD SWEARINGER**
PHOTOGRAPHS BY **ANDY LYONS**
FOOD STYLING BY **JILL LUST**

GREEN BEANS WITH LIME

For crunch, add ¼ cup sliced almonds the last 5 minutes of cooking. Stir often to toast evenly.

START TO FINISH: 30 minutes

INGREDIENTS

1	lb. fresh green beans, cut into 2-inch pieces (4 cups)
1	Tbsp. olive oil or cooking oil
1	lime

PREPARATION

1. In a large skillet cook green beans in hot oil over medium heat for 18 to 20 minutes until crisp-tender and lightly browned, using a spatula to gently lift beans occasionally to prevent them from sticking. Meanwhile, shred 1 teaspoon lime peel. Cut lime in half. Add lime peel to beans. Cook and stir for 1 minute more.
2. Lightly season beans with *salt*, drizzle with lime juice, and serve immediately. Makes 4 (½-cup) servings.

EACH SERVING: *66 cal., 4 g fat (0 g sat. fat), 0 mg chol., 67 mg sodium, 9 g carbo., 4 g fiber, 2 g pro. Daily Values: 14% vit. A, 35% vit. C, 4% calcium, 6% iron.*

Cooking in flavor

The recipes for Green Beans with Lime, Caramelized Carrots, and Onions with Pasta Nests (page 116) call for cooking the vegetables until they are lightly browned.

This method of cooking releases some of the natural sugars in the vegetables. Then, in the heat of the pan, those sugars caramelize, producing sweet and savory flavors. This technique is good for people who aren't veggie lovers; the extra sweetness can entice them to eat up.

CARAMELIZED CARROTS

Loaded with vitamin A, this side dish also boasts golden color and robust flavor.

PREP: 20 minutes
COOK: 22 minutes

INGREDIENTS

2	lb. whole small carrots, peeled, tops on, and halved lengthwise
2	Tbsp. olive oil
¼	tsp. salt
4	cloves garlic, thinly sliced
⅔	cup whipping cream
⅛	tsp. cayenne pepper Snipped fresh Italian (flat-leaf) parsley

PREPARATION

1. In a very large skillet cook carrots, cut sides down, in hot oil. Sprinkle with salt. Cook, covered, for 10 minutes. Uncover. Turn carrots; add garlic. Cover and continue cooking for 10 minutes more or until carrots are tender and both sides are golden brown. During cooking, gently shake skillet occasionally to prevent carrots from sticking. Transfer carrots to a serving plate; cover and keep warm.
2. Add cream and cayenne pepper to skillet. Bring to boiling. Reduce heat; boil gently, uncovered, for 2 to 4 minutes until cream is slightly thickened. Pour over carrots. Sprinkle with parsley. Serve immediately. Makes 8 (½-cup) servings.

EACH SERVING: *146 cal., 11 g fat (5 g sat. fat), 27 mg chol., 160 mg sodium, 12 g carbo., 3 g fiber, 2 g pro. Daily Values: 350% vit. A, 10% vit. C, 5% calcium, 2% iron.*

TO PEEL OR NOT TO PEEL?

Large carrots—the type sold whole in 1- or 2-pound cellophane bags—should generally be peeled because the skin can be tough. Small baby carrots, sold in bunches, can be eaten peel and all. Does the skin offer extra nutrition? Not too much, nutritionists say, but it does add a little fiber to your diet.

CARAMELIZED CARROTS

ONIONS WITH PASTA NESTS

WINE-POACHED BEETS

ONIONS WITH PASTA NESTS

Coiled pasta goes by several names: bird's nest pasta, coiled angel hair, and, in the Hispanic section of grocery stores, fideos.

PREP: 15 minutes
COOK: 37 minutes

INGREDIENTS
1   Tbsp. butter
1   Tbsp. olive oil
2   lb. sweet onions, sliced
     ½ inch thick and separated
     into rings
½   tsp. salt
¼   tsp. ground black pepper
4   oz. dried coiled pasta or
     angel hair pasta
1¼   cups water

PREPARATION
1. In a 12-inch skillet heat butter and olive oil over medium heat until butter melts. Add onions, salt, and pepper. Cook, covered, for 15 minutes, stirring occasionally. Uncover. Cook for 10 to 15 minutes more or until onions are tender and browned, stirring frequently. Remove onions from skillet; set aside.
2. Add pasta to hot skillet. Cook and stir for 4 minutes or until pasta is browned. Add cooked onions and water to skillet. Bring to boiling; reduce heat. Cover and cook for 5 minutes. Uncover. Cook for 3 to 4 minutes more or until pasta is tender, stirring occasionally. Serve immediately. Makes 4 (¾-cup) servings.

EACH SERVING: *233 cal., 7 g fat (2 g sat. fat), 8 mg chol., 478 mg sodium, 38 g carbo., 3 g fiber, 6 g pro. Daily Values: 2% vit. A, 18% vit. C, 5% calcium, 9% iron.*

Onions by the season

Look for these two types of cooking onions: sweet onions such as Walla Walla and Maui, which are available spring through fall, and the stronger-flavor fall/winter onions (also called "storage" onions). Use both types interchangeably in recipes—except in recipes that call for raw sweet onions. Sweet onions can be stored in the fridge for several weeks. Store fall/winter onions in a cool, dry place up to several months.

LOW FAT

WINE-POACHED BEETS

PREP: 25 minutes
COOK: 45 minutes

INGREDIENTS
¾   cup dry red wine, such as
     Merlot or Shiraz, or apple
     juice
½   cup water
1   Tbsp. packed brown sugar
2½   lb. beets, peeled and cut up
     Salt and ground black pepper
     Honey (optional)
1   Tbsp. snipped fresh parsley
     Lemon wedges (optional)

PREPARATION
1. In a large saucepan combine ½ cup of the wine, the water, and brown sugar. Bring to boiling, stirring to dissolve sugar. Add beets. Return to boiling; reduce heat. Simmer, covered, for 45 minutes until beets are tender and can be pierced with a fork, stirring occasionally. Drain. Transfer beets to bowl. Season to taste with salt and pepper.
2. Splash with remaining ¼ cup wine. If desired, drizzle with honey. Sprinkle with parsley. If desired, serve with lemon wedges. Makes 8 to 10 (½-cup) servings.

EACH SERVING: *66 cal., 4 g fat (0 g sat. fat), 0 mg chol., 67 mg sodium, 9 g carbo., 4 g fiber, 2 g pro. Daily Values: 14% vit. A, 35% vit. C, 4% calcium, 6% iron.*

BEETS AND COLOR

Beets are available in a variety of colors, from the familiar royal purple to shades of red, pink, and yellow. There are even striped varieties; 'Chioggia' and 'Candy Cane' are two of the best-known. Golden-color beets tend to be slightly sweeter than dark varieties. When shopping, look for small to medium, well-shaped beets that are firm and have smooth skins. Avoid very large beets because they can be tough. To store, trim any green leaves but leave the root end intact. Place, unwashed, in an open plastic bag or plastic bag with holes up to 1 week in the refrigerator.

BY **NANCY WALL HOPKINS**
PHOTOGRAPHS BY **ANDY LYONS**
FOOD STYLING BY **JILL LUST**

Party Dips

Stir some fun into your favorite sour cream concoction.

1. MANDARIN ORANGE slices, toasted coconut, finely shredded lime peel

2. PEACHES (chopped), toasted pecans, brown sugar

3. AVOCADO (chopped), chopped red onion, garlic salt

4. SPINACH (finely chopped), Parmesan cheese, cracked peppercorns

5. PEANUTS (chopped), Thai chili sauce, lime juice

6. CUCUMBER (chopped), chopped tomato, snipped fresh cilantro

7. STRAWBERRIES (sliced), strawberry preserves, snipped fresh mint

8. SMOKED ALMONDS (chopped), dried fruit pieces, curry powder, garlic salt

9. BACON (cooked, crumbled), crumbled blue cheese, finely chopped celery

10. HARD-COOKED EGG (chopped), snipped fresh dill, lemon pepper

BHG
BASICS

Sour Cream Dip: Beat together one 8-oz. pkg. softened cream cheese and one 8-oz. carton dairy sour cream with electric mixer until fluffy. Add desired ingredients from above.

JUNE

LUSCIOUS GRILLED FOOD—FROM MAIN DISHES
TO DESSERTS—IS A WELCOME WAY TO START
THE SUMMER SEASON IN GRAND STYLE.

**STEAK AND
GRILLED NECTARINES**
page 123

Fruit + Fire

Plus

CORN-MANGO SALAD
page 124

ICE BUCKET CHERRY SUNDAES
page 126

SUMMER'S BEST BBQ BEANS
page 134

BY **NANCY WALL HOPKINS**
PHOTOGRAPHS BY **TINA RUPP**
FOOD STYLING BY **SUSAN BROWN DRAUDT**
PROP STYLING BY **SUE MITCHELL**
RECIPES BY **DAVID BONOM**

fruit + fire

GRILLING BRINGS OUT BOLD FLAVORS AND EXTRA SWEETNESS
FROM NECTARINES, MANGOES, EVEN GRAPES—EXPERIENCE IT
YOURSELF WITH THESE ENTRÉES, SIDES, AND DESSERTS.

Sizzling, juicy, melty goodness is the reward of grill-kissed fruit.

SCALLOP AND PINEAPPLE KABOBS

PREP: 20 minutes   MARINATE: 15 minutes   GRILL: 8 minutes

INGREDIENTS

2   tsp. finely shredded lime peel
¼   cup lime juice
¼   cup snipped fresh cilantro
2   small green and/or red jalapeño chile peppers, seeded, and finely chopped (See Note, page 76)
2   tsp. sugar
½   tsp. salt
½   tsp. ground black pepper
⅓   cup canola oil
16   sea scallops (about 1½ lb.)
12   large fresh pineapple chunks
1   avocado, peeled, seeded, and cut into 8 chunks

PREPARATION

1. For marinade, in a small bowl combine lime peel and juice, cilantro, jalapeño, sugar, salt, and black pepper. Whisk in oil; set aside. In a bowl combine scallops, pineapple, and avocado. Toss with 2 tablespoons of the marinade; reserve remaining marinade to serve with kabobs. Marinate for 15 minutes, stirring often. Thread pieces onto four 12-inch skewers.
2. Grill on the greased rack of an uncovered grill directly over medium-high heat for 8 minutes, turning once halfway through grilling. Transfer to a platter. Serve with reserved marinade. Makes 4 servings.

EACH SERVING: *423 cal., 26 g fat (2 g sat. fat), 56 mg chol., 572 mg sodium, 19 g carbo., 4 g fiber, 30 g pro. Daily Values: 11% vit. A, 66% vit. C, 6% calcium, 6% iron.*

Thread scallops and chunks of **pineapple** and avocado onto skewers, then flavor with lime-, jalapeño-, and cilantro-laced marinade to create *Scallop and Pineapple Kabobs.* The kabobs grill in only 8 minutes.

SCALLOP AND PINEAPPLE KABOBS

Toss juicy **nectarines** with a sweet-hot chili powder blend and sear on the grill. Pile them on a grilled ribeye and add bacon. With *Steak and Grilled Nectarines,* who needs potatoes?

STEAK AND GRILLED NECTARINES

STEAK AND GRILLED NECTARINES

PREP: 20 minutes **GRILL:** 12 minutes

INGREDIENTS

1	Tbsp. sugar
1½	tsp. salt
1	to 1½ tsp. chili powder
1	tsp. ground cumin
½	tsp. freshly ground black pepper
⅛	to ¼ tsp. cayenne pepper
4	6- to 8-oz. boneless beef ribeye steaks, cut ½ inch thick
2	firm ripe nectarines, pitted
2	tsp. water
8	slices bacon

PREPARATION

1. In a bowl combine sugar, salt, chili powder, cumin, black pepper, and cayenne pepper. Reserve 1 teaspoon; sprinkle remaining over both sides of meat. Set aside. Cut each nectarine into 8 wedges; toss with reserved seasoning mixture and the 2 teaspoons water.
2. For a charcoal grill, place bacon in a 10-inch cast-iron skillet and place directly over medium coals. Cook for 8 to 10 minutes, turning often. (For a gas grill, preheat grill. Reduce heat to medium. Cook as above.) Remove skillet and bacon; drain bacon on paper towels.
3. Place steaks on the rack of an uncovered grill directly over medium coals. Grill, turning once. (Allow 4 to 6 minutes for medium rare.) Place nectarines on grill the last 3 to 5 minutes of grilling, turning often. Transfer steaks to plates; top with bacon and nectarines. Makes 4 servings.

EACH SERVING: *353 cal., 17 g fat (6 g sat. fat), 108 mg chol., 1,155 mg sodium, 11 g carbo., 1 g fiber, 38 g pro. Daily Values: 9% vit. A, 7% vit. C, 3% calcium, 22% iron.*

APRICOT-ONION DIP

PREP: 15 minutes **GRILL:** 20 minutes

INGREDIENTS

4	apricots, pitted and cut into wedges
2	tsp. olive oil
¾	tsp. chili powder
1	large sweet onion, cut into ½-inch slices
¾	cup dairy sour cream
⅓	cup mayonnaise
⅛	tsp. ground coriander
⅛	tsp. cayenne pepper
	Baguette slices, toasted
	Snipped fresh chives (optional)

PREPARATION

1. In a medium bowl toss apricot wedges with 1 teaspoon of the oil and the chili powder. Brush onion slices with remaining oil.
2. For a charcoal grill, grill apricot wedges on the rack of an uncovered grill directly over medium coals for 3 to 4 minutes per side. Grill onion slices for 7 to 8 minutes per side. (For a gas grill, preheat grill. Reduce heat to medium. Place apricots and onions on grill rack. Cover; grill as above.) Remove; cool.
3. In a bowl combine sour cream, mayonnaise, ½ teaspoon *salt*, coriander, and cayenne. Chop onion into pieces; stir into sour cream mixture. Chop apricots; spoon over dip. Serve with baguette slices and, if desired, chives. Makes 12 (¼-cup) servings.

EACH SERVING: *86 cal., 8 g fat (3 g sat. fat), 7 mg chol., 138 mg sodium, 3 g carbo., 1 g pro. Daily Values: 7% vit. A, 3% vit. C, 2% calcium, 1% iron.*

Grill fresh apricots for an out-of-the-ordinary appetizer—3 minutes over the coals brings out their juicy sweetness. Then chop and stir the fruit into basic sour cream-mayo-onion dip zipped with coriander and cayenne. *Apricot-Onion Dip* tastes great with grilled baguette slices or sweet potato chips.

APRICOT-ONION DIP

FAST!

CORN-MANGO SALAD

START TO FINISH: 30 minutes

INGREDIENTS

4	medium ears of corn, husked and cleaned
2	to 3 large mangoes
1	medium red onion
	Olive oil
2	Tbsp. fresh lemon juice
1	tsp. sugar
½	tsp. curry powder
6	cups fresh arugula

PREPARATION

1. Cut corn kernels from cobs. Seed and peel mangoes; cut into 12 slices. Peel onion; cut into 6 wedges, leaving root end intact.
2. For a charcoal grill, place a 9- to 10-inch cast-iron skillet on rack directly over medium-hot coals. Heat for 3 minutes. Add corn and 1 teasoon olive oil. Cook and stir for 2 to 4 minutes. (For gas grill, preheat grill. Reduce heat to medium-hot. Place cast-iron skillet on rack directly over heat for 3 minutes. Add corn. Grill as above.) Remove from grill; transfer kernels to 6 serving bowls. Set aside.
3. In a bowl combine mango slices and onion wedges; drizzle with 1 tablespoon olive oil. Toss. For a charcoal grill, place mango and onion on the rack of an uncovered grill directly over medium coals. Grill mango for 3 to 5 minutes, turning often. Grill onion for 6 to 8 minutes, turning often. (For a gas grill, reduce heat to medium. Place mango and onion on rack directly over heat. Cover; grill as above.) Transfer mango and onion to a bowl.
4. For dressing, in a bowl combine lemon juice, sugar, curry, ½ teaspoon *salt,* and ⅛ teaspoon *ground black pepper*. Whisk in 3 tablespoons olive oil until combined. Add 1 tablespoon dressing to mango mixture; toss. Spoon mango mixture over corn. Drizzle arugula with remaining dressing; toss. Add to bowls. Serves 6.

EACH SERVING: *190 cal., 11 g fat (2 g sat. fat), 0 mg chol., 206 mg sodium, 25 g carbo., 3 g fiber, 2 g pro. Daily Values: 17% vit. A, 46% vit. C, 3% calcium, 4% iron.*

CORN-MANGO SALAD

KID FRIENDLY

HONEY-GLAZED CHICKEN

PREP: 20 minutes MARINATE: 15 minutes GRILL: 50 minutes

INGREDIENTS

4	bone-in chicken breast halves
5	Tbsp. balsamic vinegar
1	Tbsp. extra virgin olive oil
3	cloves garlic, minced
½	tsp. salt
¼	tsp. ground black pepper
¼	cup honey
2	tsp. finely shredded orange peel
¼	tsp. salt
1	lb. seedless grapes, divided into 4 bunches
1	Tbsp. sugar or honey
	Blue cheese and honey (optional)

PREPARATION

1. Place chicken in a large resealable plastic bag. For marinade, in a bowl combine 2 tablespoons of the vinegar, the oil, garlic, the ½ teaspoon salt, and the pepper; pour over chicken. Seal bag; turn bag to coat chicken. Marinate for 15 minutes.
2. Meanwhile, in another bowl stir together remaining vinegar, honey, orange peel, and the ¼ teaspoon salt.
3. For a charcoal grill, arrange medium-hot coals around drip pan. Test for medium heat above pan. Remove chicken from bag; discard marinade. Place chicken, skin sides up, on grill rack over drip pan. Cover; grill for 25 minutes. Brush with honey mixture. Cover and grill for 25 minutes more or until an instant-read thermometer registers 170°F. Brush with honey mixture until the last 5 minutes of grilling. (For a gas grill, preheat grill. Reduce heat to medium. Adjust for indirect cooking. Place chicken, skin sides up, on rack on unlit side. Cover; grill as above.)
4. Meanwhile, toss grapes with sugar; place on rack over coals. Cover; grill for 2 to 3 minutes, turning once. Transfer chicken and grapes to platter. If desired, serve with blue cheese and honey. Makes 4 servings.

EACH SERVING: *622 cal., 25 g fat (6 g sat. fat), 144 mg chol., 559 mg sodium, 49 g carbo., 1 g fiber, 49 g pro. Daily Values: 4% vit. A, 27% vit. C, 6% calcium, 13% iron.*

Pair corn with **mango** for a snappy combo. Prepare the corn and mango early in the day and refrigerate. Just before dinner, grill them and toss with arugula. Curry lifts the flavor of the vinaigrette and makes *Corn-Mango Salad* a worthy accompaniment to spicy bratwurst and summer sausages.

Think you know everything about grapes? Grilling them may be a revelation. Yes, it wrinkles them a tad, but it also mellows the sweet-and-tart goodness. For *Honey-Glazed Chicken*, add a bunch or two alongside the chicken during the last 2 to 3 minutes of grilling. Just before serving, dress up the platter with a wedge of blue cheese and an extra drizzle of honey.

KID FRIENDLY

ICE BUCKET CHERRY SUNDAES

PREP: 10 minutes **FREEZE:** 4 hours **GRILL:** 12 minutes
COOL: 10 minutes

INGREDIENTS

1   quart vanilla ice cream
       Finely shredded peel and juice from 2 oranges
24   oz. mixed fresh sweet cherries, pitted (about 4 cups), or
       4 cups frozen pitted dark sweet cherries
¼   cup sugar

PREPARATION

1. Scoop ice cream into an ice bucket. Cover and freeze for 4 to
6 hours or overnight. Meanwhile, in a bowl stir together orange
juice, 2 teaspoons of the orange peel, the cherries, and sugar.
Transfer to a large cast-iron skillet.
2. For a charcoal grill, place the skillet on the rack of an uncovered
grill directly over medium coals. Cook cherry mixture, stirring
occasionally, for 12 to 15 minutes or until mixture thickens slightly.
(For a gas grill, preheat grill. Reduce heat to medium. Place skillet
on rack. Cover; grill as above.) Cool cherry mixture for 10 minutes.
To serve, spoon cherry mixture over prescooped ice cream. If
desired, add remaining orange peel. Makes 8 servings.

EACH SERVING: *344 cal., 18 g fat (11 g sat. fat), 98 mg chol.,*
68 mg sodium, 43 g carbo., 2 g fiber, 5 g pro. Daily Values: 37% vit. A,
35% vit. C, 14% calcium, 4% iron.

ICE BUCKET CHERRY SUNDAES

KID FRIENDLY

GRILLED PEACH PIE

PREP: 30 minutes **GRILL:** 1½ hours **COOL:** 30 minutes

INGREDIENTS

3½   lb. peaches, peeled, halved, and pitted
1   Tbsp. canola oil
½   cup sugar
¼   cup snipped fresh basil
3   Tbsp. cornstarch
1   Tbsp. lemon juice
1   15-oz. pkg. rolled refrigerated unbaked piecrust (2 crusts)
       Nonstick cooking spray
1   egg, lightly beaten
1   Tbsp. sugar

PREPARATION

1. For a charcoal grill, arrange medium-hot coals on one side of grill.
Test for medium heat above empty side. Brush peach halves with
oil. Grill halves, cut sides down, on rack directly over coals for
3 minutes. Remove. Cut peach halves into wedges. In a bowl toss
peaches with the ½ cup sugar, basil, cornstarch, and lemon juice.
2. On a floured surface, roll each crust to 12-inch diameter. Coat a
9- to 10-inch cast-iron skillet with cooking spray. Line skillet with
one crust; dough should come three-fourths up the sides of the pan.
Place peach mixture into piecrust in skillet. With a knife, cut several
slits in center of second crust to vent steam. Place second crust over
peaches. Tuck any extra dough at edges between side of skillet and
bottom crust. Crimp edge. Brush top of pie with beaten egg and
sprinkle with the 1 tablespoon sugar.
3. Place skillet on rack over empty side of grill. Cover and grill for
1½ hours until crust is golden, rotating once halfway through
grilling. (For gas grill, preheat grill. Reduce heat to medium. Adjust
for indirect cooking. Grill as above.) Cool the pie on a wire rack for
30 to 40 minutes before serving. Makes 12 servings.

EACH SERVING: *263 cal., 11 g fat (4 g sat. fat), 24 mg chol.,*
151 mg sodium, 39 g carbo., 2 g fiber, 2 g pro. Daily Values: 9% vit. A,
14% vit. C, 1% calcium, 2% iron.

Cherries cooked over hot coals in a
cast-iron skillet become the juicy topping for *Ice
Bucket Cherry Sundaes.* Beforehand scoop ice
cream into a bucket or bowl to stash in the
freezer. When the cherries go into the skillet
with a little sugar and orange peel, take out the
ice cream, ladle up the cherries, and let guests
dip as they please.

After 3 minutes on the grill, tumble peaches into a prepared piecrust set in a cast-iron skillet for *Grilled Peach Pie*. Top with the second crust, flute the edges, place the skillet on the grill, cover, and let it go for an hour and a half. P.S. Whipped cream is optional, but very welcome.

GRILLED PEACH PIE

CHILI CHICKEN AND PASTA

READY IN
20
MINUTES

Garden Fresh

Simple dinners to suit the season

BY **NANCY WALL HOPKINS**
PHOTOGRAPHS BY **ANDY LYONS**
FOOD STYLING BY **JILL LUST**
RECIPES BY **MARYELLYN KRANTZ**

FAST!

CHILI CHICKEN AND PASTA

START TO FINISH: 20 minutes

INGREDIENTS

6   oz. dried angel hair pasta
3   ears of corn, husked and cleaned
4   small skinless, boneless chicken breast halves
1½ tsp. chili powder
¼   tsp. salt
¼   tsp. ground black pepper
¼   cup olive oil or cooking oil
3   Tbsp. lime juice
2   medium tomatoes, sliced

PREPARATION

1. Cook pasta in boiling salted water according to package directions. Cut corn kernels off cob; add to pasta the last 2 minutes of cooking. Drain; rinse with cold water.
2. Meanwhile, sprinkle chicken with 1 teaspoon of the chili powder, the salt, and pepper. In a large skillet cook chicken in 1 tablespoon of the hot oil over medium heat for 8 to 10 minutes or until chicken is no longer pink (170°F), turning once.
3. For dressing, combine the remaining ½ teaspoon chili powder, the remaining 3 tablespoons oil, and the lime juice. Divide pasta mixture among 4 plates. Add tomato slices and chicken. Drizzle with dressing. Makes 4 servings.

EACH SERVING: *480 cal., 17 g fat (3 g sat. fat), 66 mg chol., 232 mg sodium, 49 g carbo., 4 g fiber, 35 g pro. Daily Values: 19% vit. A, 28% vit. C, 3% calcium, 15% iron.*

FAST!

MEATBALLS ON CIABATTA

START TO FINISH: 20 minutes

INGREDIENTS

⅓   cup extra virgin olive oil
¼   cup lemon juice
1   bunch fresh Italian (flat-leaf) parsley, large stems removed
2   cloves garlic
1   16- to 18-oz. pkg. frozen cooked Italian-style meatballs, thawed
6   ciabatta rolls, split and toasted
½   head romaine lettuce, torn into bite-size pieces

PREPARATION

1. In a food processor combine oil, lemon juice, parsley, and garlic. Cover; process until finely chopped. Season with *salt* and *ground black pepper.* Transfer parsley mixture to a large skillet. Add meatballs. Cover and heat through over medium heat. Spoon some of the parsley mixture over the meatballs occasionally.
2. Stack ciabatta halves, toasted sides up, on plates. Top with romaine. Using a slotted spoon, remove meatballs from skillet; place on romaine. Drizzle with parsley mixture in skillet. Makes 6 servings.

EACH SERVING: *534 cal., 31 g fat (10 g sat. fat), 49 mg chol., 1,002 mg sodium, 43 g carbo., 6 g fiber, 20 g pro. Daily Values: 5% vit. A, 6% vit. C, 1% calcium, 29% iron.*

MEATBALLS ON CIABATTA

FAST! **LOW FAT**

GINGER TILAPIA

START TO FINISH: 20 minutes

INGREDIENTS

½	cup cider vinegar
¼	cup packed brown sugar
2	tsp. grated fresh ginger
2	medium cucumbers, sliced
4	4-oz. tilapia fillets, ½ to ¾ inch thick
1	6-oz. carton plain yogurt
2	Tbsp. snipped fresh mint
	Shredded lemon peel (optional)
	Coarsely ground black pepper (optional)

PREPARATION

1. Preheat broiler. In a medium bowl stir together vinegar, brown sugar, ginger, and ¼ teaspoon *salt* until sugar is dissolved; remove ¼ cup. Add cucumbers to remaining vinegar mixture; toss.

2. Spray the rack of an unheated broiler pan with *nonstick cooking spray*. Arrange fish on rack; brush with reserved vinegar mixture. Broil 4 inches from heat for 4 to 6 minutes or until fish flakes easily.

3. In a bowl combine yogurt and mint. With a slotted spoon, add cucumbers to plates. Top with fish, yogurt mixture, and, if desired, lemon peel and pepper. Makes 4 servings.

EACH SERVING: *210 cal., 3 g fat (1 g sat. fat), 59 mg chol., 388 mg sodium, 23 g carbo., 0 g fiber, 26 g pro. Daily Values: 2% vit. A, 8% vit. C, 12% calcium, 10% iron.*

GINGER TILAPIA

VEGGIE GARDEN WRAPS

SHRIMP AND ASPARAGUS SALAD

START TO FINISH: 20 minutes

INGREDIENTS

12	oz. thin fresh asparagus spears, trimmed
6	cups watercress, tough stems removed
1	16-oz. pkg. frozen peeled cooked shrimp with tails, thawed
2	cups cherry tomatoes, halved
¾	cup bottled raspberry vinaigrette
	Sea salt and cracked black pepper

PREPARATION

1. In a large skillet cook asparagus in a small amount of lightly salted boiling water for 3 minutes. Drain in colander. Run under cold water. Divide asparagus among 4 plates; layer with watercress, shrimp, and tomatoes. Drizzle with vinaigrette. Sprinkle with salt and pepper. Makes 4 servings.

EACH SERVING: *257 cal., 8 g fat (1 g sat. fat), 227 mg chol., 360 mg sodium, 14 g carbo., 2 g fiber, 33 g pro. Daily Values: 58% vit. A, 51% vit. C, 14% calcium, 25% iron.*

VEGGIE GARDEN WRAPS

START TO FINISH: 20 minutes

INGREDIENTS

½	cup mayonnaise
3	to 4 Tbsp. purchased dried tomato pesto
8	to 12 6-inch corn tortillas
2	6-oz. pkg. refrigerated grilled chicken breast strips
2	small yellow summer squash, cut into sticks
1	medium sweet pepper, cut into strips
	Fresh cilantro sprigs (optional)

PREPARATION

1. In a bowl stir together mayonnaise and pesto; divide into 4 small bowls. Place tortillas on a microwave-safe plate; cover with paper towels. Microwave on 100% power (high) for 30 to 45 seconds or until tortillas are warm.

2. Divide chicken, squash sticks, sweet pepper strips, and warm tortillas among 4 shallow bowls. If desired, garnish with cilantro. Serve with pesto mixture. Makes 4 servings.

EACH SERVING: *481 cal., 30 g fat (6 g sat. fat), 66 mg chol., 1,021 mg sodium, 30 g carbo., 5 g fiber, 24 g pro. Daily Values: 6% vit. A, 49% vit. C, 8% calcium, 10% iron.*

SHRIMP AND ASPARAGUS SALAD

Summer Light

Fresh, healthful versions of favorite picnic sides.

BY **STEPHEN EXEL**
PHOTOGRAPHS BY **ANDY LYONS**
FOOD STYLING BY **JILL LUST**
RECIPES BY **LAURA MARZEN**

FAST! LOW FAT

CORN SALAD

Fresh spinach boosts antioxidants and fiber, and the corn builds in natural sweetness.

START TO FINISH: 20 minutes

INGREDIENTS

¼ cup lime juice
1 Tbsp. honey
1 fresh jalapeño chile pepper, seeded and finely chopped (See Note, page 76)
3 Tbsp. snipped fresh cilantro or 1 Tbsp. snipped fresh mint
¼ tsp. salt
6 ears of corn, husked and cleaned, or 3 cups frozen whole kernel corn, thawed
1½ cups fresh baby spinach leaves
1 large tomato, seeded and chopped
¾ cup seeded, chopped cucumber

PREPARATION

1. In a large bowl whisk together lime juice and honey until well combined. Stir in jalapeño pepper, cilantro, and salt.
2. Carefully cut corn kernels off cobs. Add to lime juice mixture in the bowl. Stir in spinach, tomato, and cucumber. Serve immediately. Makes 9 (⅔-cup) servings.

EACH SERVING: 59 cal., 1 g fat (0 g sat. fat), 0 mg chol., 78 mg sodium, 13 g carbo., 2 g fiber, 2 g pro. Daily Values: 16% vit. A, 17% vit. C, 1% calcium, 3% iron.

TEST KITCHEN

TIP When making this salad more than 2 hours ahead of time, toss the apple slices in lemon juice to keep them crisp and fresh looking.

LOW FAT

TWO-TONE COLESLAW

PREP: 20 minutes **CHILL:** 2 hours

INGREDIENTS

⅔ cup light mayonnaise
3 Tbsp. cider vinegar
1 Tbsp. snipped fresh dill or 1 tsp. dried dillweed
½ tsp. salt
½ tsp. coarsely ground black pepper
4 cups shredded green cabbage
4 cups shredded red cabbage
2 large apples, cored and thinly sliced
1 cup chopped sweet onion
  Fresh dill sprigs (optional)

PREPARATION

1. For dressing, in a very large bowl stir together mayonnaise, vinegar, dill, salt, and pepper. Stir in green and red cabbage, apple, and onion. Cover; chill for at least 2 hours or up to 48 hours. If desired, garnish with fresh dill sprigs. Makes 12 servings.

EACH SERVING: 75 cal., 5 g fat (1 g sat. fat), 5 mg chol., 198 mg sodium, 9 g carbo., 2 g fiber, 1 g pro. Daily Values: 7% vit. A, 8% vit. C, 3% calcium, 3% iron.

TWO-TONE COLESLAW

BHG BASICS

Don't strip potatoes of fiber and nutrients. Cook and eat them with the skin on.

POTATO SALAD WITH A TWIST

LOW FAT **KID FRIENDLY**

SUMMER'S BEST BBQ BEANS

PREP: 15 minutes **COOK:** 25 minutes

INGREDIENTS
      Nonstick cooking spray
1   medium onion, halved and thinly sliced (½ cup)
1   red or green sweet pepper, seeded and chopped (¾ cup)
2   large ripe tomatoes, chopped (2 cups)
3   15- to 16-oz. cans kidney beans, rinsed and drained
1   8-oz. can tomato sauce
1   8-oz. can crushed pineapple, undrained
1   Tbsp. molasses or maple syrup
1   Tbsp. Worcestershire sauce

PREPARATION
1. Coat a large saucepan with cooking spray. Heat over medium heat. Add onion and sweet pepper. Cook and stir for 5 minutes or until tender. Stir in tomato, beans, tomato sauce, undrained pineapple, molasses, and Worcestershire sauce.
2. Bring to boiling; reduce heat. Simmer, covered, for 10 minutes. Uncover; simmer for 10 minutes more or until desired consistency. Makes 10 servings.

EACH SERVING: *140 cal., 0 g fat (0 g sat. fat), 0 mg chol., 351 mg sodium, 31 g carbo., 8 g fiber, 10 g pro. Daily Values: 9% vit. A, 31% vit. C, 5% calcium, 12% iron.*

SUMMER'S BEST BBQ BEANS

LOW FAT

POTATO SALAD WITH A TWIST

PREP: 15 minutes **COOK:** 15 minutes **CHILL:** 4 hours

INGREDIENTS
2   lb. tiny white new potatoes or fingerling potatoes
1   cup plain low-fat yogurt
½   cup sliced green onion
¼   cup lemon juice
½   tsp. salt
½   tsp. cumin seeds (optional)
¼   tsp. ground black pepper
2   medium red, yellow, or green sweet peppers, seeded and cut into bite-size strips
1   avocado, seeded, peeled, and cut into thin wedges
2   Tbsp. cooked, chopped bacon (optional)

PREPARATION
1. Halve any large potatoes. In a large saucepan cook potatoes, covered, in enough salted boiling water to cover for 15 minutes or until tender. Drain; cool to room temperature.
2. Meanwhile, for dressing, in a bowl combine yogurt, onion, lemon juice, salt, cumin seeds (if desired), and black pepper. Add potatoes and sweet pepper strips. Toss to coat. Cover; chill for at least 4 hours or up to 24 hours. Gently stir in avocado just before serving. If desired, sprinkle with cooked bacon pieces. Makes 12 (¾-cup) servings.

EACH SERVING: *103 cal., 3 g fat (1 g sat. fat), 1 mg chol., 118 mg sodium, 18 g carbo., 3 g fiber, 3 g pro. Daily Values: 14% vit. A, 95% vit. C, 5% calcium, 5% iron.*

Sweet Tart

Pair the tart flavor of rhubarb with sweetness and you get a delicious push-pull of opposites on your tongue. Available now until the end of summer, it brightens up desserts and gives zip to cheese, ham, pork, and fish dishes.

RHUBARB SAUCE

Serve with cheese as an appetizer or alone as a lively accompaniment to plain grilled chicken or pork chops.

PREP: 20 minutes
COOK: 40 minutes

INGREDIENTS

2	large red onions, coarsely chopped
1/3	cup vinegar
1/3	cup dried cherries or golden raisins
1/4	cup granulated sugar
1/4	cup packed brown sugar
1/4	cup water
1	Tbsp. lime juice
1/4	tsp. salt
1/8	tsp. ground ginger
3	cups fresh rhubarb cut into 1/2-inch pieces or 3 cups frozen rhubarb, thawed and drained

PREPARATION

1. In a medium saucepan combine all ingredients except rhubarb. Bring to boiling; reduce heat. Cover; simmer for 25 minutes, stirring occasionally. Add rhubarb; cover and simmer for 10 minutes.
2. Uncover; simmer until thickened, about 5 minutes more if using fresh rhubarb or about 15 minutes more if using frozen rhubarb. Cool. Cover and store in refrigerator for up to 1 week. Makes 2 1/2 cups (about ten 1/4-cup servings).

EACH SERVING: *74 cal., 0 g fat (0 g sat. fat), 0 mg chol., 64 mg sodium, 18 g carbo., 1 g fiber, 1 g pro. Daily Values: 3% vit. A, 8% vit. C, 4% calcium, 2% iron.*

Rev 'em with rhubarb

1. Enhance the appeal of chocolate by adding 1 cup finely chopped rhubarb to chocolate cake mix.

2. Jazz up ginger ale or martinis with a splash of rhubarb syrup: Cook 2 cups rhubarb, 3 cups sugar, and 1 cup water for 20 minutes. Strain out pulp.

3. Make pie memorable. Substitute 1 cup chopped rhubarb for 1 cup sliced apple in a favorite apple pie recipe.

4. Microwave a handful of chopped rhubarb until tender; toss chunks with a vinaigrette.

BY **RICHARD SWEARINGER**
PHOTOGRAPHS BY **VEER, ANDY LYONS**
FOOD STYLING BY **JILL LUST**

Grilling Fever

In June we just can't get enough easy outdoor meals.
Try these new tricks, tastes, and twists for 3 summer faves.

BY **RICHARD SWEARINGER**
PHOTOGRAPHS BY **ANDY LYONS**
FOOD STYLING BY **CHARLES WORTHINGTON**

GARDEN BURGER

GARDEN BURGER

PREP: 20 minutes
GRILL: 14 minutes

INGREDIENTS

2	Tbsp. olive oil
2	Tbsp. red wine vinegar
1	tsp. snipped fresh thyme
¼	tsp. cracked black pepper
2	medium yellow summer squash, cut lengthwise (¼- to ½-inch slices)
1	lb. 90-percent lean ground beef
4	hamburger buns
2	to 4 oz. blue cheese Arugula or lettuce

PREPARATION

1. For dressing, in a bowl whisk oil, vinegar, thyme, and pepper. Brush squash with some dressing.
2. In a bowl combine beef, ¼ teaspoon *salt,* and ¼ teaspoon *ground black pepper.* Shape into four ¾-inch-thick patties.
3. For a charcoal grill, grill patties on the rack of an uncovered grill directly over medium coals for 14 to 18 minutes or until meat is done (160°F); turn once. Cook squash alongside beef for 7 to 10 minutes or until tender; turn once. (For gas grill, preheat grill. Reduce heat to medium. Cover and grill as above.)
4. To serve, drizzle dressing over cut sides of bun tops. Layer remaining ingredients on buns. Makes 4 burgers.

EACH BURGER: *426 cal., 24 g fat (8 g sat. fat), 82 mg chol., 592 mg sodium, 24 g carbo., 2 g fiber, 28 g pro. Daily Values: 6% vit. A, 10% vit. C, 16% calcium, 22% iron.*

Marinade basics

- Don't marinate at room temperature for more than 15 minutes.

- Don't exceed suggested time for marinade; meat can become mushy in acidic marinades.

MARGARITA-CHICKEN SALAD

PREP: 25 minutes
MARINATE: 2 hours
GRILL: 12 minutes

INGREDIENTS

4	skinless, boneless chicken breast halves
1½	cups margarita drink mix (without alcohol)
1	tsp. ground cumin
1	tsp. finely shredded lime peel
½	cup mayonnaise
2	Tbsp. lime juice
⅛	tsp. cayenne pepper
4	medium tomatoes, sliced
2	medium avocados, halved, seeded, peeled, and sliced
½	of a medium red onion, thinly sliced
¼	tsp. cracked black pepper

PREPARATION

1. Place chicken in a plastic bag set in a shallow dish. In a bowl combine margarita mix, cumin, and lime peel. Pour over chicken; seal bag. Refrigerate for 2 to 8 hours. Drain and discard the marinade.
2. For a charcoal grill, grill chicken on the rack of uncovered grill directly over medium coals for 12 to 15 minutes or until chicken is no longer pink (170°F), turning once halfway through grilling. (For a gas grill, preheat grill. Reduce heat to medium. Place chicken on grill rack over heat. Cover; grill as above.) Remove chicken. Cool slightly.
3. In a medium bowl combine mayonnaise, lime juice, and cayenne. Coarsely chop chicken. Add to mayonnaise mixture. Toss gently. Line 4 salad plates with tomato slices. Top tomatoes with chicken, avocados, and red onion. Sprinkle with black pepper. Makes 4 servings.

EACH SERVING: *584 cal., 38 g fat (7 g sat. fat), 92 mg chol., 241 mg sodium, 28 g carbo., 8 g fiber, 36 g pro. Daily Values: 24% vit. A, 51% vit. C, 5% calcium, 10% iron.*

FORGET FLARE-UPS

To minimize flames leaping from the grill, prevent fats and oils from falling onto coals or grates as much as possible. Techniques to try:

- Trim most of the fat from edges of steaks and chops.

- Drain marinated food to allow excess oil to run off.

- If flare-ups do occur, move meat away from flames or off grill entirely until fire subsides. Resume cooking at a lower heat, if necessary.

MARGARITA-CHICKEN SALAD

THREE-HERB STEAK

GAS GRILL, CHARCOAL FLAVOR

Charcoal gives food a unique smoky flavor, and your gas grill can do the same, says grilling expert Judith Fertig, coauthor of *Weeknight Grilling with the BBQ Queens: Making Meals Fast and Fabulous.* Her tips:

■ Add about ⅓ cup wood chunks, chips, or pellets to the grill. (*Always* consult the owners manual first.)

■ To hold the chips, either purchase a metal smoker box or make your own packet from foil.

■ Wrap chips tightly in a single thickness of foil and poke a small hole for smoke to escape.

■ Place wrapped wood as close as possible to burners either on rack of grill or next to burners. (For a smoker box, follow manufacturer's directions.)

■ Set flame to medium-high, close lid, and wait until smoke appears. Reduce heat to medium, add food, and cook with lid closed.

Season it right

Rubs, herbs, and spice blends are key to great-tasting grilling. This summer look for new blends from a variety of spice companies.

THREE-HERB STEAK

PREP: 20 minutes **CHILL:** 1 hour
GRILL: 15 minutes
STAND: 5 minutes

INGREDIENTS

½	cup snipped fresh parsley
¼	cup olive oil
¼	cup snipped fresh basil
1	Tbsp. snipped fresh oregano
1	to 2 tsp. cracked black pepper
½	tsp. salt
2	beef top loin steaks, cut 1½ inches thick
2	medium red or yellow sweet peppers, cut into ½-inch rings and seeds removed
1	Tbsp. olive oil
	Salt and ground black pepper

PREPARATION

1. In a bowl combine parsley, ¼ cup olive oil, basil, oregano, cracked pepper, and ½ teaspoon salt. Trim fat from meat. Pat about two-thirds of the herb mixture onto both sides of steaks. Cover and refrigerate 1 hour. Meanwhile, brush pepper rings with the 1 tablespoon olive oil. Season with salt and black pepper.

2. For a charcoal grill, grill steaks on the rack of an uncovered grill to desired doneness, turning once. Allow 15 to 19 minutes for medium rare (145°F) or 18 to 23 minutes for medium (160°F). Grill pepper rings next to steaks the last 8 to 10 minutes of grilling or until peppers are tender, turning once. Remove steaks from grill and sprinkle with remaining herb mixture. Cover; let stand for 5 to 10 minutes.

3. Serve with sweet pepper rings. Slice steaks across grain of meat. Makes 6 servings.

EACH SERVING: *307 cal., 19 g fat (5 g sat. fat), 77 mg chol., 313 mg sodium, 3 g carbo., 1 g fiber, 29 g pro. Daily Values: 35% vit. A, 138% vit. C, 2% calcium, 16% iron.*

BY **NANCY WALL HOPKINS**
PHOTOGRAPHS BY **ANDY LYONS**
FOOD STYLING BY **JILL LUST**

1

Lemonade

Get creative with your basic lemonade:
Add fruits, juices, herbs, and spices.

2

3

4

6

5

7

8

10

9

1. GINGER
Fresh gingerroot,
ripe pear slices,
sugarcane stalk
for stirring

2. WATERMELON
Watermelon puree,
watermelon slice

3. LAVENDER
Dried lavender,
fresh lavender leaves

4. PEACH TEA
Equal parts
lemonade, peach
nectar, and iced tea;
peach slices

5. BLACKBERRY
Fresh blackberries,
fresh sage leaves

6. KIWI-MELON
Sliced kiwifruit,
honeydew puree,
honeydew slice

7. RASPBERRY
Raspberry juice,
fresh raspberries

8. KEY LIME
Limeade, key lime
slices, mint leaves

9. LEMON DROP
Crushed lemon drops,
sugar, lemon slice

10. PAPAYA
Guava juice, fresh
papaya slice

BHG
BASICS

**For basic
lemonade:** In a large
pitcher stir together
3 cups cold water,
1 cup lemon juice,
and ¾ cup sugar until
sugar is dissolved.
Add flavors as above.
Chill; serve over ice
with garnishes.

JULY

TAKE YOUR INDEPENDENCE DAY CELEBRATIONS
AND WEEKEND MEALS OUTDOORS AND ENJOY
FRESH PRODUCE AND MEALS FROM THE GRILL.

SMOTHERED STEAK
page 144

All-Star Sizzle

Plus

Build a Better—

Celebrate—

Everyday Easy—

Fresh Now—

Good and Healthy—

GINGER PEACH GLAZED CHICKEN
page 148

HONEY WHEAT BEER MARINATED PORK CHOPS AND CHEDDAR
page 152

What's Cooking—

all-star sizzle

FROM COAST TO COAST, AMERICANS LOOK TO THEIR ROOTS FOR GRILLING INSPIRATION. SAMPLE EIGHT GREAT DISHES FROM COOKS WHO KNOW THEIR COALS.

BY **RICHARD SWEARINGER**
PHOTOGRAPHS BY **IAIN BAGWELL**
FOOD STYLING BY **WILLIAM SMITH**
PROP STYLING BY **KAREN JOHNSON**

connecticut

In Norma Castro's Bridgeport backyard, **hearty onion, garlic, sweet peppers, and sausage top** Smothered Steak. That combination is called "sofrito" in Puerto Rico, where Norma lived as a child before moving north 30 years ago.

SMOTHERED STEAK
page 144

NORMA CASTRO'S
SMOTHERED STEAK

PREP: 30 minutes **CHILL:** 1 hour **GRILL:** 17 minutes

INGREDIENTS
1 2-lb. beef flank steak
   Salt and freshly ground black pepper
2 tsp. finely shredded lime peel
4 oz. bulk Italian sausage
2 cups chopped onion (2 large)
2 red, yellow, and/or green sweet peppers, chopped
3 cloves garlic, minced
¼ cup snipped fresh cilantro
¼ cup cider vinegar

PREPARATION
1. Trim fat from meat. Score both sides of steak in diamond pattern, making shallow diagonal cuts at 1-inch intervals. Sprinkle with salt, black pepper, and peel. Wrap in plastic wrap; refrigerate 1 hour.
2. For a charcoal grill, grill steak on the rack of an uncovered grill directly over medium coals for 17 to 21 minutes for medium (160°F), turning once halfway through grilling. (For a gas grill, preheat grill. Reduce heat to medium. Grill steak on rack directly over heat. Cover and grill as above.)
3. Meanwhile, for pepper and sausage topper, preheat a large cast-iron skillet directly over medium coals. Add sausage; cook for 3 minutes, stirring occasionally. Add onion, sweet pepper, and garlic. Cook for 10 minutes or until vegetables are crisp-tender, stirring occasionally. Stir in cilantro and vinegar (vinegar will sizzle).
4. To serve, thinly slice steak; top with peppers and sausage. Makes 6 servings.

EACH SERVING (WITH ¼ CUP PEPPERS AND SAUSAGE): 351 cal., 19 g fat (7 g sat. fat), 76 mg chol., 321 mg sodium, 8 g carbo., 2 g fiber, 36 g pro. Daily Values: 29% vit. A, 136% vit. C, 6% calcium, 16% iron.

SMOTHERED STEAK

LOW FAT

HAYLEY MATSON-MATHES'
HULI-HULI PORK

"Huli-huli" means "turn-turn" in Hawaiian, a reference to the cooking method of this popular fundraising dish. Typically huli-huli is made with chicken; Hayley's innovation is the switch to pork.

PREP: 20 minutes **MARINATE:** 4 hours **GRILL:** 35 minutes
STAND: 10 minutes

INGREDIENTS
2 pork tenderloins (1 to 1¼ lb. each)
¾ cup ketchup
⅓ cup reduced-sodium soy sauce
3 Tbsp. packed brown sugar
3 Tbsp. lime juice or sweet mirin cooking wine (available in the Asian food section of supermarkets)
1 Tbsp. grated fresh ginger
4 cloves garlic, minced
   Lime wedges and fresh herbs

PREPARATION
1. Place pork in a large heavy resealable plastic bag set in a shallow dish; set aside.
2. For marinade, in a small bowl combine ketchup, soy sauce, brown sugar, lime juice, ginger, and garlic. Transfer ¾ cup of the marinade to a small container; cover and chill until needed. Pour remaining marinade over pork; seal bag. Refrigerate for 4 to 24 hours, turning the bag occasionally.
3. Drain pork, reserving marinade. For a charcoal grill, arrange hot coals around a drip pan. Place pork on the grill rack over pan. Cover and grill over medium-high heat for 20 minutes. Brush with marinade from bag. Cover and grill for 15 to 20 minutes more or until an instant-read thermometer registers 155°F when inserted into the thickest part of the meat. (For a gas grill, preheat grill. Reduce heat to medium-high. Adjust for indirect cooking. Grill as above.) Remove pork from grill. Cover with foil; let stand for 10 minutes before slicing. (Meat temperature will rise 5°F during standing.)
4. Meanwhile, place reserved ¾ cup marinade in a small saucepan; bring to boiling. Transfer to a serving dish and pass with pork. Serve with lime wedges and fresh herbs. Makes 6 to 8 servings.

EACH SERVING: 206 cal., 4 g fat (1 g sat. fat), 74 mg chol., 652 mg sodium, 17 g carbo., 0 g fiber, 25 g pro. Daily Values: 5% vit. A, 9% vit. C, 2% calcium, 10% iron.

HULI-HULI PORK

"When you spot a cloud of cooking smoke on the horizon, you get in your car and drive toward it as fast as you can because someone is making huli-huli," says **Hayley Matson-Mathes** of Honolulu. In Hayley's version, pork is marinated in soy sauce, lime juice, and brown sugar.

montana

In Billings, Stella Fong drew on her cultural heritage to create this **easy five-ingredient Grilled Shrimp Salad.** The lettuce is grilled too—combining a Chinese taste for cooked lettuce with the flair for grilling Stella acquired growing up in California.

GRILLED SHRIMP SALAD

FAST!

STELLA FONG'S
GRILLED SHRIMP SALAD

PREP: 15 minutes GRILL: 5 minutes

INGREDIENTS
¼ cup olive oil
½ tsp. kosher salt or ¼ tsp. salt
1 lb. fresh or frozen large shrimp, peeled and deveined
2 hearts of romaine lettuce, halved lengthwise
¼ cup finely shredded Parmesan cheese
2 lemons
   Olive oil
   Salt and ground black pepper

PREPARATION
1. In a bowl whisk together the ¼ cup olive oil and ½ teaspoon salt. Set aside. Thread shrimp onto four metal skewers, leaving a ¼-inch space between each shrimp. Brush oil mixture over shrimp and cut sides of lettuce.
2. For a charcoal grill, grill shrimp on the rack of an uncovered grill directly over medium coals for 5 to 8 minutes or until shrimp are opaque, turning once halfway through grilling. Grill lettuce, cut sides down, for 2 to 4 minutes or until grill marks develop on lettuce and the inside leaves are slightly wilted. (For a gas grill, preheat grill. Reduce heat to medium. Cover; grill shrimp and lettuce as above.)
3. Place lettuce in serving bowl. Remove shrimp from skewers. Add shrimp to bowl with lettuce; sprinkle with cheese. Squeeze juice of one lemon over shrimp and lettuce. Drizzle with additional olive oil. Sprinkle with salt and pepper. Cut remaining lemon into wedges and serve with salad. Makes 4 servings.

EACH SERVING: *267 cal., 20 g fat (3 g sat. fat), 133 mg chol., 514 mg sodium, 2 g carbo., 0 g fiber, 19 g pro. Daily Values: 15% vit. A, 20% vit. C, 12% calcium, 13% iron.*

PETER MCKEE'S
HERB-SMOKED SALMON

STAND: 1 hour PREP: 20 minutes GRILL: 8 minutes

INGREDIENTS
1 cup alder or hickory wood chips
3 or 4 thyme sprigs
6 4- to 5-oz. fresh or frozen skin-on salmon fillets, 1 inch thick
2 Tbsp. butter
1 Tbsp. finely snipped fresh thyme
1 Tbsp. packed brown sugar
1 Tbsp. lemon juice
¼ tsp. salt
¼ tsp. ground black pepper
1 recipe Red Pepper Rice with Grilled Squash

PREPARATION
1. Soak wood chips and thyme sprigs in water to cover 1 hour before grilling. Drain. Coat unheated grill rack with *nonstick cooking spray* or *cooking oil*. Thaw fish, if frozen. Rinse; dry with paper towels.
2. In a microwave-safe bowl microwave butter on 100% power (high) for 30 seconds until butter is melted. Stir in snipped thyme, brown sugar, lemon juice, salt, and pepper. Microwave for 30 seconds more. Stir to dissolve sugar. Brush over fish.
3. For a charcoal grill, sprinkle wood chips and thyme sprigs directly over medium coals. Grill fish, skin sides up, on prepared grill rack directly over coals for 3 minutes. Turn skin sides down. Grill for 5 to 7 minutes more or until fish flakes easily when tested with a fork. (For a gas grill, preheat grill. Reduce heat to medium. Add wood chips according to manufacturer's directions; include thyme sprigs with wood. Place fish on prepared grill rack over heat. Cover; grill as above.) Serve with Red Pepper Rice with Grilled Squash. Serves 6.
RED PEPPER RICE WITH GRILLED SQUASH: Brush 2 quartered sweet peppers and 2 halved summer squash or zucchini with olive oil; sprinkle lightly with salt and ground black pepper. Add to grill rack with salmon, turning when salmon is turned. Grill for 8 minutes. Remove from grill. Chop peppers; toss with 3 cups hot cooked rice and 2 teaspoons snipped fresh thyme. Slice squash crosswise. Serve with Herb-Smoked Salmon.

EACH SERVING: *431 cal., 21 g fat (6 g sat. fat), 77 mg chol., 297 mg sodium, 33 g carbo., 2 g fiber, 26 g pro. Daily Values: 10% vit. A, 84% vit. C, 4% calcium, 14% iron.*

Peter McKee loves traditional Southern barbecue, but he lives near Seattle—a town where king salmon isn't just a species, it's culinary royalty. So Peter, a lawyer, combines fish and smoke. The salmon is prepared Northwest-style with a baste of butter and thyme; wood chips and thyme sprigs added to coals give the fish a just-right touch of Southern smoke.

HERB-SMOKED SALMON

LOW FAT · KID FRIENDLY

FRED THOMPSON'S

GINGER PEACH GLAZED CHICKEN

PREP: 15 minutes **GRILL:** 50 minutes

INGREDIENTS

2½	to 3 lb. meaty chicken pieces (breast halves, thighs, and drumsticks)
½	cup peach preserves, large pieces snipped
1	Tbsp. white wine vinegar
1	Tbsp. prepared horseradish
1	tsp. grated fresh ginger

PREPARATION

1. Skin chicken, if desired. Sprinkle chicken lightly with *salt* and *ground black pepper*. For a charcoal grill, arrange medium-hot coals around a drip pan. Place chicken on grill rack over pan. Cover and grill over medium heat for 40 minutes. (For a gas grill, preheat grill. Reduce heat to medium. Adjust for indirect cooking. Grill as above.)

2. Meanwhile, in a small microwave-safe bowl combine preserves, vinegar, horseradish, ginger, ½ teaspoon *salt*, and ½ teaspoon *ground black pepper*. Microwave, uncovered, on 100% power (high) for 30 to 60 seconds or until preserves are melted, stirring once.

3. Brush preserves mixture onto chicken. Cover. Grill for 10 to 20 minutes more or until chicken is no longer pink (180°F for thighs and drumsticks, 170°F for breast halves). Brush occasionally with preserves mixture. Spoon any remaining preserves mixture over chicken. Makes 4 to 6 servings.

EACH SERVING: *356 cal., 9 g fat (3 g sat. fat), 115 mg chol., 565 mg sodium, 28 g carbo., 1 g fiber, 37 g pro. Daily Values: 8% vit. C, 3% calcium, 10% iron.*

GINGER PEACH GLAZED CHICKEN

GENE MATTIUZZO'S

MUSHROOM CHICKEN

PREP: 30 minutes **GRILL:** 50 minutes

INGREDIENTS

1	to 1¼ lb. chopped fresh mushrooms, such as button, cremini, and/or shiitake
1	clove garlic, minced
2	tsp. snipped fresh oregano or ¼ tsp. dried oregano, crushed
2	Tbsp. olive oil
2	Tbsp. dry Marsala wine (optional)
1	tsp. anchovy paste or soy sauce
¼	tsp. salt
¼	tsp. freshly ground black pepper
2½	to 3 lb. meaty chicken pieces (breast halves, thighs, and drumsticks)
	Lemon halves
	Fresh oregano sprigs (optional)

PREPARATION

1. In a large skillet cook mushrooms, garlic, and oregano in hot oil over medium heat for 6 minutes or until tender, stirring occasionally. Remove from heat. Stir in Marsala (if desired), anchovy paste, salt, and pepper. Return to heat; cook and stir for 2 minutes more. Remove from heat. Cool.

2. Loosen skin of each chicken piece on one side. Stuff mushroom mixture under skin. Sprinkle the chicken lightly with *salt* and *ground black pepper*.

3. For a charcoal grill, arrange medium-hot coals around a drip pan. Place chicken, bone sides down, on grill rack over drip pan. Cover and grill over medium heat for 50 to 60 minutes or until chicken is no longer pink (180°F for thighs and drumsticks, 170°F for breast halves). (For a gas grill, preheat grill. Reduce heat to medium. Adjust for indirect cooking. Place chicken on grill rack; grill as above.)

4. Serve chicken with lemon halves and, if desired, oregano. Makes 4 to 6 servings.

EACH SERVING: *328 cal., 16 g fat (4 g sat. fat), 116 mg chol., 437 mg sodium, 4 g carbo., 1 g fiber, 41 g pro. Daily Values: 5% vit. C, 3% calcium, 12% iron.*

"Growing up, the peach harvest in the Sandhills of North Carolina was a big deal," says Fred Thompson. "My parents always planned a day trip around the harvest." It was those memories that led him to create Ginger Peach Glazed Chicken. "In the South **vinegar and horseradish were always around to add a little kick to food.**"

california

Mushroom Chicken comes straight from Gene Mattiuzzo's childhood: As a kid he'd hunt wild mushrooms in the woods near his home in Fort Bragg. Tucked under the skin, **mushrooms and oregano flavor the chicken** while the meat slowly cooks on the grill. Now the mushrooms are from the supermarket, but the oregano grows at the back door.

Meredith Deeds, a recent transplant to Texas, combines big, bold flavors of the Lone Star State with a favorite dish from her native California. "This Tex-Mex-inspired Cowboy Steak, with its spicy chili rub and fresh salsa, reminds me of the wonderful *carne asada* of my youth," Meredith says.

**COWBOY STEAK
SUMMER SALSA**

MEREDITH DEEDS'
COWBOY STEAK

PREP: 25 minutes **CHILL:** 1 hour **GRILL:** 10 minutes
STAND: 10 minutes

INGREDIENTS
¼   cup ancho chili powder or chili powder
2   Tbsp. paprika
6   cloves garlic, minced
1   tsp. salt
1   tsp. coarsely ground black pepper
2   Tbsp. olive oil
4   10- to 12-oz. beef ribeye steaks, cut 1 inch thick
    Snipped fresh parsley
1   recipe Summer Salsa (right)

PREPARATION
1. For the spice rub, in a small bowl combine chili powder, paprika, garlic, salt, and pepper. Stir in olive oil to make a paste that will cling to the steaks.
2. Trim fat from steaks. Coat both sides of steaks with spice rub. Wrap steaks tightly with plastic wrap; refrigerate for 1 hour.
3. For a charcoal grill, place steaks on the rack of an uncovered grill directly over medium coals. Grill, turning once halfway through grilling time. Allow 10 to 12 minutes for medium rare (145°F) or 12 to 15 minutes for medium (160°F). (For a gas grill, preheat grill. Reduce heat to medium. Place meat on grill rack over heat. Cover and grill as above.) Let stand for 10 minutes. Sprinkle with parsley and serve with Summer Salsa. Makes 8 servings.

EACH SERVING (WITH ¼ CUP SALSA): *310 cal., 16 g fat (5 g sat. fat), 83 mg chol., 490 mg sodium, 10 g carbo., 5 g fiber, 31 g pro. Daily Values: 90% vit. A, 25% vit. C, 6% calcium, 28% iron.*

SUMMER SALSA

PREP: 20 minutes **CHILL:** 2 hours

INGREDIENTS
1   lb. tomatoes, seeded and chopped
½   cup chopped red onion (1 small)
¼   cup snipped fresh parsley
2   Tbsp. lime juice
2   cloves garlic, minced
1   to 2 serrano chile peppers, seeded and minced*
¼   tsp. salt

PREPARATION
1. In a medium bowl combine chopped tomatoes, onion, parsley, lime juice, garlic, chile pepper, and salt. Cover and refrigerate for 2 hours to allow flavors to blend. Serve with Cowboy Ribeyes (left). Makes 2½ cups salsa (ten ¼-cup servings).
*NOTE: Because hot chile peppers, such as serranos, contain volatile oils that can burn your skin and eyes, avoid direct contact with chiles as much as possible. When working with chile peppers, wear plastic or rubber gloves. If your bare hands do touch chile peppers, wash your hands well with soap and water.

EACH SERVING: *13 cal., 0 g fat (0 g sat. fat), 0 mg chol., 62 mg sodium, 3 g carbo., 1 g fiber, 2 g pro. Daily Values: 10% vit. A, 16% vit. C, 1% calcium, 1% iron.*

CARLA SNYDER'S
HONEY WHEAT BEER MARINATED PORK CHOPS AND CHEDDAR

PREP: 25 minutes **MARINATE:** 4 hours **GRILL:** 37 minutes

INGREDIENTS

4   bone-in pork loin chops or pork rib chops, cut 1¼ to 1½ inches thick (about 10 to 12 oz. each)
1   12-oz. bottle honey wheat beer
2   cloves garlic, minced
1   Tbsp. olive oil
¼   tsp. salt
½   tsp. coarsely ground black pepper
4   oz. white cheddar cheese, shredded, or blue cheese, crumbled (1 cup)
2   green onions, thinly sliced
2   Tbsp. chopped walnuts, toasted
     Salt and ground black pepper

PREPARATION

1. Place pork chops in a 2-gallon heavy resealable plastic bag set in a 4-quart bowl; set aside. For marinade, in a small bowl combine beer, garlic, oil, salt, and pepper; pour over pork. Seal bag; marinate in the refrigerator for 4 hours or up to 24 hours, turning bag occasionally. Drain pork chops, discarding marinade.
2. For a charcoal grill, arrange medium-hot coals around a drip pan. Check for medium heat above pan. Place pork on grill rack over drip pan. Cover; grill for 35 to 40 minutes or until done (160°F). (For a gas grill, preheat grill. Reduce heat to medium. Adjust for indirect cooking. Place pork on unheated side of grill rack. Cover and grill as above.)
3. Meanwhile, for topping, in a small bowl stir together cheese, green onion, and nuts. Spoon cheese mixture over chops. Cover and grill for 2 to 3 minutes more or until cheese is melted. Season to taste with salt and pepper. Makes 4 servings.

EACH SERVING: *428 cal., 17 g fat (8 g sat. fat), 160 mg chol., 595 mg sodium, 2 g carbo., 0 g fiber, 61 g pro. Daily Values: 7% vit. A, 3% vit. C, 23% calcium, 8% iron.*

THRILL TO THE GRILL—TIPS FROM OUR ALL-STAR GRILLERS

FRED THOMPSON
STORMY WEATHER

Don't get bothered if the weather is a little cranky. In cold weather increase cooking times slightly. If it's windy place the grill perpendicular to the wind flow. You'll probably need more charcoal, and keep a closer watch on the fire's temperature.

STELLA FONG
DRIZZLE ON THE OIL

Drizzle leafy vegetables with olive oil and sprinkle with salt before grilling. Or try roasted sesame oil in place of the olive oil. It contributes a nice nutty flavor that really complements the smoky flavor from the grill.

PETER MCKEE
ALDER FOR SMOKING

For authentic Pacific Northwest smoked flavor, I like to use Northwest red alder wood chips. If alder wood is not available to you, it can be found online at *thehomechef.net.*

MEREDITH DEEDS
SEAR, DON'T BURN!

It's so important to get a hot bed of coals going so you can sear the steak. Keep the grill not far from the coals but not too close because a rub can burn. A good crust helps keep flavor in and the internal temperature where you want it.

ohio

"Clevelanders like their food highly flavored—no subtle seasonings here," says Carla Snyder. Her Honey Wheat Beer Marinated Pork Chops and Cheddar honors the hearty cooking of eastern European immigrants who flocked to the region's steel mills. Just before serving, **shreds of cheese are sprinkled on, melting into a luscious sauce.**

HONEY WHEAT BEER MARINATED PORK CHOPS AND CHEDDAR

Backyard Dinners

Quick meals you can take out on the deck

READY IN
20
MINUTES

BY **NANCY WALL HOPKINS**
PHOTOGRAPHS BY **ANDY LYONS**
FOOD STYLING BY **JILL LUST**
RECIPES BY **MARYELLYN KRANTZ**

CAJUN TURKEY AND MELON

CAJUN TURKEY AND MELON

START TO FINISH: 20 minutes

INGREDIENTS

2	turkey breast tenderloins, split in half horizontally (about 1 lb.)
1	Tbsp. olive oil
1½	tsp. Cajun seasoning
6	cups torn mixed salad greens
1½	cups sliced cantaloupe
1	cup fresh blueberries
	Crumbled farmer cheese (optional)
	Purchased salad dressing of your choice

PREPARATION

1. Brush turkey pieces with olive oil. Sprinkle with Cajun seasoning. For a charcoal grill, grill turkey on the rack of an uncovered grill directly over medium coals for 12 to 15 minutes or until turkey is no longer pink (170°F), turning once halfway through grilling. (For a gas grill, preheat grill. Reduce heat to medium. Place turkey on rack over heat. Cover and grill as above.)
2. To serve, slice turkey. Arrange greens on a serving platter along with turkey, cantaloupe, and berries. If desired, top with cheese. Pass salad dressing. Makes 4 servings.

EACH SERVING: *359 cal., 22 g fat (4 g sat. fat), 68 mg chol., 161 mg sodium, 14 g carbo., 3 g fiber, 29 g pro. Daily Values: 56% vit. A, 52% vit. C, 6% calcium, 12% iron.*

CORNMEAL-CRUSTED PORK

START TO FINISH: 20 minutes

INGREDIENTS

½	cup yellow cornmeal
1	egg, lightly beaten
1	lb. pork tenderloin, cut into ½-inch slices
2	Tbsp. olive oil
12	oz. fresh green beans, trimmed
2	medium zucchini and/or yellow summer squash, thinly bias-sliced
2	Tbsp. fresh oregano leaves (optional)

PREPARATION

1. In a shallow dish combine cornmeal, ½ teaspoon *salt,* and ½ teaspoon *ground black pepper*. In another shallow dish combine egg and 1 tablespoon *water*. Dip pork into egg mixture and then into cornmeal mixture to coat.
2. Heat oil in a large skillet over medium-high heat. Add pork. Cook for 2 minutes per side or until no pink remains. Transfer to a platter. Add beans and zucchini to skillet; cook and stir for 6 minutes or until tender. Season with *salt* and *pepper*. Toss. Serve with pork. If desired, sprinkle with oregano. Makes 4 servings.

EACH SERVING: *310 cal., 6 g fat (3 g sat. fat), 127 mg chol., 385 mg sodium, 21 g carbo., 5 g fiber, 29 g pro. Daily Values: 17% vit. A, 52% vit. C, 6% calcium, 19% iron.*

CORNMEAL-CRUSTED PORK

FAST!

CHICKEN SANDWICHES

START TO FINISH: 20 minutes

INGREDIENTS

8	oz. asparagus spears, trimmed
2	Tbsp. plus 1 tsp. olive oil
4	small skinless, boneless chicken breast halves
4	4-inch portobello mushroom caps, stems removed
8	slices Italian bread, toasted
1	8-oz. tub cream cheese spread with chives

PREPARATION

1. Place asparagus in the center of a doubled large sheet of heavy foil; drizzle with the 1 teaspoon olive oil. Sprinkle with *salt* and *ground black pepper*. Seal foil, leaving space for steam to escape.

2. Brush chicken and mushrooms with about 2 tablespoons olive oil; sprinkle with *salt* and *pepper*. For a charcoal grill, place chicken, mushrooms, and foil packet on the rack of an uncovered grill directly over medium coals. Grill for 15 minutes or until an instant-read thermometer inserted in chicken registers 170°F and mushrooms are tender; turn chicken and mushrooms once. Remove chicken, mushrooms, and foil packet; slice mushrooms.

3. Spread one side of bread slices with cream cheese. Stack 4 slices with chicken, remaining bread, mushrooms, and asparagus. Makes 4 servings.

EACH SERVING: *583 cal., 29 g fat (15 g sat. fat), 121 mg chol., 751 mg sodium, 40 g carbo., 4 g fiber, 37 g pro. Daily Values: 17% vit. A, 52% vit. C, 6% calcium, 19% iron.*

CHICKEN SANDWICHES

CATFISH WITH SUMMER SUCCOTASH

CHIPOTLE STEAK

START TO FINISH: 20 minutes

INGREDIENTS

2   6- to 8-oz. beef shoulder petite tenders
2   tsp. adobo sauce
1   canned chipotle pepper in adobo sauce, chopped
¼   cup olive oil
¼   cup cider vinegar
3   medium tomatoes (about 1 lb.), cut into thick slices
2   medium avocados, halved, seeded, peeled, and sliced
½   of a small red onion, thinly sliced

PREPARATION

1. Sprinkle steaks with *salt* and *ground black pepper*. Spread each with 1 teaspoon of the adobo sauce. For a charcoal grill, grill steaks on the rack of an uncovered grill directly over medium coals, turning once. Allow 12 to 15 minutes for medium (160°F).
2. For dressing, in a screw-top jar combine chopped chipotle pepper, oil, and vinegar. Shake to combine. To serve, slice steaks. Serve with slices of tomato, avocado, and onion; drizzle with dressing. Makes 4 servings.

EACH SERVING: *421 cal., 33 g fat (6 g sat. fat), 50 mg chol., 221 mg sodium, 13 g carbo., 7 g fiber, 20 g pro. Daily Values: 19% vit. A, 34% vit. C, 3% calcium, 15% iron.*

CATFISH WITH SUMMER SUCCOTASH

START TO FINISH: 20 minutes

INGREDIENTS

2   cups frozen lima beans
4   4- to 6-oz. catfish fillets, about ½ inch thick
   Olive oil
   Garlic salt
   Ground black pepper
1   cup purchased corn relish
1   cup fresh baby spinach

PREPARATION

1. Cook lima beans according to package directions. Drain in a colander; rinse under cold water to cool.
2. Meanwhile, rinse fish; pat dry with paper towels. Brush fish with olive oil. Sprinkle with garlic salt and pepper. Place in a well-greased grill basket. For a charcoal grill, place basket on the rack of an uncovered grill directly over medium coals. Grill for 6 to 9 minutes or until fish flakes easily when tested with a fork, turning basket halfway through grilling. (For a gas grill, preheat grill. Reduce heat to medium. Place grill basket on grill rack directly over heat; cover and grill as above.)
3. Place fish on plates. In a large bowl toss together cooked lima beans, corn relish, and spinach. Serve with fish. Makes 4 servings.

EACH SERVING: *372 cal., 12 g fat (3 g sat. fat), 53 mg chol., 509 mg sodium, 41 g carbo., 5 g fiber, 24 g pro. Daily Values: 18% vit. A, 16% vit. C, 5% calcium, 15% iron.*

CHIPOTLE STEAK

Goodness on the Go

Whip up a refreshing, energy-packed smoothie for fast-action fuel.

BY **STEPHEN EXEL**
PHOTOGRAPHS BY **ANDY LYONS**
FOOD STYLING BY **JILL LUST**

CHERRY-BERRY SMOOTHIES

FAST! | KID FRIENDLY

CHERRY-BERRY SMOOTHIES

This icy smoothie combines colorful berries and fruits for a tasty daily supply of antioxidants.

START TO FINISH: 15 minutes

INGREDIENTS

1½ cups fresh strawberries, hulled
1 cup pitted dark sweet cherries or frozen unsweetened pitted dark sweet cherries

1 cup fresh raspberries, chilled
1 cup pomegranate juice, chilled
½ cup fresh blueberries, chilled

PREPARATION

1. In a blender combine strawberries, cherries, raspberries, pomegranate juice, and blueberries. Cover and blend until almost smooth. Pour into glasses. Makes 4 (8-ounce) servings.

EACH SERVING: *104 cal., 0 g fat (0 g sat. fat), 0 mg chol., 3 mg sodium, 25 g carbo., 4 g fiber, 1 g pro. Daily Values: 1% vit. A, 85% vit. C, 2% calcium, 5% iron.*

MINTY WATERMELON TEA SLUSH

Leaving the mint leaves whole instead of snipping them keeps the tea from discoloring.

PREP: 15 minutes **FREEZE:** 2 hours

INGREDIENTS

1½	cups water
2	bags Red Zinger or other red herb tea
2	Tbsp. packed fresh mint leaves
4	cups cubed watermelon
1	Tbsp. lemon juice
	Sugar (optional)

PREPARATION

1. In a small saucepan bring ¾ cup of the water to boiling. Remove from heat. Add tea bags and mint to the saucepan. Steep for 3 to 5 minutes. Strain tea mixture through a fine-mesh sieve, discarding tea bags and mint. Stir in remaining ¾ cup water. Pour into ice cube trays. Freeze for 2 hours or until solid.

2. In a blender combine watermelon cubes and lemon juice. Cover and blend until mixture begins to liquefy. With motor running, add frozen tea cubes, a few at a time, through the opening in the lid until smoothie is slushy. Pour into glasses; stir before serving. If desired, sweeten to taste with sugar. Makes 4 (8-ounce) servings.

EACH SERVING: *47 cal., 0 g fat (0 g sat. fat), 0 mg chol., 2 mg sodium, 12 g carbo., 1 g fiber, 1 g pro. Daily Values: 17% vit. A, 23% vit. C, 1% calcium, 2% iron.*

FAST!

GREEN BLAST SMOOTHIES

This delicious drink has a sweet-tart side from grapes and apple juice.

START TO FINISH: 10 minutes

INGREDIENTS

4	cups fresh baby spinach
2	cups seedless green grapes
1	medium banana, cut up
¾	cup seeded, chopped green sweet pepper
½	cup unsweetened apple juice

PREPARATION

1. In a blender or food processor combine spinach, grapes, banana, sweet pepper, and apple juice. Cover and blend or process until slightly pulpy and nearly smooth. Makes 4 (6-ounce) servings.

EACH SERVING: *109 cal., 0 g fat (0 g sat. fat), 0 mg chol., 27 mg sodium, 27 g carbo., 3 g fiber, 2 g pro. Daily Values: 60% vit. A, 71% vit. C, 4% calcium, 8% iron.*

 FAST! **LOW FAT**

MANGO-GINGER SMOOTHIES

Nonfat milk powder powers up this drink to about one-fourth the daily guidelines for dairy. To use fresh mangoes instead of frozen, seed, peel, and cut two mangoes into chunks. Place on a baking sheet lined with waxed paper. Cover; freeze for 2 hours or until solid.

START TO FINISH: 10 minutes

INGREDIENTS

2	cups frozen mango chunks
1	cup cubed fresh pineapple
1	6-oz. carton plain low-fat yogurt
½	cup fat-free milk
¼	cup nonfat dry milk powder (optional)
2	Tbsp. honey
¼	tsp. ground ginger

PREPARATION

1. In a blender combine mango chunks, pineapple cubes, yogurt, milk, milk powder (if desired), honey, and ginger. Cover and blend until smooth. Makes 4 (6-ounce) servings.

EACH SERVING: *142 cal., 1 g fat (1 g sat. fat), 3 mg chol., 45 mg sodium, 32 g carbo., 0 g fiber, 4 g pro. Daily Values: 15% vit. A, 62% vit. C, 13% calcium, 2% iron.*

TEST KITCHEN TIP

For a healthful option to pudding pops, make frozen smoothie pops by pouring a smoothie into an ice tray and freezing. Add wooden sticks when nearly firm.

MIX-AND-MATCH SMOOTHIES

Choose from each column for signature smoothies. Blend ¼ cup liquid, ½ cup creamy ingredient, 1 to 1½ cups fruit, flavor to taste, and 2 to 3 teaspoons nutrition bonus.

Liquid	Creamy	Fruit	Flavor	Nutrition Bonus
Milk	Banana	Berries	Mint	Instant breakfast powder
Juice	Yogurt	Grapes	Ginger	Peanut butter
Tea	Tofu	Stone fruit	Cocoa powder	Cottage cheese
Soymilk	Low-fat ice cream	Melons	Cinnamon	Almond butter

It's the Berries

Raspberries, blueberries, blackberries—savor their seasonal sweetness in salads, drinks, and this red, white, and blue triple-decker treat.

BY **RICHARD SWEARINGER**
PHOTOGRAPHS BY **COLLEEN DUFFLEY**
FOOD STYLING BY **BROOKE LEONARD**

BERRY-LEMON NAPOLEONS

BERRY-LEMON NAPOLEONS

PREP: 25 minutes **BAKE:** 8 minutes

INGREDIENTS

	Butter-flavor nonstick cooking spray
2	Tbsp. sugar
½	tsp. ground cardamom or cinnamon
8	sheets frozen phyllo dough (about 14×9-inch rectangles), thawed
⅓	cup lemon low-fat yogurt
3	Tbsp. lemon curd
⅓	cup whipping cream or 1 cup frozen whipped dessert topping, thawed
2	cups fresh red raspberries, blackberries, and/or blueberries

PREPARATION

1. Preheat oven to 350°F. Lightly coat two baking sheets with cooking spray; set aside. In a small bowl stir together sugar and cardamom; set aside. Stack 2 sheets of phyllo dough on a large cutting board. Lightly coat top sheet of phyllo with cooking spray. Sprinkle about one-fourth of the sugar mixture onto phyllo stack. Top with 2 more phyllo sheets. Lightly coat with cooking spray; sprinkle with sugar mixture. (Keep remaining phyllo covered with plastic wrap until needed.)

2. Cut phyllo sheets lengthwise into three equal strips, then crosswise into three pieces to make nine rectangles (about 4½×3 inches). Transfer to the prepared baking sheets. Repeat with remaining phyllo sheets and sugar mixture. Bake rectangles for 8 to 10 minutes or until golden. Transfer to a wire rack to cool.

3. Meanwhile, for lemon filling, in a bowl stir together yogurt and lemon curd; set aside. In a small bowl beat whipping cream until soft peaks form; fold into yogurt mixture.

4. To assemble, place a phyllo rectangle stack on each of 6 dessert plates. Spread a slightly rounded tablespoon of the lemon filling on each rectangle. Divide half of the berries among rectangles. Top each with another phyllo rectangle and then another tablespoon of lemon filling. Divide remaining berries among rectangles. Cover each stack with another phyllo rectangle. Serve immediately. Makes 6 servings.

EACH SERVING: *166 cal., 7 g total fat (4 g sat. fat), 26 mg chol., 82 mg sodium, 26 g carbo., 4 g fiber, 2 g pro. Daily Values: 4% vit. A, 18% vit. C, 4% calcium, 4% iron.*

PICKING THE BERRY BEST

WHAT'S IN SEASON Peak season for fresh American-grown berries lasts from 2 to 6 months:
Blackberries: June–August
Blueberries: late May–October
Boysenberries: late June–early August
Raspberries: May–September
Strawberries: June–September

HOW TO CHOOSE When picking your own, select berries that separate easily from their stems.

HOW TO STORE Refrigerate berries in a single layer, loosely covered, for up to 2 days. Rinse just before using. Use within 2 to 3 days and allow berries to come to room temperature for the best flavor.

BHG BASICS
Cutting phyllo dough requires a sharp knife—press down firmly to cut. Don't saw, which tears the dough.

Brownie Points

A fudgy treat customized with fruit, candy, or spices is a rich reward for everyday occasions.

BY **STEPHEN EXEL** PHOTOGRAPH BY **ANDY LYONS**
FOOD STYLING BY **CHARLES WORTHINGTON**

TEST KITCHEN TIP
To melt 1 cup chocolate pieces, place in microwave-safe bowl and microwave on 70% power (medium-high) for 1 minute; stir. Microwave for 1½ to 3 minutes more, stirring every 15 seconds, until chocolate is melted and smooth.

KID FRIENDLY

ULTIMATE BROWNIES

PREP: 25 minutes **BAKE:** 35 minutes

INGREDIENTS

3   oz. unsweetened chocolate
½   cup butter
1   cup sugar
2   eggs
1   tsp. vanilla
⅔   cup all-purpose flour
¼   tsp. baking soda
    Stir-ins (right)
1   cup dark chocolate pieces
½   cup chopped nuts (optional)
1   recipe Chocolate Drizzle (right) (optional)

PREPARATION

1. Preheat oven to 350°F. Coarsely chop unsweetened chocolate. In a medium saucepan melt chocolate and butter over low heat, stirring occasionally. Remove from heat; cool.
2. Line an 8×8×2-inch baking pan with foil. Coat with *nonstick cooking spray*; set aside. Stir sugar into melted chocolate mixture until sugar is dissolved. Add eggs, 1 at a time, beating with a wooden spoon just until combined. Stir in vanilla.
3. In a bowl stir together flour and baking soda. Add spice stir-ins. Add flour mixture to chocolate mixture; stir just until combined. Stir in chocolate pieces and, if desired, nuts. Add sweet stir-ins. Spread into prepared pan.
4. Bake about 35 minutes or until edges are set and begin to pull away from sides of pan. Cool in pan on a wire rack. If

desired, spoon Chocolate Drizzle across top. Cut into bars. Makes 16 brownies.
SPICE STIR-INS: To flour mixture, add 1 teaspoon ground cinnamon or ground ancho chili powder, 2 teaspoons finely shredded orange peel, or 1 tablespoon instant espresso coffee powder.
SWEET STIR-INS: To batter, add ½ cup dried fruit soaked in sparkling wine for 30 minutes, drained and chopped, or ¾ cup candy-coated peanut butter pieces.
CHOCOLATE DRIZZLE: In a bowl stir together ½ cup sifted powdered sugar, 1 tablespoon unsweetened cocoa powder, ¼ teaspoon vanilla, and 1½ teaspoons milk. Stir in additional milk, 1 teaspoon at a time, until icing is drizzling consistency.

EACH BROWNIE: *227 cal., 13 g fat (8 g sat. fat), 43 mg chol., 71 mg sodium, 28 g carbo., 2 g fiber, 3 g pro. Daily Values: 4% vit. A, 2% calcium, 9% iron.*

Tossed Salad

A crisp, lightly dressed salad starts with a basic wooden bowl.

BY **STEPHEN EXEL** PHOTOGRAPH BY **ANDY LYONS** FOOD STYLING BY **JILL LUST**

SALAD BOWL

Maintain a wooden salad bowl by seasoning with olive oil three to four times a year.

GARLIC

Flavor the greens by rubbing the bowl with a half clove of garlic, which mixes with the dressing as the salad is tossed.

LETTUCE

Contrast crunchy lettuce, such as romaine or iceberg, with soft lettuce—butterhead or red leaf. Tear—don't cut—the leaves, wash, and dry completely to prevent greens from wilting. Use 12 cups of lettuce to serve 8 to 10 people.

HERBS

Lightly crush fresh herbs—basil, parsley, and mint—to release flavor.

TOMATO AND CUCUMBER

Finally add tomato wedges and cucumber for a fresh taste and texture. Toss the salad lightly one last time with salad servers or tongs just until it is coated with dressing. Season with additional salt and pepper.

OLIVE OIL, RED WINE VINEGAR, AND LEMON

Sprinkle 3 tablespoons of room-temperature good-quality extra virgin olive oil over the leaves and toss. Dissolve a pinch of salt and black pepper in 3 tablespoons red wine vinegar; sprinkle over the salad and toss again. Vinegar's acidity balances olive oil's fruitiness. A squeeze of lemon concentrates the flavors.

TEST KITCHEN TIP

Look for salad bowls crafted from tight-grain woods that lend easily to cleaning, such as birch, walnut, or cherry. To clean, wash in warm sudsy water and air-dry. Do not place in dishwasher or soak.

EGGPLANT DIP

Bumper Crop

When market stalls are heaping with fresh
vegetables, make the most of the bounty with
recipes that save some of the abundance for later.

BY **STEPHEN EXEL**
PHOTOGRAPHS BY **ANDY LYONS**
FOOD STYLING BY **JILL LUST**

EGGPLANT DIP

Top grilled meats and poultry with dip .

PREP: 45 minutes **ROAST:** 40 minutes
COOL: 1 hour

INGREDIENTS

4	1-lb. eggplants
4	garlic bulbs
1	cup extra virgin olive oil
4	tsp. salt
4	red sweet peppers, stemmed, seeded, and coarsely chopped
⅔	cup lemon juice
½	cup snipped fresh Italian (flat-leaf) parsley
¼	cup snipped fresh oregano

PREPARATION

1. Preheat oven to 400°F. Wash eggplants; cut into ¼-inch pieces. Remove top ½ inch from garlic bulbs to expose cloves. Place garlic on a 12-inch foil square; drizzle with 1 tablespoon of the olive oil. Wrap garlic in foil.

2. Arrange eggplant in two 15×10×1-inch baking pans. Drizzle with ¼ cup of the olive oil; sprinkle with salt. Place eggplant and garlic in oven. Roast for 20 minutes. Turn eggplant; add sweet pepper. Roast 20 minutes more. Remove vegetables and garlic from oven; cool.

3. In a bowl combine vegetables. In a small bowl squeeze garlic pulp from cloves; mash pulp. Add remaining oil and lemon juice to garlic; whisk to combine. Toss oil mixture, parsley, and oregano with eggplant mixture.

4. Serve immediately or let stand for up to 1 hour. Cover; chill remaining dip for up to 3 days. Let stand at room temperature for 30 minutes before serving. (Or transfer to a freezer container; cover and freeze for up to 3 months. Thaw in the refrigerator before serving; let stand at room temperature for 30 minutes.) Makes about 40 (¼-cup) servings.

EACH SERVING: *66 cal., 8 g fat (1 g sat. fat), 0 mg chol., 235 mg sodium, 4 g carbo., 2 g fiber, 1 g pro. Daily Values: 9% vit. A, 8% vit. C, 1% calcium, 1% iron.*

EGGPLANT

To avoid bitter-tasting eggplant, select medium-size fruit that is shiny and firm, which indicates dense, sweet flesh. Use eggplants within a day or two of purchase. Store overnight at room temperature or in a cool place in the kitchen; do not refrigerate.

PICKLED GREEN BEANS

To preserve other vegetables, substitute carrot sticks or cauliflower florets.

PREP: 45 minutes **CHILL:** 4 hours

INGREDIENTS

3	lb. green beans and/or yellow wax beans
3	cups water
3	cups cider vinegar
1	Tbsp. pickling salt
3	Tbsp. snipped fresh dill
½	tsp. cayenne pepper
6	cloves garlic, sliced

PREPARATION

1. Wash beans; drain. If desired, trim ends. Place beans in an 8-quart Dutch oven. Add boiling water to cover. Return to boiling. Cook, uncovered, for 3 minutes; drain. Place beans in a large bowl.

2. In a large saucepan combine the 3 cups water, the vinegar, pickling salt, dill, cayenne pepper, and garlic. Bring to boiling. Pour over beans in bowl. Cool to room temperature. Transfer to a glass container. Cover; chill for at least 4 hours before serving. Store in refrigerator up to 2 weeks. Makes 40 (1-ounce) servings.

EACH SERVING: *14 cal., 0 g fat (0 g sat. fat), 0 mg chol., 148 mg sodium, 2 g carbo., 1 g fiber, 1 g pro. Daily Values: 4% vit. A, 8% vit. C, 1% calcium, 2% iron.*

GREEN BEANS

These pods vary in size from tiny French *haricots verts* to foot-long Chinese long beans and familiar string beans. Regardless of size, choose beans that snap when broken. Store beans in the refrigerator, tightly wrapped, for up to 5 days.

PICKLED GREEN BEANS

> Big-batch recipes keep summer lingering long after the season has passed.

AUGUST

FOR AN INSTANT MIDSUMMER COOLDOWN,
TRY AN EASY ICE CREAM TREAT MADE WITH THE
PURCHASED FROZEN PRODUCT.

VANILLA DREAM FLOATS
page 171

Tasty Freeze

SHERBET FRUIT POPS
page 169

MINT ICE CREAM WAFFLE SUNDAES
page 176

BASIL CHICKEN STACK-UPS
page 181

tasty freeze

Give your favorite store-bought ice cream the glamour treatment, transforming everyday flavors into dazzling desserts.

BY **STEPHEN EXEL**
PRODUCED BY **NANCY WALL HOPKINS**
PHOTOGRAPHS BY **GEMMA COMAS** AND **ANDY LYONS**
FOOD STYLING BY **CHARLES WORTHINGTON** AND **JILL LUST**
PROP STYLING BY **KAREN JOHNSON** AND **SUE MITCHELL**

SHERBET FRUIT POPS

KID FRIENDLY

CHOCOLATE CUPCAKE ICE CREAM SANDWICHES

PREP: 10 minutes **FREEZE:** 1 hour

INGREDIENTS

6	purchased or homemade unfrosted chocolate cupcakes
2	to 3 cups chocolate chip ice cream
1	10-oz. jar maraschino cherries, drained and chopped (½ cup)
⅓	cup chopped pecans, toasted
⅓	cup seedless raspberry jam

PREPARATION

1. Remove papers, if present, and slice cupcakes in half horizontally. Place cupcakes on a tray or baking sheet lined with waxed paper. Cover with waxed paper; freeze for 1 hour. Line another tray or shallow baking pan with waxed paper. Using a miniature ice cream scoop (#60, about 2 teaspoons), scoop ice cream and place on prepared tray (you should have 18 to 24 small scoops). Cover with waxed paper and freeze for 1 hour.
2. Meanwhile, in a small bowl combine cherries, pecans, and jam.
3. For each serving, place a cupcake bottom in a dessert dish. Top with 2 or 3 scoops of ice cream. Top with cherry mixture, cupcake top, and remaining scoops of ice cream. Makes 6 servings.

EACH SERVING: *477 cal., 22 g fat (7 g sat. fat), 52 mg chol., 316 mg sodium, 66 g carbo., 2 g fiber, 6 g pro. Daily Values: 5% vit. A, 3% vit. C, 8% calcium, 6% iron.*

LOW FAT **KID FRIENDLY**

SHERBET FRUIT POPS

PREP: 15 minutes **FREEZE:** 6 hours

INGREDIENTS

10	5-oz. paper cups
3	peeled and chopped kiwifruits
1	Tbsp. sugar
1	quart raspberry or tangerine sherbet
2	to 4 Tbsp. orange juice
10	flat wooden craft sticks

PREPARATION

1. Arrange cups on a baking pan. In a small bowl combine kiwifruits and sugar. Divide chopped kiwi among cups. In a large bowl use an electric mixer on low speed to beat together the sherbet and orange juice until combined. Spoon sherbet mixture over kiwi, filling cups.
2. Cover each cup with a square of foil. Use a table knife to make a small hole in the center of each foil square. Slide a wooden craft stick through each hole and into fruit mixture in cup. Freeze at least 6 hours or overnight.
3. To serve, remove foil; carefully tear away cups. Serve immediately. Makes 10 pops.

EACH POP: *129 cal., 2 g fat (1 g sat. fat), 0 mg chol., 36 mg sodium, 28 g carbo., 3 g fiber, 1 g pro. Daily Values: 2% vit. A, 39% vit. C, 5% calcium, 1% iron.*

CHOCOLATE CUPCAKE ICE CREAM SANDWICHES

**DULCE DE LECHE
ICE CREAM TORTE**

DULCE DE LECHE ICE CREAM TORTE

"Dulce de leche" (pronounced DOOL-say day LAY-chay) is a Spanish phrase for milk that's been cooked down into a caramelized sauce.

PREP: 25 minutes **FREEZE:** 5 hours to overnight

INGREDIENTS

2   cups finely crushed purchased shortbread or pecan shortbread cookies (about 10 oz.)
3   Tbsp. butter, melted
2   pints dulce de leche ice cream
$^2/_3$ cup roasted, lightly salted cashews, coarsely chopped
1   recipe Pineapple Topping

PREPARATION

1. In a medium bowl combine cookie crumbs and butter. Press half of the cookie crumb mixture (about 1 cup) evenly onto bottom of an 8×8×1$^7/_8$-inch disposable foil pan* or 9×9×2-inch baking pan. Set aside. Soften half of the ice cream (see tip, below). Carefully spread softened ice cream over cookie crumb layer in pan. Top with half of the nuts. Sprinkle remaining cookie crumb mixture over layers in pan. Cover and freeze for 1 to 2 hours or until firm.
2. Soften remaining ice cream; carefully spread over frozen layers in pan. Cover and freeze overnight or until very firm.
3. To serve, top with remaining cashews. Cut into squares and serve with Pineapple Topping. Makes 9 servings.
PINEAPPLE TOPPING: In a large skillet melt 2 tablespoons butter. Add 3 tablespoons packed brown sugar. Cook and stir until sugar is dissolved. Add 2 cups peeled, cored, and cubed fresh pineapple; stir to coat. Serve at once or cover and chill for up to 3 days; reheat chilled sauce before serving.
*NOTE: If using the foil pan, use a spatula to cut ice cream torte into servings; a sharp knife will cut through the foil pan.

EACH SERVING: *440 cal., 25 g fat (10 g sat. fat), 41 mg chol., 349 mg sodium, 50 g carbo., 1 g fiber, 6 g pro. Daily Values: 8% vit. A, 21% vit. C, 11% calcium, 9% iron.*

TEST KITCHEN TIP To soften ice cream, spoon ice cream into chilled large bowl. Use wooden spoon to press ice cream against sides of bowl until softened.

For a quick and easy cooldown combo, top cookie dough ice cream with cream soda for a **Vanilla Dream Float.** Cream soda comes in amber and clear varieties; both have the same old-fashioned flavor and give the float its smooth vanilla taste.

VANILLA DREAM FLOATS

PREP: 10 minutes

INGREDIENTS

1½ pints cookie dough ice cream
2 12-oz. cans or bottles cream soda

PREPARATION

1. Place 2 large scoops of ice cream in bottom of each of four 8-ounce glasses. Fill each glass with cream soda. Makes 4 servings.

EACH SERVING: *333 cal., 14 g fat (8 g sat. fat), 38 mg chol., 112 mg sodium, 48 g carbo., 0 g fiber, 5 g pro. Daily Values: 12% vit. A, 10% calcium, 3% iron.*

Why have just one dessert when you can sample three? These itty-bitty sundae-style **Tasting Trios** make a splashy dinner finale. Fill tiny plastic shot glasses with these combos: peaches and coconut, popcorn and caramel, or pears and crystallized ginger. Then add miniature scoops of vanilla, peach, or mango ice cream and dig in.

TASTING TRIOS

KID FRIENDLY

TASTING TRIOS

PREP: 30 minutes **FREEZE:** 2 hours

INGREDIENTS

1   pint vanilla, peach, and/or mango ice cream
24 1-oz. disposable plastic shot glasses

PREPARATION

1. Line a 15×10×1-inch baking pan with waxed paper. Using a miniature ice cream scoop (#60, about 2 teaspoons), scoop ice cream and place in prepared pan (you should have 24 small scoops). Cover loosely with waxed paper and freeze for at least 2 hours. Prepare desired combinations below. Serve at once. Makes 8 servings (3 treats per serving).

PEAR-GINGER: Divide ¾ cup coarsely crushed sugar cookies among 8 plastic shot glasses. Sprinkle with 2 tablespoons finely chopped crystallized ginger. Top with vanilla ice cream and add slivers of fresh pear.

PEACH: Peel, pit, and coarsely chop 2 small peaches; toss with 1 tablespoon sugar. Divide mixture among 8 plastic shot glasses. Top with scoops of vanilla ice cream and toasted coconut chips.*

POPCORN: Divide ½ cup popped popcorn among 8 plastic shot glasses. Drizzle with 2 tablespoons purchased caramel ice cream topping. Top with peach or mango ice cream and add additional popcorn.

*TO TOAST COCONUT: Preheat oven to 350°F. Place 2 tablespoons raw chip coconut in an 8×8×2-inch baking pan. Bake for 5 to 6 minutes or until toasted, stirring once.

EACH SERVING (PEAR-GINGER VARIATION): *187 cal., 10 g fat (6 g sat. fat), 53 mg chol., 59 mg sodium, 22 g carbo., 1 g fiber, 2 g pro. Daily Values: 7% vit. A, 1% vit. C, 7% calcium, 2% iron.*

KID FRIENDLY

TROPICAL TREAT SANDWICHES

PREP: 35 minutes **BAKE:** 6 minutes per batch **FREEZE:** 5 hours

INGREDIENTS

1   18-oz. pkg. refrigerated sugar cookie dough
½   cup all-purpose flour
2   tsp. milk
4   tsp. coarse sugar or 1 tsp. granulated sugar
1¾   quarts tropical fruit or rainbow sherbet

PREPARATION

1. Preheat oven to 350°F. In a mixing bowl combine cookie dough and flour; knead with hands until well combined. On a lightly floured surface, roll dough, half at a time, into a 14×10-inch rectangle. Using a fluted pastry wheel or pizza cutter, cut into 3×2-inch rectangles. Place on ungreased baking sheets. Prick with a fork. Brush with milk; sprinkle with sugar.
2. Bake for 6 to 7 minutes or until edges are lightly browned. Cool on cookie sheet for 1 minute. Transfer to a wire rack and let cool completely.
3. Place a baking sheet or 15×10×1-inch pan in the freezer. Cut carton from sherbet. Place sherbet on chilled baking sheet. With a very sharp knife, cut in half lengthwise. Cut again into 1-inch slices. Halve each slice crosswise (you should have 20 slices). Return baking sheet with sherbet slices to freezer for 1 hour or until firm.
4. To assemble sandwiches, place a sherbet slice between 2 cookies, sugar-sprinkled sides out. Wrap in plastic wrap; freeze for 4 hours or until firm. Cookies may be frozen for up to 3 months. Makes 20 sandwiches.

EACH SANDWICH: *214 cal., 6 g fat (2 g sat. fat), 7 mg chol., 132 mg sodium, 38 g carbo., 0 g fiber, 2 g pro. Daily Values: 32% vit. C, 5% calcium, 3% iron.*

TROPICAL TREAT SANDWICHES

DOUBLE MELON BOWLS

DOUBLE MELON BOWLS

PREP: 25 minutes FREEZE: overnight STAND: 20 minutes

INGREDIENTS

2   cups cubed, seeded watermelon
1   medium cantaloupe (about 3 pounds), halved and seeded
1   quart vanilla frozen yogurt or ice cream, softened
     (see tip, page 170)
     Sea salt or kosher salt (optional)

PREPARATION

1. Place watermelon cubes in a single layer on a tray or in a shallow baking pan; freeze for 2 to 3 hours or until firm. Transfer to a freezer bag or container until needed.

2. With a large spoon, remove flesh from cantaloupe, leaving a ¼-inch shell; set fruit aside. Cut thin slice from bottom of each cantaloupe shell so shell sits flat. Place shells, upside down, on a paper towel-lined tray; set aside.

3. Place cantaloupe fruit in a food processor or blender; cover and process or blend until smooth. Place fruit mixture in a fine-mesh sieve set over a bowl. Let stand for 5 minutes to remove excess liquid; discard liquid. You should have about 1 cup pulp.

4. In a bowl gently fold pulp into softened frozen yogurt until just combined. Divide frozen yogurt mixture evenly between cantaloupe shells. Place shells on a baking sheet or tray. Cover and freeze overnight until very firm.

5. Before serving, let shells stand at room temperature for 20 to 30 minutes to soften slightly. Top with watermelon cubes. If desired, sprinkle watermelon lightly with salt. Scoop into serving bowls. Makes 6 to 8 servings.

EACH SERVING: *188 cal., 4 g fat (2 g sat. fat), 13 mg chol., 59 mg sodium, 36 g carbo., 1 g fiber, 4 g pro. Daily Values: 87% vit. A, 78% vit. C, 15% calcium, 2% iron.*

LEMON DROP SHAKES

START TO FINISH: 5 minutes

INGREDIENTS

½   of a small lemon, thinly sliced
2   Tbsp. crushed lemon drop candies
1   Tbsp. sugar
1   quart vanilla ice cream
1½   cups lemonade

PREPARATION

1. Rub rim of 6 juice-size glasses with one lemon slice. In a shallow dish combine crushed lemon drops and sugar; dip glass rims in mixture and set aside.

2. In a blender combine ice cream and lemonade. Cover and blend until smooth. Pour ice cream mixture into glasses. Top with remaining lemon slices. Makes 6 (⅔-cup) servings.

EACH SERVING: *403 cal., 23 g fat (15 g sat. fat), 131 mg chol., 108 mg sodium, 45 g carbo., 0 g fiber, 5 g pro. Daily Values: 19% vit. A, 1% vit. C, 17% calcium, 3% iron.*

LEMON DROP SHAKES

FAST! **KID FRIENDLY**

MINT ICE CREAM WAFFLE SUNDAES

START TO FINISH: 5 minutes

INGREDIENTS

4   giant waffle ice cream cones
1   quart mint or pistachio ice cream
1   12-oz. jar dark chocolate or fudge ice cream topping,
     or ½ cup Berry Sauce
     Fresh raspberries, blackberries, and/or blueberries
     Fresh mint leaves

PREPARATION

1. Place each waffle cone in a tall cup or bowl. Scoop ice cream into cones. Top with ice cream topping or Berry Sauce. Add berries to top of sundae. Sprinkle with mint leaves. Makes 4 sundaes.

BERRY SAUCE: In a medium saucepan stir together one 12-ounce package frozen unsweetened raspberries, 1 cup fresh or frozen blackberries, 1 cup fresh or frozen blueberries, and ½ cup sugar over medium heat. Bring to boiling; reduce heat. Simmer, uncovered, until thickened, about 15 minutes. Remove from heat; cool slightly. Place berry mixture in a blender. Cover and blend until smooth. Store leftover sauce, tightly covered, for up to 2 weeks in the refrigerator. Makes 2 cups.

EACH SUNDAE (WITH CHOCOLATE TOPPING): 467 cal., 17 g fat (9 g sat. fat), 25 mg chol., 135 mg sodium, 73 g carbo., 4 g fiber, 7 g pro. Daily Values: 4% vit. A, 10% vit. C, 11% calcium, 20% iron.

KID FRIENDLY

NEAPOLITAN SUNDAES

PREP: 20 minutes   **BAKE:** 3 minutes per batch

INGREDIENTS

1   Tbsp. sugar
½   tsp. ground cinnamon
½   of a 4- to 5-oz. pkg. refrigerated ready-to-use crepes (5)
2   Tbsp. butter, melted
1   rectangular half-gallon carton Neapolitan ice cream
1   recipe Sweetened Whipped Cream
     Maraschino cherries
1   11.75-oz. jar hot fudge ice cream topping, warmed

PREPARATION

1. Preheat oven to 375°F. Grease 2 large baking sheets; set aside. In a small bowl stir together sugar and cinnamon. Brush both sides of crepes with butter and sprinkle with sugar mixture. Cut each crepe into quarters and arrange on prepared baking sheets. Bake 1 baking sheet at a time for 3 to 4 minutes or until crepes are lightly browned. Cool on sheets. Remove and set aside. (Handle baked crepes gently; they are delicate and break easily.)

2. Cut ice cream crosswise into 10 slices; halve slices crosswise again. To serve, layer crepe pieces and ice cream slices in bowls. Add sweetened whipped cream and cherries. Pass ice cream topping. Makes 10 sundaes.

SWEETENED WHIPPED CREAM: In a chilled large mixing bowl use a large whisk or electric mixer to beat 1 cup whipping cream, 2 tablespoons powdered sugar, and ½ teaspoon vanilla until stiff peaks form. Makes 2 cups.

EACH SUNDAE: 457 cal., 25 g fat (15 g sat. fat), 88 mg chol., 203 mg sodium, 66 g carbo., 1 g fiber, 5 g pro. Daily Values: 15% vit. A, 19% calcium, 3% iron.

MINT ICE CREAM WAFFLE SUNDAES

READY IN
20
MINUTES

Summer Pleasers

These quick dinners are just right for alfresco dining.

BY **NANCY WALL HOPKINS** PHOTOGRAPHS BY **IAIN BAGWELL**
FOOD STYLING BY **WILLIAM SMITH** RECIPES BY **MARYELLYN KRANTZ**

BARBECUE-SAUCED BURGERS

FAST! KID FRIENDLY
BARBECUE-SAUCED BURGERS

START TO FINISH: 20 minutes

INGREDIENTS
1	lb. lean ground beef
1	to 2 Tbsp. horseradish mustard
¼	tsp. salt
¼	tsp. ground black pepper
3	to 4 oz. white cheddar cheese, sliced
4	hamburger buns, split and toasted
¼	cup bottled barbecue sauce
	Arugula, tomato slices, and/or red onion slices (optional)

PREPARATION

1. In a large bowl combine beef, horseradish mustard, salt, and pepper; mix well. Shape into four ¾-inch-thick patties.

2. For a charcoal grill, grill patties on the rack of an uncovered grill directly over medium coals for 14 to 18 minutes or until done (160°F), turning once. (For a gas grill, preheat grill. Reduce heat to medium. Place patties on the grill rack over heat. Cover and grill as above.) Top burgers with cheese during the last 1 minute of grilling. Serve on buns with barbecue sauce. If desired, add arugula, tomato, and/or onion. Makes 4 servings.

EACH SERVING: *476 cal., 27 g fat (12 g sat. fat), 99 mg chol., 722 mg sodium, 26 g carbo., 2 g fiber, 31 g pro. Daily Values: 10% vit. A, 9% vit. C, 25% calcium, 24% iron.*

FAST!
TURKEY AND BACON SALAD

START TO FINISH: 20 minutes

INGREDIENTS
5	slices low-sodium bacon
2	cups sugar snap peas
½	cup light mayonnaise
1	Tbsp. Dijon-style mustard
1	Tbsp. cider vinegar
1	Tbsp. snipped fresh dill
1	small head romaine lettuce, coarsely chopped or torn
8	oz. roast turkey breast, cut into strips

PREPARATION

1. Line a 9-inch microwave-safe plate with paper towels. Arrange bacon in a layer on towels. Cover with additional towels. Microwave on 100% power (high) for 4 minutes or until crisp. Remove plate from microwave. Set bacon aside to cool. Meanwhile, cook peas, covered, in boiling salted water for 2 minutes or until crisp-tender; drain. Crumble 1 bacon slice; set aside. Break remaining into pieces.

2. In a bowl combine mayonnaise, mustard, vinegar, and dill. Stir in crumbled bacon. Arrange romaine on 4 plates. Add peas, turkey strips, and bacon pieces. Serve with dressing. Makes 4 servings.

EACH SERVING: *258 cal., 14 g fat (3 g sat. fat), 68 mg chol., 601 mg sodium, 9 g carbo., 3 g fiber, 23 g pro. Daily Values: 69% vit. A, 29% vit. C, 6% calcium, 11% iron.*

TURKEY AND BACON SALAD

GRILLED PORK AND PINEAPPLE

START TO FINISH: 20 minutes

INGREDIENTS

4   ¾-inch-thick boneless top loin pork chops
1   peeled and cored fresh pineapple
3   Tbsp. orange marmalade
½   cup plain yogurt
¼   cup roasted, lightly salted cashew halves, coarsely chopped

PREPARATION

1. Sprinkle pork with *salt* and *ground black pepper*. Cut pineapple into ½-inch-thick slices; set aside.

2. For a charcoal grill, grill chops on the rack of an uncovered grill directly over medium coals for 4 minutes. Turn; add pineapple. Brush chops and pineapple with 2 tablespoons of the marmalade. Grill for 3 to 5 minutes more or until an instant-read thermometer inserted in pork registers 160°F, turning pineapple.

3. Meanwhile, combine yogurt and remaining marmalade. Arrange pineapple and chops on plates. Top with yogurt mixture; sprinkle with nuts. Makes 4 servings.

EACH SERVING: *317 cal., 7 g fat (2 g sat. fat), 80 mg chol., 313 mg sodium, 29 g carbo., 2 g fiber, 35 g pro. Daily Values: 2% vit. A, 72% vit. C, 10% calcium, 7% iron.*

GRILLED PORK AND PINEAPPLE

CHICKEN WITH APRICOTS

[FAST!]

BASIL CHICKEN STACK-UPS

START TO FINISH: 20 minutes

INGREDIENTS

3	to 4 medium tomatoes
1	2- to 2½-lb. purchased roasted chicken
1	avocado, seeded, peeled, and sliced
¼	cup extra virgin olive oil
1	medium lime, quartered
½	cup small fresh basil leaves
	Salt and cracked black pepper

PREPARATION

1. Cut tomatoes into slices and chunks. Divide among 4 individual plates. Using 2 forks, gently pull chicken meat off bones; shred in large pieces. Discard bones and skin. Top tomatoes with chicken and avocado.

2. Drizzle with olive oil. Squeeze juice from lime quarters over tomato, chicken, and avocado. Sprinkle with basil leaves, salt, and cracked black pepper. Makes 4 servings.

EACH SERVING: 470 cal., 31 g fat (6 g sat. fat), 120 mg chol., 270 mg sodium, 9 g carbo., 5 g fiber, 41 g pro. Daily Values: 24% vit. A, 21% vit., C, 5% calcium, 14% iron.

[FAST!] [LOW FAT]

CHICKEN WITH APRICOTS

START TO FINISH: 20 minutes

INGREDIENTS

1¼	cups dried orzo (8 oz.)
1	15-oz. can unpeeled apricot halves in light syrup
4	skinless, boneless chicken breast halves
1½	tsp. curry powder
	Salt and ground black pepper
2	Tbsp. olive oil
6	green onions

PREPARATION

1. Cook orzo according to package directions; drain. Drain apricots, reserving ½ cup syrup.

2. Meanwhile, sprinkle chicken with ½ teaspoon of the curry powder, salt, and pepper. In a large skillet heat oil over medium heat. Add chicken; cook for 8 minutes or until no longer pink (170°F), turning once. Add apricots the last 2 minutes. Transfer chicken and apricots to plates.

3. Cut tops of 2 onions into diagonal slices; set aside. Chop remaining onions. Add chopped onion and remaining curry powder to skillet; cook 1 minute. Stir in reserved syrup and cooked orzo. Add to plates. Sprinkle with onion tops. Makes 4 servings.

EACH SERVING: 514 cal., 10 g fat (2 g sat. fat), 82 mg chol., 330 mg sodium, 64 g carbo., 5 g fiber, 41 g pro. Daily Values: 34 % vit. A, 12% vit. C, 6% calcium, 15 % iron.

BASIL CHICKEN STACK-UPS

Strong and Sweet

A daily bowl of juicy berries builds
your antioxidant defenses.

BY **STEPHEN EXEL** PHOTOGRAPHS BY **ANDY LYONS**
FOOD STYLING BY **JILL LUST** RECIPES BY **LAURA MARZEN**

UPSIDE-DOWN BERRY CORNMEAL CAKE

ARUGULA SALAD WITH BERRY DRESSING

Berries are the base of this salad dressing. Whole berries also complement most green salads—toss raspberries on spinach and blueberries with Boston or Bibb lettuce.

PREP: 25 minutes

INGREDIENTS

1	cup strawberries, hulled and halved
2	Tbsp. balsamic vinegar
1	Tbsp. canola oil
1	tsp. honey
	Dash salt
2	Tbsp. chopped pistachio nuts
1	4-oz. log goat cheese (chèvre)
4	cups arugula leaves
¾	cup blackberries, blueberries, and/or raspberries
¼	cup thin strips of shaved jicama* (optional)

PREPARATION

1. For berry dressing, in a blender combine ¾ cup of the strawberries, vinegar, oil, honey, and salt. Cover; blend until smooth. Set aside. Spread pistachio nuts on piece of waxed paper. Roll goat cheese in nuts until well coated. Slice goat cheese crosswise into 8 slices.
2. Place arugula and remaining strawberries in serving dish. Top with blackberries, cheese slices, and jicama. Drizzle berry dressing. Makes 4 servings.
*NOTE: Peel jicama and cut into strips with a vegetable peeler.

EACH SERVING: *166 cal., 12 g fat (5 g sat. fat), 13 mg chol., 147 mg sodium, 10 g carbo., 3 g fiber, 7 g pro. Daily Values: 11% vit. A, 50% vit. C, 9% calcium, 7% iron.*

UPSIDE-DOWN BERRY CORNMEAL CAKE

For extra sweetness, whisk together ⅓ cup powdered sugar, 2 teaspoons milk, and 1 teaspoon lemon juice. Lightly brush on warm cake.

PREP: 20 minutes **BAKE:** 40 minutes
COOL: 5 minutes

INGREDIENTS

2	to 2½ cups fresh blueberries, raspberries, and/or blackberries
1⅓	cups all-purpose flour
½	cup yellow cornmeal
1	Tbsp. finely snipped fresh basil
2	tsp. baking powder
¼	tsp. salt
2	eggs, lightly beaten
½	cup sugar
⅔	cup milk
⅓	cup canola oil
	Fresh basil and/or mint (optional)

PREPARATION

1. Preheat oven to 350°F. Grease an 8-inch round cake pan; line bottom with parchment paper and grease the paper. Arrange 1½ cups of the berries in bottom of pan; set aside. In a bowl stir together flour, cornmeal, basil, baking powder, and salt. Set aside.
2. In a bowl whisk together eggs, sugar, milk, and oil. Add egg mixture all at once to flour mixture. Stir until combined; pour over berries. Spread evenly.
3. Bake for 40 to 45 minutes or until a wooden pick inserted near center comes out clean. Cool cake in pan 5 minutes. Run knife around edge of pan to loosen sides. Invert. Remove parchment. Top with remaining berries and, if desired, basil and/or mint. Makes 10 servings.

EACH SERVING: *227 cal., 9 g fat (1 g sat. fat), 43 mg chol., 152 mg sodium, 35 g carbo., 2 g fiber, 3 g pro. Daily Values: 2% vit. A, 8% vit. C, 10% calcium, 8% iron.*

BERRY BENEFITS

Because of their low calorie count, berries are a good diet treat. Their antioxidants—natural compounds that protect cells from damage-causing free radicals—help the body fight a variety of diseases, including lung, skin, and cervical cancers; heart disease; high blood pressure; and age-related mental decline.

Fruit	Calories per Cup	Good Stuff
Strawberries	47	vitamin C, fiber, folate
Blackberries	46	vitamin C, fiber, C3G
Blueberries	84	anthocyanins, fiber
Raspberries	45	vitamin C, gallic acid

ARUGULA SALAD WITH BERRY DRESSING

GRILLED SALMON WITH GARDEN MAYONNAISE

Go Fish!

Fast and light is in season. It's time for fresh seafood suppers that cook in 35 minutes or less.

BY **STEPHEN EXEL** PHOTOGRAPHS BY **ANDY LYONS** FOOD STYLING BY **JILL LUST**

SELECTING SEAFOOD: THE NOSE KNOWS

Look for shiny, taut, bright skin and flesh that's firm and elastic with a moist appearance. Ask to smell the fish; avoid a strong "fishy" odor.

FAST!

GRILLED SALMON WITH GARDEN MAYONNAISE

Basic seasonings—salt, pepper, and olive oil—enhance grilled salmon and asparagus. Top them with Garden Mayonnaise laced with tarragon and green onion.

PREP: 10 minutes **GRILL:** 8 minutes

INGREDIENTS

4	6- to 8-oz. skinless salmon fillets, cut 1 inch thick
12	oz. fresh asparagus spears
1	Tbsp. olive oil
	Sea salt
	Freshly ground black pepper
1	recipe Garden Mayonnaise

PREPARATION

1. Rinse fish; pat dry. Snap off and discard woody bases from asparagus. Brush asparagus and both sides of salmon with oil. Season both with salt and pepper.
2. For a charcoal grill, grill salmon on the greased rack of uncovered grill directly over medium coals. Place asparagus on grill next to salmon. Grill salmon and asparagus for 8 to 12 minutes or until asparagus is tender and fish flakes easily with a fork, turning fish once halfway through grilling and turning asparagus occasionally. (For a gas grill, preheat grill. Reduce heat to medium. Place salmon and asparagus on the grill rack. Cover; grill as above.)
3. To serve, arrange asparagus on plates. Top with salmon. Spoon Garden Mayonnaise mixture on top of salmon. Makes 4 servings.
GARDEN MAYONNAISE: In a small bowl combine ½ cup finely chopped celery (1 stalk), ¼ cup thinly sliced green onion, ⅓ cup mayonnaise, 1 tablespoon lemon juice, and 2 teaspoons snipped fresh tarragon or ½ teaspoon dried tarragon, crushed. Makes ¾ cup.
EACH SERVING (WITH 3 TABLESPOONS GARDEN MAYONNAISE): *501 cal., 36 g fat (7 g sat. fat), 107 mg chol., 313 mg sodium, 6 g carbo., 3 g fiber, 36 g pro. Daily Values: 21% vit. A, 28% vit. C, 6% calcium, 18% iron.*

FAST!

MUSTARD-DILL FISH

PREP: 15 minutes **COOK:** 9 minutes

INGREDIENTS

4	catfish fillets (about 1½ lb. total)
	Salt and ground black pepper
¼	cup Dijon-style mustard
3	Tbsp. snipped fresh dill
2	Tbsp. olive oil
4	medium tomatoes, chopped
2	cloves garlic, very thinly sliced or chopped

PREPARATION

1. Rinse fish; pat dry. Season fish with salt and pepper. In a bowl combine Dijon-style mustard, 2 tablespoons of the dill, and 1 tablespoon of the oil. Spread mustard mixture over both sides of the fish.
2. In a bowl combine tomato, garlic, and remaining oil and dill; season to taste with salt and pepper.
3. Heat a cast-iron or nonstick skillet over medium-high heat. Add fish to skillet. Cook for 8 to 10 minutes or until fish flakes easily with a fork, turning once. Transfer to a plate. Add tomato mixture to skillet. Cook and stir 1 minute. Serve tomato mixture with fish. Serves 4.

EACH SERVING: *328 cal., 20 g fat (4 g sat. fat), 79 mg chol., 602 mg sodium, 5 g carbo., 2 g fiber, 28 g pro. Daily Values: 22% vit. A, 28% vit. C, 3% calcium, 7% iron.*

MUSTARD-DILL FISH

LOW FAT

SHRIMP TACOS WITH TOMATO SALSA

Toss shrimp and green beans with Jamaican jerk seasoning, a blend of chiles, thyme, cinnamon, ginger, cloves, and garlic.

START TO FINISH: 35 minutes

INGREDIENTS

8	6-inch corn tortillas
1	recipe Tomato Salsa
8	oz. fresh green beans, trimmed and halved crosswise
1	tsp. Jamaican jerk seasoning
1	lb. medium to large shrimp, peeled and deveined
1	Tbsp. olive oil

PREPARATION

1. Preheat oven to 350°F. Wrap tortillas in heavy foil. Heat in oven for 10 minutes. Meanwhile, prepare Tomato Salsa; set aside.

2. In a bowl toss beans with ½ teaspoon of the jerk seasoning. In another bowl toss shrimp with remaining ½ teaspoon seasoning. In a large skillet heat oil over medium-high heat. Add green beans; cook and stir for 3 minutes. Add shrimp to skillet; cook and stir for 2 to 3 minutes more or until shrimp are opaque.

3. To serve, fill each warm tortilla with ⅓ cup shrimp and green bean mixture. Serve with Tomato Salsa. Makes 4 (2 tortillas each plus ⅔ cup salsa) servings.

TOMATO SALSA: In a bowl combine 1½ cups chopped, seeded tomato; 1 cup chopped, seeded cucumber; ⅓ cup thinly sliced green onion; ¼ cup snipped fresh cilantro; 3 tablespoons lime juice; and ¼ teaspoon salt.

EACH SERVING: *274 cal., 7 g fat (1 g sat. fat), 129 mg chol., 381 mg sodium, 33 g carbo., 7 g fiber, 22 g pro. Daily Values: 30% vit. A, 42% vit. C, 13% calcium, 20% iron.*

SHRIMP TACOS WITH TOMATO SALSA

CHOOSE IT AND USE IT

Ideally you should cook fresh fish the day you buy it. If that's not possible, wrap the fish loosely in plastic wrap and store in the coldest part of the refrigerator. Use within two days.

Corn on the Cob

Season up summer's best side dish with these surprising flavors.

1

2

3

4

5

6

7

8

9

10

1. HUMMUS, roasted red pepper, olive tapenade

2. FRESH SAGE, rosemary leaves, butter

3. GUACAMOLE, freshly squeezed lime juice

4. CINNAMON, granulated sugar, melted butter

5. CURRY POWDER, chopped pistachios, melted butter

6. COARSE SEA SALT, cracked black pepper, cumin seeds, olive oil

7. MAYONNAISE, Mexican Cojita cheese, ground chili powder

8. PESTO SAUCE, freshly grated Parmesan cheese

9. FRUIT CHUTNEY, melted butter

10. HERBED PEPPER SEASONING BLEND, butter

BY **NANCY WALL HOPKINS**
PHOTOGRAPHS BY **ANDY LYONS**
FOOD STYLING BY **JILL LUST**

BHG BASICS

To grill corn, peel back husks; do not remove. Discard silk. Rinse and dry corn. Fold husks around ears; tie with string. Grill on rack of uncovered grill over medium coals for 25 minutes, turning occasionally, until kernels are tender.

SEPTEMBER

THE NEW SCHOOL YEAR BRINGS A HOST OF ACTIVITIES, INCLUDING TAILGATING EVENTS. CHECK OUT THESE RECIPES TO GET YOUR TAILGATE PLAN STARTED.

ZESTY CHICKEN WRAPS
page 200

Tailgating U

POTATO AND SQUASH SALAD
page 195

BAKED SWEET POTATO AND CHILI WEDGES
page 199

BEAN-POTATO CHOWDER
page 204

Tailgating U

Kick off a championship party season with this winning mix of recipes.

BY **STEPHEN EXEL**
PHOTOGRAPHS BY **COLLEEN DUFFLEY**
FOOD STYLING BY **SUSAN SUGARMAN**
PROP STYLING BY **SUE MITCHELL**

FIELD GOAL:
SET FOODS OUT
ALL AT ONCE SO
EVERYONE IS FREE
TO DIG IN WHEN THE
MOOD STRIKES.
BUT REMEMBER, FOOD
SAFETY SCORES BIG:
DON'T LEAVE
PREPARED FOODS OUT
MORE THAN TWO
HOURS—LESS IF THE
WEATHER IS HOT.

MEET THE TEAM

For the best tailgating spread, we asked for advice straight from the experts: culinary students from Johnson & Wales University Culinary Arts Program in Denver, Colorado. Avid food and football fans in a city known for sports, they scored with these inventive, spirited recipes with big flavors that will rank high at your pregame mixer. So your tailgate is more fun and less fuss, these cooking aces built in strategies for make-ahead and toting. Not hitting the parking lot before the game? The recipes are just as delicious when the gang gathers at home for some TV quarterbacking.

PHOTOS **EDMUND BARR**

ASPEN HOFFMAN

"Eventually I would like to open my own restaurant and feature Mexican specialties."

DAVE FISCHER

"After 15 years of designing medical equipment, I decided to become a chef."

DENNIS TAYLOR

"My interest in cooking started with baking with my grandmother for Thanksgiving dinner."

ANNA ESPINOZA

"I credit my cooking skills to my mom, who always tasted my food, yummy or not."

CARL BLACKBIRD

"I plan to use my culinary degree to pursue a career in healthy-lifestyle training."

REDMOND COLE

"I took my first cooking class in high school and instantly fell in love. Baking is my passion."

ASPEN HOFFMAN'S
CHILI-SOUR CREAM DIP

PREP: 20 minutes **CHILL:** overnight

INGREDIENTS
1	16-oz. carton dairy sour cream
2	7-oz. cans diced green chiles, drained
¼	cup snipped fresh cilantro
¼	cup bottled salsa
2	cloves garlic, minced
2	tsp. finely shredded lime peel
1	tsp. mild or hot chili powder
½	tsp. salt
	Bottled hot pepper sauce
	Assorted vegetable dippers

PREPARATION
1. In a large bowl combine sour cream, chiles, cilantro, salsa, garlic, lime peel, chili powder, salt, and bottled hot pepper sauce to taste. Cover and chill overnight. Serve with vegetable dippers. Makes 15 (¼-cup) servings.

TAILGATE PLAN: Place in an insulated container with an ice pack. Serve within 4 hours.

EACH SERVING: *73 cal., 7 g fat (4 g sat. fat), 13 mg chol., 193 mg sodium, 3 g carbo., 0 g fiber, 2 g pro. Daily Values: 7% vit. A, 18% vit. C, 8% calcium, 1% iron.*

ASPEN HOFFMAN'S
BONANZA BEAN DIP

Cotija is a salty Mexican cheese.

PREP: 30 minutes **CHILL:** up to 24 hours

INGREDIENTS
1	16-oz. can refried beans
¼	tsp. cayenne pepper
1	recipe Lime Guacamole
4	oz. Cotija cheese, crumbled (1 cup), or 1 cup shredded Monterey Jack cheese
1	8-oz. carton dairy sour cream
1	cup halved cherry tomatoes
1	2.25-oz. can sliced pitted ripe olives, well drained
½	cup sliced green onion
⅓	cup shredded Monterey Jack cheese
	Green onion tops (optional)
	Lime wedges

PREPARATION
1. In a bowl combine beans and cayenne. In half of the bottom of a 2-quart rectangular baking dish spread bean mixture in an even layer. Spoon Lime Guacamole in other half of baking dish, spreading evenly. Sprinkle both with Cotija cheese. Spread sour cream over all. Cover; chill for up to 24 hours.

2. Before serving, sprinkle tomatoes, olives, and sliced onion over sour cream. Sprinkle Monterey Jack cheese over tomatoes. If desired, sprinkle onion tops over the dip. Pass lime wedges. Makes 8 to 10 (½-cup) servings.

LIME GUACAMOLE: In a bowl combine 4 avocados, halved, seeded, peeled, and coarsely mashed; 1 medium tomato, chopped; ¼ cup finely chopped onion; 1 jalapeño chile pepper, seeded and finely chopped (See Note, page 76); 1 tablespoon minced garlic (6 cloves); 1 teaspoon finely shredded lime peel; 2 tablespoons lime juice; ½ teaspoon salt; ⅛ teaspoon ground black pepper; and ⅛ teaspoon bottled hot pepper sauce.

TAILGATE PLAN: Prepare as in Step 1; cover and chill the mixture for up to 24 hours. Chill toppers in separate containers. Place dip and toppers in an insulated carrier with ice packs. Add toppers on site.

EACH SERVING: *311 cal., 24 g fat (6 g sat. fat), 33 mg chol., 433 mg sodium, 20 g carbo., 9 g fiber, 12 g pro. Daily Values: 22% vit. A, 32% vit. C, 25% calcium, 13% iron.*

CHILI-SOUR CREAM DIP

Chili-Sour Cream Dip
The game plan: In just minutes stir up a chili-and-salsa-based dip at home. Steam and chill the veggie dippers, then pack them all to travel. You can also serve the dip with chips or on a burger.

Bonanza Bean Dip

Start pregame festivities scooping up a Southwestern-style munchie. Lime- and jalapeño-spiced guacamole is the hidden surprise in this favorite standby. Don't forget seasoned chips or baked tortillas for digging in.

Potato and Squash Salad

This Caribbean-influenced autumn salad is spiced with thyme, basil, and pepper. Serve it room temperature on a bed of spinach at the game site. At home pair the salad with grilled chicken or pork chops.

DAVE FISCHER'S
POTATO AND SQUASH SALAD

PREP: 25 minutes **COOK:** 8 minutes

INGREDIENTS

1	1¼- to 1½-lb. butternut squash, peeled, halved, seeded, and cubed (about 4 cups)
2	cups peeled, cubed sweet and/or white potato (2 medium)
1	cup water
½	cup chopped red sweet pepper
½	cup thin wedges yellow onion
2	cloves garlic, minced
¼	cup olive oil
1	Tbsp. packed brown sugar
1	tsp. snipped fresh thyme
1	tsp. snipped fresh basil
½	tsp. salt
¼	tsp. crushed red pepper
¼	tsp. ground black pepper
5	cups spinach leaves
	Snipped fresh thyme (optional)

PREPARATION

1. In a large skillet combine squash and potato cubes. Add the water. Bring to boiling; reduce heat. Simmer, covered, for 8 to 10 minutes or until vegetables are tender. Drain. Set aside.
2. In the same skillet cook sweet pepper, onion, and garlic in hot oil over medium heat until onion is tender, stirring occasionally. Stir in brown sugar. Remove from heat. Stir in 1 teaspoon thyme, the basil, salt, crushed red pepper, and black pepper.
3. In the skillet combine sweet pepper and potato mixtures. Place spinach in a bowl. Top with the potato mixture. If desired, sprinkle with thyme. (Or let potato mixture stand at room temperature, covered, for up to 2 hours before serving over spinach.) Makes 8 to 10 (1-cup) servings.
TAILGATE PLAN: Place potato mixture and spinach in separate airtight containers. Assemble salad on site.

EACH SERVING: *134 cal., 7 g fat (1 g sat. fat), 0 mg. chol., 182 mg sodium, 18 g carbo., 3 g fiber, 2 g pro. Daily Values: 262% vit. A, 53% vit. C, 6% calcium, 7% iron.*

REDMOND COLE'S
PEACH AND POUND CAKE SANDWICHES

A homemade pound cake is a super treat, but if time is an issue, substitute one from your favorite bakery.

PREP: 1¼ hours **BAKE:** 60 minutes **COOL:** 1 hour

INGREDIENTS

½	cup butter
3	eggs
½	cup dairy sour cream
1½	cups all-purpose flour
¼	tsp. baking powder
⅛	tsp. baking soda
1	cup sugar
½	tsp. vanilla
1	recipe Lemon Butter
3	medium fresh peaches or pears, pitted or cored and sliced
1	to 2 cups fresh strawberries, sliced
½	cup purchased caramel ice cream topping

PREPARATION

1. Allow butter, eggs, and sour cream to stand at room temperature for 30 minutes. Meanwhile, grease and lightly flour a 9×5×3-inch loaf pan; set aside. In a bowl combine flour, baking powder, and baking soda; set aside.
2. Preheat oven to 325°F. In a mixing bowl beat butter with an electric mixer on medium to high speed for 30 seconds. Gradually add sugar, beating for 10 minutes or until very light and fluffy. Beat in vanilla. Add eggs, 1 at a time, beating 1 minute after each addition and scraping bowl frequently. Alternately add flour mixture and sour cream to butter mixture, beating on low to medium speed after each addition just until combined. Pour batter into prepared pan.
3. Bake for 60 to 75 minutes or until a wooden toothpick inserted near center of cake comes out clean. Cool on a wire rack for 10 minutes. Remove from pan; cool thoroughly on a wire rack.
4. To assemble sandwiches, slice cake into ½-inch slices. Spread Lemon Butter on one side of 8 cake slices. Top with peach and strawberry slices. Drizzle with caramel topping. Top with remaining cake slices. Makes 8 servings.
LEMON BUTTER: In a medium mixing bowl beat ¼ cup softened butter with an electric mixer on medium to high speed for 30 seconds. Add 1½ teaspoons finely shredded lemon peel. Beat until combined. Gradually drizzle in 1 teaspoon lemon juice; beat until combined. Use immediately or cover and chill butter for up to 1 week. Let stand at room temperature for 30 minutes before using.
TAILGATE PLAN: Pack a knife and corer for fruit. Wrap whole cake tightly in plastic wrap. Transport fruits whole. Or slice fruit at home and dip into a mixture of 1 cup water and 2 tablespoons lemon juice; drain. Place in an airtight container. Pack butter and fruits in an insulated carrier with ice packs.

EACH SERVING: *469 cal., 22 g fat (13 g sat. fat), 131 mg chol., 258 mg sodium, 64 g carbo., 2 g fiber, 4 g pro. Daily Values: 18% vit. A, 25% vit. C, 6% calcium, 10% iron.*

PEACH AND POUND CAKE SANDWICHES

LIGHT MY FIRE

SET UP THE GRILL AT LEAST TWO FEET OR MORE AWAY FROM YOUR VEHICLE. USE A CHIMNEY STARTER AND NEWSPAPER OR PARAFFIN CUBES TO START THE COALS. FINALLY WAIT UNTIL COALS ARE COMPLETELY COOL BEFORE DISPOSING OF COAL ASHES.

DENNIS TAYLOR'S
ONION-AND-MUSHROOM-STUFFED BURGER

Toast the rolls or buns directly over hot coals during the last 1 to 2 minutes of grilling.

PREP: 50 minutes **GRILL:** 25 minutes

INGREDIENTS

1½	cups sliced onion (about 3 medium)
8	oz. fresh button or cremini mushrooms, sliced (3 cups)
1	Tbsp. olive oil
2	Tbsp. snipped fresh parsley
2½	lb. 85% lean ground beef
⅓	cup Worcestershire sauce
4	cloves garlic, minced
1½	tsp. salt
1	tsp. ground black pepper
16	slices applewood smoked bacon (about 1 lb.) (optional)
8	slices Swiss, provolone, and/or Colby and Monterey Jack cheese (optional)
8	kaiser rolls or hamburger buns, split and toasted Tomato slices (optional)

PREPARATION

1. In very large skillet cook onion and mushrooms in hot oil over medium heat for 15 to 20 minutes or until all of the liquid has evaporated and onion and mushrooms are tender and golden brown, stirring occasionally. Remove from heat. Stir in parsley; set aside to cool slightly.

2. In very large mixing bowl mix beef, Worcestershire sauce, garlic, salt, and pepper until just combined (do not overmix). Shape mixture into 16 (3½-inch-diameter) patties. Spoon filling onto half of the patties to ½ inch of the edge. Top with remaining patties; pinch to seal. If desired, place 2 bacon slices over each stuffed patty in a crisscross pattern, tucking ends under.

3. For a charcoal grill, arrange medium-hot coals around a drip pan. Test for medium heat above pan. Place patties over drip pan on grill rack. Cover and grill for 25 to 30 minutes or until done (160°F). (For a gas grill, preheat grill. Reduce heat to medium. Adjust for indirect grilling. Grill as above.) If desired, top with cheese. Cover; cook for 1 to 2 minutes more or until cheese melts.

4. Serve burgers on rolls. If desired, add tomato slices. Makes 8 servings.

TAILGATE PLAN: After assembling stuffed burger patties, place them in an airtight container; separate layers with waxed paper. Seal container and chill for up to 24 hours before transporting to the tailgate gathering. If using, pack cheese and tomatoes separately in airtight containers. Place in an insulated carrier with ice packs.

EACH SERVING: *516 cal., 26 g fat (9 g sat. fat), 96 mg chol., 954 mg sodium, 37 g carbo., 2 g fiber, 33 g pro. Daily Values: 2% vit. A, 10% vit. C, 10% calcium, 32% iron.*

FILL IT UP To make these stuffed burgers, top one patty with an even spoonful of the onion-mushroom mixture (do not mound), leaving about a half inch to the edge. Top with second patty and gently press the edges together so the patties adhere to one another.

ONION-AND-MUSHROOM-
STUFFED BURGER

Baked Sweet Potato and Chili Wedges

Just before heading to the game, baste potato wedges with a spicy-sweet orange juice mixture while baking. Serve with cilantro sour cream.

CARL BLACKBIRD'S

BAKED SWEET POTATO AND CHILI WEDGES

Serve these as an appetizer or side dish.

PREP: 20 minutes **BAKE:** 25 minutes

INGREDIENTS

- 3½ lb. sweet potatoes (5 to 6 large)
- 2 Tbsp. olive oil
- 1 tsp. sea salt or ¾ tsp. salt
- ¼ tsp. ground black pepper
- ½ cup orange juice
- 3½ tsp. chili powder
- 1 Tbsp. honey
- 1 8-oz. carton dairy sour cream
- ⅓ cup snipped fresh cilantro

PREPARATION

1. Preheat oven to 450°F. Cut each unpeeled potato into 1-inch-thick wedges. Place in a large resealable plastic bag; toss with oil, salt, and pepper. Arrange potatoes in two 13×9×2-inch disposable foil pans.

2. Meanwhile, in a small bowl combine orange juice, 3 teaspoons of the chili powder, and honey; set aside.

3. Bake potato wedges, uncovered, for 25 to 30 minutes or until tender, brushing three times with orange juice mixture and shaking the pan occasionally.

4. Meanwhile, in a small bowl combine sour cream, remaining ½ teaspoon chili powder, and the cilantro. Transfer potatoes to a serving dish; serve with sour cream mixture. Serve immediately or at room temperature. Makes 8 to 10 servings.

TAILGATE PLAN: Place potatoes in an airtight container. Do not chill. Place the sour cream mixture in an airtight container and place in an insulated container with ice packs.

EACH SERVING (ABOUT 6 WEDGES): *233 cal., 10 g fat (4 g sat. fat), 12 mg chol., 306 mg sodium, 35 g carbo., 5 g fiber, 3 g pro. Daily Values: 421% vit. A, 26% vit. C, 8% calcium, 7% iron.*

CARL BLACKBIRD'S

ARTICHOKE AND PEPPER TOASTS

PREP: 20 minutes **BAKE:** 25 minutes

INGREDIENTS

- 2 14-oz. cans artichoke hearts, drained and chopped
- 1 cup bottled roasted red sweet peppers, drained and chopped
- 1½ cups shredded mozzarella cheese (6 oz.)
- ½ cup grated fresh Parmesan cheese
- 1 cup fresh basil, finely chopped
- ¼ cup extra virgin olive oil
- 4 cloves garlic, minced
- ½ tsp. ground black pepper
  Shaved Parmesan cheese (optional)
- 1 to 2 baguettes, sliced into ½-inch slices, brushed with olive oil, and toasted

PREPARATION

1. Preheat oven to 350°F. In a bowl combine artichoke hearts, roasted red pepper, mozzarella, grated Parmesan, basil, oil, garlic, and black pepper. Transfer mixture to a 1½-quart casserole.

2. Bake, uncovered, about 25 minutes or until heated through. If desired, top with shaved cheese. Serve at room temperature with toasted baguette slices. Makes 8 (½-cup) servings.

TAILGATE PLAN: Prepare as above or divide mixture between two 8¼×5¼×1-inch disposable foil pans before baking for easier transport. Cover with a double layer of foil. Serve the dip at room temperature.

EACH SERVING (WITH 2 SLICES TOAST): *223 cal., 12 g fat (4 g sat. fat), 14 mg chol., 559 mg sodium, 19 g carbo., 2 g fiber, 10 g pro. Daily Values: 6% vit. A, 72% vit. C, 20% calcium, 7% iron.*

Artichoke and Pepper Toasts

The garlicky, cheesy spread is prebaked before the party. Have plenty of toasted baguette slices on hand so guests won't be tempted to double-dip! To tote, wrap the casserole and toasts separately in double layers of foil and place in an insulated container.

ZESTING The recipes for Lime Vinaigrette (*right*), Chili-Sour Cream Dip, and Lime Guacamole (*page 192*) call for shredded lime peel, or "zest." To get the most flavorful peel, carefully drag the lime across the surface of the shredder, avoiding scraping into the white layer, or pith, which has a bitter taste.

ANNA ESPINOZA'S
ZESTY CHICKEN WRAPS
PREP: 40 minutes   **MARINATE:** 2 hours   **COOK:** 6 minutes per batch

INGREDIENTS

2½	lb. skinless, boneless chicken breast tenders
1	recipe Lime Vinaigrette
4	plum tomatoes, coarsely chopped
1	cup fresh corn kernels or frozen corn
1	cup coarsely chopped, peeled jicama
¾	cup chopped, peeled mango (1 mango)
½	cup chopped red onion
2	Tbsp. snipped fresh mint
2	to 3 Tbsp. canola oil
8	10- to 11-inch flour tortillas
⅓	cup bottled lime-flavored mayonnaise
	Mint leaves

PREPARATION

1. Divide chicken tenders between two resealable plastic bags set in a shallow dish. Reserve ¼ cup Lime Vinaigrette. Pour the remaining vinaigrette over chicken, dividing evenly between the bags; seal bags. Marinate in the refrigerator for 2 to 4 hours, turning bags occasionally.

2. Meanwhile, for salsa, in a large resealable plastic bag or covered storage container combine reserved ¼ cup Lime Vinaigrette, tomato, corn, jicama, mango, red onion, and mint. Cover and chill for 2 to 4 hours.

3. Drain chicken, discarding vinaigrette. In a large skillet cook chicken, uncovered, about one-third at a time in hot oil over medium heat for 6 to 8 minutes or until chicken is no longer pink. Remove from skillet; let stand until cool enough to handle. Halve pieces lengthwise. Transfer to a covered container; refrigerate for up to 24 hours or until ready to serve.

4. Spread tortillas lightly with mayonnaise. Divide chicken evenly among the tortillas. Remove salsa mixture with a slotted spoon and place on top of chicken. Top with mint leaves and roll up to serve. Makes 8 wraps.

LIME VINAIGRETTE: In a medium bowl combine 1 tablespoon finely shredded lime peel, 1 cup lime juice, 3 tablespoons canola oil, 2 teaspoons ground cumin, and ¼ teaspoon salt.

TAILGATE PLAN: Pack chicken, salsa, and mayonnaise separately in airtight containers in an insulated carrier with ice packs. Assemble wraps on site.

EACH WRAP: *467 cal., 18 g fat (3 g sat. fat), 92 mg chol., 363 mg sodium, 34 g carbo., 3 g fiber, 39 g pro. Daily Values: 13% vit. A, 35% vit. C, 8% calcium, 16% iron.*

Zesty Chicken Wraps

This unbeatable meal lineup includes tortillas filled with lime-marinated chicken tenders and homemade tomato-mango salsa. For the freshest wrap, pack the prepared ingredients separately and assemble when you're ready to eat.

BEEF AND BLUE PIZZA

READY IN
20
MINUTES

Back-to-School Dinners
Weeknight-friendly recipes for busy, on-the-go families.

BY **NANCY WALL HOPKINS** RECIPES BY **MARYELLYN KRANTZ** PHOTOGRAPHS BY **ANDY LYONS** FOOD STYLING BY **JILL LUST**

FAST!

BEEF AND BLUE PIZZA

START TO FINISH: 20 minutes

INGREDIENTS
½   of a medium red onion, cut into thin slivers
2   Tbsp. olive oil
1   12-inch Italian bread shell (such as Boboli)
8   oz. thinly sliced cooked roast beef
1   small red sweet pepper, seeded and chopped
4   oz. crumbled blue cheese
¼   tsp. pizza seasoning (optional)

PREPARATION
1. Position the oven rack in center of the oven. Preheat oven to 425°F. In a large skillet cook onion in 1 tablespoon of the oil over medium-high heat for 3 to 5 minutes or just until onion is tender. Place bread shell on a baking sheet; brush with remaining oil. Bake for 5 minutes.
2. Meanwhile, stack beef slices on a cutting board; slice into strips. Top bread shell with beef, sweet pepper, onion, cheese, and, if desired, pizza seasoning. Change oven setting to broil. Broil pizza for 4 to 5 minutes or until toppings are heated through and crust is browned. Cut into wedges. Makes 4 servings.

EACH SERVING: *523 cal., 20 g fat (7 g sat. fat), 56 mg chol., 1,637 mg sodium, 54 g carbo., 1 g fiber, 31 g pro. Daily Values: 23% vit. A, 96% vit. C, 34% calcium, 10% iron.*

FAST! **LOW FAT**

CHICKEN TORTELLINI TOSS

START TO FINISH: 20 minutes

INGREDIENTS
2   9-oz. pkg. refrigerated cheese tortellini
4   cups broccoli and/or cauliflower florets
1   14.5 oz. can diced tomatoes with Italian herbs
½   of a 10-ounce jar dried tomato pesto (½ cup)
1   9-oz. pkg. frozen roasted or grilled chicken breast strips, thawed
     Shaved Parmesan (optional)

PREPARATION
1. In a 4-quart Dutch oven cook tortellini according to package directions, adding the broccoli the last 3 minutes of cooking. Drain. Return to Dutch oven. Stir in undrained tomatoes, tomato pesto, and chicken. Cook, stirring occasionally, just until heated through. If desired, garnish with Parmesan cheese. Makes 4 servings.

EACH SERVING: *468 cal., 10 g fat (4 g sat. fat), 81 mg chol., 1,372 mg sodium, 61 g carbo., 5 g fiber, 33 g pro. Daily Values: 28% vit. A, 169% vit. C, 32% calcium, 20 % iron.*

CHICKEN TORTELLINI TOSS

FAST! **LOW FAT**

BEAN-POTATO CHOWDER

START TO FINISH: 20 minutes

INGREDIENTS

1	20-oz. pkg. refrigerated diced potatoes with onions
1	14-oz. can vegetable broth
1	cup shredded Swiss cheese (8 oz.)
⅓	cup all-purpose flour
3	cups milk
1	tsp. dried Italian seasoning, crushed
1	15-oz. can navy beans, rinsed and drained
	Bottled roasted red sweet pepper (optional)
	Snipped fresh Italian (flat-leaf) parsley (optional)
8	slices toasted bread with cheese (optional)

PREPARATION

1. In a Dutch oven combine potatoes and broth. Cover; bring to boiling over high heat. Reduce heat. Simmer, covered, for 4 minutes. In a bowl toss together cheese and flour. Gradually stir in milk. Add milk mixture and Italian seasoning to potatoes in the Dutch oven. Cook and stir over medium heat until thickened and bubbly. Stir in beans; cook and stir for 1 minute more. If desired, top with roasted pepper and parsley and serve with toasted bread. Makes 4 servings.

EACH SERVING: 494 cal., 12 g fat (7 g sat. fat), 40 mg chol., 1,344 mg sodium, 70 g carbo., 9 g fiber, 25 g pro. Daily Values: 16% vit. A, 27% vit. C, 50% calcium, 19% iron.

BEAN-POTATO CHOWDER

SESAME-CRUSTED COD

SESAME-CRUSTED COD

START TO FINISH: 20 minutes

INGREDIENTS

1	lb. cod fillets, ¾ inch thick
	Salt and ground black pepper
2	Tbsp. sesame seeds
3	Tbsp. butter, melted
1	12-oz. pkg. trimmed fresh tender young green beans
1	orange, halved and sliced
3	cloves garlic, thinly sliced

PREPARATION

1. Preheat broiler. Rinse cod; pat dry. Cut into 4 portions; place on the unheated rack of a broiler pan. Sprinkle with salt and pepper. Stir sesame seeds into melted butter. Set aside 1 tablespoon of the butter mixture for vegetables. Brush cod with half of the remaining butter mixture. Broil 6 inches from the heat for 4 minutes; turn fish. Brush with remaining half of the butter mixture. Broil 5 to 6 minutes more or until fish flakes easily when tested with a fork.

2. Meanwhile, in a skillet heat reserved 1 tablespoon butter mixture over medium-high heat. Add beans and orange slices. Cover and cook for 2 minutes. Uncover and add garlic. Cook for 5 to 6 minutes or until beans are tender, stirring often. Serve bean mixture with cod. Makes 4 servings.

EACH SERVING: *241 cal., 12 g fat (6 g sat. fat), 72 mg chol., 274 mg sodium, 12 g carbo., 4 g fiber, 23 g pro. Daily Values: 19% vit. A, 55% vit. C, 11% calcium, 12% iron.*

PORK-VEGGIE SANDWICHES

START TO FINISH: 20 minutes

INGREDIENTS

1	18.4-oz. peppercorn-seasoned pork tenderloin
1	ripe avocado, halved, seeded, and peeled
¼	tsp. salt
⅛	tsp. ground black pepper
1	10-inch focaccia, cut into quarters and split horizontally
½	of a medium red onion, thinly sliced
1	large tomato, cored and sliced

PREPARATION

1. Preheat broiler. Slice tenderloin into ½-inch-thick slices; flatten slightly with the palm of your hand. Arrange slices on the unheated rack of a broiler pan. Broil 4 inches from the heat for 4 to 6 minutes or until just slightly pink in center, turning once.

2. Meanwhile, in a small bowl mash avocado with a fork. Stir in salt and pepper.

3. Spread bottoms of bread quarters with avocado mixture. Layer onion, pork, and tomato on top of avocado mixture. Add bread tops; halve. Makes 4 servings (2 pieces each).

EACH SERVING: *476 cal., 14 g fat (4 g sat. fat), 61 mg chol., 925 mg sodium, 57 g carbo., 7 g fiber, 35 g pro. Daily Values: 8% vit. A, 19% vit. C, 13% calcium, 13% iron.*

PORK-VEGGIE SANDWICHES

CHILI–CORN SNACK MIX

Good-For-You Snacks

Sensible snacking can help you maintain a
healthful diet and still satisfy your cravings.

BY **STEPHEN EXEL** PHOTOGRAPHS BY **ANDY LYONS** FOOD STYLING BY **JILL LUST** RECIPES BY **LAURA MARZEN**

CHILI-CORN SNACK MIX

START TO FINISH: 15 minutes

INGREDIENTS

1	Tbsp. canola oil
1	Tbsp. lime juice
1	tsp. chili powder
2	cups toasted high-fiber corn cereal and/or crispy corn and rice cereal
1	cup tiny pretzel knots
½	cup whole almonds
¼	cup dehydrated corn kernels
¼	cup snipped dried apricots or whole dried cherries

PREPARATION

1. In a large skillet heat oil, lime juice, and chili powder over medium heat for 30 seconds. Add cereal, pretzels, and almonds. Cook for 4 to 6 minutes or until cereal and almonds are very lightly browned, stirring frequently. Remove from heat. Stir in corn and apricots. Spread mixture on foil to cool. Makes 8 (½-cup) servings.

EACH SERVING: *125 cal., 7 g fat (1 g sat. fat), 0 mg chol., 133 mg sodium, 16 g carbo., 3 g fiber, 3 g pro. Daily Values: 5% vit. A, 2% vit. C, 3% calcium, 20% iron.*

PEANUT BUTTER-BANANA TRIFLES

START TO FINISH: 10 minutes

INGREDIENTS

1¾	cups plain low-fat yogurt
2	Tbsp. smooth peanut butter
1	to 2 Tbsp. honey
2	large bananas, sliced
2	cups lightly sweetened multigrain clusters

PREPARATION

1. In a bowl whisk together yogurt, peanut butter, and honey until smooth. Divide half of the yogurt mixture among four 6-ounce glasses or custard cups. Top with half of the banana slices and half of the multigrain clusters. Repeat layers. Serve immediately. Makes 4 servings.

EACH SERVING: *283 cal., 7 g fat (2 g sat. fat), 6 mg chol., 215 mg sodium, 45 g carbo., 6 g fiber, 13 g pro. Daily Values: 2% vit. A, 10% vit. C, 23% calcium, 7% iron.*

PEANUT BUTTER-BANANA TRIFLES

TEST KITCHEN TIP
The trifles' yogurt mixture can be made and chilled for up to 24 hours ahead of time. Assemble the trifles just before serving.

FAST! **KID FRIENDLY**

ITALIAN POPCORN

START TO FINISH: 5 minutes

INGREDIENTS

1   100-calorie-size bag unpopped microwave popcorn
       Nonstick cooking spray
2   Tbsp. grated Parmesan cheese
½   tsp. dried Italian seasoning, crushed
⅛   tsp. crushed red pepper (optional)

PREPARATION

1. Prepare popcorn according to package directions. While popcorn is still hot, transfer to a large bowl. Remove any uncooked kernels. Lightly coat popcorn with nonstick cooking spray. Toss; repeat until all kernels are well coated with nonstick spray. Sprinkle popcorn with Parmesan cheese, Italian seasoning, and, if desired, crushed red pepper; toss gently to coat. Serve immediately (do not store). Makes 1 serving.

EACH SERVING: *145 cal., 4 g fat (2 g sat. fat), 9 mg chol., 325 mg sodium, 22 g carbo., 3 g fiber, 7 g pro. Daily Values: 1% vit. A, 12% calcium, 3% iron.*

ITALIAN POPCORN

TEST KITCHEN TIP
Because this recipe is best served hot, make as much of it as you need at one time. It doubles and triples easily, so it's a quick-and-easy crowd-pleaser for casual gatherings.

APPLE CRUNCH MIX

FAST! **KID FRIENDLY**

APPLE CRUNCH MIX

Use cinnamon-flavor cereal and baked apple pieces for this easy-to-prepare snack mix.

PREP: 5 minutes

INGREDIENTS

2   cups cinnamon-flavor oat square cereal
⅔   cup original- or cinnamon-flavor crisp baked apple pieces
½   cup shelled lightly salted pistachio nuts or coarsely chopped toasted pecans
¼   cup golden raisins

PREPARATION

1. In a medium bowl combine cereal, apple pieces, nuts, and raisins. Store in an airtight container at room temperature for up to 1 week. Makes 6 (½-cup) servings.

CHOCOLATE CRUNCH MIX: In a medium bowl combine 2 cups sweetened oat square cereal, 1 tablespoon unsweetened dark or regular cocoa powder, and 1 teaspoon powdered sugar; toss to coat. Add ⅔ cup original-flavor crisp baked apple pieces, ½ cup dry-roasted peanuts, and ¼ cup dried cranberries or dried banana chips. Makes 6 (½-cup) servings.

EACH SERVING: *164 cal., 6 g fat (1 g sat. fat), 0 mg chol., 94 mg sodium, 25 g carbo., 3 g fiber, 5 g pro. Daily Values: 4% vit. A, 4% vit. C, 5% calcium, 35% iron.*

Artichoke Dip

Warm spices and fresh, crunchy texture brighten up this potluck favorite.

BY **STEPHEN EXEL** PHOTOGRAPHS BY **ANDY LYONS** FOOD STYLING BY **JILL LUST**

CHEESE & MAYO
Lite mayonnaise keeps the creamy base low in calories. Stir together with coarsely grated Parmesan cheese to make it high in flavor.

SEASONINGS
Seasoning with a crushed peppercorn blend and smoked paprika adds aromatic punch (and color straight out of potluck tradition).

GARLIC
Three or four roasted garlic cloves complement the artichokes with gutsy taste.

ARTICHOKE HEARTS
To bring out their sweetness, brush thawed frozen artichoke hearts with olive oil and broil them for 2 to 3 minutes before stirring them into the mixture.

PARSLEY
Snipped fresh Italian (flat-leaf) parsley scattered over the top of the baked dip gives a hit of color.

LEMON ZEST
Refreshing citrus flavor comes from a sprinkle of lemon peel.

BANANA PEPPERS
Add about ⅔ cup jarred banana pepper slices for mild heat and extra texture.

BASIC ARTICHOKE DIP
In a 1½-quart casserole combine three 9-ounce packages frozen artichoke hearts, thawed and chopped; 1½ cups mayonnaise; and 2 cups shredded Parmesan cheese. Season. Bake, uncovered, in a 400°F oven for 25 to 30 minutes or until the dip is golden.

Sandwiches All Day

These lunchtime classics are also a delicious, convenient meal any time of day.

BY **RICHARD SWEARINGER** RECIPES BY **STEPHEN EXEL** PHOTOGRAPHS BY **ANDY LYONS** FOOD STYLING BY **JILL LUST**

ITALIAN MUFFULETTA

This sandwich is traditionally made with chopped olive "salad." Our muffuletta substitutes easier-to-find pepperoncini salad peppers.

PREP: 20 minutes **CHILL:** 2 hours

INGREDIENTS

3   Tbsp. olive oil
2   Tbsp. white wine vinegar
2   tsp. snipped fresh oregano
1   tsp. Dijon-style mustard
¼   tsp. crushed red pepper
12   slices crusty sourdough bread
2   medium tomatoes, sliced
6   oz. thinly sliced Italian fontina or provolone cheese
6   oz. thinly sliced prosciutto or mortadella
2   cups loosely packed fresh basil leaves
5   pepperoncini salad peppers, seeded and thinly sliced

PREPARATION

1. For dressing, in a screw-top jar combine oil, vinegar, oregano, mustard, and crushed red pepper. Cover; shake well. Set aside.

2. On 6 of the bread slices layer tomatoes, cheese, prosciutto, basil, and pepperoncini salad peppers.

3. Shake dressing and drizzle over peppers. Top with remaining 6 bread slices. Wrap tightly. Chill for up to 2 hours before serving. Makes 6 sandwiches.

EACH SANDWICH: *354 cal., 24 g fat (8 g sat. fat), 85 mg chol., 1,596 mg sodium, 13 g carbo., 2 g fiber, 22 g pro. Daily Values: 28% vit. A, 13% vit. C, 24% calcium, 7% iron.*

FAST!

GREENS, EGGS, AND HAM SANDWICHES

Add a dash of water to the eggs and cover to cook them more evenly.

START TO FINISH: 30 minutes

INGREDIENTS

4   slices whole grain bread, cut ½ inch thick
2   Tbsp. stone-ground mustard
4   oz. thinly sliced capacola or other fully cooked ham
3   to 4 oz. Gruyère or Swiss cheese, thinly sliced
1   Tbsp. butter or margarine
4   eggs
1   Tbsp. water
½   cup arugula or spinach leaves, stems removed

PREPARATION

1. Preheat broiler. Place bread slices on a baking sheet. Broil 3 to 4 inches from heat for 1 to 2 minutes per side until toasted. Remove from oven. Spread mustard on one side of each slice. Top with ham and cheese. Broil about 2 minutes more or until cheese is melted.

2. Meanwhile, for fried eggs, in a large skillet melt butter over medium heat.* Break eggs into skillet. Sprinkle lightly with *salt* and *ground black pepper*. When whites are set, add water. Cover skillet and cook eggs for 2 to 3 minutes or until yolks begin to set but are not hard.

3. Place prepared bread slices on dinner plates. Top with a fried egg and a few arugula leaves. Makes 4 sandwiches.

*NOTE: If desired, omit the butter or margarine and coat a large nonstick skillet with nonstick cooking spray.

EACH SANDWICH: *298 cal., 18 g fat (8 g sat. fat), 254 mg chol., 954 mg sodium, 15 g carbo., 1 g fiber, 18 g pro. Daily Values: 8% vit. A, 3% vit. C, 22% calcium, 11% iron.*

GREENS, EGGS, AND HAM SANDWICHES

PEPPER AND ONION HOT BEEF SANDWICHES

PEPPER AND ONION HOT BEEF SANDWICHES

Made with convenient precooked pot roast, these sandwiches and a side salad make a hearty dinner.

PREP: 25 minutes   COOK: 20 minutes

INGREDIENTS

1   cup thinly sliced red onion
1   small yellow and/or red sweet pepper, cut into thin bite-size strips
2   cloves garlic, minced
1   Tbsp. butter
1   16- or 17-oz. pkg. refrigerated cooked beef pot roast with juices
½   cup lightly packed basil leaves
4   kaiser rolls or onion rolls, toasted
1   recipe Basil Mayonnaise

PREPARATION

1. In a large skillet cook onion, sweet pepper, and garlic in hot butter over medium heat for 5 minutes or until nearly tender. Add pot roast with juices. Bring to boiling; reduce heat. Simmer, covered, about 10 minutes or until pot roast is heated through.

2. Transfer pot roast to a cutting board; keep warm. Remove vegetables from skillet with a slotted spoon, reserving juices in skillet. Simmer juices until reduced to ¼ cup, about 5 minutes. Cut pot roast into bite-size pieces. Divide basil leaves and pot roast among roll bottoms. Top with vegetable mixture and some of the juices. Spread Basil Mayonnaise on roll tops. Replace roll tops. Makes 4 sandwiches.

BASIL MAYONNAISE: In a small bowl stir together ¼ cup light mayonnaise or salad dressing, 2 tablespoons snipped fresh basil, and a dash freshly ground black pepper.

EACH SANDWICH: *425 cal., 18 g fat (6 g sat. fat), 73 mg chol., 784 mg sodium, 39 g carbo., 2 g fiber, 29 g pro. Daily Values: 10% vit. A, 77% vit. C, 8% calcium, 21% iron.*

SHRIMP PO' BOY

SHRIMP PO' BOY

Consider this sweet and spicy make-ahead for lunch.

PREP: 25 minutes **CHILL:** up to 1 hour **BROIL:** 1 minute

INGREDIENTS

1	lb. peeled cooked shrimp
1	medium papaya or mango, seeded, peeled, and coarsely chopped
1/3	cup mayonnaise or light mayonnaise
1	serrano or jalapeño chile pepper, seeded and finely chopped (see Note, page 76)
1	green onion, thinly sliced
1	tsp. finely shredded lime peel
1	Tbsp. lime juice
1/8	tsp. salt
1/8	tsp. freshly ground black pepper
1	18- to 24-inch baguette
4	Bibb or romaine lettuce leaves
2	Tbsp. shredded coconut, toasted

PREPARATION

1. Remove and discard shrimp tails, if present. If desired, coarsely chop the shrimp. In a medium bowl combine shrimp, papaya, mayonnaise, serrano pepper, onion, lime peel, lime juice, salt, and black pepper. Cover and chill for up to 1 hour.

2. Preheat broiler. Cut baguette into 4 equal-size rolls. Slice in half lengthwise. Remove some of the bread from bottom half of each roll, leaving a thick shell. Place all rolls, cut sides up, on broiler pan or baking sheet; broil 3 to 4 inches from the heat for 1 to 2 minutes or until toasted. Place a lettuce leaf on bottom of each roll. Spoon shrimp mixture onto lettuce; sprinkle with coconut. Place tops of rolls on shrimp mixture. Makes 4 sandwiches.

EACH SANDWICH: *681 cal., 25 g fat (5 g sat. fat), 235 mg chol., 1,136 mg sodium, 78 g carbo., 5 g fiber, 35 g pro. Daily Values: 19% vit. A, 49% vit. C, 16% calcium, 42% iron.*

FAST! **KID FRIENDLY**

GRILLED CHEESE AND FRUIT SANDWICHES

Add fruit and jam to the classic sandwich—they are natural flavor companions to cheese.

PREP: 15 minutes **GRILL:** 3 to 4 minutes

INGREDIENTS

8	slices white or egg bread, cut 1/2 inch thick
2	Tbsp. softened butter
1/4	cup fig or plum jam
4	oz. thinly sliced Havarti or Monterey Jack cheese
1	small pear or apple, thinly sliced
2	Tbsp. sliced almonds or chopped pecans, toasted

PREPARATION

1. Spread one side of each bread slice lightly with softened butter. Spread other side of 4 of the bread slices with jam. Top jam sides of bread with cheese. Top cheese with pear and almonds. Top with remaining bread slices, buttered sides up.

2. Preheat an indoor electric grill. Place sandwiches on grill rack. If using a covered grill, close lid. Grill sandwiches until bread is golden and cheese is melted. (For a covered grill, allow 3 to 4 minutes. For an uncovered grill, allow about 6 minutes, turning once halfway through grilling.) Or place sandwiches on a griddle over medium heat. Cook for 5 to 6 minutes or until golden and cheese melts, turning once. Makes 4 sandwiches.

EACH SANDWICH: *400 cal., 20 g fat (4 g sat. fat), 50 mg chol., 528 mg sodium, 46 g carbo., 3 g fiber, 13 g pro. Daily Values: 4% vit. A, 6% vit. C, 25% calcium, 12% iron.*

GRILLED CHEESE AND FRUIT SANDWICHES

Caramel Apples

Easy dress-ups for a favorite autumn treat.

BY **NANCY WALL HOPKINS**
PHOTOGRAPH BY **ANDY LYONS**
FOOD STYLING BY **JILL LUST**

4. BANANA CHIPS, drizzle of smooth peanut butter

5. MILK AND DARK chocolates (melted)

6. CHOPPED PECANS (toasted), shaved coconut (toasted)

7. APPLE PIE SPICE or chili powder (dusting)

8. TOFFEE CHOCOLATE BAR (crushed)

9. GRANOLA CEREAL, candy-coated milk chocolate pieces

10. ORANGE ZEST (coarsely shredded), drizzle of honey

1. RED CINNAMON CANDIES

2. PEANUTS, salted or honey-roasted

3. WHITE CHOCOLATE (melted)

BHG BASICS

To make enough caramel for 8 apples: Unwrap two 14-ounce packages vanilla caramels; melt in a small saucepan over low heat with 2 tablespoons of water; stir frequently. Dip apple in hot caramel, spooning caramel over apple. Cool for 30 minutes on buttered foil. Top as desired.

OCTOBER

CHECK OUT THE PHOTOS AND DESCRIPTIONS OF CLASSIC AND NEW APPLE VARIETIES ALONG WITH DELICIOUS RECIPES FOR USING THIS FRUIT FAVORITE.

CARAMEL APPLE PIE
page 224

Apple-licious!

Plus

Build a Better—

Everyday Easy—

Good and Healthy—

Ten to Try—

APPLE-GLAZED ROAST CHICKEN
page 218

APPLE-CHEDDAR SOUP
page 222

STEAK WITH SWEET POTATO-MANGO CHUTNEY
page 229

Apple-icious!

AN APPLE A DAY JUST ISN'T ENOUGH DURING HARVEST SEASON, ESPECIALLY WITH DELICIOUS NEW RECIPES FOR SOUPS, SALADS, MAIN COURSES, AND DESSERTS.

BY **RICHARD SWEARINGER**   PHOTOGRAPHS BY **ANDY LYONS**   FOOD STYLING BY **JILL LUST**   PROP STYLING BY **SUE MITCHELL**

Braeburn

Jazz

Granny Smith

Cameo

Pacific Queen

Golden Delicious

Fuji

Take Your Pick

A REFRESHER COURSE ON CLASSIC AND NEW VARIETIES

Braeburn Firm and crisp. The go-to apple for baking and cooking. Makes a great sauce.

Granny Smith Tart and crisp. Another great choice for all-around cooking.

Jazz Cross between Braeburn and Royal Gala. One of the newest on the market. Best raw and in salads.

Pacific Queen Sweet, light, and crisp. Eat out-of-hand or in salads.

Cameo Sweet and spicy. Wonderful in pies and for cooking.

Fuji Crisp and very sweet. A good baking and salad apple.

Golden Delicious The unsung hero of apples. Delicious to eat fresh and an excellent all-around apple for cooking.

FAST!

APPLE PECAN SALAD

Store any extra dressing in the refrigerator for up to 2 days.

START TO FINISH: 25 minutes

INGREDIENTS

	Nonstick cooking spray
3	Tbsp. packed brown sugar
3	Tbsp. finely chopped pecans
3	small sweet apples, halved and cored
1	Tbsp. butter, melted
1/3	cup canola oil
1/4	cup apple cider
1/4	cup cider vinegar
1	Tbsp. honey
1/4	tsp. salt
1/4	tsp. ground black pepper
6	cups mesclun mix or mixed salad greens
1/4	cup coarsely chopped pecans, toasted (optional)

PREPARATION

1. Preheat oven to 425°F. Line a baking sheet with foil; lightly coat with cooking spray. In a bowl combine brown sugar and finely chopped pecans. Place apple halves, cut sides up, on baking sheet. Brush tops of apples with butter; sprinkle with brown sugar mixture. Bake for 15 minutes or just until tender when pierced with a fork.
2. Meanwhile, for dressing, in a screw-top jar combine oil, cider, vinegar, honey, salt, and pepper. Cover; shake well.
3. Arrange greens on a platter; top with apple halves. Spoon melted sugar and pecans from baking sheet over the salad. Shake dressing; drizzle desired amount on salad. If desired, sprinkle with coarsely chopped pecans. Pass remaining dressing. Makes 6 servings.

EACH SERVING: 380 cal., 30 g fat (4 g sat. fat), 8 mg chol., 328 mg sodium, 28 g carbo., 4 g fiber, 4 g pro. Daily Values: 4% vit. A, 19% vit. C, 6% calcium, 7% iron.

APPLE PECAN SALAD

APPLE-GLAZED ROAST CHICKEN

Cook rice in the oven along with the chicken. Make sure the casserole has a tight-fitting lid so the rice remains moist while cooking.

PREP: 30 minutes **ROAST:** 2¼ hours

INGREDIENTS

1	cup cider vinegar
1	cup apple jelly
1	tsp. apple pie spice
1	5-lb. whole roasting chicken
	Salt
6	small tart baking apples, halved and cored, if desired
2¼	cups water
1	6-oz. pkg. long grain and wild rice mix
1	Tbsp. butter
½	tsp. freshly ground black pepper
3	green onions, thinly sliced
	Sage leaves (optional)

PREPARATION

1. For glaze, in a medium saucepan stir together vinegar and jelly. Heat and stir over medium heat until boiling. Boil gently, uncovered, for 20 minutes until syrupy and reduced to about 1 cup, stirring frequently. Remove from heat. Stir in apple pie spice. Divide glaze in half; set aside. (Glaze will thicken as it stands; stir before brushing on chicken and apples.)
2. Preheat oven to 325°F. Skewer neck skin of chicken to back; tie legs to tail. Twist wing tips under back. Place chicken, breast side up, on rack in a roasting pan. Sprinkle with salt. Roast, uncovered, for 1¼ hours. Cut string. Place apples around chicken.
3. Meanwhile, in a 1-quart casserole combine the water, rice and seasoning mix, and butter; cover. Set aside. Brush chicken and apples with some of one portion of the glaze. Sprinkle with pepper. Roast chicken and rice together in oven for 1 to 1¼ hours more or until an instant-read thermometer registers 180°F when inserted into thickest part of thigh and juices run clear, brushing with remainder of glaze portion twice. Stir green onion into rice. Transfer rice to platter; top with chicken and apples. Cover with foil to keep warm.
4. For sauce, skim fat from juices in roasting pan; discard fat. Pour remaining reserved glaze portion into pan. Using a wooden spoon, scrape up any brown bits stuck to bottom of pan (place pan on stovetop over medium heat, if necessary, to heat glaze). Strain; season to taste with salt and pepper. Transfer to a gravy boat. If desired, garnish chicken with sage leaves. Makes 6 servings.

EACH SERVING: 885 cal., 25 g fat (8 g sat. fat), 331 mg chol., 1,041 mg sodium, 81 g carbo., 5 g fiber, 87 g pro. Daily Values: 4% vit. A, 16% vit. C, 15% calcium, 65% iron.

THE OVEN COAXES OUT WARM, CARAMEL FLAVORS AND TONES DOWN SWEETNESS —PERFECT FOR BOTH DINNER AND DESSERT.

The glimmering, crispy skin of *Apple-Glazed Roast Chicken* gets its flavor from a sweet-tart blend of apple jelly and cider vinegar.

The gooey goodness of *Apple Upside-Down Cake* bakes up from a no-fuss, one-bowl batter spiced with ginger and cinnamon.

APPLE UPSIDE-DOWN CAKE

PREP: 25 minutes **BAKE:** 50 minutes **COOL:** 25 minutes

INGREDIENTS

- 1/3 cup butter, cut up
- 1/3 cup packed brown sugar
- 6 very small red cooking apples (1¼ to 1½ lb.), halved and, if desired, cores removed
- 1⅓ cups all-purpose flour
- 2/3 cup granulated sugar
- 2 tsp. baking powder
- 1 tsp. ground ginger
- 1 tsp. ground cinnamon
- 2/3 cup milk
- ¼ cup butter, softened
- 1 egg
- 1 tsp. vanilla
  Vanilla ice cream (optional)

PREPARATION

1. Preheat oven to 350°F. Place ⅓ cup butter in a 9×9×2-inch baking pan. Place in oven for 5 minutes or until butter melts. Sprinkle brown sugar over butter; stir. Arrange 9 of the apple halves in mixture, cut sides down. Bake for 10 to 15 minutes or until bubbly.

2. Meanwhile, peel remaining apples. Coarsely shred; set aside. In a mixing bowl combine flour, granulated sugar, baking powder, ginger, and cinnamon. Add shredded apple, milk, ¼ cup butter, egg, and vanilla. Beat with an electric mixer on low speed until combined; beat on medium speed for 1 minute. Spoon batter over apples and spread evenly (apples may be exposed; some butter may come to surface).

3. Bake about 35 minutes or until a wooden toothpick inserted near center comes out clean. Cool in pan on a wire rack for 5 minutes. Loosen edges; invert onto a platter. Spoon any topping in pan over top of cake. Cool for 20 minutes. If desired, serve with ice cream. Makes 9 servings.

EACH SERVING: *313 cal., 13 g fat (8 g sat. fat), 56 mg chol., 157 mg sodium, 47 g carbo., 2 g fiber, 3 g pro. Daily Value: 9% vit. A, 5% vit. C, 6% calcium, 7% iron.*

FAST!

APPLE-SAUSAGE RIGATONI

START TO FINISH: 25 minutes

INGREDIENTS

- 6 oz. dried rigatoni (about 2 cups)
- 8 oz. cooked smoked sausage, halved lengthwise and cut into 1-inch pieces
- 1½ lb. Golden Delicious apples, cored and cut into ½-inch slices
- ½ cup whipping cream
- ½ cup crumbled Gorgonzola or other blue cheese
  Snipped fresh basil (optional)

PREPARATION

1. In a 4-quart Dutch oven cook pasta according to package directions; drain. Set aside.

2. In the same Dutch oven cook sausage until lightly browned. Add apples; cook, stirring occasionally, for 5 to 7 minutes or until apples are lightly golden. Stir in cooked pasta, cream, and cheese. Heat through. If desired, garnish with basil. Makes 4 servings.

EACH SERVING: *613 cal., 34 g fat (16 g sat. fat), 92 mg chol., 1,056 mg sodium, 56 g carbo., 5 g fiber, 26 g pro. Daily Values: 14% vit. A, 14% vit. C, 13% calcium, 13% iron.*

APPLE-SAUSAGE RIGATONI

FAST! **KID FRIENDLY**

PEANUT BUTTER-APPLE-BACON SANDWICHES

Applewood-smoked bacon adds amazing autumn flavor.

START TO FINISH: 30 minutes

INGREDIENTS

¼	cup peach preserves
	Dash cayenne pepper (optional)
8	slices whole grain bread
1	large yellow or green crisp apple, cored and very thinly sliced
8	slices applewood-smoked bacon or other bacon, crisp-cooked and drained
¼	cup creamy peanut butter
2	to 3 Tbsp. butter, softened

PREPARATION

1. In a small bowl stir together preserves and, if desired, cayenne pepper. Place 4 slices of bread on a work surface; spread slices with preserves. Top with apple slices and bacon. Spread one side of remaining bread slices with peanut butter; place, spread sides down, over apples and bacon. Spread sandwich tops with some of the butter.

2. Preheat griddle or very large skillet over medium heat. Place sandwiches, buttered sides down, on griddle. Carefully spread unbuttered bread with butter. Cook for 2 to 3 minutes per side or until bread is golden and sandwiches are heated through. Makes 4 servings.

EACH SERVING: *470 cal., 23 g fat (7 g sat. fat), 33 mg chol., 831 mg sodium, 59 g carbo., 8 g fiber, 18 g pro. Daily Values: 4% vit. A, 6% vit. C, 32% calcium, 34% iron.*

KID FRIENDLY

APPLE-CHEDDAR SOUP

PREP: 20 minutes **COOK:** 20 minutes

INGREDIENTS

½	cup finely chopped onion (1 medium)
1	Tbsp. butter
2	medium baking potatoes, peeled and diced
2	cups apple cider
1	tsp. snipped fresh thyme or ½ tsp. dried thyme, crushed
½	tsp. salt
	Dash cayenne pepper
1	medium cooking apple, peeled, cored, and coarsely chopped
½	cup milk
2	Tbsp. all-purpose flour
4	oz. sharp cheddar cheese, shredded (1 cup)
	Apple slices
	Green peppercorns

PREPARATION

1. In a large saucepan cook onion in hot butter over medium heat until tender. Stir in diced potatoes, cider, thyme, salt, and cayenne pepper. Bring to boiling; reduce heat. Simmer, covered, for 15 minutes. Add chopped apple; simmer, covered, 5 minutes more or until diced potatoes are tender. In a small bowl combine milk and flour; stir into soup. Cook and stir until bubbly. Slowly add cheese, whisking until cheese is melted.

2. Divide soup among serving dishes; top with apple slices and peppercorns. Makes 4 to 6 side-dish servings.

EACH SERVING: *352 cal., 16 g fat (10 g sat. fat), 48 mg chol., 527 mg sodium, 32 g carbo., 4 g fiber, 12 g pro. Daily Values: 12% vit. A, 31% vit. C, 27% calcium, 9% iron.*

PEANUT BUTTER-APPLE-BACON SANDWICHES

CORING AND CUTTING APPLES

An apple corer, teaspoon, or small ice cream scoop makes short work of coring apples. For Chunky Applesauce recipe (*page 225*), the apples can be cut into medium-size chunks— no artistry required!

APPLE-CHEDDAR SOUP

CARAMEL APPLE PIE

Mix a variety of cooking apples, such as Braeburn, Granny Smith, Fuji, and Golden Delicious, for a sweet and tart flavor.

PREP: 45 minutes **ROAST:** 7 minutes per batch **BAKE:** 65 minutes

INGREDIENTS

- 1/3 cup butter, melted
- 1 tsp. ground cinnamon
- 4 lb. cooking apples, cored and cut into 1/4-inch slices (about 12 cups)
- 1 recipe Oat Pastry (right) or one 15-oz. pkg. rolled refrigerated unbaked piecrust (2 crusts)
- 1/2 cup packed brown sugar
- 2 Tbsp. all-purpose flour
- 1/2 tsp. salt
- 1 egg, lightly beaten
- 1 Tbsp. water
- 1 12-oz. jar caramel ice cream topping (about 1 cup)

PREPARATION

1. Preheat oven to 475°F. In a very large bowl combine butter and cinnamon; add apples and toss gently to coat. Spread apples evenly in a parchment paper- or foil-lined large roasting pan or two 15×10×1-inch baking pans. Roast (one pan at a time if using baking pans) 4 to 5 inches from heat for 7 to 10 minutes or until apples start to brown on edges, turning once halfway through. Cool apples in pan(s). Reduce oven temperature to 375°F.

2. Prepare Oat Pastry or let refrigerated pastry stand at room temperature according to package directions. Line a 9-inch pie plate with half of the pastry as directed.

3. In a very large bowl stir together brown sugar, flour, and salt. Add apple slices and any juices; stir to coat. Transfer to the pastry-lined pie plate. On a lightly floured surface roll remaining dough to a 14-inch circle; cut slits for steam to escape. Place on top of fruit filling. Trim top pastry to 1/2 inch beyond edge of pie plate. Fold top pastry edge under bottom pastry; crimp edge. Brush top with a mixture of beaten egg and the water. Cover edge of pie with foil to prevent overbrowning.

4. Place pie on middle rack in the oven and place a foil-lined baking sheet on lower rack beneath pie. Bake for 30 minutes; remove foil from pie. Bake for 35 to 40 minutes more or until top is golden and filling is bubbly. Remove to a wire rack. While warm, drizzle with some of the caramel topping. Cool completely. Serve with remaining topping. Makes 8 servings.

EACH SERVING (WITH OAT PASTRY): *645 cal., 26 g fat (10 g sat. fat), 47 mg chol., 656 mg sodium, 102 g carbo., 7 g fiber, 9 g pro. Daily Values: 9% vit. A, 18% vit. C, 7% calcium, 15% iron.*

OAT PASTRY

Make sure to use quick-cooking oats rather than regular rolled oats in this pastry.

START TO FINISH: 15 minutes

INGREDIENTS

- 2 cups all-purpose flour
- 1/2 cup quick-cooking rolled oats
- 1 tsp. salt
- 2/3 cup shortening
- 8 to 10 Tbsp. cold water

PREPARATION

1. In a medium bowl stir together flour, oats, and salt. Using a pastry blender, cut in shortening until pieces are pea size.

2. Sprinkle 1 tablespoon of the water over part of mixture; gently toss with a fork. Push moistened dough to side of bowl. Repeat, using 1 tablespoon water at a time, until all of the dough is moistened. Divide in half; form each half into a ball.

3. On a lightly floured surface flatten 1 dough ball. Roll from center to edge into 12-inch circle.

4. To transfer pastry, wrap around a rolling pin; unroll into a 9-inch pie plate, being careful not to stretch pastry. Trim pastry even with rim of pie plate. Fill pie plate with filling.

5. On a lightly floured surface roll remaining dough to a 14-inch circle; cut slits for steam to escape. Place on top of fruit filling; trim to 1/2 inch beyond edge of pie plate. Fold top crust under bottom crust; crimp edge. Makes pastry for 2-crust pie.

CARAMEL APPLE PIE

CURRIED CIDER-PORK STEW

CURRIED CIDER-PORK STEW

PREP: 35 minutes COOK: 1 hour

INGREDIENTS
2	lb. boneless pork shoulder
4	medium red and/or green crisp-tart cooking apples
1	Tbsp. cooking oil
1	large onion, cut into thin wedges
2	tsp. curry powder
1	14-oz. can chicken broth
$^2/_3$	cup apple cider or apple juice
$^1/_4$	tsp. salt
$^1/_4$	tsp. ground black pepper
12	oz. baby carrots with tops, trimmed, or packaged peeled baby carrots
2	stalks celery, sliced
1	1½-lb. butternut squash, peeled, seeded, and cubed (2 cups) Dairy sour cream, shredded orange peel, snipped fresh oregano, and/or freshly ground black pepper (optional)

PREPARATION

1. Trim fat from pork; cut pork into 1-inch cubes. Peel, core, and chop 2 of the apples; set aside. In a 4-quart Dutch oven brown pork, half at a time, in hot oil; return all pork to pan. Add chopped apple, onion, and curry powder; cook and stir for 2 minutes. Add broth, cider, salt, and pepper. Bring to boiling; reduce heat. Simmer, covered, for 30 minutes, stirring occasionally.

2. Add carrots and celery to pork mixture; return to boiling. Reduce heat; simmer, covered, for 20 minutes, stirring occasionally. Cut remaining apples into ¼-inch wedges. Add apples and squash to pork mixture. Cover; cook for 10 to 12 minutes or until pork and vegetables are tender. If desired, serve with sour cream, orange peel, oregano, and/or pepper. Makes 6 servings.

EACH SERVING: *379 cal., 14 g fat (4 g sat. fat), 102 mg chol., 526 mg sodium, 31 g carbo., 6 g fiber, 32 g pro. Daily Values: 322 % vit. A, 52% vit. C, 10% calcium, 19% iron.*

LOW FAT **KID FRIENDLY**

CHUNKY APPLESAUCE

The stovetop version of this recipe creates a chunky, sprightly sauce; the slow-cooker preparation gives a mellow, rich alternative.

PREP: 15 minutes COOK: 20 minutes

INGREDIENTS
6	sprigs fresh thyme
4	lb. red and/or green cooking apples, cored and cut into chunks
½	cup water
½	to ¾ cup granulated sugar Brown sugar (optional) Fresh thyme sprigs (optional)

PREPARATION

1. Tie thyme sprigs with clean kitchen string. In an 8-quart Dutch oven combine apple chunks, water, and tied thyme sprigs. Bring to boiling; reduce heat. Simmer, covered, for 20 minutes or until apples just begin to break up, stirring occasionally. Remove thyme.

2. With a potato masher or large spoon mash apples slightly. (Or process with an immersion blender or process, half at a time, in a food processor.) Sweeten to taste with granulated sugar. Stir before serving. If desired, sprinkle with brown sugar and thyme. Or cool completely and store in the refrigerator for up to 3 weeks. Makes about 12 (½-cup) servings.

SLOW COOKER METHOD: Place apple chunks in a 5- or 6-quart slow cooker. Stir in ½ cup sugar and 4 to 6 inches stick cinnamon (omit thyme and water). Cover; cook on high-heat setting for 3½ to 4 hours or until apples are very tender. Cool mixture for 1 hour; remove cinnamon. Mash slightly with a potato masher. (Or process with an immersion blender or process, half at a time, in a food processor.) Sweeten to taste with granulated sugar. Stir before serving.

TO FREEZE: Quick-cool the applesauce by placing Dutch oven or the slow cooker liner after the 1 hour cooling in a sink filled with ice water; stir mixture to cool. Ladle into 7 wide-top half-pint freezer containers, leaving a ½-inch headspace; seal, label, and freeze for up to 6 months.

EACH SERVING: *106 cal., 0 g fat (0 g sat. fat), 0 mg chol., 2 mg sodium, 28 g carbo., 3 g fiber, 4 g pro. Daily Values: 2 % vit. A, 13% vit. C, 1% calcium, 2% iron.*

CHUNKY APPLESAUCE

Autumn Dinners

Fresh and simple recipes for busy, on-the-go families.

BY **NANCY WALL HOPKINS**
RECIPES BY **MARYELLYN KRANTZ**
PHOTOGRAPHS BY **ANDY LYONS**
FOOD STYLING BY **JILL LUST**

READY IN
20
MINUTES

TURKEY SPINACH TOSS

FAST! **LOW FAT**

TURKEY SPINACH TOSS

START TO FINISH: 20 minutes

INGREDIENTS

2   8-oz. turkey breast tenderloins, halved horizontally
¼   tsp. coarsely ground black pepper
2   Tbsp. butter
2   oz. thinly sliced deli ham, cut into bite-size pieces
½   cup orange juice
2   9- to 10-oz. pkg. fresh spinach
1   orange, cut into wedges
    Salt
    Ground black pepper

PREPARATION

1. Season turkey with ¼ teaspoon pepper. In a very large skillet heat butter over medium-high heat; add turkey. Cook for 12 minutes or until no longer pink (170°F); turn once.

2. Remove turkey from skillet. Slice into strips; cover and keep warm. Add ham to skillet; cook and stir for 1 minute or until heated and starting to crisp. With a slotted spoon remove ham from skillet. Add juice to skillet; bring to boiling.

3. Add spinach, half at a time, to skillet; cook for 1 minute or until just wilted. Add orange wedges with second batch of spinach. Using tongs, remove from skillet and divide among plates. Sprinkle with salt and pepper. Top with turkey and ham. Drizzle with remaining juices from skillet. Makes 4 servings.

EACH SERVING: *244 cal., 8 g fat (4 g sat. fat), 94 mg chol., 528 mg sodium, 9 g carbo., 3 g fiber, 34 g pro. Daily Values: 244% vit. A, 87% vit. C, 15% calcium, 28% iron.*

FAST!

RAVIOLI WITH ZUCCHINI

START TO FINISH: 20 minutes

INGREDIENTS

1   9-oz. pkg. refrigerated whole wheat or plain cheese ravioli
½   cup walnuts, coarsely chopped
2   Tbsp. olive oil
2   medium zucchini, halved lengthwise and sliced
6   green onions, cut diagonally into ¼-inch slices
⅓   cup milk
1   cup finely shredded Parmesan cheese (4 oz.)
    Salt and ground black pepper

PREPARATION

1. Cook ravioli in 4 cups boiling salted water for 6 to 8 minutes or until tender; drain.

2. Meanwhile, in a large skillet cook walnuts in hot oil over medium heat for 2 to 3 minutes; remove with a slotted spoon. Add zucchini and green onion. Cook and stir 2 to 3 minutes or until crisp-tender.

3. Add pasta, walnuts, milk, and ¾ cup of the cheese to pan. Cook and toss 1 minute. Season to taste with salt and pepper. Transfer to serving bowls; sprinkle with remaining cheese. Makes 4 servings.

EACH SERVING: *466 cal., 29 g fat (9 g sat. fat), 59 mg chol., 859 mg sodium, 33 g carbo., 6 g fiber, 21 g pro. Daily Values: 12% vit. A, 35% vit. C, 41% calcium, 14% iron.*

RAVIOLI WITH ZUCCHINI

FAST!

WILTED CABBAGE AND BRATS

START TO FINISH: 20 minutes

INGREDIENTS

½ of a 2-lb. napa cabbage, cut into 4 wedges, core intact
2 Tbsp. olive oil
6 cooked smoked bratwurst links, halved diagonally
2 small apples, cored and cut into wedges
2 Tbsp. Dijon-style mustard
½ cup dairy sour cream
1 Tbsp. snipped fresh sage

PREPARATION

1. In a large skillet cook cabbage in 1 tablespoon of the hot oil over medium heat for 8 minutes or until tender.
2. Meanwhile, in a 4- to 5-quart Dutch oven cook bratwurst and apples in remaining 1 tablespoon hot oil for 2 minutes. In a small bowl whisk together ¼ cup *water* and mustard; add to Dutch oven. Bring to boiling; reduce heat. Simmer, covered, for 4 to 6 minutes or until apples are tender, stirring occasionally.
3. Use a slotted spoon to transfer cabbage, bratwurst, and apples to bowls. In a small bowl combine sour cream and sage; whisk in cooking juices. Serve mixture over bratwurst. Makes 4 servings.

EACH SERVING: *456 cal., 38 g fat (10 g sat. fat), 88 mg chol., 1,046 mg sodium, 13 g carbo., 2 g fiber, 15 g pro. Daily Values: 12% vit. A, 57% vit. C, 13% calcium, 8% iron.*

WILTED CABBAGE AND BRATS

STEAK WITH SWEET POTATO-MANGO CHUTNEY

FAST!

CHICKEN WITH CAPERS

START TO FINISH: 20 minutes

INGREDIENTS

4	skinless, boneless chicken breast halves (about 1½ lb.)
1	Tbsp. Dijon-style mustard
4	Tbsp. olive oil
	Salt and ground black pepper
½	cup seasoned fine dry bread crumbs
8	oz. fresh green beans, trimmed
2	lemons, 1 sliced and 1 juiced
1	Tbsp. capers

PREPARATION

1. Place each chicken breast half between sheets of plastic wrap. Lightly pound with the flat side of a meat mallet to an even thickness. Brush chicken with mustard; sprinkle evenly with salt, pepper, and bread crumbs to coat.

2. Heat 2 tablespoons of the oil in a large skillet over medium heat. Add chicken. Cook 4 minutes per side or until no pink remains (170°). Transfer to plates. Add remaining 2 tablespoons oil to skillet. Cook green beans in oil for 4 minutes or until crisp-tender; add lemon slices to beans in skillet the last minute. Transfer to plates. Add lemon juice and capers to skillet; heat through. Drizzle on chicken. Makes 4 servings.

EACH SERVING: 362 cal., 16 g fat (3 g sat. fat), 99 mg chol., 546 mg sodium, 13 g carbo., 4 g fiber, 42 g pro. Daily Values: 8% vit. A, 64% vit. C, 7% calcium, 14% iron.

FAST! LOW FAT

STEAK WITH SWEET POTATO-MANGO CHUTNEY

START TO FINISH: 20 minutes

INGREDIENTS

1	large sweet potato, peeled and diced (12 oz.)
4	6-oz. boneless beef round steaks, about ¾ inch thick
	Salt
	Steak seasoning
⅓	cup mango chutney
¼	cup dried cranberries

PREPARATION

1. In a medium saucepan bring 3 cups lightly salted water to boiling. Add sweet potato. Simmer, covered, for 8 to 10 minutes or until tender. Drain; keep warm.

2. Meanwhile, preheat a large nonstick skillet over medium-high heat. Season steaks with salt and steak seasoning. Add steaks to skillet; reduce heat to medium. Cook for 8 to 10 minutes. (If steaks brown too quickly, reduce heat to medium-low.) Transfer steaks to plates; cover to keep warm.

3. Add cooked potato to skillet. Cook and stir for 2 minutes. Add chutney and cranberries; heat through. Serve mixture with steaks. Makes 4 servings.

EACH SERVING: 344 cal., 5 g fat (2 g sat. fat), 70 mg chol., 418 mg sodium, 32 g carbo., 4 g fiber, 40 g pro. Daily Values: 330% vit. A, 34% vit. C, 8% calcium, 23% iron.

CHICKEN WITH CAPERS

The Whole Truth

Fiber- and vitamin-rich whole grains bring key health benefits to the nutritional party.

BY **STEPHEN EXEL** PHOTOGRAPHS BY **ANDY LYONS** FOOD STYLING BY **JILL LUST** RECIPES BY **LAURA MARZEN**

SESAME-GINGER WHEAT BERRY SALAD

SESAME-GINGER WHEAT BERRY SALAD

Wheat berries have a nutty, grassy taste and a chewy texture.

PREP: 15 minutes **COOK:** 45 minutes

INGREDIENTS

1 ¼ cups water
½ cup wheat berries
1 cup canned black beans, rinsed and drained
½ of a medium mango, seeded, peeled, and chopped
¾ cup thin bite-size carrot strips
¼ cup mango chutney
2 Tbsp. rice vinegar
2 tsp. toasted sesame oil
¼ tsp. ground ginger
   Salt (optional)
1 small head napa cabbage, coarsely shredded

PREPARATION

1. In a medium saucepan combine the water and wheat berries. Bring to boiling; reduce heat. Simmer, covered, for 45 to 60 minutes or until tender. Drain liquid. Stir in black beans, mango, carrots, chutney, vinegar, oil, and ginger. If desired, season with salt. Serve with cabbage. Makes 4 (²/₃-cup) servings.

EACH SERVING: *226 cal., 3 g fat (0 g sat. fat), 0 mg chol., 332 mg sodium, 45 g carbo., 8 g fiber, 9 g pro. Daily Values: 88% vit. A, 52% vit. C, 10% calcium, 11% iron.*

SPICY BARLEY AND RICE

PREP: 10 minutes **COOK:** 45 minutes

INGREDIENTS

½ cup chopped onion (1 medium)
2 tsp. olive oil
²/₃ cup regular (pearl) barley
1 14-oz. can reduced-sodium chicken broth
1 ³/₄ cups water
¼ cup brown rice
1 Tbsp. small fresh thyme sprigs or ½ tsp. dried thyme, crushed
½ to 1 tsp. finely chopped chipotle pepper in adobo sauce
2 cups torn fresh spinach
⅓ cup pecans or walnuts, toasted and coarsely chopped

PREPARATION

1. In a large saucepan cook onion in hot oil over medium heat about 5 minutes or until tender, stirring occasionally. Add barley; cook and stir for 3 minutes or until barley starts to brown.
2. Carefully add broth, the water, brown rice, dried thyme (if using), and chipotle pepper. Bring to boiling; reduce heat. Simmer, covered, about 45 minutes or until barley and rice are tender and most of the liquid is absorbed.
3. Stir in fresh thyme (if using). Remove from heat. Let stand for 5 minutes. Stir in spinach and pecans just before serving. Makes 6 (²/₃-cup) servings.

EACH SERVING: *168 cal., 7 g fat (1 g sat. fat), 0 mg chol., 173 mg sodium, 24 g carbo., 5 g fiber, 5 g pro. Daily Values: 19% vit. A, 8% vit. C, 3% calcium, 8% iron.*

Twice the Benefit Whole grains contain antioxidant levels that can match or exceed those in fruits and vegetables. Teaming oats and apples for breakfast or barley and broccoli for supper scores a double hit of healthy eating.

SPICY BARLEY AND RICE

LOW FAT

SQUASH-QUINOA SOUP

Quinoa is a tiny beadlike grain with delicate flavor and slight crunch.

PREP: 15 minutes **COOK:** 17 minutes

INGREDIENTS

12	oz. skinless, boneless chicken breast halves, cut into 1-inch pieces
⅓	cup finely chopped shallot or onion
2	tsp. olive oil or canola oil
2	14-oz. cans reduced-sodium chicken broth
1	5.5-oz. can apricot nectar
1	lb. butternut squash, peeled, halved, seeded, and cut into 1-inch cubes
¾	cup quinoa, rinsed and drained
1	tsp. ground cumin
2	small zucchini, halved lengthwise and cut into 1-inch pieces
	Salt and ground black pepper

PREPARATION

1. In a large saucepan cook chicken and shallot in hot oil over medium heat for 2 to 3 minutes or until shallot is tender, stirring occasionally. Add broth, apricot nectar, squash, quinoa, and cumin. Bring to boiling; reduce heat. Simmer, covered, for 5 minutes. Add zucchini. Cover and cook about 10 minutes more or until squash and quinoa are tender. Season to taste with salt and pepper. Makes 6 (1⅓-cup) servings.

EACH SERVING: *226 cal., 4 g fat (1 g sat. fat), 33 mg chol., 454 mg sodium, 31 g carbo., 3 g fiber, 19 g pro. Daily Values: 155% vit. A, 33% vit. C, 67% calcium, 18% iron.*

SQUASH-QUINOA SOUP

SWISS OATMEAL

BULGUR-MUSHROOM STOVETOP PILAF

PREP: 15 minutes **COOK:** 45 minutes

INGREDIENTS
- ½ cup chopped onion (1 medium)
- 1 Tbsp. olive oil
- 1 14-oz. can chicken broth
- 1 cup apple juice
- ½ cup wild rice, rinsed
- 2 cups quartered or sliced stemmed shiitake, cremini, or button mushrooms
- ½ cup bulgur
- 1 medium red or green sweet pepper, seeded and chopped
- ½ cup snipped fresh Italian (flat-leaf) parsley
- ¼ cup chopped walnuts, toasted
- Freshly cracked black pepper
- 1 oz. feta cheese, crumbled (¼ cup)

PREPARATION
1. In a large saucepan cook onion in hot oil about 5 minutes or until tender, stirring occasionally. Add broth, apple juice, and wild rice. Bring to boiling; reduce heat. Simmer, covered, for 30 minutes.
2. Stir in mushrooms and bulgur. Cook, covered, for 10 to 15 minutes more or until grains are tender and most of the liquid is absorbed. Stir in sweet pepper; remove from heat. Cover; let stand 5 minutes. Stir in parsley and walnuts. Season to taste with black pepper. Sprinkle with feta cheese. Makes 6 (¾-cup) servings.

EACH SERVING: *196 cal., 7 g fat (1 g sat. fat), 5 mg chol., 327 mg sodium, 29 g carbo., 5 g fiber, 7 g pro. Daily Values: 25% vit. A, 68% vit. C, 5% calcium, 8% iron.*

LOW FAT

SWISS OATMEAL

This oatmeal uses steel-cut oats, which retain more nutrients because they are minimally processed. Preparing the oatmeal ahead means no prep time at breakfast.

PREP: 15 minutes **CHILL:** 12 hours **COOK:** 8 minutes + 10 minutes

INGREDIENTS
- 1½ cups water
- ¾ cup steel-cut oats
- ¾ cup fat-free milk
- 1 6-oz. carton plain low-fat yogurt
- 3 Tbsp. honey
- ¼ tsp. apple pie spice or pumpkin pie spice
- ⅛ tsp. salt
- ½ cup assorted dried fruit, such as cranberries; blueberries; snipped apples, apricots, or plums (prunes); and/or dried fruit bits
- ⅓ cup coarsely chopped almonds, toasted
- Sliced banana (optional)

PREPARATION
1. In a medium saucepan combine the water and oats. Bring to boiling; reduce heat. Simmer, uncovered, for 8 minutes (oats will not be tender). Remove from heat; transfer to a bowl. Cool 5 minutes. Stir in milk, yogurt, 2 tablespoons of the honey, apple pie spice, salt, and dried fruit. Cover; chill at least 12 hours or up to 3 days.
2. Heat oatmeal in a saucepan over low heat for 10 minutes. Or oatmeal may be served at room temperature by letting it stand 15 minutes after removing from the refrigerator.
3. Stir in the remaining 1 tablespoon honey. Divide among serving bowls. Top with almonds and, if desired, sliced banana. Makes 5 (⅔ cup) servings.

EACH SERVING: *228 cal., 5 g fat (1 g sat. fat), 3 mg chol., 102 mg sodium, 38 g carbo., 4 g fiber, 8 g pro. Daily Values: 2% vit. A, 1% vit. C, 13% calcium, 3% iron.*

BULGAR-MUSHROOM STOVETOP PILAF

Garden Wrap

When you're on a roll for lunch, fresh and crisp is the way to go.

BY **STEPHEN EXEL** PHOTOGRAPH BY **ANDY LYONS** FOOD STYLING BY **CHARLES WORTHINGTON**

HERBED CREAM CHEESE
Spread the tortilla with room temperature herbed cream cheese or a favorite spreadable cheese. The cheese creates a firm foundation to keep ingredients in place and the tortilla from splitting.

FLAVORED TORTILLA
Add an extra layer of flavor with a spinach, sundried tomato, or herbed tortilla.

WHOLE LEAF LETTUCE
Line the wrap with fresh whole leaf lettuce leaves such as red leaf, romaine, or Bibb. The leaves will contain any dressing and keep the tortilla from getting soggy.

FROM THE DELI
Top lettuce with sliced turkey breast or ham. Choose smoked varieties for richer flavor.

VEGGIE STRIPS
Cut fresh red sweet pepper and cucumber into thin, long strips to prevent them from falling out of the rolled wrap. Shredded carrots add more delicious crunch.

BALSAMIC VINAIGRETTE AND SEASONINGS
Toss vegetables with balsamic vinaigrette to enhance their natural flavors. Season with cracked black pepper and sea salt.

THAT'S A WRAP
To make a wrap, place ingredients in the center of the tortilla. Place the tortilla so the fillings are horizontal. Starting at the bottom, tightly roll the tortilla up over the fillings. Tuck in the ends.

BY
NANCY WALL HOPKINS
PHOTOGRAPH BY
ANDY LYONS
RECIPES BY
JILL LUST

Mac 'n' Cheese
Jazz up the ultimate comfort food.

1. HERBED
Croutons, herbs, olive oil

2. ITALIAN
Mushrooms, roasted red peppers, Parmesan cheese

3. HARVEST
Sauteed apples, toasted walnuts, sage

4. SMOKY
Smoked white cheddar, hickory-smoked bacon, almonds

5. NEW ENGLAND
Lobster, crab, melted butter

6. PIZZA
Pepperoni, mozzarella, tomato sauce, pizza seasoning

7. DENVER
Ham, green peppers, onions, cheddar, hard-cooked egg

8. SOUTH OF THE BORDER
Chorizo sausage, avocado, grape tomatoes (diced)

9. GREEK
Roasted chicken, herbed feta, green olives, roasted sweet peppers.

10. GARDEN
Asparagus, broccoli, carrots, spinach, banana pepper rings

BHG BASICS

For Macaroni and Cheese, combine 2½ cups milk, 2 Tbsp. flour, and ⅛ tsp. black pepper. Heat; stir until thickened. Stir in 1½ cups each shredded Cheddar and American cheeses. Stir in 4 cups cooked macaroni. Transfer to casserole; bake in a 350°F oven until bubbly for 25 to 30 minutes.

NOVEMBER

WHEN IT'S TIME TO PLAN THE HOLIDAY DINNER, FEATURE A SUCCULENT ROASTED TURKEY WITH ALL THE TRIMMINGS FOR A HOMESPUN FEAST.

Simple & Pure

Plus

Build a Better—

Everyday Easy—

Ten to Try—

What's Cooking—

**LEMON-GLAZED
SWEET POTATOES**
page 245

**PARSLEYED
GREEN BEANS**
page 247

simple & pure

BY **SCOTT PEACOCK** PHOTOGRAPHS BY **JAMES BAIGRIE** FOOD STYLING BY **JILL LUST** PROP STYLING BY **LESLIE SIEGEL**

PRODUCED BY **NANCY WALL HOPKINS**

SIMPLE ROAST TURKEY

THANKSGIVING JUST GOT A WHOLE LOT EASIER—AND FAR MORE DELICIOUS. LEARN HOW SOUTHERN CHEF SCOTT PEACOCK COAXES PURE AND SIMPLE FLAVORS FROM YOUR ALL-TIME FAVORITE FEAST.

SIMPLE ROAST TURKEY

Chef Scott Peacock says, "Citrus fruits, vegetables, and garlic add a subtle perfume to the turkey."

PREP: 30 minutes **ROAST:** 2¾ hours **REST:** 20 minutes

INGREDIENTS

1	10- to 12-lb. turkey, brined for 24 to 36 hours*
6	Tbsp. unsalted butter, room temperature
½	tsp. salt
½	tsp. freshly ground black pepper
1½	tsp. dried thyme, crushed
	Freshly squeezed juice of 1 lemon
	Freshly squeezed juice of 1 orange
1	large yellow onion, quartered
2	stalks celery with leaves, cut into large pieces
3	bay leaves
5	cloves garlic, unpeeled
2	cups chicken broth

PREPARATION

1. Preheat oven to 325°F. Rinse brined turkey* under cold water; pat dry, inside and out, with paper towels. In bowl mix softened butter, salt, pepper, and thyme. Stir in citrus juices (not all juice will be incorporated). Rub turkey with seasoned butter, inside and out. Fill cavity with onion, celery, bay leaves, and garlic. Skewer turkey neck skin to back. Tuck drumstick ends under band of skin across tail, if available. If there is no band of skin, tie drumsticks securely to tail. Twist wing tips under back. Place turkey, breast side up, on rack in roasting pan. Insert an oven-going meat thermometer into center of inside thigh muscle not touching bone. Pour chicken broth into the roasting pan.

2. Roast turkey 45 minutes undisturbed. Spoon pan juices over turkey. Roast 1 hour more, spooning juices over turkey every 20 minutes. Cut band of skin or string; spoon juices over turkey. Roast 1 to 1½ hours more or until thickest part of thigh reaches an internal temperature of 165°F and thigh juices run clear, spooning juices over every 20 minutes. Remove from oven; transfer turkey to serving platter. Tent loosely with foil, shiny side down. Let rest 20 to 30 minutes. Remove vegetables from inside cavity; discard.

3. While turkey rests, pour drippings from roasting pan into heatproof glass measuring cup or fat separator; skim fat. Reserve separated fat for Thanksgiving Gravy (page 244). Return drippings to pan; heat through, scraping up brown bits. Measure for use in Thanksgiving Gravy. Makes 8 servings (plus leftovers).

***To brine turkey:** For a 10- to 12-pound turkey, thoroughly dissolve 1½ cups kosher salt in 1½ gallons water. (Use this formula to make enough brine to fully submerge turkey, increasing salt/water combination in proportion to size of bird.) Refrigerate the brining turkey, breast side down; soak for 24 to 36 hours. Use a weighted dinner plate to keep turkey submerged. Or turn bird a few times during brining.

Note: Scott prefers a simply presented roast turkey. To add color to your serving platter, brush halved oranges and lemons, celery, and unpeeled garlic cloves with olive oil and roast alongside the bird in a separate pan during the last half hour of cooking. Place roasted fruits and vegetables on the serving platter.

EACH SERVING (ABOUT 3 OZ.): *257 cal., 12 g total fat (5 g sat. fat), 80 mg chol., 77 mg sodium, 13 g carbo., 4 g fiber, 25 g pro. Daily Values: 6% vit. A, 90% vit. C, 8% calcium, 11 iron.*

ROASTED SQUASH SOUP

Scott says, "The soup may be made two days in advance and gently reheated."

PREP: 10 minutes **BAKE:** 1 hour **COOK:** 40 minutes

INGREDIENTS

2½	lb. butternut or acorn squash, or sugar pumpkin
1½	tsp. salt
2	Tbsp. unsalted butter
1½	cups diced onion (3 medium)
½	tsp. dried thyme, crushed
1	small bay leaf
3½	cups chicken broth
1	Tbsp. honey
⅓	cup whipping cream
½	tsp. freshly grated nutmeg

PREPARATION

1. Preheat oven to 350°F. Split squash in half lengthwise. With a spoon, scrape out seeds and fibers from cavity of squash. Season cut sides of squash with 1 teaspoon of the salt; place, flesh sides down, in a lightly buttered baking dish or 15×10×1-inch baking pan lined with parchment paper.

2. Add ½ cup water to baking pan. Bake 1 to 1½ hours until skin is brown and flesh is tender when pierced with a knife. Remove from oven; let rest until cool enough to handle. Scoop out flesh and discard skin.

3. In a large saucepan or Dutch oven heat butter until foaming. Add onion and season with remaining ½ teaspoon salt. Sprinkle thyme over onion. Add bay leaf. Cook over medium heat, stirring often, until onion is tender and translucent (do not allow pieces to color), about 20 minutes.

4. Add squash. Season with additional salt and *ground black pepper*. Cook 5 minutes, stirring often.

5. Add broth; bring to simmering. Simmer, uncovered, 20 minutes, stirring occasionally. Season to taste. Remove bay leaf. Stir in honey. Cool slightly. Puree soup, half at a time, in a blender or food processor.

6. Rinse pot and dry. Return soup to pot; bring to simmering. Stir in ¼ cup of the cream and ¼ teaspoon of the grated nutmeg; heat through. Taste for seasoning and add salt, pepper, and honey as needed. Drizzle with remaining cream; sprinkle with remaining nutmeg. Makes 6 (1-cup) servings.

To reheat soup: Cook over medium heat, stirring occasionally until heated through.

EACH SERVING: *188 cal., 9 g total fat (6 g sat. fat), 28 mg chol., 716 mg sodium, 26 g carbo., 4 g fiber, 4 g pro. Daily Values: 344% vit. A, 61% vit. C, 10% calcium, 8% iron.*

Roasted Squash Soup

"Slow roasting the fresh squash brings out the rich flavor with ease," says Scott. This velvety soup can be made up to two days ahead, then reheated to serve.

"The Thanksgiving feast

embodies who we are now and from where we have come. When I was growing up, carefully considered dishes were as much an expression of emotion as culinary feats. Particular dishes were lovingly made for particular family members, everyone having his favorite. When I cook today I try to honor this by coaxing out the simple flavors of good, honest food—all the while looking for that link to those long-ago meals. While striving for simplicity, I hope to uncover the memories folded into these traditional dishes." —*Scott Peacock*

A Perfect Plate
Clockwise from top of plate: Slathered Eggs (page 243), Chestnut Dressing (page 244), Simple Roast Turkey (page 240), Cranberry Relish (page 243), Honestly Good Mashed Potatoes (page 243), Thanksgiving Gravy (page 244), Parsleyed Green Beans (page 247), and Lemon-Glazed Sweet Potatoes (page 245).

SLATHERED EGGS

Scott says, "This cooking method yields tender, medium-cooked eggs with yolks that are slightly creamy in the center."

PREP: 25 minutes **STAND:** 43 minutes

INGREDIENTS

8   to 10 large eggs
1   Tbsp. finely sliced chives, or 2 tsp. chives and
     1 tsp. fresh tarragon, finely chopped
1/2 cup mayonnaise

PREPARATION

1. Let eggs stand at room temperature for 30 minutes. In a large saucepan place eggs in single layer. Cover with 1 1/2 inches water. Add 2 tablespoons *salt* to water. Bring to boiling over high heat. Remove from heat; cover with a tight-fitting lid. Let sit 8 to 9 minutes; drain. Roll eggs in saucepan to crack shells. Place eggs in ice water. Let eggs sit in water 5 minutes; peel.

2. Stir chives into mayonnaise; set aside.

3. Split each egg lengthwise; place on serving dish (trim off a small amount from uncut side of each egg half to keep eggs from rolling). Season with *salt* and *freshly ground black pepper*. Slather each egg generously with mayonnaise mixture. Sprinkle with additional herbs. Makes 8 to 10 servings.

EACH SERVING (1 EGG): *177 cal., 16 g total fat (4 g sat. fat), 217 mg chol., 137 mg sodium, 1 g carbo., 0 g fiber, 6 g pro. Daily Values: 6% vit. A, 3% calcium, 3% iron.*

CRANBERRY RELISH

Scott says, "I like cranberry sauce that's chunky and textured. For a smoother sauce, cook all ingredients together for a longer time."

PREP: 10 minutes **COOK:** 10 minutes

INGREDIENTS

24   oz. fresh cranberries (6 cups)
1   cup full-bodied red wine or cranberry juice
1 1/2 cups granulated sugar
1/4 tsp. salt
1   cinnamon stick
1   Tbsp. finely grated orange zest

PREPARATION

1. Wash cranberries; drain. Remove any spoiled berries. In a wide nonreactive skillet combine wine, sugar, salt, and cinnamon stick. Bring to simmering, stirring to dissolve sugar; cook 1 minute. Add cranberries; cook, stirring constantly, until they begin to pop, 3 to 5 minutes. Add orange zest; cook a few seconds longer. Remove from heat. Cool. Remove cinnamon stick. For a thicker relish, smash berries slightly with the back of a spoon. Makes 4 1/2 to 5 cups.
Note: Relish can be made 1 week in advance. Cover the cooled relish and store in the refrigerator.

EACH SERVING (1/4 CUP): *94 cal., 0 g total fat (0 g sat. fat), 0 mg chol., 33 mg sodium, 22 g carbo., 2 g fiber. Daily Values: 9% vit. C, 1% iron.*

HONESTLY GOOD MASHED POTATOES

Scott says, "If you make the mashed potatoes ahead of time, hold them in a slow cooker set on low. Follow instructions for thinning potatoes so they are creamy when served."

PREP: 25 minutes **COOK:** 15 minutes

INGREDIENTS

5   medium all-purpose potatoes (about 2 1/2 pounds), peeled
     and sliced 1/2 inch thick
1   tsp. salt
3/4 cup milk
1/2 cup whipping cream
6   Tbsp. unsalted butter, cut up
     Unsalted butter

PREPARATION

1. In a saucepan add potatoes with enough water to cover. Add the salt. Bring to boiling; reduce heat. Simmer, covered, 15 to 20 minutes or until tender. Drain well. Let stand in colander 5 minutes to dry and cool slightly. Meanwhile, in a small saucepan combine milk and cream. Heat just until hot.

2. In a mixing bowl beat potatoes with the whip attachment of an electric stand mixer just until potatoes break. Add 3 tablespoons of the butter; mix on low speed just until incorporated. Add remaining 3 tablespoons butter; beat again.

3. Slowly beat in milk mixture, adding only as much as potatoes can absorb. On medium speed, beat until potatoes are light and fluffy. Do not overmix. Season to taste with salt and moisten with more milk mixture, if needed.

4. Cover potatoes; set aside until ready to serve. To reheat, transfer potatoes to a medium nonstick saucepan and heat over medium-low heat until reheated, gently stirring occasionally. If necessary, thin mashed potatoes with additional hot milk mixture before serving. Top with additional butter before serving. Makes 6 to 8 servings.

EACH SERVING (3/4 CUP): *295 cal., 20 g total fat (12 g sat. fat), 60 mg chol., 417 mg sodium, 27 g carbo., 2 g fiber, 4 g pro. Daily Values: 14% vit. A, 34% vit. C, 7% calcium, 6% iron.*

THANKSGIVING GRAVY

Scott says: "Make the turkey broth early in the day and refrigerate until ready to use."

PREP: 30 minutes **COOK:** 13 minutes

INGREDIENTS

Pan juices from turkey roasting pan (see Simple Roast Turkey recipe, page 240)
About 6 cups Turkey Broth or chicken broth
¼ cup fat from pan juices or ¼ cup unsalted butter
⅔ cup all-purpose flour
Reserved pan juices from Simple Roast Turkey (optional)

PREPARATION

1. Measure pan juices; add enough broth to make 6 cups. Set aside.
2. In a large saucepan heat fat from pan juices or butter until melted. Whisk in flour. Cook over moderately high heat, stirring or whisking constantly, until a deep and even brown, about 8 minutes (mixture may seem crumbly at first but will soften and break down as it cooks).
3. Remove from heat. Whisk in broth and reserved pan juices. Return to heat; bring to simmering, stirring until the gravy thickens. Taste for seasoning, adding *salt* and *ground black pepper* as needed. Simmer gently, uncovered, 5 minutes more. Makes 5½ to 6 cups.
Turkey Broth: Cut turkey neck into 2-inch pieces. In a large pot heat 1 tablespoon butter until hot and foaming. Add neck and giblets. Cook, stirring often, until deeply brown all over. Add 1 small onion, diced; 1 stalk celery, diced; ½ teaspoon salt; ¼ teaspoon dried thyme, crushed; and 1 bay leaf. Cook 5 minutes until vegetables begin to brown. Add 4 cups chicken broth, 3 cups water, and 1 cup dry white wine. Bring to a gentle boil. Skim fat from broth; reduce heat to simmering. Cook, partially covered, 1½ to 2 hours. Strain broth. Makes about 6 cups.

EACH SERVING (¼ CUP): *57 cal., 3 g total fat (2 g sat. fat), 18 mg chol., 162 mg sodium, 4 g carbo., 0 g fiber, 2 g pro. Daily Values: 29% vit. A, 1% vit. C, 0% calcium, 3% iron.*

CHESTNUT DRESSING

Scott says, "Order fresh or dried chestnuts from Allen Creek Farm at chestnutsonline.com."

PREP: 35 minutes **BAKE:** 50 minutes

INGREDIENTS

12 oz. good white bread, crusts trimmed and cut into ½-inch cubes (about 8 cups)
12 Tbsp. (1½ sticks) unsalted butter
1¼ cups chopped celery, including some of the tender inner leaves
1¼ cups diced onion (3 medium)
1 tsp. salt
½ tsp. ground black pepper
1 Tbsp. dried leaf sage, crushed
1 tsp. dried thyme, crushed
3 cups peeled, roasted chestnuts,* coarsely chopped, or 12 oz. dried chestnuts, rehydrated** and coarsely chopped
2 eggs, lightly beaten
¾ to 1¼ cups chicken broth

PREPARATION

1. Preheat oven to 325°F. Place bread in a large mixing bowl; set aside.
2. In a saucepan over medium heat melt 4 tablespoons of the butter. Add celery, onion, salt, and pepper. Cook 2 to 3 minutes, stirring often. Add sage and thyme. Cook 5 to 7 minutes or until vegetables are tender but not colored.
3. Add vegetables to bread cubes; gently toss. Melt remaining butter; pour over mixture. Fold in chestnuts. Taste for seasoning. Fold in beaten eggs. Add chicken broth to moisten dressing well without making soupy.
4. Turn dressing into buttered 2-quart baking dish. Cover with foil; bake 30 minutes. Uncover; bake 20 to 25 minutes or until dressing is golden and heated through. (If needed, baste dressing with additional broth during final minutes of baking.) Makes 8 to 10 servings (plus leftovers).
*To roast chestnuts: Using 1¼ pounds chestnuts in shells, cut an X in the flat side of each chestnut with a sharp knife. (This allows shell to peel easily and prevents the nut from exploding during cooking.) Arrange nuts in a single layer on an ungreased baking sheet. Bake in a 425°F oven for 15 minutes, tossing once or twice. Cool slightly; peel while warm.
**To rehydrate dried chestnuts: Rinse dried chestnuts. In a large saucepan bring 6 cups water to boiling. Add chestnuts. Return to boiling; boil gently, uncovered, 10 minutes. Remove from heat. Let stand 1 hour. Drain. Discard any chestnuts with hard centers.

EACH SERVING (¾ CUP): *293 cal., 14 g total fat (8 g sat. fat), 66 mg chol., 437 mg sodium, 38 g carbo., 3 g fiber, 7 g pro. Daily Values: 9% vit. A, 18% vit. C, 4% calcium, 9% iron.*

LEMON-GLAZED SWEET POTATOES

PREP: 15 minutes **COOK:** 18 minutes **BAKE:** 40 minutes

INGREDIENTS

6	medium sweet potatoes (4 lb.)
¾	cup water
⅓	cup granulated sugar
⅓	cup packed light brown sugar
½	tsp. salt
3	Tbsp. lemon juice
½	tsp. freshly grated nutmeg
3	Tbsp. unsalted butter
1	Tbsp. finely shredded lemon peel

PREPARATION

1. Preheat oven to 350°F. In a large pot place potatoes with enough water to cover. Bring to boiling. Reduce heat and simmer for 10 to 12 minutes or just until potatoes are tender but not soft. (Potatoes should be tender on outside but resistant in center when pierced with the tip of a paring knife.) Drain potatoes; cool.

2. Meanwhile, in nonreactive saucepan combine the ¾ cup water, the sugars, and salt. Bring to boiling, stirring just until sugars are dissolved. Simmer 8 minutes; remove from heat. Stir in lemon juice, nutmeg, and 2 tablespoons of the butter.

3. Butter a large shallow glass or ceramic baking dish with the remaining butter. Peel potatoes; cut crosswise into ¾-inch-thick slices. Arrange slices in a single layer in the baking dish; pour lemon mixture over slices. Bake for 40 to 50 minutes, basting occasionally, until potatoes are well glazed and begin to caramelize on edges. Remove from oven; cool slightly before serving. Serve hot or warm garnished with shredded lemon peel. Makes 6 to 8 servings.

EACH SERVING (¾ CUP): *330 cal., 6 g total fat (4 g sat. fat), 15 mg chol., 320 mg sodium, 68 g carbo., 7 g fiber, 4 g pro. Daily Values: 621% vit. A, 1% vit. C, 8% calcium, 9% iron.*

LEMON-GLAZED SWEET POTATOES

ICEBOX BISCUITS

ICEBOX BISCUITS

Scott says, "For light, fluffy biscuits try homemade baking powder. Sift ¼ cup cream of tartar with 2 tablespoons baking soda 3 times. Store 6 to 8 weeks in a tightly sealed jar at room temperature away from sunlight."

PREP: 40 minutes **RISE:** 30 minutes **BAKE:** 10 minutes per batch

INGREDIENTS

1	package active dry yeast
¼	cup warm water (105°F to 115°F)
5	cups all-purpose flour
¼	cup sugar
1	Tbsp. baking powder
1	tsp. baking soda
1	Tbsp. kosher salt
¾	cup lard, chilled, or ½ cup shortening plus ¼ cup butter, chilled
2	cups buttermilk, chilled
3	Tbsp. melted butter

PREPARATION

1. Dissolve yeast in the warm water; let stand 5 minutes.

2. In a bowl combine flour, sugar, baking powder, baking soda, and salt. Whisk to mix well. Using your fingers, quickly work chilled lard into dry ingredients until flour mixture resembles large peas. Stir in dissolved yeast and buttermilk; mix just until well blended.

3. Turn dough onto a floured surface; knead 6 or 7 times. Roll out to ½-inch thickness. Pierce rolled dough completely through at ½-inch intervals with a floured dinner fork. Cut out biscuits with a 2½- to 3-inch cutter, taking care not to twist cutter, which will seal the sides of biscuit and inhibit rising.

4. Place biscuits on greased baking sheet about ½ inch apart. Cover with tea towel. Let rise 30 to 45 minutes until almost doubled.

5. Preheat oven to 450°F. Bake for 10 to 12 minutes, rotating pan halfway through baking, until biscuits are golden brown. Remove from oven. Brush generously with melted butter. Serve hot. Makes about 30 biscuits.

EACH BISCUIT: *232 cal., 11 g total fat (5 g sat. fat), 14 mg chol., 474 mg sodium, 28 g carbo., 1 g fiber, 2 g pro. Daily Values: 1% vit. A, 5% calcium, 9% iron.*

Parsleyed Green Beans

"Two teaspoons of garlic, a pinch of salt, and a few grinds of pepper are all you need to finish these green beans," says Scott. You'll save prep time by cooking the beans one day ahead.

PARSLEYED GREEN BEANS

Scott says, "Chopping the garlic with a good pinch of salt helps soak up the garlic flavor and tranfer it to the beans."

PREP: 25 minutes **COOK:** 10 minutes

INGREDIENTS

1½   lb. green beans, washed and trimmed
1   Tbsp. salt
3   Tbsp. unsalted butter
2   tsp. fresh garlic, finely chopped with pinch of salt
2   Tbsp. chopped parsley
     Fresh Italian (flat-leaf) parsley (optional)

PREPARATION

1. Fill a large pot with water; bring to a rolling boil. Add beans and the 1 tablespoon salt. Cook, uncovered, for 5 to 8 minutes or until tender but still vibrant green and slightly resistant to the bite. Drain beans; immediately submerge in a bowl of lightly salted ice water to stop cooking and set color. When thoroughly chilled, drain well. (Beans can be prepared to this point 1 day ahead and refrigerated.)
2. In a wide skillet heat butter over medium-high heat until hot and foaming. Add beans. Cook, tossing often, until heated through. Sprinkle with garlic, chopped parsley, a generous amount of *salt,* and a few grinds of *black pepper.* Cook 1 minute longer, tossing frequently to distribute flavorings and avoid burning the garlic. If desired, sprinkle with additional parsley. Serve immediately. Makes 6 to 8 servings.

EACH SERVING (ABOUT ¾ CUP): *90 cal., 6 g total fat (4 g sat. fat), 15 mg chol., 80 mg sodium, 9 g carbo., 4 g fiber, 2 g pro. Daily Values: 20% vit. A, 27% vit. C, 5% calcium, 7% iron.*

LOW FAT

SCOTT'S HOLIDAY SALAD

Scott says, "The flavor of this salad will remind you of a bread-and-butter pickle."

PREP: 40 minutes **CHILL:** 4 hours

INGREDIENTS

½   cup cold water
2   envelopes unflavored gelatin
½   cup champagne vinegar or white vinegar
1   cup sugar
1   tsp. kosher salt
3   cups peeled and seeded cucumbers, cut into ¼-inch pieces
½   cup thinly sliced green onions, white and green parts
½   cup celery, cut into ¼-inch pieces
     Vegetable oil or cooking spray

PREPARATION

1. Pour the ½ cup cold water into a bowl. Sprinkle gelatin over water to soften; let stand about 10 minutes.
2. In nonreactive saucepan combine 1 cup *water,* the vinegar, sugar, and salt. Cook and stir over medium heat until hot and sugar is dissolved. Remove from heat; add softened gelatin mixture, stirring until dissolved. Transfer to a large bowl.
3. Place bowl over a very large bowl of ice water. Stir the mixture occasionally until completely cold and just beginning to thicken, about 10 minutes.
4. Stir cucumber, onion, and celery into cold mixture. Pour into a 6- to 8-cup nonreactive mold or dish that has been lightly oiled. Wrap mold with plastic wrap; refrigerate 4 hours or overnight.
5. To unmold, dip mold briefly (10 seconds or less) into hot water. Invert mold onto a serving dish. Makes 8 servings.

EACH SERVING (½ CUP): *117 cal., 0 g total fat (0 g sat. fat), 0 mg chol., 254 mg sodium, 27 g carbo., 2 g pro. Daily Values: 3% vit. A, 4% vit. C, 2% calcium, 2% iron.*

SCOTT'S HOLIDAY SALAD

Buttermilk Pudding

Not too filling, not too sweet—this old-fashioned dessert topped with Caramel Oranges has a smooth, silky texture and a zippy, refreshing tang from buttermilk. "It's a superb way to end a big meal," says Scott. Brown Sugar-Pecan Shortbreads are buttery, mildly sweet plate mates.

BUTTERMILK PUDDING

PREP: 1 hour **CHILL:** 2 hours

INGREDIENTS

2	envelopes unflavored gelatin
¼	cup milk or cold water
2	cups whipping cream
1	cup sugar
½	cup crème fraîche or dairy sour cream
2	cups buttermilk
¼	cup freshly squeezed lemon juice
¾	tsp. vanilla
¼	tsp. salt
5	tsp. finely shredded lemon peel (2 lemons)
1	recipe Caramel Oranges (right)

PREPARATION

1. In a bowl combine gelatin and milk to moisten. Set aside. In a small saucepan combine whipping cream and sugar. Cook and stir over medium heat until sugar is completely dissolved and cream just comes to a simmer. Remove immediately from heat; stir in softened gelatin until completely dissolved. Set aside; let cool 5 minutes.

2. Transfer cream mixture to a bowl. Add crème fraîche; whisk until blended. Whisk in buttermilk, lemon juice, vanilla, and salt. Strain mixture. Stir in lemon peel. Spoon pudding into 8 serving dishes. Cover with plastic wrap; refrigerate until set, 2 hours or overnight. Top with Caramel Oranges. Makes 8 servings.

EACH SERVING (WITHOUT CARAMEL ORANGES): *370 cal., 28 g total fat (18 g sat. fat), 105 mg chol., 267 mg sodium, 25 g carbo., 0 g fiber, 5 g pro. Daily Values: 26% vit. A, 10% vit. C, 12% calcium, 1% iron.*

BROWN SUGAR-PECAN SHORTBREADS

Scott says, "Store shortbread in an airtight container at room temperature up to 1 week."

PREP: 25 minutes **BAKE:** 15 minutes **COOL:** 5 minutes

INGREDIENTS

2	cups unbleached all-purpose flour
¼	cup packed light brown sugar
½	tsp. salt
1	cup unsalted butter, chilled
1	cup chopped pecans
	Powdered sugar (optional)

PREPARATION

1. Preheat oven to 350°F. Lightly butter twenty-four 1¾-inch mini muffin cups; set aside.

2. In a mixing bowl stir together flour, sugar, and salt. Cut butter into 1-inch pieces; add to flour. Beat with an electric mixer on low speed 5 to 7 minutes or until thoroughly blended, scraping sides of bowl occasionally (mixture will resemble fine crumbs and begin to cling together). Add pecans. Press mixture together to form dough.

3. Divide dough into 24 portions; press into muffin pans. Bake for 15 to 20 minutes or until light brown. Cool 5 minutes in pans. Carefully turn out of pans. Cool completely on wire racks. Dust with powdered sugar before serving. Makes 24 shortbreads.

EACH SHORTBREAD: *146 cal., 11 g total fat (5 g sat. fat), 20 mg chol., 51 mg sodium, 11 g carbo., 1 g fiber, 2 g pro. Daily Values: 5% vit A, 1% calcium, 4% iron.*

LOW FAT

CARAMEL ORANGES

PREP: 25 minutes **CHILL:** 2 hours

INGREDIENTS

4	large navel oranges
½	cup granulated sugar
¼	cup water

PREPARATION

1. Carefully peel oranges. Holding oranges over a bowl to catch juices, cut between orange membrane with a sharp knife and extract individual sections. Place orange sections in a wide nonreactive dish; pour juice over orange sections. Discard membranes.

2. In a small saucepan combine sugar and water. Stir gently over low heat just until sugar dissolves, being careful not to splash sugar up sides of saucepan. Increase heat to bring to boiling. Reduce heat to medium and boil gently for 13 to 14 minutes or until mixture is a light amber-hue caramel color, shaking pan occasionally to heat evenly (do not stir). Cool 1 minute. Pour caramel over orange sections; cool 5 minutes (caramel will harden). Cover and chill for 2 to 3 hours or up to 24 hours (most of the caramel will dissolve in orange juice).

3. Serve orange sections and caramel-flavored sauce with Buttermilk Pudding. Makes 8 servings.

EACH SERVING: *90 cal., 0 g total fat (0 g sat. fat), 0 mg chol., 0 mg sodium, 23 g carbo., 2 g fiber, 0 g pro. Daily Values: 4% vit. A, 77% vit. C, 4% calcium.*

Meet the Thanksgiving Chef

Scott Peacock is executive chef at Watershed restaurant in Decatur, Georgia. In 2007 Scott was awarded Best Chef in the Southeast by the James Beard Foundation.

Harvest Dinners

Rib-sticking, no-fuss meals for busy weeknights.

BY **NANCY WALL HOPKINS**
PHOTOGRAPHS BY **ANDY LYONS**
FOOD STYLING BY **JILL LUST**
RECIPES BY **MARYELLYN KRANTZ**

READY IN
20
MINUTES

TURKEY TORTILLA SOUP

FAST! **LOW FAT**

TURKEY TORTILLA SOUP

START TO FINISH: 20 minutes

INGREDIENTS

3	6-inch corn tortillas, cut into strips
2	Tbsp. cooking oil
1	cup purchased red or green salsa
2	14-oz. cans reduced-sodium chicken broth
2	cups cubed cooked turkey (12 oz.)
1	large zucchini, coarsely chopped
	Lime wedges (optional)
	Sour cream and fresh cilantro (optional)

PREPARATION

1. In a large skillet cook tortilla strips in hot oil until crisp; remove with a slotted spoon and drain on paper towels.
2. In a large saucepan combine salsa and chicken broth; bring to boiling over medium-high heat. Stir in turkey and zucchini; heat through. Serve in bowls; top with tortilla strips. If desired, garnish with lime wedges, sour cream, and cilantro. Makes 4 servings.

EACH SERVING: *262 cal., 11 g fat (2 g sat. fat), 53 mg chol., 920 mg sodium, 16 g carbo., 3 g fiber, 26 g pro. Daily Values: 6% vit. A, 21% vit. C, 6% calcium, 11% iron.*

FAST!

PORK AND POTATOES WITH TOMATO RELISH

START TO FINISH: 20 minutes

INGREDIENTS

1	24-oz. pkg. refrigerated mashed potatoes
4	boneless pork loin chops, ¾ inch thick
2	Tbsp. olive oil or cooking oil
1	large red onion, quartered and sliced (2 cups)
2	tomatoes, cut into thin wedges
¼	cup red wine vinaigrette salad dressing

PREPARATION

1. Prepare potatoes according to microwave package directions.
2. Meanwhile, season chops with *salt* and *ground black pepper*. In a very large skillet heat oil over medium-high heat. Add pork chops; cook 3 minutes. Turn; add onion. Cook 10 minutes more or until chops are done (160°F), turning to brown evenly. Stir onion occasionally. Transfer chops to serving plates.
3. Add tomato and vinaigrette to onion; cook and stir 1 minute more. Serve on chops with mashed potatoes. Makes 4 servings.

EACH SERVING: *433 cal., 20 g fat (3 g sat. fat), 62 mg chol., 624 mg sodium, 32 g carbo., 3 g fiber, 31 g pro. Daily Values: 10% vit. A, 68% vit. C, 6% calcium, 11% iron.*

PORK AND POTATOES WITH TOMATO RELISH

FAST! **KID FRIENDLY**

CHICKEN WITH PARMESAN NOODLES

START TO FINISH: 20 minutes

INGREDIENTS

1	9-oz. pkg. refrigerated angel hair pasta
4	large carrots, thinly sliced
2	Tbsp. butter
1½	lb. skinless, boneless chicken breast halves
¼	cup purchased basil pesto
¼	cup finely shredded Parmesan cheese
	Olive oil (optional)
	Fresh basil (optional)

PREPARATION

1. Cook pasta according to package directions.
2. Meanwhile, in a very large skillet cook carrot in 1 tablespoon melted butter over medium heat for 3 minutes. Cut chicken into 1-inch cubes. Add chicken; cook and stir for 4 to 5 minutes or until no pink remains in chicken. Add pesto; toss to coat.
3. Drain pasta. Return to pan; toss with remaining butter. Serve with chicken mixture. Sprinkle with cheese and *ground black pepper*. If desired, drizzle with olive oil and top with basil. Makes 4 servings.

EACH SERVING: *567 cal., 19 g fat (8 g sat. fat), 164 mg chol., 452 mg sodium, 47 g carbo., 5 g fiber, 52 g pro. Daily Values: 388% vit. A, 11% vit. C, 19% calcium, 16% iron.*

CHICKEN WITH PARMESAN NOODLES

CATFISH PO'BOYS

SAUCY BEANS AND EGGPLANT

FAST!

START TO FINISH: 20 minutes

INGREDIENTS

1	small eggplant (about 10 to 12 oz.), cut into 8 slices
3	Tbsp. olive oil
¼	cup seasoned fine dry bread crumbs
1	cup instant brown rice
	Sliced green onion (optional)
1	15-oz. can navy or Great Northern beans, rinsed and drained
1	26-oz. jar roasted garlic pasta sauce
	Crumbled feta cheese (optional)

PREPARATION

1. Brush eggplant lightly with half of the oil; sprinkle with *salt* and *ground black pepper*. Coat with crumbs. In a very large skillet cook eggplant in remaining oil over medium-high heat 5 minutes per side. Turn often.

2. Cook rice according to package directions; if desired, stir in green onion. In another saucepan combine beans and pasta sauce; heat through. Serve eggplant slices with rice and beans. If desired, top with feta cheese and sprinkle with pepper. Makes 4 servings.

EACH SERVING: *511 cal., 14 g fat (2 g sat. fat), 0 mg chol., 1,099 mg sodium, 82 g carbo., 13 g fiber, 17 g pro. Daily Values: 15% vit. A, 20% vit. C, 16% calcium, 30% iron.*

FAST!

CATFISH PO'BOYS

START TO FINISH: 20 minutes

INGREDIENTS

1	to 1¼ lb. catfish fillets
	Salt and ground black pepper
½	cup fine dry bread crumbs
2	Tbsp. olive oil
4	hoagie buns, split and toasted
2	medium red and/or yellow sweet peppers, cored and sliced into rings
4	oz. Monterey Jack cheese with jalapeño peppers, shredded (1 cup)
1	cup purchased deli coleslaw
	Bottled hot pepper sauce (optional)
	Small hot peppers (optional)

PREPARATION

1. Cut catfish into 3-inch pieces. Season lightly with salt and pepper. Coat with bread crumbs. In a very large skillet cook catfish in hot oil for 6 to 8 minutes, turning once, until golden and fish flakes easily when tested with a fork.

2. Divide catfish among buns. Top with sweet pepper rings, cheese, and coleslaw. If desired, pass hot pepper sauce and serve with hot peppers. Makes 4 servings.

EACH SERVING: *675 cal., 30 g fat (10 g sat. fat), 86 mg chol., 1,004 mg sodium, 67 g carbo., 4 g fiber, 35 g pro. Daily Values: 49% vit. A, 144% vit. C, 33% calcium, 20% iron.*

SAUCY BEANS AND EGGPLANT

Easy Holiday Baking

Your foolproof guide to creating the best desserts of the season.

BY **RICHARD SWEARINGER**
PHOTOGRAPHS BY **ANDY LYONS**
FOOD STYLING BY **JILL LUST,**
SUSAN BROWN DRAUDT, AND
CHARLES WORTHINGTON
RECIPES BY **DAVID BONOM**

CRANBERRY BLONDIES

If using a wire whisk, allow butter to soften at room temperature for an hour.

PREP: 30 minutes **BAKE:** 25 minutes
COOL: 1 hour

INGREDIENTS

	Nonstick cooking spray
½	cup butter, softened
½	cup granulated sugar
½	cup packed brown sugar
¾	tsp. baking powder
¼	tsp. baking soda
¼	tsp. salt
2	eggs
1	tsp. vanilla
1	cup all-purpose flour
½	cup dried cranberries
½	cup coarsely chopped white chocolate
1	cup fresh cranberries
1	recipe Cinnamon Whipped Cream (optional)

PREPARATION

1. Preheat oven to 350°F. Line an 11×7×1½-inch or a 9×9×2-inch baking pan with foil; coat foil with cooking spray and set aside.

2. In a large mixing bowl beat butter with a wire whisk or electric mixer until softened. Whisk or beat in sugars, baking powder, soda, and salt. Whisk or beat in eggs and vanilla until combined. With whisk or with electric mixer on low speed, beat in flour.

3. Stir in dried cranberries and white chocolate. Spread batter in prepared pan. Sprinkle with fresh cranberries; press in lightly with a spatula. Bake for 25 to 30 minutes or until a wooden toothpick inserted near center comes out clean.

4. Cool in pan on a wire rack for 1 hour. Lift with foil to remove from pan. Cut into bars. If desired, serve with Cinnamon Whipped Cream. Makes 12 bars.

Cinnamon Whipped Cream: In a chilled medium mixing bowl combine ½ cup whipping cream and ¼ teaspoon ground cinnamon; beat with an electric mixer on medium speed until soft peaks form.

EACH BAR (WITHOUT WHIPPED CREAM):
*246 cal., 11 g fat (7 g sat. fat),
57 mg chol., 175 mg sodium, 35 g carbo.,
1 g fiber, 2 g pro. Daily Values: 6% vit. A,
2% vit. C, 5% calcium, 5% iron.*

SIMPLE SECRETS

ADDING CRANBERRIES Scatter them evenly over surface of batter and press lightly with spatula (stirring would cause cranberries to leave red streaks in the bars).

CHOCOLATY HARVEST FRUIT-TOPPED CAKE

PREP: 30 minutes **BAKE:** 30 minutes
COOL: 10 minutes **CHILL:** 1 hour

INGREDIENTS

1	8-oz. carton dairy sour cream
1	cup water
2/3	cup canola oil
2	cups sugar
2	eggs
1	tsp. vanilla
2	tsp. baking powder
1/2	tsp. baking soda
1/2	tsp. salt
2	cups all-purpose flour
3/4	cup unsweetened cocoa powder
3/4	tsp. freshly ground black pepper
1/2	tsp. ground cinnamon
1/2	tsp. ground allspice
1/2	tsp. ground nutmeg
1/8	tsp. ground cloves
8	oz. semisweet chocolate
1	cup whipping cream
1	recipe Fruit Topping (right)
2/3	cup caramel-flavor ice cream topping

PREPARATION

1. Preheat oven to 350°F. Grease and flour two 9×1½-inch round cake pans.

2. In a very large bowl combine sour cream, the water, oil, sugar, eggs, vanilla, baking powder, baking soda, and salt. Whisk until well combined. Add flour, cocoa powder, pepper, cinnamon, allspice, nutmeg, and cloves; whisk vigorously until smooth. Divide batter between prepared pans.

3. Bake 30 to 35 minutes until tops spring back when lightly touched in centers. Cool in pans on wire racks for 10 minutes. Remove from pans and cool completely.

4. Finely chop chocolate. In a saucepan over medium-high heat bring whipping cream to boiling. Remove from heat and stir in chocolate until smooth. Cool to room temperature; chill until spreadable, about 1 hour. Meanwhile, prepare Fruit Topping.

5. To assemble, place a cake layer on a serving plate. Spread with half of the chocolate-cream mixture. Top with the second layer. Spread with remaining chocolate mixture. Arrange fruit in a single layer on top of cake. Pour caramel topping over the fruit. Serve immediately. (Cake does not store well after fruit is added.) Makes 12 servings.

EACH SERVING: *651 cal., 31 g fat (12 g sat. fat), 71 mg chol., 223 mg sodium, 93 g carbo., 5 g fiber, 5 g pro. Daily Values: 9% vit. A, 3% vit. C, 7% calcium, 17% iron.*

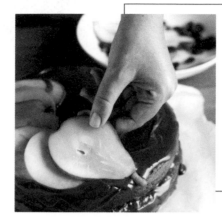

SIMPLE SECRETS

FRUIT TOPPING Thinly slice 1 unpeeled pear lengthwise and 1 unpeeled cooking apple horizontally. In a medium saucepan combine 2 cups apple juice and 1 cup sugar; bring to boiling over medium-high heat. Add sliced fruit and ⅓ cup dried cranberries; return to boiling. Reduce heat. Simmer, covered, for 2 minutes. Remove from heat; let stand 5 minutes. Strain and discard liquid. Cool to room temperature.

CHOCOLATY HARVEST FRUIT-TOPPED CAKE

Topped with poached apples, pears, and cranberries, this cake makes an enchanting centerpiece for any gathering.

SWEET POTATO SPICE LOAF

SWEET POTATO SPICE LOAF

For even browning and best shape, bake in a metal loaf pan.

PREP: 30 minutes
BAKE: 65 minutes
COOL: 2 hours

INGREDIENTS

3	eggs
$\frac{1}{2}$	cup buttermilk
	Nonstick cooking spray
2	cups all-purpose flour
1	tsp. baking powder
1	tsp. ground cinnamon
$\frac{1}{2}$	tsp. baking soda
$\frac{1}{4}$	tsp. salt
$\frac{1}{4}$	tsp. ground allspice
$\frac{1}{4}$	tsp. ground nutmeg
$\frac{3}{4}$	cup butter, cut up
1	cup sugar
1	tsp. vanilla
2	cups shredded fresh unpeeled sweet potato (about 10 oz.)
1	recipe Clementine Peel

PREPARATION

1. Let eggs and buttermilk stand at room temperature for 30 minutes. Preheat oven to 350°F. Lightly coat 9×5×3-inch baking pan with cooking spray; coat lightly with *flour*. Set aside. In a bowl combine flour, baking powder, cinnamon, baking soda, salt, allspice, and nutmeg; set aside.
2. In a large microwave-safe bowl microwave butter on 10% power (low) for $1\frac{1}{2}$ to $2\frac{1}{2}$ minutes or until very soft but not melted, checking and rearranging if necessary every 30 seconds.
3. Add sugar; whisk until well combined. Add eggs, buttermilk, and vanilla; whisk until well mixed (mixture may look curdled). Add flour mixture. Whisk until combined. Fold in sweet potato. Spoon into prepared pan and spread evenly.
4. Bake for 65 to 70 minutes or until top springs back when lightly touched and split in top appears dry. Cool on wire rack 10 minutes. Remove from pan. Cool completely, about 2 hours. Top loaf with Clementine Peel before slicing. Makes 12 servings.

Clementine Peel: With a vegetable peeler, remove strips of peel from 1 clementine or orange. In a small microwave-safe bowl combine peel strips with $\frac{1}{4}$ cup honey. Microwave on 100% power (high) for 30 to 40 seconds or until warm. Cover. Let stand while the cake cools.

EACH SERVING: 312 cal., 13 g total fat (8 g sat. fat), 84 mg chol., 254 mg sodium, 45 g carbo., 2 g fiber, 3 g pro. Daily Values: 72% vit. A, 11% vit. C, 7% calcium, 8% iron.

Citrus and seasonal produce like sweet potatoes add fresh flavor to winter baking.

SIMPLE SECRETS

1. NO-PEEL SWEET POTATOES As you grate sweet potatoes, the skin is cut up so finely that it blends itself into the batter and adds a touch of texture to the cake.

2. CITRUS SKILL To remove peel from clementines in long strips, hold the peeler stationary and slowly rotate the fruit away from you. Gently rock the peeler back and forth to cut into the zest.

GINGER PEAR MUFFINS

GINGER PEAR MUFFINS

PREP: 25 minutes **BAKE:** 15 minutes
COOL: 10 minutes

INGREDIENTS

1½   cups all-purpose flour
1   tsp. baking powder
1   tsp. ground ginger
1   tsp. ground cinnamon
½   tsp. baking soda
¼   tsp. salt
⅔   cup mild-flavor molasses
¼   cup butter, melted
¼   cup packed brown sugar
1   egg
½   cup boiling water
2   small pears, cut into 6 wedges each
       Raw sugar (optional)
3   ounces dark or bittersweet chocolate,
       broken into small pieces

PREPARATION

1. Preheat oven to 350°F. Coat twelve
2½-inch muffin cups with *nonstick
cooking spray* and *flour*.
2. In a large bowl combine flour, baking
powder, ginger, cinnamon, baking soda, and
salt. In a second bowl whisk together
molasses, butter, brown sugar, and egg. Pour
into flour mixture. Stir until combined.
Whisk in the boiling water. Divide evenly
among muffin cups. Add 1 pear wedge to
each muffin, pressing in lightly.
3. Bake for 15 to 18 minutes or until a
wooden toothpick inserted into centers
comes out clean. If desired, sprinkle with
raw sugar. Add chocolate pieces to top of
muffins. Cool in pan on rack for 10 minutes.
Use a table knife to smooth melted
chocolate. Remove from cups. Cool
completely on wire rack. Makes 12 muffins.

EACH MUFFIN: *221 cal., 7 g fat (4 g sat. fat),
29 mg chol., 163 mg sodium, 39 g carbo.,
2 g fiber, 1 g pro. Daily Values: 3% vit. A,
2% vit. C, 6% calcium, 11% iron.*

SIMPLE SECRETS

1. PLACING FRUIT Gently lay pear slices
on top of the batter and press lightly. This
ensures they'll stand up during baking.

2. ADD CHOCOLATE As soon as muffins
come out of the oven, place chocolate
pieces on their tops; it may take a few
moments for chocolate to soften to
spreadable consistency.

MAPLE-CINNAMON PUMPKIN PIE

PREP: 30 minutes BAKE: 55 minutes

INGREDIENTS

1	recipe Pastry for Single-Crust Pie
1	15-oz. can pumpkin
½	cup sugar
¼	cup pure maple syrup or maple-flavor syrup
1	tsp. ground cinnamon
½	tsp. salt
3	eggs, lightly beaten
1	cup milk
1	recipe Maple Whipped Cream and sunflower kernels (optional)

PREPARATION

1. Preheat oven to 375°F. Prepare and roll out Pastry for Single-Crust Pie.
2. For filling, in a bowl combine pumpkin, sugar, maple syrup, cinnamon, and salt. Add eggs; beat with a fork until combined. Gradually add milk; stir until combined.
3. Carefully pour filling into pastry shell. Cover edge of piecrust with foil. Bake for 30 minutes. Remove foil. Bake for 25 to 30 minutes more or until knife inserted near center comes out clean. Cool on wire rack. Cover and refrigerate within 2 hours.
4. If desired, serve with Maple Whipped Cream and sunflower kernels. Makes 8 servings..

Pastry for Single-Crust Pie: In a bowl stir together 1½ cups all-purpose flour and ¼ teaspoon salt. Using a pastry blender cut in ½ cup shortening until pieces are pea size. Sprinkle 1 tablespoon cold water over part of the flour mixture; gently toss with a fork. Push moistened dough to side of the bowl. Repeat, using 1 tablespoon water at a time (4 to 5 tablespoons total), until flour mixture is moistened. Form dough into a ball. On a floured surface flatten with hands. Roll dough from center to edges into 13-inch circle. To transfer pastry, wrap around a rolling pin. Unroll into a 9-inch pie plate (for Fresh Pear and Cranberry Pie use a deep-dish pan). Ease pastry into pie plate without stretching. Trim pastry to 1 inch beyond edge of pie plate. Fold under extra.

Maple Whipped Cream: In chilled medium bowl combine 1 cup whipping cream and 1 tablespoon pure maple syrup. With mixer on medium speed beat until soft peaks form.

EACH SERVING (WITHOUT MAPLE WHIPPED CREAM): *276 cal., 11 g total fat (3 g sat. fat), 82 mg chol., 361 mg sodium, 39 g carbo., 2 g fiber, 6 g pro. Daily Values: 168% vit. A, 4% vit. C, 7% calcium, 12% iron.*

MAPLE-CINNAMON PUMPKIN PIE

FRESH PEAR AND CRANBERRY PIE

PREP: 35 minutes BAKE: 70 minutes
COOL: 1½ hours

INGREDIENTS

1	recipe Pastry for Single-Crust Pie (left)
8	cups sliced red and/or green ripe pears (7 to 8 pears; 3 to 3½ lb. total)
1	cup fresh cranberries
¼	cup sugar
3	Tbsp. cornstarch
2	Tbsp. apple cider or water
¼	tsp. ground nutmeg
1	Tbsp. sugar
2	Tbsp. caramel-flavor ice cream topping, plus additional for drizzling

PREPARATION

1. Prepare and roll out Pastry for Single-Crust Pie. Crimp and form high edge to keep filling from bubbling over. Preheat oven to 375°F.
2. Arrange half of the pears in pastry shell; sprinkle with ½ cup of the cranberries. Arrange remaining pears on top of cranberries. In a bowl stir together ¼ cup sugar, cornstarch, cider, and nutmeg; drizzle evenly over pears. Cover with foil.
3. Bake for 40 minutes. Remove foil; sprinkle with 1 tablespoon sugar. Bake, uncovered, for 30 to 35 minutes more or until pears are tender and juices are bubbly. Remove from oven. Place on a wire rack.
4. Meanwhile, in a small saucepan combine remaining cranberries and 2 tablespoons caramel topping. Bring to boiling. Cook 1 minute. Remove from heat. Spoon over hot pie.
5. Serve warm. Drizzle with additional caramel topping. Makes 8 servings.

EACH SERVING: *357 cal., 13 g fat (3 g sat. fat), 0 mg chol., 93 mg sodium, 59 g carbo., 6 g fiber, 1 g pro. Daily Values: 15% vit. A, 14% vit. C, 2% calcium, 8% iron.*

FRESH PEAR AND CRANBERRY PIE

BUILD A BETTER

Green Bean Casserole

Update this family classic with fresh vegetables and creamy cheeses.

BY **STEPHEN EXEL** PHOTOGRAPH BY **ANDY LYONS** FOOD STYLING BY **JILL LUST**

TEST KITCHEN TIP
For a sweeter flavor, use a greater proportion of cream cheese to goat cheese. Go the other way for a tangier taste. For more earthy flavor, use portobello mushrooms in place of button.

GREEN BEANS
Start with fresh whole beans, trimmed, or frozen green beans. Cook in a small amount of boiling water (just enough to cover) for about 3 minutes.

MUSHROOMS AND RED SWEET PEPPER
In a casserole combine green beans with fresh button mushrooms and sliced red sweet pepper. Toss with olive oil and soy sauce or balsamic vinegar to coat. Roast in 375°F oven for 15 minutes.

ONIONS AND BREAD CRUMBS
Sweeten onion wedges by sauteing in olive oil and brown sugar just until tender. Toss cooked onions with dry bread crumbs to coat for classic onion ring crispiness.

CHEESE
For a note of tanginess, blend softened cream cheese with goat cheese. Toss with warm vegetables and place in baking dish. Top with onions. Bake in 400°F oven for 5 to 8 minutes just until heated through.

FRESH ITALIAN (FLAT-LEAF) PARSLEY
Scatter snipped fresh leaves across the top for a peppery flavor.

TO SERVE 10 TO 12 PERSONS, use 2 lb. green beans, 1 large onion, 1 small sweet pepper, 6 oz. mushrooms, and 6 oz. cheese.

BY **NANCY WALL HOPKINS**
PHOTOGRAPH BY **ANDY LYONS**
FOOD STYLING BY **JILL LUST**

Gravy

Try one stir-in on Thanksgiving and another with leftovers. Mashed potatoes never had it so good.

1. HERB GARDEN
Rosemary, thyme, sage

2. ITALIAN
Sausage, roasted red sweet pepper, parsley

3. STEAK HOUSE
Caramelized red onion, steak sauce, blue cheese

4. TROPICAL
Cashews, mangoes, chili-garlic sauce

5. MEDITERRANEAN
Lemon zest, capers, olive oil

6. MUSHROOM
Cremini, shiitake, and dried morel mushrooms; cream

7. BISTRO
Red pears, peppercorns, brandy

8. HARVEST
Dried fruit, sauteed cipollini onions

9. SOUTHWEST
Roasted pumpkin seeds, chopped chipotle peppers in adobo sauce, chile powder

10. SPICY
Sliced jalapeño peppers, chopped tomato

BHG BASICS

Turkey Gravy:
After you've roasted the turkey, scrape pan drippings and brown bits from the pan into a measuring cup. Skim and reserve fat.

Pour ¼ cup fat into a medium saucepan (discard remaining fat). Stir in ¼ cup flour. Add enough chicken broth to remaining drippings in the measuring cup to equal 2 cups. Add broth all at once to saucepan.

Cook and stir over medium heat until thickened and bubbly. Cook and stir for 1 minute more. Season to taste with salt and pepper.

DECEMBER

CELEBRATE THE SEASON WITH A TRADITIONAL ROAST BEEF DINNER MADE DRESSY AND MODERN. OR PREPARE 20-MINUTE DISHES FOR EVERYDAY MEALS DURING THE HOLIDAYS.

CREAMY MUSHROOM SOUP
page 265

All Aglow

Plus

Everyday Easy—

CHRISTMAS RIB ROAST WITH DRIED FRUITS
page 265

HONEY-SAUCED SHRIMP AND VEGGIES
page 270

CRIMSON SIPPER
page 267

KIELBASA AND ORZO
page 271

All aglow

GATHER EVERYONE FOR A FEAST THAT'S MERRY AND BRIGHT, COMFY AND WARM. WE'VE MADE THE HOLIDAY TABLE EVEN MORE ENCHANTING BY SPRINKLING A LITTLE GRACIOUS GLIMMER AND LOW-KEY GLAMOUR THROUGHOUT THE FEAST.

STEAMED MILK CHOCOLATE PUDDING
page 267

PRODUCED BY **COLLEEN DUFFLEY**
RECIPES BY **STEPHEN EXEL**
WRITING BY **WINIFRED MORANVILLE**

CHRISTMAS RIB ROAST WITH DRIED FRUITS

PREP: 40 minutes **ROAST:** 1¾ hours **STAND:** 15 minutes

INGREDIENTS

1	6-lb. beef rib roast
1	Tbsp. anise seeds, lightly crushed
3	Tbsp. olive oil
3	Tbsp. Dijon-style mustard
3	cloves garlic, minced
3	cups dried figs, apricots, and/or pears
12	red boiling onions, peeled and halved
2⅓	cups orange juice
3	fresh pears, cored and cut into wedges
1	Tbsp. all-purpose flour
	Fresh rosemary sprigs

PREPARATION

1. Preheat oven to 325°F. If desired, trim fat from roast. In a small bowl combine anise seeds, olive oil, 2 tablespoons of the mustard, garlic, ¾ teaspoon *salt*, and ¼ teaspoon *ground black pepper*. Spread 2 tablespoons of the mixture over roast; set remaining mustard mixture aside. Place roast on a rack in a shallow roasting pan. Roast, uncovered, for 1¾ to 2¼ hours for medium rare (135°F) or 2¼ to 2¾ hours for medium (150°F).

2. Meanwhile, in a large bowl combine dried fruit, halved onions, ⅓ cup of the orange juice, and reserved mustard mixture. Toss to coat. Fold a 36×18-inch piece of heavy-duty foil in half to make an 18-inch square. Place fruit mixture in center of foil. Bring up opposite edges of foil; seal with a double fold. Double-fold remaining edges to completely enclose mixture, leaving space for steam to build. Add foil packet to oven rack beside roast for the last 1 hour of roasting time. Place pear wedges in roasting pan beside roast the last 30 minutes of roasting; stir pears once.

3. Remove roast to a serving platter. Use a slotted spoon to remove pears from pan; add to platter with roast. Cover; let stand 15 minutes. Remove foil packet from oven; set aside. Drain all but 1 tablespoon fat from roasting pan. Whisk flour into reserved fat in roasting pan. Whisk together remaining 2 cups orange juice with remaining 1 tablespoon mustard. Add orange juice mixture to roasting pan. Place over two burners on stove. Heat over medium-high heat, scraping up any brown bits from bottom of pan. Whisk until thickened and bubbly; whisk for 1 to 2 minutes more or until desired consistency. Strain, if desired. Serve with roast, pears, and onion mixture. Garnish with fresh rosemary. Makes 12 servings.

EACH SERVING: *397 cal., 15 g total fat (5 g sat. fat), 75 mg chol., 312 mg sodium, 38 g carbo., 5 g fiber, 28 g pro. Daily Values: 2% vit. A, 46% vit. C, 9% calcium, 22% iron.*

CREAMY MUSHROOM SOUP

CREAMY MUSHROOM SOUP

Bring back the sit-down starter! Gathering around the table over this lusciously rich soup—updated with roasted red peppers—gives everyone the chance to relax and ease into the festivities together.

PREP: 20 minutes **COOK:** 15 minutes

INGREDIENTS

¼	cup butter
1	medium white onion, chopped (½ cup)
4	cloves garlic, minced
2	bay leaves
2	tsp. snipped fresh rosemary
1½	lb. fresh button mushrooms, coarsely chopped
2	14-oz. cans chicken broth or vegetable broth
	Salt and freshly ground black pepper
2	cups whipping cream
1	cup bottled roasted red sweet peppers, drained
2	Tbsp. olive oil
	Snipped fresh rosemary

PREPARATION

1. In a large saucepan melt butter. Add onion, garlic, bay leaves, and the 2 teaspoons rosemary; cook over medium heat about 5 minutes or until onion is tender. Add mushrooms. Cook and stir 5 minutes more. Add broth. Bring to boiling; reduce heat. Simmer, uncovered, for 5 to 10 minutes more or until mushrooms are tender. Remove and discard bay leaves. Cool soup mixture slightly.

2. Place one-third of the soup in a food processor or blender. Cover and process or blend until almost smooth. Repeat with remaining soup. Return all of the mixture to the saucepan. Season to taste with salt and pepper. Bring just to boiling. Whisk in cream; heat through.

3. In a small bowl mash roasted red peppers with a potato masher or finely chop. Stir in olive oil. To serve, ladle soup into bowls. Top with mashed red pepper and garnish with snipped rosemary. Makes 12 servings.

EACH SERVING: *217 cal., 21 g total fat (12 g sat. fat), 66 mg chol., 408 mg sodium, 5 g carbo., 1 g fiber, 0 g pro. Daily Values: 14% vit. A, 61% vit. C, 3% calcium, 3% iron.*

CHRISTMAS RIB ROAST WITH DRIED FRUITS

CHEDDAR AND ONION PUDDING

HONEY-GLAZED CARROTS

ORANGE-SAUCED BROCCOLI

CHEDDAR AND ONION PUDDING

PREP: 30 minutes **BAKE:** 20 minutes

INGREDIENTS

2	medium onions, each cut into 8 wedges with root end attached
1	Tbsp. olive oil
3	Tbsp. butter
1	clove garlic, minced
3	eggs
1½	cups milk
⅓	cup all-purpose flour
4	oz. white cheddar cheese, shredded
1	Tbsp. snipped fresh sage
	Fresh sage leaves (optional)

PREPARATION

1. Preheat oven to 400°F. In a large skillet place onions in hot oil; season with *salt* and *ground black pepper*. Cook 5 minutes over medium-low heat; stir occasionally. Add 2 tablespoons of the butter and the garlic; cook until tender, about 8 minutes, stirring occasionally. Remove from heat; set aside.
2. Grease ten to twelve 5- to 7-ounce ramekins or custard cups with remaining butter; arrange in a 15×10×1-inch or two 13×9×2-inch baking pan(s); set aside. In a large mixing bowl whisk eggs and milk together. Whisk in flour until smooth. Add cheese and snipped sage; stir to combine.
3. Spoon onion mixture into prepared dishes. Pour batter over (about ¼ cup per dish). Bake for 20 to 25 minutes or until puffed and golden brown. Remove puddings from oven. Let stand about 10 minutes. Serve warm. If desired, garnish with fresh sage leaves. Makes 10 to 12 servings.

EACH SERVING: *150 cal., 11 g total fat (6 g sat. fat), 87 mg chol., 190 mg sodium, 7 g carbo., 0 g fiber, 6 g pro. Daily Values: 8% vit. A, 3% vit. C, 14% calcium, 4% iron.*

FAST! LOW FAT

HONEY-GLAZED CARROTS

Glazed carrots—always a favorite—brighten up for the holidays with light touches of crushed red pepper and fresh lemon peel.

START TO FINISH: 30 minutes

INGREDIENTS

6	cups water
3	lb. baby carrots with tops trimmed to 2 inches, peeled or scrubbed
2	Tbsp. butter
3	to 4 Tbsp. honey
1	tsp. finely shredded lemon peel
½	tsp. crushed red pepper
½	tsp. salt
	Crushed red pepper (optional)

PREPARATION

1. In a very large skillet bring the water to boiling. Add carrots. Return to boiling; reduce heat. Simmer, covered, for 8 to 10 minutes or until carrots are just tender. Drain carrots. Pat dry with paper towels.
2. To glaze carrots, in the same skillet combine butter, honey, lemon peel, ½ teaspoon crushed red pepper, and salt. Stir constantly over medium heat until butter is melted and mixture bubbles. Carefully add carrots. Toss gently for 2 to 3 minutes or until carrots are thoroughly coated with glaze and heated through.
3. To serve, transfer carrots to a shallow bowl or platter. Drizzle with remaining glaze from the skillet. If desired, sprinkle with crushed red pepper. Makes 12 servings.

EACH SERVING: *75 cal., 2 g total fat (1 g sat. fat), 5 mg chol., 180 mg sodium, 14 g carbo., 3 g fiber, 1 g pro. Daily Values: 341% vit. A, 10% vit. C, 3% calcium, 2% iron.*

FAST!

ORANGE-SAUCED BROCCOLI

Every holiday table needs some sparkling green. Why not try broccoli rabe for something new? It's amazing how much "wow" this assertive veggie will add!

PREP: 15 minutes **COOK:** 8 minutes

INGREDIENTS

3	cups water
¾	tsp. salt
12	cups broccoli florets and/or broccoli rabe cut into 1½-inch pieces*
1	cup whipping cream
1	Tbsp. frozen orange juice concentrate, thawed
½	tsp. cracked black pepper
⅓	cup sliced almonds, toasted

PREPARATION

1. In a 4-quart Dutch oven bring water and salt to boiling. Add broccoli. Return to boiling; reduce heat. Cook, covered, for 8 to 10 minutes or until crisp-tender. Drain. Transfer to a serving bowl.
2. Add cream to Dutch oven. Bring to boiling. Boil gently, uncovered, for 3 minutes or until thickened, stirring occasionally. Stir in the orange juice concentrate and pepper. Spoon over broccoli; sprinkle with almonds. Makes 10 to 12 servings.
***TIP:** You will need approximately 2 pounds of broccoli or 1½ pounds broccoli rabe to equal 12 cups.

EACH SERVING: *141 cal., 11 g total fat (6 g sat. fat), 33 mg chol., 162 mg sodium, 9 g carbo., 3 g fiber, 4 g pro. Daily Values: 21% vit. A, 167% vit. C, 8% calcium, 5% iron.*

CRIMSON SIPPER

CRIMSON SIPPER

PREP: 10 minutes **COOK:** 10 minutes **CHILL:** 4 hours

INGREDIENTS

2 pints pomegranate juice (4 cups)
1½ cups sugar
12 fresh sage leaves, lightly crushed
2 2×½-inch strips lemon peel*
1 cup lemon juice
  Ice
1 750 ml bottle dry (brut) sparkling wine or club soda, chilled
  Fresh sage leaves

PREPARATION

1. In a large saucepan heat pomegranate juice, sugar, sage leaves, and lemon peel to boiling, stirring to dissolve sugar. Reduce heat. Simmer, uncovered, for 10 minutes. Remove from heat; stir in lemon juice. Transfer to a glass pitcher or container; cover and chill at least 4 hours or up to 1 week.

2. To serve, remove and discard sage leaves and lemon peel. Add ice to 6-ounce cocktail glasses. Fill half full with pomegranate mixture and add about ¼ cup sparkling wine or club soda. Stir well before drinking. Garnish with fresh sage leaves. Makes 12 (6-ounce) servings.

*TIP: Avoid picking up the white pith of the lemon when cutting off the peel; it will add a bitter flavor to the beverage.

EACH SERVING: *205 cal., 0 g total fat (0 g sat. fat), 0 mg chol., 7 mg sodium, 41 g carbo., 0 g fiber, 0 g pro. Daily Values: 2% vit. A, 34% vit. C, 1% calcium, 3% iron.*

STEAMED MILK CHOCOLATE PUDDING

PREP: 25 minutes **STEAM:** 1½ hours **COOL:** 40 minutes

INGREDIENTS

1¾ cups all-purpose flour
1½ tsp. baking powder
1 tsp. ground ginger
½ tsp. ground nutmeg
½ tsp. ground cinnamon
¼ cup butter, softened
1 cup sugar
2 eggs
2 egg whites
6 oz. milk chocolate, melted and cooled
1¼ cups milk
1 recipe Cranberry-Kumquat Compote
  Whipped cream and orange peel twist (optional)

PREPARATION

1. Grease and flour a 2½-quart heatproof glass mixing bowl or a 10-cup steamed pudding mold with cover; set aside.

2. In a small mixing bowl stir together flour, baking powder, ginger, nutmeg, and cinnamon; set aside.

3. In a large mixing bowl beat butter with an electric mixer on medium to high speed for 30 seconds. Add sugar; beat until combined. Add eggs and egg whites, 1 at a time, beating on low speed after each addition just until combined. Stir in melted chocolate.

4. Add flour mixture and milk alternately to butter mixture, beating on low speed after each addition just until combined. Pour batter into prepared bowl or mold. Cover with greased foil or put lid on mold; press foil tightly against edge of bowl.

5. Place bowl or mold on a rack in a deep kettle. Add water to a depth of about 1 inch up sides of bowl or mold. Cover the kettle and bring water to boiling; reduce heat to simmering. Steam for 1½ to 1¾ hours or until a long wooden pick or skewer inserted in center of pudding comes out clean. Check water level about every 30 minutes, adding boiling water to the kettle as necessary.

6. Remove the bowl or mold from kettle and remove foil or top. Cool the pudding for 10 minutes; unmold onto a serving platter. Let stand for 30 to 40 minutes on a wire rack to cool slightly. Serve warm with Cranberry-Kumquat Compote. If desired, serve with whipped cream and garnish with orange peel. Makes 12 servings.

CRANBERRY-KUMQUAT COMPOTE: In a medium saucepan combine 2 cups halved and seeded kumquats or cut-up clementines, 1 cup packed brown sugar, 1 cup cranberry juice, one 2- or 3-inch stick cinnamon, and 1 bay leaf. Bring to boiling; reduce heat. Simmer, uncovered, about 3 minutes or until kumquats are slightly softened. Stir in 2 cups fresh cranberries and ½ cup dried cherries. Bring to boiling; reduce heat. Simmer, uncovered, about 8 minutes until sauce begins to thicken. Remove and discard cinnamon and bay leaf. Serve warm or at room temperature. If desired, stir in ½ cup chopped toasted pecans before serving.

EACH SERVING: *394 cal., 10 g total fat (6 g sat. fat), 51 mg chol., 112 mg sodium, 72 g carbo., 3 g fiber, 4 g pro. Daily Values: 12% vit. A, 34% vit. C, 11% calcium, 10% iron.*

STEAMED MILK CHOCOLATE PUDDING

Weeknight Specials

On the table in a flash—with enticing seasonal flavors and color.

BY **NANCY WALL HOPKINS**
WRITTEN BY **PEG SMITH**
FOOD STYLING BY **JILL LUST**
RECIPES BY **MARYELLYN KRANTZ**

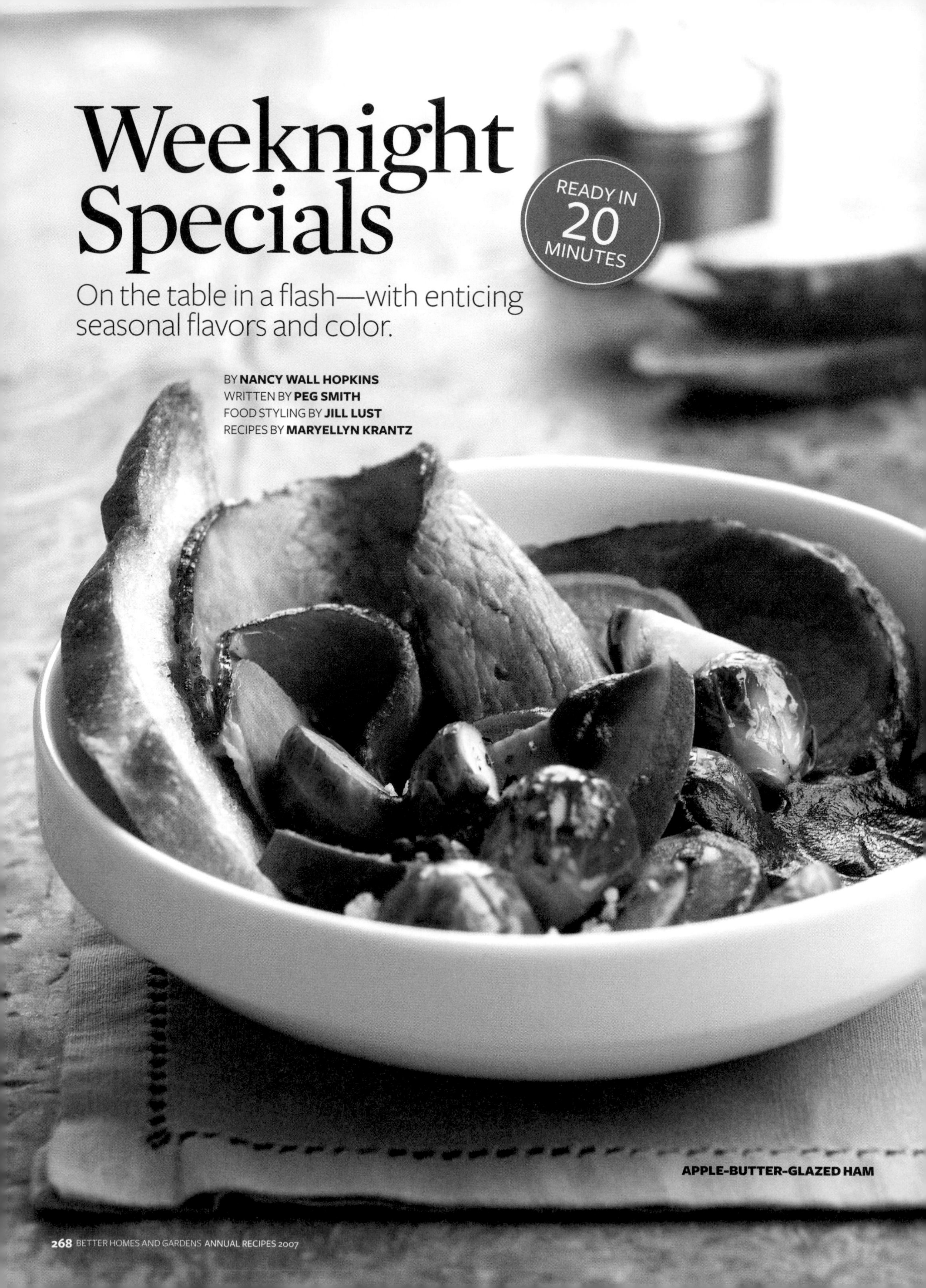

APPLE-BUTTER-GLAZED HAM

APPLE-BUTTER-GLAZED HAM

START TO FINISH: 20 minutes

INGREDIENTS

2	medium sweet potatoes, peeled and cut into 1-inch cubes
12	oz. fresh Brussels sprouts, trimmed and halved
1	to 1¼ lb. sliced cooked ham, about ¼ inch thick
2	Tbsp. butter, melted
½	cup apple butter
2	Tbsp. cider vinegar
	Salt and ground black pepper
	Baguette slices (optional)

PREPARATION

1. In a large saucepan cook potato cubes and Brussels sprouts in lightly boiling salted water for 8 to 10 minutes or just until tender. Drain the vegetables.

2. Meanwhile, in a very large skillet cook ham in melted butter over medium-high heat for 4 to 5 minutes, turning occasionally. Remove from skillet and place on serving plates with vegetables; keep warm. Stir apple butter and vinegar into the skillet; heat through. Serve with ham and vegetables. Season to taste with salt and pepper. If desired, serve with baguette slices. Makes 4 servings.

EACH SERVING: *513 cal., 16 g total fat (7 g sat. fat), 80 mg chol., 1,664 mg sodium, 71 g carbo., 8 g fiber, 23 g pro. Daily Values: 181% vit. A, 104% vit. C, 10% calcium, 17% iron.*

CHICKEN WITH CHERRY-GINGER CHUTNEY

START TO FINISH: 20 minutes

INGREDIENTS

4	medium skinless, boneless chicken breast halves, each cut into 4 pieces
½	tsp. ground ginger
1	Tbsp. olive oil or cooking oil
½	cup dried tart red cherries
1	large apple, thinly sliced horizontally and seeds removed
⅓	cup coarsely chopped walnuts
¼	cup water
3	Tbsp. vinegar
4	tsp. packed brown sugar

PREPARATION

1. Sprinkle chicken lightly with *salt, ground black pepper*, and ¼ teaspoon of the ground ginger.

2. In a large skillet cook chicken in hot oil over medium heat for 12 minutes or until chicken is no longer pink (170°F). Transfer chicken to a serving platter; cover and keep warm. Add cherries, apple, and walnuts to skillet; cook, stirring frequently, for 2 minutes. In a small bowl stir together the water, vinegar, brown sugar, and remaining ginger. Add to skillet. Cook and stir for 1 minute. Serve with chicken. Makes 4 servings.

EACH SERVING: *364 cal., 12 g total fat (2 g sat. fat), 82 mg chol., 249 mg sodium, 30 g carbo., 3 g fiber, 35 g pro. Daily Values: 6% vit. A, 7% vit. C, 5% calcium, 10% iron.*

CHICKEN WITH CHERRY-GINGER CHUTNEY

FAST! LOW FAT

HONEY-SAUCED SHRIMP AND VEGGIES

START TO FINISH: 20 minutes

INGREDIENTS

1	12-oz. pkg. peeled fresh baby carrots
8	oz. broccoli, trimmed and cut up (3 cups)
1	lb. peeled and deveined medium shrimp
1	cup cherry tomatoes
1	Tbsp. cooking oil
⅓	cup honey
2	Tbsp. bottled chili garlic sauce
2	Tbsp. orange juice

PREPARATION

1. In a large saucepan cook carrots, covered, in boiling lightly salted water for 5 minutes. Add broccoli; cook for 3 to 4 minutes more or until vegetables are just tender. Drain.

2. Meanwhile, in a large skillet cook and stir shrimp and tomatoes in hot oil for 3 to 4 minutes or until shrimp are opaque. Transfer to a serving platter along with carrot mixture. In the same skillet combine honey, chili garlic sauce, and orange juice; heat through. Spoon over shrimp and vegetable mixtures. Makes 4 servings.

EACH SERVING: *319 cal., 6 g total fat (1 g sat. fat), 172 mg chol., 361 mg sodium, 43 g carbo., 5 g fiber, 26 g pro. Daily Values: 254% vit. A, 127% vit. C, 13% calcium, 23% iron.*

HONEY-SAUCED SHRIMP AND VEGGIES

BEEF AND RED ONION SANDWICHES

KIELBASA AND ORZO

START TO FINISH: 16 minutes

INGREDIENTS

1	lb. cooked kielbasa, halved lengthwise and cut into 2-inch lengths
1	Tbsp. cooking oil
1	cup dried orzo (rosamarina)
1	14-oz. can beef broth
½	cup water
1	tsp. dried Italian seasoning, crushed
2	medium zucchini, halved lengthwise and coarsely chopped (2½ cups)
⅓	cup 1-inch pieces green onion and/or finely chopped red sweet pepper (optional)
	Salt and ground black pepper

PREPARATION

1. In a large skillet brown kielbasa in hot oil for 2 minutes over medium-high heat; stir in orzo. Cook and stir 1 minute.

2. Stir in beef broth, the water, and Italian seasoning. Bring to boiling; reduce heat. Simmer, covered, about 8 minutes or until orzo is tender, adding the zucchini the last 4 minutes of cooking and stirring occasionally.

3. Uncover; stir in green onion and/or sweet pepper. Season to taste with salt and pepper. Makes 4 servings.

EACH SERVING: *417 cal., 24 g total fat (8 g sat. fat), 79 mg chol., 1,815 mg sodium, 30 g carbo., 2 g fiber, 21 g pro. Daily Values: 6% vit. A, 59% vit. C, 3% calcium, 17% iron.*

BEEF AND RED ONION SANDWICHES

START TO FINISH: 20 minutes

INGREDIENTS

8	sliced dried tomatoes or dried tomato halves (not oil packed)
2	Tbsp. olive oil
12	oz. beef sirloin steak, about ¾ inch thick
1	small red onion, thinly sliced
	Salt and ground black pepper
4	square bagels or ciabatta rolls, split
¼	cup mayonnaise
1	cup mixed salad greens

PREPARATION

1. Preheat broiler. Place tomatoes in a small bowl; cover with water. Microwave on 100% power (high) for 1 minute. Meanwhile, brush oil on steak and onion slices; season with salt and pepper. Arrange steak and onion on the unheated rack of a broiler pan. Broil 3 to 4 inches from heat for 12 to 16 minutes or until desired doneness, turning once. Thinly slice beef across the grain into bite-size pieces.

2. Meanwhile, drain tomatoes. Spread split sides of rolls lightly with mayonnaise. Top roll bottoms with steak, onion, drained tomatoes, salad greens, and roll tops. Makes 4 servings.

EACH SERVING: *451 cal., 22 g total fat (4 g sat. fat), 51 mg chol., 681 mg sodium, 40 g carbo., 3 g fiber, 26 g pro. Daily Values: 4% vit. A, 6% vit. C, 8% calcium, 25% iron.*

KIELBASA AND ORZO

Prize Tested RECIPES®

HERE ARE THE BEST 2007 READER RECIPES. CHECK OUT THE SELECTION OF GREAT-TASTING WINNING RECIPES.

CHEWY BUTTERSCOTCH BROWNIES
page 312

Categories

DEVILED EGG SALAD
page 286

SASSY TURKEY BURGERS
page 290

PISTACHIO BAKED SALMON
page 276

COCONUT LEMONADE
page 300

FRUGAL EXTRAVAGANCE

HEARTY PORK STEW

PREP: 25 minutes **BAKE:** 50 minutes

- 1½ lb. lean pork stew meat, cut into 1-inch pieces
- 1 tsp. dried sage, crushed
- 1 tsp. dried mint, crushed
- ¼ cup butter
- 8 oz. fresh button mushrooms, halved or quartered
- 1 cup chopped onion (1 large)
- 4 cloves garlic, minced
- 1 14-oz. can chicken broth
- 1 bay leaf
- 1 lb. carrots, coarsely chopped
- 3 Tbsp. all-purpose flour
- 1 Tbsp. Worcestershire sauce
  Hot cooked noodles (optional)

1. Preheat oven to 350°F. Sprinkle pork with sage and mint. In a very large oven-going skillet brown pork in 1 tablespoon of the butter over medium-high heat, turning often. Remove pork from skillet. Add mushrooms, onion, and garlic to skillet. Cook and stir until onion is tender. Stir in browned pork, broth, and bay leaf. Bring pork mixture to boiling. Remove from heat; cover. Place skillet in oven. Bake for 30 minutes. Stir in chopped carrots; cover and bake for 20 minutes more or until carrots are crisp-tender.

2. In a small saucepan melt remaining 3 tablespoons butter over medium-low heat. Remove from heat. Stir in flour and Worcestershire sauce. Remove skillet from oven. Return skillet to stovetop; uncover. Stir in flour mixture. Bring pork mixture to boiling over medium heat, stirring occasionally. Reduce heat. Simmer, uncovered, for 2 minutes or until the mixture is slightly thickened. Remove and discard bay leaf. If desired, serve stew over hot cooked noodles. Makes 6 servings.

EACH SERVING: *409 cal., 16 g total fat (8 g sat. fat), 118 mg chol., 504 mg sodium, 36 g carbo., 4 g fiber, 29 g pro. Daily Values: 206% vit. A, 14% vit. C, 6% calcium, 20% iron.*

LIGHT 'N' TANGY ASIAN SALAD

PREP: 30 minutes **BAKE:** 15 minutes

- 1 recipe Sweet and Tangy Dressing
- 14 cups torn romaine lettuce or packaged torn mixed salad greens
- 8 green onions, sliced
- 2 cups chopped cooked chicken or turkey breast
- 1 small daikon, peeled, halved lengthwise, and thinly sliced, or 1 cup sliced radishes
- 3 Tbsp. butter
- 2 3-oz. pkg. chicken- or oriental-flavor ramen noodles
- 1 cup dry-roasted peanuts

1. Preheat oven to 350°F. Prepare Sweet and Tangy Dressing; cool. In a 4- or 5-quart bowl combine lettuce, onion, chicken, and daikon. Cover and refrigerate until serving time.

2. Place butter in a 15×10×1-inch baking pan. Place in oven for 1 to 2 minutes or until butter is melted. Break ramen noodles into small pieces. (Use one seasoning packet for Sweet and Tangy Dressing, below. Discard the other seasoning packet.) Stir noodles and peanuts into hot butter. Bake about 15 minutes or until crisp and slightly browned, stirring once; cool. Sprinkle over lettuce mixture. Drizzle with dressing. Toss well to combine. Serve immediately. Makes 12 (1¾-cup) servings.

SWEET AND TANGY DRESSING: In a small saucepan combine ⅓ cup sugar, ¼ cup sesame oil, ¼ cup cider vinegar, 2 tablespoons soy sauce, and 1 seasoning packet from ramen noodles. Bring to boiling; reduce heat. Simmer, uncovered, for 1 minute. Cool completely. Whisk before adding to salad mixture.

EACH SERVING: *293 cal., 18 g total fat (4 g sat. fat), 29 mg chol., 440 mg sodium, 23 g carbo., 3 g fiber, 13 g pro. Daily Values: 81% vit. A, 30% vit. C, 11% calcium, 13% iron.*

SOUTHWESTERN POTATO BREAKFAST BAKE

PREP: 25 minutes **BAKE:** 30 minutes
STAND: 10 minutes

    Nonstick cooking spray
5 cups frozen shredded hash brown
    potatoes (½ of a 30-oz. pkg.)
¼ tsp. seasoned salt
1 large onion, chopped (1 cup)
1 Tbsp. olive oil
2 14.5-oz. cans diced tomatoes and
    green chiles, undrained
1 tsp. chili powder
½ tsp. seasoned salt
¼ tsp. ground black pepper
8 eggs
⅓ cup milk
1 cup shredded Mexican cheese blend

1. Preheat oven to 375°F. Lightly coat a 3-quart rectangular baking dish with cooking spray. Place potatoes evenly in dish; sprinkle with ¼ teaspoon seasoned salt. Set aside.
2. In a large skillet cook onion in hot oil until tender. Add undrained tomatoes, chili powder, ½ teaspoon seasoned salt, and pepper. Bring to boiling; reduce heat. Simmer, uncovered, for 10 minutes, stirring occasionally. Spoon over potatoes in dish. In a large bowl whisk together eggs and milk; pour evenly over mixture in dish. Sprinkle with cheese.
3. Bake, uncovered, for 30 to 35 minutes or until set. Let stand for 10 minutes before serving. Makes 8 servings.

EACH SERVING: *221 cal., 11 g total fat (5 g sat. fat), 225 mg chol., 635 mg sodium, 17 g carbo., 3 g fiber, 13 g pro. Daily Values: 17% vit. A, 53% vit. C, 18% calcium, 7% iron.*

NEW YEAR'S SOUP

PREP: 25 minutes **COOK:** 45 minutes

1 cup chopped onion (1 large)
1 cup chopped carrot (2 medium)
2 cloves garlic, minced
1 Tbsp. cooking oil
2 10-oz. pkg. frozen chopped spinach
    or one 16-oz. pkg. frozen chopped
    turnip greens
2 Tbsp. cider vinegar
1 Tbsp. sugar
¼ tsp. ground black pepper
6 cups water
2 Tbsp. instant chicken bouillon
    granules
2 15.5-oz. cans black-eyed peas,
    undrained
2 cups diced cooked ham and/or
    cooked smoked sausage
¼ to ½ tsp. bottled hot pepper sauce
    (optional)
¾ cup long grain rice
    Corn bread (optional)

1. In a 5- to 6-quart Dutch oven cook onion, carrot, and garlic in hot oil over medium heat just until onion is tender. Add frozen spinach. Sprinkle with vinegar, sugar, and pepper.
2. Cook, covered, for 5 minutes, stirring once to break up spinach. Add water, bouillon granules, undrained black-eyed peas, ham, and, if desired, hot pepper sauce. Bring to boiling; reduce heat. Stir in rice. Simmer, covered, for 40 minutes. If desired, serve with corn bread. Makes 8 servings.

EACH SERVING: *247 cal., 5 g total fat (1 g sat. fat), 19 mg chol., 1,520 mg sodium, 37 g carbo., 7 g fiber, 12 g pro. Daily Values: 154% vit. A, 15% vit. C, 10% calcium, 15% iron.*

CALYPSO RICE WITH SWEET POTATOES

PREP: 20 minutes **COOK:** 1 hour

4 cups water
2 Tbsp. Jamaican jerk seasoning
2 tsp. salt
2 cups brown rice
1 15-oz. can black beans, rinsed and
    drained
1 large onion, halved and thinly sliced
2 cloves garlic, minced
2 Tbsp. cooking oil
2 large sweet potatoes, peeled and
    chopped
1 16-oz. bag frozen cut green beans
⅔ cup orange juice
1½ tsp. cornstarch
⅓ cup dried banana chips, coarsely
    crushed (optional)

1. In a medium saucepan bring the water, 2 teaspoons of the jerk seasoning, and the salt to boiling. Add brown rice. Reduce heat to low. Cook, covered, for 1 hour or until liquid is absorbed. Stir in drained black beans.
2. Meanwhile, in a very large skillet cook onion and garlic in hot oil until tender. Stir in remaining 4 teaspoons jerk seasoning and sweet potatoes. Cook and stir for 1 minute. Stir in green beans and ⅓ cup of the orange juice. Simmer, covered, for 10 minutes or until sweet potato is just tender.
3. Combine remaining orange juice and the cornstarch; add to skillet. Cook, stirring gently, just until thickened.
4. Place rice on a large platter; top with sweet potato mixture. If desired, sprinkle with crushed banana chips. Makes 8 servings.

EACH SERVING: *310 cal., 5 g total fat (1 g sat. fat), 0 mg chol., 968 mg sodium, 60 g carbo., 7 g fiber, 9 g pro. Daily Values: 122% vit. A, 34% vit. C, 8% calcium, 12% iron.*

ROASTED VEGETABLE LASAGNA

PREP: 30 minutes **BROIL:** 12 minutes
BAKE: 50 minutes **STAND:** 10 minutes

12 dried lasagna noodles
4 cups zucchini cut into
    bite-size pieces
2½ cups thinly sliced carrot
2 cups cremini or button
    mushrooms, halved
1½ cups coarsely chopped red or
    green sweet pepper
¼ cup olive oil
1 Tbsp. dried Italian seasoning,
    crushed
½ tsp. salt
½ tsp. ground black pepper
1 12-oz. carton cottage cheese
1 egg, beaten
½ cup grated Parmesan cheese
1 26-oz. jar marinara sauce
3 cups shredded mozzarella cheese
    (12 oz.)

1. Cook noodles according to package directions; drain. Place on waxed paper.
2. Meanwhile, preheat broiler. In a very large bowl combine zucchini, carrot, mushrooms, and sweet pepper. Drizzle vegetables with olive oil; sprinkle with Italian seasoning, salt, and black pepper. Toss well to combine. Place vegetable mixture in a shallow roasting pan.
3. Broil vegetables 5 to 6 inches from the heat for 6 minutes. Stir vegetables and broil 6 to 8 minutes more or until light brown and tender. Set vegetables aside.
4. Preheat oven to 375°F. In a medium bowl combine cottage cheese, egg, and ¼ cup of the Parmesan cheese; set aside.
5. Grease a 3-quart rectangular baking dish. Place one-third of the marinara sauce in the bottom of the prepared dish. Layer 4 of the noodles on top of sauce. Top with half of the roasted vegetables, one-third of the sauce, and one-third of the mozzarella cheese. Add 4 more noodles, all of the cottage cheese mixture, and one-third of the mozzarella. Add 4 more noodles, the remaining vegetables, sauce, and mozzarella. Sprinkle with remaining Parmesan cheese.
6. Bake, covered, for 30 minutes. Uncover and bake about 20 minutes more or until heated through. Let stand for 10 minutes before serving. Makes 9 servings.

EACH SERVING: *420 cal., 21 g total fat (8 g sat. fat), 3 mg chol., 1,020 mg sodium, 37 g carbo., 3 g fiber, 22 g pro. Daily Values: 147% vit. A, 101% vit. C, 32% calcium, 15% iron.*

CRUNCHY KITCHEN FAVORITES

PRIZE TESTED RECIPES® $400 WINNER

HEATHER POOLE, KEIZER, ORE..

PRIZE TESTED RECIPES® $200 WINNER

J. GREGORY HORGAN, SOUTHPORT, N.C..

PISTACHIO BAKED SALMON

PREP: 20 minutes **BAKE:** 6 to 8 minutes per ½-inch thickness

- 1 cup salted dry-roasted pistachio nuts, chopped
- ½ cup packed brown sugar
- 3 Tbsp. lemon juice
- 1 tsp. dried dillweed
- 1 tsp. coarsely ground black pepper
- 6 6-oz. skinless salmon fillets
- ¼ cup purchased refrigerated basil pesto (optional)

1. Preheat oven to 425°F. In a small bowl combine pistachio nuts, brown sugar, lemon juice, dillweed, and pepper; set aside.
2. Place salmon fillets in a greased foil-lined 15×10×1-inch baking pan. Turn under any thin edges to make fillets a uniform thickness. Measure thickness of fish. Spoon pistachio mixture evenly on top of fillets and gently press in place to form a crust.
3. Bake for 6 to 8 minutes per ½-inch thickness of fish or until fish flakes easily when tested with a fork. If desired, pass pesto with fish. Makes 6 servings.
EACH SERVING: *391 cal., 16 g total fat (2 g sat. fat), 88 mg chol., 208 mg sodium, 25 g carbo., 2 g fiber, 39 g pro. Daily Values: 5% vit. A, 7% vit. C, 7% calcium, 15% iron.*

CRUNCHY CHICKEN SALAD

PREP: 20 minutes **CHILL:** 2 hours

- 3 cups coarsely shredded cooked chicken
- 2 to 3 stalks celery, coarsely chopped
- ⅓ cup finely chopped onion (1 small)
- ½ cup mayonnaise
- 1 Tbsp. olive oil
- ¼ tsp. salt
- ¼ tsp. ground black pepper
- ½ cup salted mixed nuts, coarsely chopped
- ¾ cup broken peanut brittle
  Flatbread (optional)

1. In a large bowl stir together chicken, celery, onion, mayonnaise, olive oil, salt, and pepper. Cover and chill for at least 2 hours.
2. Just before serving, stir in nuts and peanut brittle. (Salad can be chilled for up to 2 hours after adding nuts.) If desired, serve with flatbread. Makes 4 (1-cup) servings.
EACH SERVING: *605 cal., 43 g total fat (7 g sat. fat), 104 mg chol., 572 mg sodium, 7 g carbo., 2 g fiber, 35 g pro. Daily Values: 4% vit. A, 3% vit. C, 4% calcium, 16% iron.*

CHOCOLATE-COVERED-PEANUT SHORTCAKES

PREP: 30 minutes **BAKE:** 10 minutes

- 2 cups all-purpose flour
- 2 Tbsp. granulated sugar
- 1 Tbsp. baking powder
- ⅓ cup creamy honey-roasted peanut butter
- 2 Tbsp. shortening
- ⅔ cup milk
- 3 cups vanilla, chocolate, or other favorite flavor ice cream, softened*
- 1½ cups chocolate-covered peanuts
- ¾ cup coarsely chopped pecans, toasted
  Powdered sugar

1. Preheat oven to 425°F. In a large bowl combine flour, granulated sugar, baking powder, and ½ teaspoon *salt*. Using a pastry blender, cut in peanut butter and shortening until mixture resembles coarse crumbs. Make a well in center of flour mixture. Add milk all at once. Using a fork, stir just until moistened. Turn dough out onto a lightly floured surface. Knead dough by folding and gently pressing for four to six strokes or just until dough holds together. Pat or lightly roll dough to ½-inch thickness. Using a floured 3½-inch round cutter, cut into 6 biscuits.

2. Place biscuits 1 inch apart on a lightly greased baking sheet. Bake for 10 to 12 minutes or until golden brown. Transfer biscuits to a wire rack; cool completely.

3. To serve, split biscuits in half horizontally. Place biscuit bottoms on 6 dessert plates. In a large bowl stir together ice cream, peanuts, and pecans. Spoon ice cream mixture on top of biscuit bottoms. Add biscuit tops. Sprinkle with powdered sugar. Serve shortcakes immediately. Makes 6 shortcakes.

***TO SOFTEN ICE CREAM:** Place ice cream in a large chilled mixing bowl; stir with a wooden spoon until soft but not melted, pressing ice cream against side of bowl.

EACH SHORTCAKE: *778 cal., 48 g total fat (16 g sat. fat), 74 mg chol., 443 mg sodium, 76 g carbo., 6 g fiber, 17 g pro. Daily Values: 11% vit. A, 23% calcium, 17% iron.*

MACADAMIA-COCONUT TARTS

PREP: 40 minutes **BAKE:** 8 minutes
CHILL: 1 hour

- Nonstick cooking spray
- 1½ cups macadamia nuts
- 1½ cups flaked coconut, toasted
- 8 sheets frozen phyllo dough (14×9-inch rectangles), thawed
- ⅓ cup butter, melted
- 1 8-oz. pkg. cream cheese, softened
- ⅓ cup cream of coconut
- 2 Tbsp. milk (optional)

1. Preheat oven to 350°F. Lightly coat twelve 2½-inch muffin cups with nonstick spray. Set aside. Finely chop ½ cup of the macadamia nuts and ½ cup of the coconut; combine and set aside ⅓ cup for topping. Coarsely chop remaining nuts; set aside.

2. Brush 1 sheet of phyllo dough with butter; sprinkle with about 2 teaspoons of the nut-coconut mixture. Repeat two more times and end with a sheet of phyllo. Brush with butter. Repeat to make a second stack of 4 phyllo sheets. Cut each stack in half lengthwise. Cut crosswise into thirds (12 rectangles total). Press 1 rectangle into each prepared muffin cup, pleating phyllo as necessary to form a cup. Bake for 8 minutes or until golden. Cool for 5 minutes in pan. Remove from pan; cool completely.

3. In a large mixing bowl beat cream cheese until smooth; gradually beat in cream of coconut. If desired, beat in enough milk to make filling desired consistency. Stir in chopped macadamia nuts and remaining coconut. Spoon filling into prepared phyllo shells. Sprinkle with reserved nut-coconut mixture. Cover and chill for 1 to 4 hours. Makes 12 tarts.

EACH TART: *318 cal., 30 g total fat (14 g sat. fat), 34 mg chol., 196 mg sodium, 11 g carbo., 2 g fiber, 4 g pro. Daily Values: 8% vit. A, 1% vit. C, 3% calcium, 7% iron.*

NUTTY TABBOULEH

PREP: 25 minutes **CHILL:** 4 hours
STAND: 15 minutes

- ¾ cup uncooked bulgur
- 1 6-oz. jar marinated artichoke hearts
- 1 small zucchini, coarsely chopped
- 2 medium carrots, coarsely shredded
- ½ cup thinly sliced green onion (4)
- 1 Tbsp. white wine vinegar or lemon juice
- ¼ cup fresh basil, cut into thin strips, or 2 teaspoons dried basil, crushed
- 1 cup walnuts, pecans, or almonds, toasted and chopped
- 1 small tomato, seeded and chopped

1. Place bulgur in a colander; rinse with cold water and drain. Drain artichokes, reserving liquid. Coarsely chop the artichokes. In a large bowl combine bulgur, artichokes, zucchini, carrot, and green onion.

2. In a screw-top jar combine artichoke liquid, vinegar, ¼ cup *water*, ¼ teaspoon *salt*, ⅛ teaspoon *ground black pepper*, and, if using, dried basil. Cover and shake well. Pour over bulgur mixture. Toss lightly to coat. Cover and chill for 4 to 24 hours. Bring to room temperature, about 15 minutes. Stir in fresh basil (if using), nuts, and tomato. Makes 10 to 12 servings.

EACH SERVING: *140 cal., 9 g total fat (1 g sat. fat), 0 mg chol., 124 mg sodium, 14 g carbo., 4 g fiber, 4 g pro. Daily Values: 46% vit. A, 16% vit. C, 3% calcium, 5% iron.*

FAST!

SPICY CAJUN PECANS

PREP: 10 minutes **BAKE:** 15 minutes

- 4 cups pecan halves
- 2 Tbsp. cooking oil
- 1 Tbsp. Worcestershire sauce
- 2 tsp. lemon juice
- 2 tsp. garlic salt
- 2 tsp. paprika
- ½ tsp. onion salt
- ½ tsp. cayenne pepper
- ½ tsp. dried thyme, crushed
- ¼ tsp. ground black pepper

1. Preheat oven to 350°F. Spread pecans in a 13×9×2-inch baking pan. In a small bowl combine oil, Worcestershire sauce, lemon juice, garlic salt, paprika, onion salt, cayenne, thyme, and black pepper; drizzle over nuts. Toss to coat nut halves.

2. Bake, uncovered, for 15 minutes or until nuts are toasted, stirring occasionally. Spread on a piece of foil to cool. Store the nuts in an airtight container for up to 1 week. Makes 16 (¼-cup) servings.

EACH SERVING: *205 cal., 21 g total fat (2 g sat. fat), 0 mg chol., 183 mg sodium, 4 g carbo., 3 g fiber, 3 g pro. Daily Values: 3% vit. A, 1% vit. C, 2% calcium, 5% iron.*

SWEET AND SPICY CAJUN PECAN MIX: Prepare as above, except omit lemon juice, reduce oil to 1 tablespoon, and add 2 tablespoons dark corn syrup.

FAST!

WALNUT, CUCUMBER, AND EGG SALAD APPETIZERS

START TO FINISH: 30 minutes

- 4 hard-cooked eggs, finely chopped
- ½ cup peeled, seeded, and finely chopped cucumber
- ⅔ cup walnuts, toasted and coarsely chopped
- 2 Tbsp. snipped fresh chives
- 2 Tbsp. mayonnaise
- 2 Tbsp. dairy sour cream
- 2 tsp. snipped fresh dill or ½ tsp. dried dillweed
- 1 tsp. Dijon-style mustard
- ¼ tsp. garlic salt
- ⅛ tsp. ground black pepper
- 24 ¼-inch-thick slices baguette-style French bread, toasted, or ¼-inch-thick diagonal cucumber slices

1. In a bowl combine eggs, cucumber, ¼ cup of the walnuts, the chives, mayonnaise, sour cream, dill, mustard, garlic salt, and pepper. Spoon onto bread. Sprinkle with remaining nuts. Makes 24 appetizers.

EACH APPETIZER: *63 cal., 4 g total fat (1 g sat. fat), 36 mg chol., 70 mg sodium, 4 g carbo., 0 g fiber, 2 g pro. Daily Values: 1% vit. A, 1% calcium, 2% iron.*

SPECIAL DINNERS FOR TWO

FILET WITH CRAB TOPPING

START TO FINISH: 40 minutes

- 2 bacon-wrapped beef tenderloin steaks, cut 1½ inches thick*
  Salt and ground black pepper
- ½ cup long grain rice
- 3 Tbsp. snipped fresh parsley
- 1 Tbsp. butter
- ⅓ cup half-and-half or light cream
- ½ of a 3-oz. pkg. cream cheese
- 2 Tbsp. thinly sliced green onion
- ½ tsp. seasoned pepper or herb-pepper seasoning
- 2 oz. drained and flaked canned crabmeat (about ½ cup)
- 1 tsp. lemon juice

1. Season steaks with salt and pepper. Preheat broiler. Place steaks on the unheated rack of a broiler pan. Broil 4 to 5 inches from the heat for 18 to 21 minutes for medium rare (145°F) or 22 to 27 minutes for medium (160°F), turning once halfway through cooking. (For a charcoal grill, grill steaks on the rack of an uncovered grill directly over medium coals for 15 to 19 minutes for medium rare [145°F] or 18 to 23 minutes for medium [160°F], turning once halfway through grilling. For a gas grill, preheat grill. Reduce heat to medium. Place steaks on grill rack over heat. Cover and grill as above.)

2. Meanwhile, in a medium saucepan cook rice according to package directions. Stir in 1 tablespoon of the parsley and the butter. Cover; let stand for 5 minutes. In a small saucepan combine half-and-half, cream cheese, onion, seasoning, and remaining 2 tablespoons parsley. Cook and stir over medium heat until cheese melts and mixture is smooth. Stir in crabmeat and lemon juice; heat through.

3. Place steaks on dinner plates. Pack rice mixture into 6-ounce ramekins or custard cups and invert onto plates. Spoon crab mixture over meat. Makes 2 servings.

***NOTE:** Find bacon-wrapped tenderloin steaks at the supermarket butcher's counter. If not available, wrap a slice of bacon around each steak and secure with a wooden toothpick.

EACH SERVING: *638 cal., 32 g total fat (16 g sat. fat), 173 mg chol., 588 mg sodium, 41 g carbo., 1 g fiber, 44 g pro. Daily Values: 22% vit. A, 17% vit. C, 12% calcium, 39% iron.*

CHICKEN, GREENS, AND BRIE

PREP: 30 minutes **COOK:** 11 minutes

- 3 cups torn mixed salad greens
- 1 cup seedless green grapes
- ½ cup walnut or pecan halves, toasted
- ¼ cup olive oil
- 2 Tbsp. cider vinegar, white vinegar, or rice vinegar
- 1 Tbsp. strawberry spreadable fruit
- ¼ cup purchased refrigerated basil pesto
- ¼ cup chopped walnuts or pecans, toasted
- 1 Tbsp. olive oil
- 2 skinless, boneless chicken breast halves (8 oz. total)
- 1 cup Marsala or chicken broth
- 2 1- to 2-oz. wedges Brie
- 2 slices purchased crusty country bread

1. For salad, in a large bowl combine greens, grapes, and nut halves; set aside. For dressing, in a small bowl whisk together the ¼ cup oil, vinegar, and spreadable fruit; set aside. For pesto, in a small bowl combine pesto and chopped nuts; set aside.

2. In a large skillet heat oil over medium-high heat. Add chicken; cook about 3 minutes on each side or until brown. Remove skillet from heat; drain fat. Carefully add Marsala (liquid may spatter). Return skillet to heat. Bring to boiling; reduce heat. Simmer, uncovered, for 5 to 10 minutes or until chicken is no longer pink, turning chicken once. Remove chicken from skillet; discard Marsala.

3. Toss together salad and dressing. Transfer salad to dinner plates. Arrange chicken and Brie on top of greens. Spoon pesto mixture over chicken. Serve with bread. Makes 2 servings.

EACH SERVING: *1,218 cal., 94 g total fat (13 g sat. fat), 98 mg chol., 654 mg sodium, 48 g carbo., 5 g fiber, 46 g pro. Daily Values: 13% vit. A, 19% vit. C, 15% calcium, 21% iron.*

ROSEMARY LAMB CHOPS

PREP: 20 minutes **BAKE:** 12 minutes

- ¼ cup currant jelly
- 1 medium cooking apple, peeled, cored, and coarsely chopped
- 1 Tbsp. all-purpose flour
- ½ tsp. dried rosemary, crushed
- ¼ tsp. salt
- ¼ tsp. ground black pepper
- 4 lamb loin chops
- 1 Tbsp. cooking oil
- 2 Tbsp. packed brown sugar
- 2 Tbsp. orange juice
- 1 Tbsp. cider vinegar
- ½ tsp. yellow mustard
- 1 cup hot cooked rice

1. Preheat oven to 350°F. In a small skillet combine currant jelly and apple. Cook over medium heat about 3 minutes or until apple is crisp-tender, stirring occasionally.
2. Meanwhile, in a shallow dish combine flour, rosemary, salt, and pepper. Add lamb chops to flour mixture, turning to coat. In a large oven-going skillet heat oil over medium-high heat. Add lamb chops and cook until brown, turning once.
3. Stir brown sugar, orange juice, vinegar, and mustard into apple mixture. Spoon apple mixture over chops in skillet.
4. Bake, uncovered, for 12 to 15 minutes or until chops are desired doneness (145°F for medium rare or 160°F for medium). Serve chops with rice and sauce. Makes 2 servings.
EACH SERVING: 634 cal., 17 g total fat (5 g sat. fat), 112 mg chol., 440 mg sodium, 80 g carbo., 3 g fiber, 38 g pro. Daily Values: 1% vit. A, 19% vit. C, 5% calcium, 28% iron.

CHEESE SOUFFLÉ WITH MUSHROOM-SHERRY SAUCE

PREP: 30 minutes **BAKE:** 35 minutes

- 2 Tbsp. butter
- ⅓ cup chopped onion (1 small)
- 2 cloves garlic, minced
- 2 Tbsp. all-purpose flour
- ⅛ tsp. salt
  Dash cayenne pepper
- ½ cup half-and-half or light cream
- ¾ cup shredded cheddar cheese (3 oz.)
- ¼ cup finely shredded Parmesan cheese (1 oz.)
- 2 egg yolks
- 2 egg whites
- 1 recipe Mushroom-Sherry Sauce

1. Preheat oven to 325°F. In a medium saucepan heat butter over medium heat. Add onion and garlic; cook until tender. Stir in flour, salt, and cayenne. Add half-and-half all at once. Cook and stir over medium heat until thickened and bubbly. Reduce heat to low; add cheeses, stirring to melt. Remove from heat. In a small bowl beat egg yolks with a fork. Gradually stir in cheese mixture.
2. In a medium mixing bowl beat egg whites with an electric mixer until stiff peaks form (tips stand straight). Gently fold about one-fourth of the egg whites into yolk mixture to lighten. Gradually pour yolk mixture over remaining egg whites; fold just until combined. Pour into an ungreased 3-cup soufflé dish.
3. Bake, uncovered, for 35 to 40 minutes or until a knife inserted near the center comes out clean. Serve immediately with Mushroom-Sherry Sauce. Makes 2 servings.
MUSHROOM-SHERRY SAUCE: In a small saucepan melt 2 tablespoons butter over medium heat. Add 1 cup sliced cremini or stemmed shiitake mushrooms and ¼ cup sliced green onion; cook until tender. Stir in 1 tablespoon all-purpose flour, ⅛ teaspoon salt, and a dash cayenne pepper. Add ⅔ cup half-and-half or light cream all at once. Cook and stir until thickened and bubbly; cook and stir for 1 minute more. Stir in 2 tablespoons dry sherry; heat through. Makes about 1 cup.
EACH SERVING: 766 cal., 61 g total fat (37 g sat. fat), 375 mg chol., 115 mg sodium, 24 g carbo., 2 g fiber, 28 g pro. Daily Values: 42% vit. A, 12% vit. C, 64% calcium, 12% iron.

LUSCIOUS LOBSTER WRAPS

START TO FINISH: 50 minutes

- 2 Tbsp. butter
- 1 Tbsp. finely chopped shallot
- ¼ cup mascarpone cheese
- ½ cup half-and-half or light cream
- 2 tsp. cornstarch
- 2 tsp. snipped fresh tarragon or ½ tsp. dried tarragon, crushed
- ¼ tsp. salt
- ⅛ tsp. freshly ground black pepper
- 2 6- to 8-oz. frozen lobster tails, thawed, cooked,* shelled, and cubed
- 2 oz. smoked Gouda cheese, shredded
- 2 10-inch dried tomato and basil flour tortillas, warmed**
- 1 to 2 Tbsp. half-and-half or light cream (optional)
- 1 tsp. caviar (optional)
  Fresh tarragon (optional)

1. For sauce, in a small saucepan heat 1 tablespoon of the butter over medium heat. Add shallot; cook about 3 minutes or until tender. Stir in mascarpone cheese until melted. In a small bowl stir together the ½ cup half-and-half and the cornstarch until smooth. Add half-and-half mixture to mascarpone mixture; cook and stir until thickened and bubbly. Cook and stir for 2 minutes more. Stir in tarragon, salt, and pepper. Remove from heat; keep warm.
2. In a large skillet heat remaining 1 tablespoon butter over medium heat. Add cooked lobster and cook until heated through.
3. Divide Gouda cheese between tortillas. Using a slotted spoon, place lobster on top of cheese. Add ¼ cup of sauce to each tortilla. Roll up tortillas; cut in half. If desired, stir additional half-and-half into remaining sauce to reach desired consistency. Divide sauce between plates. Place halved tortilla rolls on sauce. If desired, garnish with caviar and/or additional fresh tarragon. Makes 2 servings.
*TO COOK LOBSTER TAILS: In a Dutch oven cook lobster tails in enough boiling salted water to cover for 8 to 12 minutes or until shells turn bright red and meat is tender; drain. Submerse in ice water to cool quickly. Drain well. Using kitchen shears, cut through shells and remove the meat.
**TO WARM TORTILLAS: Preheat oven to 350°F. Wrap tortillas in foil and bake for 10 minutes. Or wrap tortillas in white paper towels and microwave on 100% power (high) for 15 seconds.
EACH SERVING: 734 cal., 43 g total fat (25 g sat. fat), 203 mg chol., 1,714 mg sodium, 45 g carbo., 3 g fiber, 45 g pro. Daily Values: 14% vit. A, 2% vit. C, 46% calcium, 8% iron.

FAST!

PORK MEDALLIONS WITH CHIPOTLE-RASPBERRY GLAZE

START TO FINISH: 25 minutes

- 8 oz. pork tenderloin
  Salt and ground black pepper
- 2 Tbsp. butter
- ½ of a medium onion, cut into thin wedges
- 1 clove garlic, minced
- ½ cup seedless raspberry jam
- 1 Tbsp. balsamic vinegar
- ½ of a chipotle pepper in adobo sauce, finely chopped
- 1 tsp. adobo sauce
- 1 cup hot cooked couscous
- ¼ cup fresh raspberries

1. Cut pork into ½-inch slices. Sprinkle lightly with salt and black pepper; set aside.
2. In a large skillet heat butter over medium heat. Add onion and garlic; cook, stirring occasionally, until tender. Add pork slices. Cook for 4 to 5 minutes or just until pork is pink in center, turning once.
3. Meanwhile, in a small bowl combine jam, vinegar, chipotle pepper, and adobo sauce; add to skillet. Simmer, uncovered, for 2 minutes, turning pork once. Season to taste with additional salt and black pepper. To serve, place couscous on plates; top with pork mixture and sprinkle with raspberries. Makes 2 servings.
EACH SERVING: 580 cal., 15 g total fat (9 g sat. fat), 104 mg chol., 354 mg sodium, 81 g carbo., 3 g fiber, 28 g pro. Daily Values: 8% vit. A, 24% vit. C, 4% calcium, 12% iron.

TACOS WITH A TWIST

FAST!

HAWAIIAN TACOS

START TO FINISH: 30 minutes

- 1 lb. bulk hot Italian sausage
- ½ cup chopped onion (1 medium)
- 2 cloves garlic, minced
  Dash bottled hot pepper sauce
- 12 taco shells, warmed
- 1 recipe Hawaiian Pineapple Salsa
- 1 cup shredded cheddar cheese (4 oz.)

1. In a large skillet cook sausage, onion, and garlic until sausage is brown and onion is tender, stirring to break up sausage. Drain fat. Stir in hot pepper sauce. Spoon sausage mixture into taco shells. Top with Hawaiian Pineapple Salsa and sprinkle with cheese. Makes 12 tacos.
HAWAIIAN PINEAPPLE SALSA: In a large bowl combine 3 plum tomatoes, seeded and chopped; 1 cup seeded, chopped cucumber or 3 tomatillos, husked and chopped; one 8-ounce can pineapple tidbits, drained; ⅓ cup chopped onion; 1 or 2 fresh jalapeño chile peppers, seeded and finely chopped;* 2 tablespoons snipped fresh cilantro; and 1 tablespoon packed brown sugar. Stir until combined. Serve immediately or cover and refrigerate for up to 2 hours. If chilled longer than 30 minutes, serve salsa with a slotted spoon.
***NOTE:** Because chile peppers contain volatile oils that can burn your skin and eyes, avoid direct contact with chiles as much as possible. Wear plastic or rubber gloves. Wash hands and nails well with soap and warm water.
EACH TACO: *259 cal., 18 g total fat (7 g sat. fat), 39 mg chol., 387 mg sodium, 16 g carbo., 2 g fiber, 9 g pro. Daily Values: 7% vit. A, 12% vit. C, 11% calcium, 6% iron.*

FAST! **LOW FAT**

PERUVIAN-STYLE CHICKEN TACOS

START TO FINISH: 30 minutes

- 1 lb. uncooked ground chicken
- ½ cup chopped onion (1 medium)
- 2 tsp. ground coriander
- 2 tsp. ground cumin
- 1 tsp. salt
- 1 14.5-oz. can diced tomatoes, undrained
- 1 medium potato, peeled and finely chopped
- ¼ cup snipped pitted dried plums (prunes)
- ¼ cup chopped pimiento-stuffed green olives
- 12 6- to 7-inch corn or flour tortillas
- 4 to 6 oz. Cotija or Monterey Jack cheese, shredded
  Chopped onion (optional)
  Snipped fresh cilantro (optional)

1. Preheat oven to 350°F. In a large skillet cook chicken and the ½ cup onion until chicken is no longer pink, stirring to break up chicken. Drain fat, if necessary. Add coriander, cumin, and salt; cook and stir for 1 to 2 minutes more or until fragrant. Add undrained tomatoes, potato, dried plums, and olives. Bring to boiling; reduce heat. Simmer, covered, for 12 to 15 minutes or until potato is tender. Uncover and cook about 5 minutes more or until most of the liquid has evaporated.
2. Meanwhile, wrap tortillas in foil and bake for 15 minutes or until heated through. To assemble, place ⅓ cup of the chicken mixture in center of each tortilla; top with cheese and, if desired, onion and cilantro. Fold tortillas in half. Makes 12 tacos.
EACH TACO: *194 cal., 10 g total fat (0 g sat. fat), 9 mg chol., 328 mg sodium, 18 g carbo., 3 g fiber, 11 g pro. Daily Values: 5% vit. A, 11% vit. C, 14% calcium, 8% iron.*

CHICKEN AND SWEET SOYBEAN TACOS

START TO FINISH: 30 minutes

- ½ of a 12-oz. pkg. frozen sweet soybeans (edamame) (1¼ cups)
- 12 oz. uncooked ground chicken or turkey
- ¼ cup orange marmalade
- 2 Tbsp. hoisin sauce
- ¼ tsp. ground ginger
- 1 3-oz. pkg. cream cheese
- 6 7- to 8-inch spinach flour tortillas
- 1 11-oz. can mandarin orange sections, drained
- ¼ cup sliced almonds, toasted
- ¼ cup sliced green onion (2)

1. Cook soybeans according to package directions; drain and set aside.

2. In a large skillet cook chicken until no longer pink, stirring to break up chicken; drain fat, if necessary. Stir in soybeans, marmalade, hoisin sauce, and ginger. Bring to boiling; reduce heat. Simmer, covered, for 5 minutes. Stir in cream cheese just until melted.

3. Divide chicken mixture among tortillas. Top with orange sections, almonds, and green onion; roll up. Makes 6 tacos.

EACH TACO: *493 cal., 20 g total fat (4 g sat. fat), 16 mg chol., 551 mg sodium, 55 g carbo., 7 g fiber, 22 g pro. Daily Values: 14% vit. A, 39% vit. C, 21% calcium, 15% iron.*

FAST!

ITALIAN-PESTO SOFT TACOS

START TO FINISH: 30 minutes

- 1 lb. bulk mild (sweet) sausage
- 2 large yellow and/or red sweet peppers, cut into bite-size strips
- 1 medium red onion, halved and sliced
- 1 6-oz. jar quartered marinated artichoke hearts, undrained
- ¼ cup purchased basil pesto
- 6 7- to 8-inch flour tortillas
- 1½ cups shredded Italian cheese blend (6 oz.)

1. In a very large skillet cook and stir sausage over medium heat until brown; drain fat. Add sweet pepper and onion. Cook and stir for 3 to 4 minutes or until vegetables are crisp-tender. Add undrained artichoke hearts and pesto; heat through. Use a slotted spoon to divide sausage mixture among tortillas. Top with cheese and roll up. Makes 6 tacos.

EACH TACO: *538 cal., 39 g total fat (14 g sat. fat), 81 mg chol., 1,036 mg sodium, 25 g carbo., 2 g fiber, 22 g pro. Daily Values: 4% vit. A, 205% vit. C, 26% calcium, 13% iron.*

FAST! LOW FAT

CHERRY-KISSED TACOS WITH FETA CHEESE SALSA

START TO FINISH: 25 minutes

- 1 lb. lean ground lamb or pork
- 1 cup finely chopped onion (1 large)
- 1 tsp. curry powder
- ½ cup mango chutney
- ½ cup dried tart red cherries, chopped
- 1 Tbsp. lemon juice
- 12 taco shells, warmed
- 1 recipe Feta Cheese Salsa

1. In a large skillet cook ground meat and onion until meat is brown and onion is tender. Drain off fat. Add curry powder; cook and stir for 1 minute.

2. Cut up large pieces of chutney. Stir chutney, cherries, lemon juice, ¼ teaspoon *salt*, and ¼ teaspoon *ground black pepper* into meat mixture. Bring to boiling; reduce heat. Simmer, covered, for 5 minutes.

3. Spoon meat mixture into taco shells. Top with Feta Cheese Salsa. Makes 12 tacos.

FETA CHEESE SALSA: In a medium bowl combine 1 medium tomato, seeded and finely chopped; ⅓ cup finely chopped cucumber; ¼ cup crumbled feta cheese; ¼ cup finely chopped red onion; ¼ cup finely chopped green sweet pepper; 1 tablespoon olive oil; 1 tablespoon lemon juice; and salt and ground black pepper to taste. Stir until combined. Serve with a slotted spoon. Makes 1½ cups.

EACH TACO: *208 cal., 10 g total fat (3 g sat. fat), 27 mg chol., 282 mg sodium, 21 g carbo., 2 g fiber, 8 g pro. Daily Values: 7% vit. A, 13% vit. C, 5% calcium, 6% iron.*

FAST!

GRILLED TUSCAN CHICKEN TACOS

START TO FINISH: 20 minutes

- 2 large skinless, boneless chicken breast halves (about 12 oz. total)
- 2 Tbsp. olive oil
- ½ tsp. lemon-pepper seasoning
- 1 8-oz. pkg. sliced fresh button mushrooms
- 1 14-oz. can artichoke hearts, drained and quartered
- 2 Tbsp. snipped dried tomatoes (not oil-packed)
- 1 tsp. dried Italian seasoning, crushed
- ½ tsp. salt
- ¼ tsp. ground black pepper
- ¼ cup dry white wine
- 3 to 4 Tbsp. bottled Caesar salad dressing
- 8 7- to 8-inch flour tortillas
- 1 cup shredded mozzarella cheese

1. Brush chicken with 1 tablespoon of the olive oil; sprinkle with lemon-pepper seasoning. For a charcoal grill, grill chicken on the rack of an uncovered grill directly over medium coals for 12 to 15 minutes or until chicken is no longer pink (170°F), turning once halfway through grilling. (For a gas grill, preheat grill. Reduce heat to medium. Place chicken on grill rack over heat. Cover; grill as above.) Cut chicken into thin strips. Cover; keep warm.

2. Meanwhile, in a large skillet heat remaining 1 tablespoon oil over medium heat. Add mushrooms, artichoke hearts, tomatoes, Italian seasoning, salt, and pepper; cook about 5 minutes or until mushrooms are tender, stirring occasionally. Carefully add wine. Bring to boiling; reduce heat. Simmer, uncovered, for 5 to 8 minutes or until most of the liquid has evaporated. Spread salad dressing over half of each tortilla. Top with chicken strips and mushroom mixture. Sprinkle with cheese. Fold other tortilla half over filling. Makes 8 tacos.

EACH TACO: *268 cal., 13 g total fat (4 g sat. fat), 36 mg chol., 687 mg sodium, 19 g carbo., 2 g fiber, 17 g pro. Daily Values: 4% vit. A, 3% vit. C, 13% calcium, 15% iron.*

SWEET SHRIMP TACOS

PREP: 20 minutes **BAKE:** 10 minutes

- 12 oz. fresh or frozen peeled and deveined medium shrimp
- 1 tsp. Jamaican jerk seasoning
- ½ cup orange juice
- 1 Tbsp. cornstarch
- 1 Tbsp. packed brown sugar
- 1 Tbsp. soy sauce
- 8 7- to 8-inch flour tortillas
- 1 Tbsp. macadamia nut oil or cooking oil
- 2 tsp. bottled minced garlic
- 1 8.8-oz. package cooked long grain and wild rice
- 1 11-oz. can mandarin orange sections or one 8-oz. can pineapple tidbits (juice pack), drained
- ⅓ cup slivered almonds, toasted
- ¼ cup shredded coconut, toasted (optional)

1. Preheat oven to 350°F. Thaw shrimp, if frozen; coarsely chop shrimp. In a medium bowl toss shrimp with jerk seasoning; set aside. In a small bowl combine orange juice, cornstarch, brown sugar, and soy sauce; set aside. Wrap tortillas in foil; bake for 10 minutes or until heated through.

2. Meanwhile, in a large skillet heat oil over medium-high heat. Add garlic and shrimp; cook and stir for 2 to 3 minutes or until shrimp are opaque. Stir orange juice mixture; add to skillet. Cook and stir until bubbly. Add rice, orange sections, and almonds; heat through.

3. Spoon shrimp mixture into warmed tortillas. If desired, top with coconut. Roll up tortillas. Makes 8 tacos.

EACH TACO: *259 cal., 8 g total fat (1 g sat. fat), 65 mg chol., 452 mg sodium, 34 g carbo., 2 g fiber, 13 g pro. Daily Values: 9% vit. A, 38% vit. C, 8% calcium, 15% iron.*

EVERYTHING ONION

MARIE BRUNO, GREENSBORO, GA.

ULTIMATE TRIPLE ONION TART

PREP: 30 minutes **BAKE:** 40 minutes **COOL:** 15 minutes

- 1 crust from a 15-oz. pkg. rolled refrigerated unbaked piecrust
- ¼ cup butter
- 1 large sweet onion, halved and thinly sliced (about 2 cups)
- 1 large leek, halved lengthwise and thinly sliced
- 2 shallots, thinly sliced
- 1 tsp. sugar
- ¾ tsp. salt
- ½ tsp. ground black pepper
- ½ tsp. ground nutmeg
- 1 3-oz. pkg. cream cheese, cubed and softened
- ¾ cup shredded Swiss cheese (3 oz.)
- ¾ cup shredded Monterey Jack cheese with jalapeño peppers (3 oz.)
- 3 eggs, lightly beaten
- ⅔ cup whipping cream

1. Preheat oven to 375°F. Let the piecrust stand according to package directions.

2. In a very large skillet heat butter over medium heat; add onion, leek, shallot, sugar, salt, pepper, and nutmeg. Cook about 8 minutes or until onion is tender, stirring occasionally. Reduce heat. Stir in cream cheese until melted. Stir in Swiss cheese and Monterey Jack cheese until combined. In a large bowl combine eggs and cream. Gradually stir in onion mixture until combined. Ease piecrust into a 9-inch pie plate; pour onion mixture into piecrust. Fold edge of crust over filling, pleating as necessary.

3. Bake, uncovered, about 40 minutes or until crust and top are golden brown and a knife inserted near the center comes out clean. Cool on a wire rack for 15 to 20 minutes. Cut into 16 wedges. Serve warm. Makes 16 appetizer servings.

EACH SERVING: *203 cal., 16 g total fat (9 g sat. fat), 79 mg chol., 256 mg sodium, 10 g carbo., 0 g fiber, 5 g pro. Daily Values: 10% vit. A, 3% vit. C, 10% calcium, 2% iron.*

MELISSA McKAY, NEW YORK, N.Y.

LOW FAT

PINEAPPLE-ONION MARMALADE

PREP: 30 minutes **COOK:** 55 minutes

- 2 lb. white onions, chopped (5 cups)
- ¼ cup cooking oil
- 1 8-oz. can crushed pineapple (juice pack), undrained
- 1 cup cider vinegar or white wine vinegar
- ¾ cup granulated sugar
- ¾ cup packed brown sugar
- ½ tsp. salt

1. In a very large skillet cook onion, uncovered, in hot oil over medium heat about 20 minutes or until very tender and beginning to brown, stirring occasionally (if necessary, reduce heat to medium-low to prevent overbrowning).

2. Add undrained pineapple, vinegar, granulated sugar, brown sugar, and salt to skillet. Bring to boiling, stirring to dissolve sugars; reduce heat. Simmer, uncovered, for 35 to 45 minutes or until thickened to desired consistency, stirring occasionally.

3. Serve marmalade warm with cooked chicken or pork or spread on toasted baguette slices. If desired, transfer marmalade to a medium bowl; cover and refrigerate for up to 5 days. Heat marmalade in a saucepan until warm before serving. Makes 2½ cups; 20 (2-tablespoon) servings.

EACH SERVING: *109 cal., 3 g total fat (0 g sat. fat), 0 mg chol., 63 mg sodium, 21 g carbo., 1 g fiber, 0 g pro. Daily Values: 6% vit. C, 2% calcium, 2% iron.*

BROILED SALMON WITH SWEET-SOUR ONION SAUCE

START TO FINISH: 40 minutes

- 1 medium sweet onion, thinly sliced
- 2 Tbsp. butter
- 3 Tbsp. cider vinegar
- ¼ cup raisins (optional)
- 1 Tbsp. snipped fresh rosemary or 1 teaspoon dried rosemary, crushed
- ½ cup chicken broth
- 1 tsp. cornstarch
- 4 6-oz. skinned salmon fillets, about 1 inch thick
- 2 Tbsp. packed brown sugar
- ½ tsp. salt
- ¼ tsp. crushed red pepper

1. For onion sauce, in a large skillet cook and stir onion in hot butter over medium heat about 10 minutes or until tender and light brown. Add vinegar. Bring onion mixture to boiling; reduce heat. Simmer, uncovered, for 5 minutes, stirring occasionally. Stir in raisins, if desired, and rosemary. In a small bowl combine broth and cornstarch; add all at once to skillet. Cook and stir until slightly thickened and bubbly. Cook and stir for 2 minutes more.

2. Meanwhile, preheat broiler. Arrange salmon fillets on the greased unheated rack of a broiler pan. Broil 3 to 4 inches from the heat for 5 minutes. Combine brown sugar, salt, and crushed red pepper. Turn salmon and sprinkle with brown sugar mixture. Broil 3 to 6 minutes more or until salmon flakes easily when tested with a fork. Serve salmon with onion sauce. Makes 4 servings.

EACH SERVING: *290 cal., 12 g total fat (5 g sat. fat), 104 mg chol., 570 mg sodium, 10 g carbo., 0 g fiber, 34 g pro. Daily Values: 8% vit. A, 2% vit. C, 4% calcium, 9% iron.*

ONION MUFFINS WITH ROSEMARY AND PINE NUTS

PREP: 15 minutes **BAKE:** 20 minutes
COOL: 5 minutes

- 1½ cups coarsely chopped sweet onion
- ⅔ cup butter
- 2 cups all-purpose flour
- ⅓ cup sugar
- 3 to 4 tsp. finely snipped fresh rosemary or 1 teaspoon dried rosemary, finely crushed
- 2 tsp. baking powder
- ½ tsp. salt
- 2 eggs, lightly beaten
- ⅓ cup milk
- ¼ cup pine nuts or slivered almonds, toasted and coarsely chopped

1. Preheat oven to 350°F. Grease twelve 2½-inch muffin cups or line with paper bake cups; set aside. In a large skillet cook onion in hot butter for 8 minutes or until tender; cool slightly.

2. In a large bowl combine flour, sugar, rosemary, baking powder, and salt. Make a well in center of flour mixture; set aside.

3. In a small bowl combine eggs and milk. Add egg mixture and onion mixture all at once to flour mixture. Stir just until moistened (the batter should be lumpy). Gently stir in pine nuts.

4. Divide batter among muffin cups. Bake about 20 minutes or until muffin tops are golden brown and a wooden toothpick inserted in centers comes out clean. Cool in muffin cups on a wire rack for 5 minutes. Remove from muffin cups; serve warm. Makes 12 muffins.

EACH MUFFIN: *232 cal., 13 g total fat (7 g sat. fat), 63 mg chol., 246 mg sodium, 24 g carbo., 1 g fiber, 4 g pro. Daily Values: 8% vit. A, 2% vit. C, 8% calcium, 8% iron.*

ROASTED ONIONS AND BEANS

PREP: 20 minutes **ROAST:** 40 minutes

- 2 large sweet onions, cut into thin wedges (4 cups)
- 2 Tbsp. olive oil
- ¾ tsp. lemon-pepper seasoning
- 1 lb. green beans, trimmed and cut into 2-inch pieces, or 3 cups frozen cut green beans, thawed
- 1 cup coarse Italian country bread crumbs
- ¼ cup chopped walnuts
- ¼ cup snipped fresh Italian (flat-leaf) parsley
- 2 Tbsp. olive oil

1. Preheat oven to 425°F. In a shallow roasting pan combine onion, 2 tablespoons oil, and lemon-pepper seasoning; toss to coat. Roast, uncovered, for 15 minutes.

2. Stir in green beans; roast for 20 minutes or until beans are tender, stirring once.

3. Meanwhile, in a small bowl combine bread crumbs, walnuts, parsley, and the 2 tablespoons oil. Stir roasted vegetables; sprinkle with crumb mixture. Roast for 5 minutes more or until golden brown. Serve vegetable mixture with a spatula. Makes 8 servings.

EACH SERVING: *139 cal., 9 g total fat (1 g sat. fat), 0 mg chol., 146 mg sodium, 13 g carbo., 3 g fiber, 2 g pro. Daily Values: 10% vit. A, 22% vit. C, 5% calcium, 6% iron.*

TWO-TONE BALSAMIC-ONION SPIRAL ROLLS

No need to make a yeast dough from scratch. These rolls get a head start with loaves of white and whole wheat frozen bread dough. Remember to allow plenty of time for the doughs to thaw following package directions.

PREP: 35 minutes **RISE:** 45 minutes
BAKE: 25 minutes **COOL:** 15 minutes

- 2 slices bacon
- 2 cups chopped onion (2 large)
- ¼ cup balsamic vinegar
- ½ cup grated Parmesan cheese
- ¼ tsp. ground black pepper
- 1 1-lb. loaf frozen white bread dough, thawed
- 1 1-lb. loaf frozen whole wheat bread dough, thawed
- 1 egg yolk, lightly beaten
- 1 Tbsp. milk

1. Grease a 13×9×2-inch baking pan; set aside. In a large skillet cook bacon until crisp. Remove bacon, reserving drippings in skillet. Drain bacon on paper towels; crumble bacon and set aside.

2. Cook onion in bacon drippings over medium heat for 5 minutes or until onion is tender. Carefully stir in vinegar. Simmer, uncovered, over medium-low heat for 1 to 2 minutes or until most of the liquid has evaporated. Remove from heat. Stir in Parmesan and pepper. Cool completely.

3. Meanwhile, on a lightly floured surface, roll each loaf of dough into a 16×10-inch rectangle. Spread onion mixture over white dough rectangle; sprinkle with bacon. Top with wheat dough rectangle. Roll up rectangles together, starting from a long side. Seal seam. Slice roll crosswise into 16 pieces. Place, cut sides down, in prepared pan.

4. Cover loosely and let dough rise in a warm place until nearly double in size (about 45 minutes).

5. Preheat oven to 375°F. In a small bowl beat together egg yolk and milk. Brush dough with egg mixture.

6. Bake about 25 minutes or until roll tops are light brown. Remove from oven. Invert onto a wire rack. Cool slightly, about 15 minutes. Invert again onto a serving platter. Serve warm. Makes 16 rolls.

EACH ROLL: *189 cal., 4 g total fat (1 g sat. fat), 18 mg chol., 237 mg sodium, 29 g carbo., 1 g fiber, 7 g pro. Daily Values: 1% vit. A, 2% vit. C, 6% calcium, 2% iron.*

SOUTHERN SPECIALTIES

SWEET POTATO PUDDING

PREP: 25 minutes **BAKE:** 1½ hours **COOL:** 30 minutes

1½ lb. sweet potatoes (1 to 2 large)
3 eggs, lightly beaten
1 cup half-and-half or milk
½ cup sugar
¼ cup yellow cornmeal
¼ cup dark corn syrup
2 Tbsp. butter, melted
1 Tbsp. vanilla
½ tsp. ground nutmeg
¼ tsp. salt
¾ cup flaked coconut
¾ cup chopped pecans

1. Preheat oven to 300°F. Lightly grease bottom and sides of a 2-quart square baking dish; set aside. Peel and coarsely shred sweet potatoes (about 4 cups). In a large bowl combine eggs, half-and-half, sugar, cornmeal, corn syrup, butter, vanilla, nutmeg, and salt. Stir in shredded sweet potato, ½ cup of the coconut, and ½ cup of the pecans. Transfer mixture to prepared baking dish. (If desired, cover and refrigerate for up to 24 hours.)

2. Bake, uncovered, for 1 hour. Sprinkle with remaining coconut and pecans. Bake, uncovered, for 30 minutes more or until a knife inserted near the center comes out clean. Cool on wire rack about 30 minutes. Serve warm. Makes 9 servings.

EACH SERVING: *307 cal., 16 g total fat (6 g sat. fat), 87 mg chol., 172 mg sodium, 37 g carbo., 3 g fiber, 5 g pro. Daily Values: 137% vit. A, 2% vit. C, 6% calcium, 6% iron.*

CREAMED COLLARD GREENS

Red Swiss chard will tint the cream pink. To avoid discoloration, choose a chard variety with white stems.

PREP: 30 minutes **COOK:** 27 minutes

3 lb. collard greens or Swiss chard
¼ cup butter
1 cup chopped onion (1 large)
2 cloves garlic, minced
1 cup whipping cream
½ tsp. salt
¼ tsp. ground black pepper

1. Trim stems from collard greens; chop leaves (about 24 cups lightly packed greens). In a very large Dutch oven cook greens in lightly salted boiling water for 20 minutes. (If using Swiss chard, cook 5 minutes.) Drain.

2. Place greens in a very large bowl of ice water. Allow to stand for a few minutes to cool, stirring occasionally. Drain in a colander, pressing out excess water. Arrange greens on a tray or baking sheet lined with paper towels; pat dry and set aside.

3. In a large skillet heat butter over medium heat. Add onion and garlic. Cook and stir about 5 minutes or until tender. Add cream, salt, and pepper. Bring to boiling; reduce heat. Simmer, uncovered, for 2 minutes or until slightly thickened. Add greens. Stir to combine; heat through. Makes 8 (½-cup) servings.

EACH SERVING: *212 cal., 18 g total fat (11 g sat. fat), 56 mg chol., 232 mg sodium, 12 g carbo., 6 g fiber, 5 g pro. Daily Values: 239% vit. A, 102% vit. C, 27% calcium, 2% iron.*

BLACK-EYED PEA CAKES WITH SPICY DRESSING

PREP: 25 minutes **BAKE:** 20 minutes

⅔ cup soft bread crumbs
¼ cup mayonnaise
1 egg, beaten
1 tsp. ground cumin
1 tsp. dried minced onion
1 tsp. coarse-grain brown mustard
1 15- to 16-oz. can black-eyed peas, rinsed, drained, and mashed
Nonstick cooking spray
⅓ cup mayonnaise
¼ cup dairy sour cream
2 Tbsp. bottled salsa
1 tsp. prepared horseradish
½ tsp. Cajun seasoning

1. Preheat oven to 425°F. In a medium bowl combine bread crumbs, the ¼ cup mayonnaise, egg, cumin, onion, and mustard; mix well. Add black-eyed peas; mix well (mixture will be soft). Lightly coat a baking sheet with cooking spray. Using a scant ¼ cup for each, drop pea mixture into 8 mounds on baking sheet. Spread each mound into a 3-inch cake. Coat cakes with additional cooking spray.

2. Bake, uncovered, for 10 minutes; turn and bake for 10 minutes more. Meanwhile, for dressing, in a small bowl stir together the ⅓ cup mayonnaise and remaining ingredients. Serve with black-eyed pea cakes. Makes 4 servings.

EACH SERVING: *456 cal., 31 g total fat (6 g sat. fat), 70 mg chol., 742 mg sodium, 34 g carbo., 6 g fiber, 11 g pro. Daily Values: 5% vit. A, 1% vit. C, 10% calcium, 9% iron.*

CORN BREAD SALAD

PREP: 20 minutes **BAKE:** 20 minutes
CHILL: 2 hours

1 8.5-oz. pkg. corn muffin mix
2 15- to 16-oz. cans pinto beans, rinsed and drained
1 15.25-oz. can whole kernel corn, drained
2 medium tomatoes, chopped
1 medium green sweet pepper, chopped
½ cup sliced green onion
8 slices bacon, crisp-cooked, drained, and crumbled
1 cup mayonnaise or salad dressing
1 8-oz. carton dairy sour cream
1 0.4-oz. envelope ranch dry salad dressing mix
2 cups shredded cheddar cheese

1. Preheat oven to 400°F. Prepare and bake muffin mix according to package directions. Cool completely and coarsely crumble.

2. In a large bowl combine beans, corn, tomato, sweet pepper, green onion, and bacon; set aside. For dressing, in a medium bowl combine mayonnaise, sour cream, and dry salad dressing mix; set aside.

3. In a 3-quart glass serving dish layer half of the corn bread, half of the bean mixture, and half of the cheese. Spread with half of the dressing. Repeat layers. Cover and chill for 2 to 24 hours. Makes 10 to 12 servings.

EACH SERVING: *564 cal., 37 g total fat (13 g sat. fat), 68 mg chol., 1,126 mg sodium, 38 g carbo., 6 g fiber, 16 g pro. Daily Values: 16% vit. A, 28% vit. C, 28% calcium, 14% iron.*

LOW FAT KID FRIENDLY

CORN BREAD MUFFINS

PREP: 25 minutes **ROAST:** 45 minutes
BAKE: 25 minutes **STAND:** 10 minutes

6 medium tomatoes
1 cup chopped onion (1 large)
3 Tbsp. olive oil
1 tsp. garlic powder
1 tsp. sea salt or ¾ tsp. salt
1 tsp. freshly ground black pepper
1 8.5-oz. pkg. corn muffin mix
4 oz. smoked cheddar cheese, shredded (1 cup)
1 cup frozen whole kernel corn, thawed
1 4-oz. can diced green chiles, drained
¼ cup milk
¼ cup dairy sour cream
1 egg, lightly beaten
Nonstick cooking spray

1. Preheat oven to 350°F. Trim ends off tomatoes; remove cores. Slice tomatoes in half horizontally to make 12 slices. Line a 15×10×1-inch baking pan with parchment paper. Place tomato slices and onion in the prepared pan. Drizzle with oil. Sprinkle with garlic powder, salt, and black pepper. Roast for 45 minutes. Remove from oven. Increase oven temperature to 400°F.

2. Meanwhile, in a bowl combine muffin mix, cheese, corn, chile peppers, milk, sour cream, and egg. Stir just until combined. Set aside. Coat twelve 3¼- to 3½-inch muffin cups with cooking spray. Place a tomato slice and some of the onion in the bottom of each muffin cup. Spoon corn mixture on top of tomato slices, filling muffin cups nearly full.

3. Bake for 25 to 30 minutes or until tops are golden brown and a wooden toothpick inserted into muffins comes out clean. Let stand in cups on wire racks for 10 minutes. Run a thin metal spatula around edges to loosen from sides of pan. Invert muffins onto a serving plate. Serve warm. Makes 24 muffins.

EACH MUFFIN: *100 cal., 5 g total fat (2 g sat. fat), 15 mg chol., 241 mg sodium, 11 g carbo., 1 g fiber, 3 g pro. Daily Values: 7% vit. A, 10% vit. C, 6% calcium, 3% iron.*

HAM WITH HORSERADISH GLAZE

PREP: 10 minutes **ROAST:** 1½ hours

1 6- to 8-lb. cooked ham with bone (rump or shank portion)
¾ cup apple jelly
¾ cup pineapple preserves
3 Tbsp. prepared horseradish
1 Tbsp. dry mustard
½ tsp. ground black pepper

1. Preheat oven to 325°F. Score ham by making cuts in a diamond pattern. Place ham on a rack in shallow roasting pan. Insert an oven-going meat thermometer into center of ham; make sure thermometer does not touch bone. Roast, uncovered, for 1¼ to 1¾ hours or until thermometer registers 130°F.

2. Meanwhile, in a small saucepan combine apple jelly, pineapple preserves, horseradish, mustard, and pepper. Heat and stir just until jelly and preserves melt. Brush some glaze over ham. Roast for 15 to 30 minutes more or until thermometer registers 140°F, brushing twice with some remaining glaze. Slice ham; serve with remaining glaze. Makes 16 to 20 servings.

EACH SERVING: *359 cal., 18 g total fat (6 g sat. fat), 90 mg chol., 1,363 mg sodium, 24 g carbo., 0 g fiber, 26 g pro. Daily Values: 1% vit. A, 4% vit. C, 2% calcium, 11% iron.*

LOW FAT

SQUASH CORN BREAD

PREP: 20 minutes **BAKE:** 25 minutes

1 cup yellow cornmeal
¾ cup whole wheat flour
1 Tbsp. sugar
2 tsp. baking powder
1 tsp. salt
½ tsp. baking soda
Nonstick cooking spray
1¼ cups buttermilk
2 eggs, lightly beaten
1½ cups finely shredded yellow summer squash (about 1 large)

1. Preheat oven to 400°F. In a large bowl stir together cornmeal, flour, sugar, baking powder, salt, and baking soda; set aside.

2. Coat a 9-inch cast-iron skillet or 9×1½-inch round metal baking pan with cooking spray. Place in the preheated oven for 2 minutes.

3. In a medium bowl combine buttermilk and eggs. Add egg mixture all at once to flour mixture. Stir just until moistened. Gently stir in squash. Pour batter into hot skillet or pan. Bake for 25 to 30 minutes or until a wooden toothpick inserted near the center comes out clean. Serve warm. Makes 8 servings.

EACH SERVING: *145 cal., 2 g total fat (1 g sat. fat), 54 mg chol., 489 mg sodium, 26 g carbo., 3 g fiber, 6 g pro. Daily Values: 3% vit. A, 7% vit. C, 8% calcium, 5% iron.*

YOUR BEST EASTER DINNER EVER

FAST!

DEVILED EGG SALAD

START TO FINISH: 30 minutes

- 7 hard-cooked eggs*
- 3 Tbsp. salad dressing or mayonnaise
- 1 Tbsp. chopped fresh dill
- 1 clove garlic, minced
- 5 dashes bottled hot pepper sauce
- ⅛ tsp. salt
- 6 cups torn Boston or Bibb lettuce
- 2 cups grape tomatoes or cherry tomatoes, halved, if desired
- 1 medium red sweet pepper, chopped
- 4 slices bacon, crisp-cooked, drained, and crumbled
- 3 green onions, sliced
- 1 recipe Dill Vinaigrette

1. Halve hard-cooked eggs lengthwise and remove yolks. Set whites aside. Place yolks in a small bowl; mash with a fork. Add salad dressing, dill, garlic, hot pepper sauce, and salt. Stuff egg white halves with yolk mixture. Set aside.

2. Arrange lettuce, tomatoes, sweet pepper, bacon, and green onion on a large serving platter. Arrange stuffed eggs on top of greens mixture. Drizzle with Dill Vinaigrette. Makes 6 to 8 servings.

DILL VINAIGRETTE: In a screw-top jar combine ⅓ cup olive oil or salad oil; 2 tablespoons tarragon vinegar; 1 tablespoon chopped fresh dill; 2 teaspoons Dijon-style mustard; 1 clove garlic, minced; ¼ teaspoon salt; and ¼ teaspoon bottled hot pepper sauce. Cover; shake well.

*TO HARD-COOK EGGS: In a large saucepan place eggs in a single layer. Add enough cold water to cover eggs by 1 inch. Bring to a rapid boil over high heat. Remove from heat and cover. Let stand for 15 minutes; drain. Run cold water over the eggs or place them in ice water until cool enough to handle; drain. Peel.

EACH SERVING: *269 cal., 22 g total fat (4 g sat. fat), 254 mg chol., 427 mg sodium, 8 g carbo., 2 g fiber, 11 g pro. Daily Values: 67% vit. A, 82% vit. C, 7% calcium, 11% iron.*

LOW FAT

CHERRY-STUFFED HAM

PREP: 35 minutes **STAND:** 15 minutes **BAKE:** 2 hours + 10 minutes

- 1 cup dried tart cherries, chopped
- ½ cup cherry juice or orange juice
- 1 3- to 4-lb. cooked boneless ham
- 1 18-oz. jar peach preserves
- 2 Tbsp. lemon juice

1. Preheat oven to 325°F. In a small saucepan combine ½ cup of the dried cherries and the cherry juice; bring to boiling. Remove from heat; let stand for 15 minutes. Drain cherries and discard juice.

2. With a sharp knife, cut three or four 1½- to 2-inch-deep slits in ham, making cuts at a right angle to the direction the ham will be sliced. Press in soaked cherries as each slit is made. Place ham on a rack in a shallow roasting pan. Insert an oven-going meat thermometer into center of ham. Cover ham with foil. Bake for 2 hours or until thermometer registers 140°F.

3. Place peach preserves in a small bowl. With kitchen shears snip any large pieces of fruit. Add remaining dried cherries and the lemon juice. Spoon ½ cup of the preserves mixture over ham. Bake, uncovered, for 10 minutes.

4. In a small saucepan heat remaining preserves mixture and pass with ham. Makes 10 to 12 servings.

EACH SERVING: *413 cal., 12 g total fat (4 g sat. fat), 78 mg chol., 1,795 mg sodium, 52 g carbo., 3 g fiber, 23 g pro. Daily Values: 8% vit. A, 19% vit. C, 5% calcium, 10% iron.*

APRICOT-GLAZED HENS WITH WHITE AND WILD RICE

PREP: 25 minutes **COOK:** 50 minutes
ROAST: 1 hour + 10 minutes

- 3 1¼- to 1½-lb. Cornish game hens, halved lengthwise
- 2 Tbsp. butter, melted
- 2 tsp. snipped fresh thyme or ¼ tsp. dried thyme, crushed
- ½ tsp. salt
- ¼ tsp. ground black pepper
- ⅓ cup apricot preserves
- 1 Tbsp. lemon juice or cider vinegar
- 1 recipe White and Wild Rice

1. Preheat oven to 375°F. Place hens, cut sides down, in a 15×10×1-inch baking pan. In a small bowl combine butter, half of the fresh or dried thyme, the salt, and pepper; brush over hens. Roast hens, covered, for 1 hour.
2. Meanwhile, for apricot glaze, in a small bowl combine preserves, lemon juice, and remaining thyme. Brush over hens. Roast, uncovered, for 10 to 15 minutes more or until juices run clear (180°F), brushing once with apricot glaze.
3. Spoon White and Wild Rice onto a serving platter. Arrange hens on top of rice. Makes 6 servings.

WHITE AND WILD RICE: In a large saucepan bring one 14-ounce can chicken broth and ¾ cup water to boiling. Stir in ½ cup wild rice; return to boiling. Simmer, covered, for 30 minutes. Stir in ½ cup uncooked long grain rice and ½ cup sliced green onion. Simmer, covered, for 20 minutes more or until rice is tender. Remove from heat; stir in ½ cup chopped toasted walnuts and 1 teaspoon snipped fresh thyme.
EACH SERVING: *589 cal., 33 g total fat (9 g sat. fat), 184 mg chol., 580 mg sodium, 37 g carbo., 2 g fiber, 35 g pro. Daily Values: 7% vit. A, 10% vit. C, 5% calcium, 15% iron.*

FAST!

ASPARAGUS WITH CITRUS-BASIL DRESSING

PREP: 15 minutes **COOK:** 1 minute

- ¾ cup light mayonnaise or salad dressing
- ¼ cup light dairy sour cream
- ½ cup snipped fresh basil
- 2 Tbsp. finely chopped oil-packed dried tomatoes
- 2 tsp. finely shredded lime or lemon peel
- 2 Tbsp. lime or lemon juice
- 2½ lb. fresh asparagus, trimmed

1. For dressing, in a medium bowl combine mayonnaise, sour cream, basil, tomatoes, lime peel, and lime juice.

2. In a Dutch oven bring 2 inches of lightly salted water to boiling. Add asparagus; return to boiling. Cook for 1 minute. Drain immediately and transfer to a serving platter. Spoon mayonnaise mixture over asparagus. Makes 10 servings.
EACH SERVING: *79 cal., 6 g total fat (1 g sat. fat), 8 mg chol., 118 mg sodium, 6 g carbo., 1 g fiber, 2 g pro. Daily Values: 12% vit. A, 10% vit. C, 3% calcium, 8% iron.*

LOW FAT

CHICKEN WITH LEMON-PARMESAN RICE

PREP: 25 minutes **COOK:** 20 minutes
STAND: 5 minutes

- 6 skinless, boneless chicken breast halves (about 2 lb. total)
  Salt
  Freshly ground black pepper
- 2 Tbsp. olive oil or cooking oil
- 2 cloves garlic, minced
- 1⅓ cups long grain rice
- 1½ cups fresh mushrooms, quartered
- ½ cup sliced green onion
- 1 8- to 9-oz. pkg. frozen artichoke hearts, thawed and quartered
- 2 14-oz. cans reduced-sodium chicken broth
- 2 tsp. finely shredded lemon peel
- 1 Tbsp. lemon juice
- 1 oz. Parmesan cheese, finely shredded
- ¼ tsp. cayenne pepper
- 1 oz. Parmesan cheese, shaved or finely shredded
  Sliced green onion tops

1. Sprinkle chicken lightly with salt and black pepper. In a very large skillet heat oil over medium heat. Add chicken breasts and cook for 2 minutes on each side; remove from skillet. Add garlic and rice; cook and stir for 1 minute. Stir in mushrooms, green onion, and artichoke hearts. Add chicken broth, lemon peel, lemon juice, shredded Parmesan cheese, and cayenne pepper. Bring to boiling.
2. Top with browned chicken. Reduce heat; cook, covered, for 20 to 25 minutes or until chicken is no longer pink (170°F) and rice is tender. Remove from heat and let stand for 5 minutes.
3. Sprinkle with shaved Parmesan cheese and green onion tops. Makes 6 servings.
EACH SERVING: *434 cal., 10 g total fat (3 g sat. fat), 96 mg chol., 635 mg sodium, 39 g carbo., 3 g fiber, 45 g pro. Daily Values: 5% vit. A, 16% vit. C, 16% calcium, 19% iron.*

THREE-CHEESE EASTER PIE

PREP: 35 minutes **BAKE:** 1 hour
STAND: 15 minutes

- 2 cups all-purpose flour
- ½ tsp. salt
- ⅔ cup shortening
- 3 to 5 Tbsp. cold water
- 1 egg yolk
- 6 eggs
- ⅔ cup half-and-half, light cream, or milk
- 6 oz. shredded Monterey Jack cheese (1½ cups)
- 4 oz. Canadian-style bacon, chopped
- ⅓ cup grated Parmesan cheese
- 4 oz. provolone cheese, shredded (1 cup)
- ¼ cup chopped green onion
- ¼ tsp. ground black pepper
- 1 egg white, lightly beaten
- 1 Tbsp. water

1. Preheat oven to 350°F. For pastry, in a large mixing bowl stir together flour and salt. Using a pastry blender, cut in shortening until pieces are pea size. Combine 3 tablespoons water and the egg yolk; sprinkle 1 tablespoon of the yolk mixture over part of the flour mixture and toss with a fork. Push moistened pastry to side of bowl. Repeat, using 1 tablespoon of mixture at a time, until flour mixture is moistened. If necessary, use additional water. Divide pastry in half and form into balls.
2. On a lightly floured surface, use your hands to slightly flatten one pastry ball. Roll pastry from center to edges into a circle 12 inches in diameter. Wrap pastry circle around the rolling pin. Unroll pastry into a 9-inch pie plate, easing it into the pie plate without stretching it.
3. For filling, in a large bowl beat 6 eggs. Stir in half-and-half, Monterey Jack cheese, Canadian bacon, Parmesan, provolone cheese, green onion, and pepper. Spoon into pastry-lined pie plate. Trim pastry even with rim of pie plate. Roll remaining pastry into a 12-inch circle. Cut slits in pastry. Place over filling. Trim to ½ inch beyond edge of plate. Fold top pastry under bottom pastry. Crimp edge as desired. Cover edge with foil to prevent overbrowning.
4. Bake for 45 minutes. Remove foil; brush with mixture of the 1 egg white and 1 tablespoon water. Bake for 15 to 20 minutes more or until crust is golden. Let stand 15 minutes before serving. Makes 8 servings.
EACH SERVING: *517 cal., 36 g total fat (14 g sat. fat), 230 mg chol., 648 mg sodium, 26 g carbo., 1 g fiber, 22 g pro. Daily Values: 12% vit. A, 2% vit. C, 35% calcium, 15% iron.*

LOW FAT **KID FRIENDLY**

MANGO-YOGURT POPS

PREP: 15 minutes **FREEZE:** 3 hours + overnight

- 2 medium-size ripe mangoes, seeded and peeled
- ½ cup water
- ¼ cup sugar
- ¼ cup lemon juice
- 3 6-oz. cartons vanilla low-fat yogurt
  Ice pop molds (2- to 3-oz. size) or 4-oz. paper cups*
  Wooden crafts sticks (optional)

1. In a blender combine mango, water, sugar, and lemon juice; cover and blend until smooth. Add yogurt; cover and blend until combined. Transfer mango mixture to a 3-quart rectangular baking dish. Cover and freeze about 3 hours, stirring two or three times, until edges are firm but center is still slightly soft.

2. Scrape mango mixture into a chilled large mixing bowl. Beat with an electric mixer on medium speed until smooth. Pour mango mixture into pop molds; cover with lids. Cover and freeze overnight. Remove from molds to serve. Makes 12 to 16 pops.

*NOTE: If using paper cups, cover each filled cup with a square of foil. Use a table knife to make a small slit in the center of each foil square. Slide a crafts stick through each hole and into the center of the mango mixture in each cup. Peel off paper to serve.

EACH POP: *75 cal., 1 g total fat (0 g sat. fat), 2 mg chol., 29 mg sodium, 16 g carbo., 1 g fiber, 2 g pro. Daily Values: 6% vit. A, 20% vit. C, 8% calcium.*

KID FRIENDLY

DOUGHNUT DELIGHTS

PREP: 15 minutes **BAKE:** 10 minutes **STAND:** 30 minutes

- ⅔ cup flaked coconut
- ½ cup bittersweet chocolate pieces
- 1½ tsp. shortening
- ¾ tsp. ground cinnamon
- 24 glazed doughnut holes

1. Preheat oven to 350°F. Spread coconut in a shallow baking pan. Bake for 10 minutes or until toasted, stirring two or three times (watch closely toward the end of baking to prevent coconut from burning). Set aside to cool.

2. In a medium microwave-safe bowl place chocolate pieces and shortening. Microwave on 50% power (medium) for 1 to 2 minutes or until chocolate is melted and smooth, stirring after each minute. Stir in cinnamon.

3. Arrange doughnut holes on a tray or baking sheet lined with waxed paper. Spoon melted chocolate over each doughnut hole and sprinkle with coconut. Let stand until set, about 30 minutes. To serve, arrange on a platter. (If desired, thread 2 doughnut holes onto a bamboo skewer; arrange in a spoke fashion on a platter. Decorate the ends of the skewers with colored curling ribbon, choosing colors to fit the occasion.) Makes 24 doughnut holes.

EACH DOUGHNUT HOLE: *121 cal., 7 g total fat (3 g sat. fat), 1 mg chol., 82 mg sodium, 13 g carbo., 1 g fiber, 2 g pro. Daily Values: 1% calcium, 2% iron.*

CHOCO-CRAN CUT-UPS

PREP: 25 minutes **CHILL:** 1 hour

- 1 16-oz. box toasted honey-flavored corn and wheat cereal flakes with oats (8 cups)
- ¾ cup chopped peanuts
- ⅔ cup dried cranberries
- 1 cup semisweet chocolate pieces
- ¼ cup honey
- 3 Tbsp. butter
- 5 cups tiny marshmallows
- 2 tsp. shortening

1. Line a 13×9×2-inch pan with foil, extending foil over edges of pan. Grease foil; set aside.

2. In a very large bowl combine cereal, peanuts, cranberries, and ½ cup of the chocolate pieces; set aside.

3. In a large microwave-safe bowl combine honey and butter. Microwave on 100% power (high) for 1 minute. Stir until butter melts. Add marshmallows; toss to coat. Microwave on high for 1½ minutes. Stir until melted and combined. Add marshmallow mixture to cereal mixture; toss to coat. Press cereal mixture firmly into prepared pan.

4. In a small bowl combine remaining chocolate pieces and shortening. Microwave on 50% power (medium) for 1 minute or until melted, stirring once. Drizzle over bars.

5. Chill 1 hour or until set. Use foil to lift from pan. Cut into bars. Store, covered, at room temperature for up to 3 days. Makes 32 bars.

EACH BAR: *144 cal., 5 g total fat (2 g sat. fat), 3 mg chol., 94 mg sodium, 24 g carbo., 1 g fiber, 2 g pro. Daily Values: 6% vit. A, 1% calcium, 16% iron.*

ROCKY ROAD POPCORN ON A STICK

PREP: 30 minutes **STAND:** 1 hour

- Nonstick cooking spray
- ½ cup miniature candy-coated milk chocolate pieces
- 3 cups popped popcorn
- ⅓ cup dry-roasted unsalted peanuts
- ⅓ cup dried cranberries
- ½ cup tiny marshmallows
- 6 oz. chocolate-flavored candy coating, chopped
- 1 Tbsp. creamy peanut butter
- 12 crafts sticks

1. Lightly coat twelve 2½-inch muffin cups with cooking spray. Divide candy-coated pieces among muffin cups. Set aside.

2. In a large bowl combine popcorn, peanuts, cranberries, and marshmallows; set aside.

3. In a small saucepan melt coating and peanut butter over low heat until smooth, stirring frequently. Pour warm mixture over popcorn mixture; stir until well coated. Quickly spoon mixture into prepared muffin cups, pressing tightly with the back of a spoon. Insert a stick into each. Let stand for at least 1 hour.

4. Use a small metal spatula or a table knife to loosen popcorn mixture from sides of muffin cups. Gently lift out of cups. Wrap each individually in plastic wrap. Serve the same day. Makes 12 servings.

EACH SERVING: *184 cal., 10 g total fat (6 g sat. fat), 1 mg chol., 16 mg sodium, 23 g carbo., 1 g fiber, 2 g pro. Daily Values: 1% vit. A, 1% calcium, 2% iron.*

TRAIL MIX TRIANGLES

PREP: 25 minutes **BAKE:** 18 minutes
COOL: 20 minutes

- 1 6-oz. pkg. purchased nut and chocolate trail mix (about 1 cup)
- 2 Tbsp. honey
- 1 Tbsp. granulated sugar
- 1 Tbsp. orange juice
- ¼ tsp. ground cinnamon
- ⅛ tsp. ground nutmeg
- 12 sheets frozen phyllo dough (14×9-inch rectangles), thawed
- ½ cup butter, melted
- Powdered sugar

1. Preheat oven to 375°F. Line a baking sheet with parchment paper; set aside. Place trail mix in a food processor or blender. Cover and process or blend until coarsely chopped. Transfer to a medium bowl. Stir in honey, granulated sugar, orange juice, cinnamon, and nutmeg; set aside.

2. Place one phyllo sheet on a work surface; brush with some of the butter. Top with another phyllo sheet and brush with more butter. Repeat with two more sheets. (Keep remaining phyllo covered with plastic wrap until needed.) Cut the phyllo stack lengthwise into thirds. Place about 1 tablespoon of the nut mixture on the short end of one of the phyllo strips. Bring a corner over filling so it lines up with the other side of the strip. Continue folding strip in a triangular shape. Repeat with remaining phyllo strips. Place triangles on prepared baking sheet. Repeat stacking, brushing, and folding with remaining phyllo sheets, butter, and filling.

3. Bake for 18 to 20 minutes or until golden. Remove and cool slightly on a wire rack. Sprinkle with powdered sugar; serve warm. Makes 9 triangles.

EACH TRIANGLE: *248 cal., 17 g total fat (8 g sat. fat), 27 mg chol., 155 mg sodium, 23 g carbo., 1 g fiber, 3 g pro. Daily Values: 6% vit. A, 2% vit. C, 2% calcium, 6% iron.*

FAST!

TIRAMISU TO GO

START TO FINISH: 20 minutes

- 6 waffle ice cream cones
- 1 Tbsp. granulated sugar
- 2 Tbsp. coffee liqueur or brandy
- 2 cups ½-inch cubes pound cake
- ½ of an 8-oz. pkg. cream cheese, softened
- ¼ cup powdered sugar
- ¼ cup dairy sour cream
- 1 Tbsp. coffee liqueur or brandy
- ¾ cup whipping cream
- ½ oz. bittersweet chocolate, grated
- 12 chocolate-covered espresso beans, coarsely chopped

1. Place a cone in each of 6 glasses or cups; set aside. In a bowl combine granulated sugar and 2 tablespoons liqueur; stir to combine. Add pound cake cubes and toss to coat.

2. In a large mixing bowl beat cheese with an electric mixer on medium to high speed until smooth. Add powdered sugar, sour cream, and 1 tablespoon liqueur. Beat until combined.

3. Beat cream until soft peaks form. Fold half of the cream into the cream cheese mixture; fold in pound cake cubes. Divide evenly among cones. Top with remaining whipped cream. Sprinkle with grated chocolate and espresso beans. Makes 6 servings.

EACH SERVING: *391 cal., 27 g total fat (16 g sat. fat), 112 mg chol., 181 mg sodium, 33 g carbo., 0 g fiber, 4 g pro. Daily Values: 18% vit. A, 6% calcium, 8% iron.*

FAST! LOW FAT

BERRY-FILLED WONTON BITES

PREP: 20 minutes **BAKE:** 8 minutes

- Nonstick cooking spray
- 24 wonton wrappers
- 2 teaspoons sugar
- ¼ cup seedless raspberry preserves
- ¼ tsp. ground cinnamon
- 1 cup fresh raspberries
- ⅔ cup small blueberries
- ¼ cup toffee-glazed sliced almonds

1. Preheat oven to 375°F. Lightly coat twenty-four 1¾-inch muffin cups with cooking spray. Press 1 wrapper into each cup. Spray wrappers with cooking spray and sprinkle with sugar. Bake for 8 to 10 minutes or until crisp. Cool slightly on wire rack; remove from cups. Cool completely. (If desired, place in an airtight container and store for up to 3 days.)

2. In a small saucepan heat preserves just until melted; stir in cinnamon. Gently fold in berries. Divide evenly among prepared cups. Serve within 4 hours of filling. Sprinkle with nuts just before serving. Makes 24 servings.

EACH SERVING: *46 cal., 1 g total fat (0 g sat. fat), 1 mg chol., 52 mg sodium, 9 g carbo., 1 g fiber, 1 g pro. Daily Values: 3% vit. C, 1% calcium, 2% iron.*

BEST SUMMER BURGER

SASSY TURKEY BURGERS

PREP: 25 minutes **GRILL:** 14 minutes

- 1 cup chopped tomato (2 medium)
- ½ cup finely chopped onion (1 medium)
- ¼ cup seeded and finely chopped fresh jalapeño chile pepper (2)*
- ¼ cup bottled salsa
- 1½ lb. uncooked ground turkey
- 8 oz. bulk pork sausage
- 2 Tbsp. Worcestershire sauce
- ½ tsp. ground cumin
- ¼ tsp. salt
- ¼ tsp. ground black pepper
- 6 hamburger buns, split and, if desired, toasted

1. For the salsa topping, in a small bowl combine tomato, ¼ cup of the onion, the jalapeño, and salsa. Cover and chill until serving time.

2. For the burgers, in a large bowl combine remaining ¼ cup onion, turkey, pork sausage, Worcestershire sauce, cumin, salt, and black pepper; mix well. Shape mixture into six ¾-inch-thick patties.

3. For a charcoal grill, place patties on the rack of an uncovered grill directly over medium coals. Grill for 14 to 18 minutes or until done (165°F), turning once halfway through grilling. (For a gas grill, preheat grill. Reduce heat to medium. Place patties on grill rack over heat. Cover; grill as above.) Top burgers with salsa mixture and serve in buns. Makes 6 burgers.

*NOTE: Because hot chile peppers contain volatile oils that can burn your skin and eyes, avoid direct contact with chiles as much as possible. When working with chile peppers, wear plastic or rubber gloves. If your bare hands touch the chile peppers, wash your hands well with soap and water.

EACH BURGER: *430 cal., 21 g total fat (6 g sat. fat), 117 mg chol., 772 mg sodium, 27 g carbo., 2 g fiber, 30 g pro. Daily Values: 8% vit. A, 17% vit. C, 10% calcium, 21% iron.*

PORK AND PEANUT BURGERS

PREP: 30 minutes **GRILL:** 10 minutes

- ½ cup finely chopped onion (1 medium)
- ¼ cup finely chopped dry-roasted peanuts
- 1 Tbsp. snipped fresh cilantro
- 1 Tbsp. grated fresh ginger
- 3 cloves garlic, minced
- 1 tsp. salt
- ¼ to ½ tsp. crushed red pepper
- 1 lb. lean ground pork
- 1 Tbsp. sesame oil
- ⅓ cup Asian sweet chili sauce or bottled chili sauce
- 1 Tbsp. creamy peanut butter
- 1 clove garlic, minced
- 1 cup shredded bok choy
- 4 French rolls or hamburger buns, split and toasted
  Chopped peanuts (optional)

1. In a medium bowl combine onion, the ¼ cup peanuts, cilantro, ginger, 3 cloves garlic, salt, and crushed red pepper. Add ground pork; mix well. Shape mixture into four ½-inch-thick patties to fit rolls. Brush patties with sesame oil; cover and set aside.

2. For sauce, in a small bowl stir together chili sauce, peanut butter, and the 1 clove garlic; set aside.

3. For a charcoal grill, place patties on the rack of an uncovered grill directly over medium coals. Grill for 10 to 13 minutes or until done (160°F), turning once halfway through grilling. (For a gas grill, preheat grill. Reduce heat to medium. Place patties on grill rack over heat. Cover; grill as above.) Or cook patties in a large skillet over medium heat for 9 to 12 minutes or until done (160°F), turning once halfway through cooking.

4. Place bok choy on roll bottoms. Top with burgers, sauce, chopped peanuts (if desired), and roll tops. Makes 4 burgers.

EACH BURGER: *574 cal., 36 g total fat (11 g sat. fat), 82 mg chol., 1,175 mg sodium, 37 g carbo., 3 g fiber, 26 g pro. Daily Values: 18% vit. A, 19% vit. C, 9% calcium, 17% iron.*

CORNMEAL-CRUSTED TUNA BURGERS

PREP: 30 minutes **BAKE:** 18 minutes

- 1½ lb. fresh tuna fillets
- ½ cup finely shredded carrot
- 2 green onions, chopped
- ½ cup panko (Japanese-style) bread crumbs
- 2 Tbsp. creamy Dijon-style mustard blend
- ½ tsp. salt
- ¼ tsp. bottled hot pepper sauce
- ¼ cup yellow cornmeal
- 1 recipe Tangy Dill Coleslaw

1. Preheat oven to 425°F. Grease a 15×10×1-inch baking pan; set aside. Finely chop tuna. In a large bowl combine tuna, carrot, green onion, ¼ cup of the bread crumbs, the mustard blend, salt, and hot pepper sauce. With wet hands, shape mixture into six ½-inch-thick patties.

2. In a shallow dish combine remaining bread crumbs and cornmeal; coat tuna patties with bread crumb mixture. Place patties in prepared pan.

3. Bake, uncovered, for 18 minutes or until done (160°F), turning patties once halfway through baking. Serve burgers with Tangy Dill Coleslaw. Makes 6 burgers.

TANGY DILL COLESLAW: In a large bowl stir together ¼ cup light mayonnaise, ¼ cup light dairy sour cream, 2 tablespoons creamy Dijon-style mustard blend, 1 tablespoon snipped fresh dill, and 1 tablespoon cider vinegar. Add one 10-ounce package finely shredded green cabbage and ¼ cup finely chopped dill pickle; mix well. Cover and refrigerate until serving time.

EACH BURGER (WITH COLESLAW): *277 cal., 10 g total fat (2 g sat. fat), 49 mg chol., 577 mg sodium, 17 g carbo., 2 g fiber, 29 g pro. Daily Values: 84% vit. A, 28% vit. C, 5% calcium, 10% iron.*

MEXI-TURKEY BURGERS

PREP: 20 minutes **GRILL:** 14 minutes

- 1 cup radishes, chopped
- 6 green onions, chopped
- 1 cup fresh cilantro, snipped
- ¼ tsp. salt
- 1 lb. uncooked ground turkey
- 1 4-oz. can whole green chiles, drained
- 4 1-oz. slices Monterey Jack cheese
- 4 large hamburger buns, split and toasted
- 1 cup shredded lettuce
- 4 tomato slices
- ½ cup bottled salsa

1. In a large bowl combine radishes, green onion, cilantro, and salt. Add ground turkey; mix well. Shape mixture into four ¾-inch-thick patties.

2. For a charcoal grill, place patties on the greased rack of an uncovered grill directly over medium coals. Grill for 14 to 18 minutes or until no longer pink (165°F), turning once halfway through grilling. Top burgers with chiles and cheese during the last 1 minute of grilling. (For a gas grill, preheat grill. Reduce heat to medium. Place patties on greased grill rack over heat. Cover; grill as above.) Serve burgers in buns with lettuce, tomato, and salsa. Makes 4 burgers.

EACH BURGER: *431 cal., 21 g total fat (8 g sat. fat), 115 mg chol., 908 mg sodium, 29 g carbo., 3 g fiber, 33 g pro. Daily Values: 53% vit. A, 50% vit. C, 37% calcium, 24% iron.*

RED-WHITE-AND-BLUE CHEESE BURGERS

PREP: 30 minutes **STAND:** 30 minutes **GRILL:** 14 minutes

- ¼ cup dried cranberries
- ¼ cup red wine vinegar or cider vinegar
- 2 lb. lean ground beef
- ¼ cup finely chopped red onion
- ¼ tsp. salt
- ¼ tsp. ground black pepper
- 4 oz. blue cheese, crumbled
- 6 kaiser rolls, split and toasted
- 1 recipe Blackberry Sauce
- 6 Bibb lettuce leaves and tomato slices

1. In a small bowl combine cranberries and vinegar. Cover and let stand at room temperature for 30 minutes to 1 hour.

2. In a large bowl combine ground beef, onion, salt, and pepper; mix well. Add undrained cranberries; mix until combined. Shape mixture into six ¾-inch-thick patties.

3. For a charcoal grill, place patties on the rack of an uncovered grill directly over medium coals. Grill for 14 to 18 minutes or until done (160°F), turning once halfway through grilling. Top each burger with some of the cheese during the last 1 minute of grilling. (For a gas grill, preheat grill. Reduce heat to medium. Place patties on grill rack over heat. Cover; grill as above.)

4. Spread rolls generously with Blackberry Sauce. Top roll bottoms with lettuce, burgers, tomato slices, and roll tops. Pass remaining Blackberry Sauce. Makes 6 burgers.

BLACKBERRY SAUCE: In a medium saucepan melt ¼ cup butter over medium heat. Stir in 1½ cups fresh or frozen blackberries, ¼ cup sugar, and ¼ teaspoon ground nutmeg. Cook and stir over medium heat about 15 minutes or until mixture is thickened.

EACH BURGER: *783 cal., 47 g total fat (21 g sat. fat), 148 mg chol., 833 mg sodium, 49 g carbo., 4 g fiber, 38 g pro. Daily Values: 31% vit. A, 19% vit. C, 19% calcium, 30% iron.*

ROSEMARY CHICKEN AND BRIE BURGERS

PREP: 25 minutes **COOK:** 10 minutes

- ⅓ cup fine dry bread crumbs
- ¼ cup finely shredded Parmesan cheese
- 2 Tbsp. snipped fresh parsley
- 2 tsp. snipped fresh rosemary
- ¼ tsp. salt
- ¼ tsp. ground black pepper
- 1¼ lb. uncooked ground chicken Nonstick cooking spray
- 3 oz. Brie cheese, rind removed and thinly sliced
- 4 kaiser rolls, split and toasted
- 2 Tbsp. mayonnaise
- 4 lettuce leaves
- 1 recipe Tomato Kabobs (optional)

1. In a large bowl combine bread crumbs, Parmesan cheese, parsley, rosemary, salt, and pepper. Add ground chicken; mix well. Shape mixture into four ½-inch-thick patties.

2. Lightly coat a grill pan or large skillet with cooking spray. Heat pan over medium heat. Add patties and cook for 10 to 12 minutes or until done (165°F), turning once halfway through cooking. Top each chicken patty with Brie cheese during the last 1 minute of cooking.

3. Spread bottom halves of rolls with mayonnaise; top with lettuce leaves, burgers, and roll tops. If desired, serve with Tomato Kabobs. Makes 4 burgers.

EACH BURGER (WITHOUT KABOB): *623 cal., 35 g total fat (6 g sat. fat), 28 mg chol., 871 mg sodium, 38 g carbo., 2 g fiber, 38 g pro. Daily Values: 20% vit. A, 7% vit. C, 21% calcium, 24% iron.*

TOMATO KABOBS: Measure four 6-inch sprigs of rosemary. Leaving ½ inch of leaves intact at the top of each sprig, use your fingers to pull remaining leaves down and away, exposing stems. Use a bamboo skewer to make a hole through the stem end of each of 16 cherry tomatoes. Thread 4 tomatoes onto each rosemary sprig.

MUSHROOMS

ANN GALVAN, IMLAY CITY, MICH.

CATHERINE WILKINSON, DEWEY, ARIZ.

FAST!

MUSHROOMS AND PASTA

START TO FINISH: 30 minutes

    3 Tbsp. butter
    1 Tbsp. olive oil
  ½ cup chopped onion (1 medium)
    3 cloves garlic, minced
  12 oz. fresh button mushrooms, halved or quartered (4½ cups)
    1 Tbsp. snipped fresh thyme or 1 tsp. dried thyme, crushed
  ½ tsp. salt
  ¼ tsp. ground black pepper
  ½ cup whipping cream
  ½ cup finely shredded Parmesan cheese (2 oz.)
    3 cups hot cooked pasta
       Snipped fresh parsley (optional)

1. For mushroom sauce, in a large skillet heat butter and oil over medium heat. Add onion and garlic. Cook for 4 to 5 minutes or until onion is tender, stirring occasionally. Stir in mushrooms, thyme, salt, and pepper. Cook for 4 to 5 minutes or until mushrooms are tender and lightly browned, stirring occasionally. Add cream. Bring just to boiling; reduce heat. Boil gently, uncovered, for 2 to 3 minutes or until sauce is thickened. Stir in cheese until melted.

2. To serve, place cooked pasta in a serving bowl. Spoon mushroom sauce over pasta. If desired, sprinkle with parsley. Makes 4 servings.

EACH SERVING: *425 cal., 27 g total fat (15 g sat. fat), 71 mg chol., 539 mg sodium, 36 g carbo., 3 g fiber, 12 g pro. Daily Values: 16% vit. A, 8% vit. C, 17% calcium, 12% iron.*

FAST!

MUSHROOMS IN GINGER SAUCE

START TO FINISH: 20 minutes

    2 Tbsp. butter
  ⅓ cup chopped green onion
  ⅓ cup chopped fresh cilantro
    1 Tbsp. grated fresh ginger
    4 cloves garlic, minced
  12 oz. fresh button mushrooms, sliced (about 3½ cups)
    2 Tbsp. soy sauce
  ¼ cup unsweetened coconut milk
    1 Tbsp. lime juice
       Steamed green beans or hot cooked rice (optional)

1. In a large skillet heat butter over medium-high heat. Add green onion, cilantro, ginger, and garlic. Cook and stir for 1 minute.

2. Stir mushrooms and soy sauce into skillet; cook for 2 minutes. Stir in coconut milk. Bring to boiling; reduce heat. Simmer, uncovered, about 5 minutes or until sauce thickens. Remove from heat. Stir in lime juice. Serve as a side dish or, if desired, over steamed green beans or hot cooked rice. Makes 6 side-dish servings.

EACH SERVING: *80 cal., 6 g total fat (5 g sat. fat), 10 mg chol., 374 mg sodium, 5 g carbo., 1 g fiber, 3 g pro. Daily Values: 9% vit. A, 9% vit. C, 2% calcium, 4% iron.*

ASIAN MUSHROOM TOSS

PREP: 15 minutes **COOK:** 8 minutes

- 1 Tbsp. peanut oil
- 1 Tbsp. toasted sesame oil
- 1 lb. fresh button mushrooms, quartered
- 1 large clove garlic, minced
- 2 Tbsp. soy sauce
- 1 Tbsp. rice vinegar
- ¼ tsp. crushed red pepper
- 2 cups hot cooked rice
- 2 Tbsp. snipped fresh cilantro
- 2 to 3 Tbsp. honey-roasted peanuts, coarsely chopped

1. In a large skillet combine peanut oil and sesame oil; heat over medium heat. Add mushrooms and garlic. Cook about 5 minutes or until tender, stirring occasionally. If necessary, cook for 2 to 3 minutes more or until most of the liquid has evaporated.

2. Add soy sauce, vinegar, and crushed red pepper to skillet; cook for 1 minute. Spoon mushroom mixture over hot cooked rice. Sprinkle with cilantro and peanuts. Makes 6 side-dish servings.

EACH SERVING: *144 cal., 6 g total fat (1 g sat. fat), 0 mg chol., 319 mg sodium, 18 g carbo., 1 g fiber, 5 g pro. Daily Values: 2% vit. A, 4% vit. C, 1% calcium, 6% iron.*

BACON-AND-CHEESE-STUFFED MUSHROOMS

Serve this knife-and-fork appetizer as the first course of a meal.

PREP: 30 minutes **BAKE:** 17 minutes

- 1½ cups soft bread crumbs (about 2 slices bread)
- 1 Tbsp. olive oil
- 6 3- to 4-inch-diameter fresh portobello mushrooms (about 1¼ lb.)
- 1 cup finely shredded Colby and Monterey Jack cheese (4 oz.)
- 4 slices bacon, crisp-cooked, drained, and crumbled
- ¼ cup bottled creamy Italian salad dressing
- 2 green onions, sliced
- 1 clove garlic, minced
- 6 cherry tomatoes, thinly sliced

1. Preheat oven to 400°F. For crumb topping, place bread crumbs in a 13×9×2-inch baking pan; toss with oil. Bake, uncovered, for 5 to 7 minutes or until lightly toasted, stirring once. Cool on a wire rack.

2. Meanwhile, clean mushrooms; remove and discard stems and gills. Pat dry with paper towels. Place mushrooms, rounded sides down, on a baking sheet.

3. In a medium bowl combine ½ cup of the toasted bread crumbs, the cheese, bacon, salad dressing, green onion, and garlic. Spoon mixture into mushroom caps. Top with tomato slices. Sprinkle with remaining crumbs. Bake for 12 to 15 minutes or until mushrooms are tender. Cut in half to serve. Makes 12 appetizer servings.

EACH SERVING: *109 cal., 8 g total fat (3 g sat. fat), 11 mg chol., 253 mg sodium, 6 g carbo., 1 g fiber, 5 g pro. Daily Values: 4% vit. A, 3% vit. C, 8% calcium, 3% iron.*

PORTOBELLO PARMIGIANA

PREP: 15 minutes **BAKE:** 15 minutes

- Nonstick cooking spray
- ½ cup grated Parmesan cheese
- ¼ cup seasoned fine dry bread crumbs
- ¼ tsp. paprika
- ⅛ tsp. garlic powder
- ⅛ tsp. ground black pepper
- 1 egg, lightly beaten
- 1 Tbsp. water
- 4 4-inch-diameter fresh portobello mushrooms
- ½ cup bottled roasted red sweet peppers, drained and cut into strips
- ½ cup pizza sauce
- 2 oz. thinly sliced prosciutto, cut into thin strips
- ½ cup shredded mozzarella cheese (2 oz.)

1. Preheat oven to 450°F. Lightly coat a 15×10×1-inch baking pan with cooking spray; set aside. In a medium bowl combine ¼ cup of the Parmesan cheese, the bread crumbs, paprika, garlic powder, and black pepper. In a small bowl whisk together egg and water.

2. Clean mushrooms and remove stems. If desired, use a small spoon to scrape out gills. Dip mushrooms into egg mixture, turning to coat, then into bread crumb mixture to coat (sprinkle with the crumb mixture as necessary to coat the mushrooms). Place mushrooms, rounded sides down, in prepared baking pan. Bake for 10 minutes.

3. Top mushrooms with sweet pepper strips. Spoon about 2 tablespoons pizza sauce over each. Top with prosciutto, mozzarella cheese, and remaining Parmesan cheese. Bake 5 minutes more or until heated through and cheese is melted. Makes 4 servings.

EACH SERVING: *190 cal., 9 g total fat (4 g sat. fat), 79 mg chol., 954 mg sodium, 13 g carbo., 2 g fiber, 16 g pro. Daily Values: 10% vit. A, 91% vit. C, 25% calcium, 9% iron.*

PORTOBELLO PESTO PIZZA

PREP: 10 minutes **BAKE:** 25 minutes

- 1 13.8-oz. pkg. refrigerated pizza dough
- ½ cup purchased basil pesto
- ¼ cup dairy sour cream
- 1½ cups shredded mozzarella cheese
- 2 fresh portobello mushrooms, stems removed, halved, and thinly sliced
- ¼ cup chopped red onion
- 1 Tbsp. olive oil
- 2 Tbsp. snipped fresh basil
- ¼ tsp. crushed red pepper (optional)

1. Preheat oven to 400°F. Grease a 15×10×1-inch baking pan. Unroll pizza dough into pan. Press dough to edges. Bake for 10 minutes or until the edges are light golden brown.

2. Remove crust from oven. In a small bowl combine pesto and sour cream. Spread mixture evenly over crust; sprinkle with cheese. In a medium bowl toss mushrooms and onion with oil; sprinkle over pizza.

3. Bake for 15 minutes more or until cheese is melted and vegetables are softened. Remove from oven. Sprinkle with basil and, if desired, crushed red pepper. Makes 6 servings.

EACH SERVING: *370 cal., 22 g total fat (7 g sat. fat), 33 mg chol., 580 mg sodium, 31 g carbo., 2 g fiber, 13 g pro. Daily Values: 8% vit. A, 1% vit. C, 23% calcium, 12% iron.*

ROASTED MUSHROOM MEDLEY

PREP: 25 minutes **ROAST:** 20 minutes

- 1 lb. assorted fresh mushrooms, such as cremini, stemmed shiitake, button, and/or porcini mushrooms, quartered
- 6 cloves garlic, peeled and thinly sliced
- 2 Tbsp. extra virgin olive oil
- 2 tsp. Worcestershire sauce
- 2 tsp. balsamic vinegar
- 1 tsp. dried oregano, crushed
- ¼ tsp. salt
- ¼ tsp. ground black pepper
- 2 Tbsp. snipped fresh Italian (flat-leaf) parsley

1. Preheat oven to 400°F. Place mushrooms in a 13×9×2-inch baking pan. Stir garlic slices into mushrooms. Drizzle mushroom mixture with oil, Worcestershire sauce, and vinegar. Sprinkle with oregano, salt, and pepper. Toss gently to coat.

2. Roast, uncovered, for 20 to 25 minutes or until mushrooms are tender, stirring twice. Stir in parsley just before serving. Makes 6 side-dish servings.

EACH SERVING: *65 cal., 5 g total fat (1 g sat. fat), 0 mg chol., 124 mg sodium, 4 g carbo., 1 g fiber, 3 g pro. Daily Values: 2% vit. A, 7% vit. C, 1% calcium, 4% iron.*

THE COOLEST SALADS EVER

LOW FAT · **KID FRIENDLY**

SUMMER STRAWBERRY SALAD

PREP: 20 minutes

    6 cups chopped romaine lettuce
    3 cups sliced fresh strawberries
    2 cups cubed fresh pineapple
    1 banana, sliced
    ¼ cup water
    ¼ cup cream of coconut*
    2 Tbsp. lemon juice
    1 Tbsp. yellow mustard
    ½ tsp. ground ginger
    ¼ cup sliced almonds, toasted (optional)

1. In a 4-quart bowl toss together romaine, strawberries, pineapple, and banana. (If desired, salad may be assembled and refrigerated, tightly covered, for up to 1 hour.)
2. For dressing, in a small bowl whisk together the water, cream of coconut, lemon juice, mustard, and ginger. Cover and refrigerate.
3. To serve, toss salad with dressing to coat. If desired, sprinkle with almonds. Makes 6 to 8 side-dish servings.
*NOTE: Look for cream of coconut with alcohol drink mixers in the supermarket.
EACH SERVING: *111 cal., 4 g total fat (3 g sat. fat), 0 mg chol., 35 mg sodium, 20 g carbo., 4 g fiber, 2 g pro. Daily Values: 66% vit. A, 131% vit. C, 4% calcium, 7% iron.*

FAST!

SPRING MANGO CHICKEN SALAD

START TO FINISH: 30 minutes

     6 cups torn mixed salad greens
     2 cups fresh blueberries
     1 mango, seeded, peeled, and cut up*
    12 to 16 oz. chicken breast tenderloins
        Salt and ground black pepper
     2 Tbsp. purchased garlic butter or 2 Tbsp. butter and 1 clove garlic, mashed
     2 cups broccoli florets
     ½ cup bottled blue cheese Italian vinaigrette salad dressing
        Crumbled blue cheese (optional)

1. Arrange greens on a serving platter. Top with blueberries and mango; set aside.
2. Season chicken breast tenderloins with salt and ground black pepper. In a large skillet cook chicken in 1 tablespoon of the hot garlic butter over medium heat for 6 to 8 minutes or until no longer pink, turning once. Transfer chicken to a cutting board and slice. Arrange chicken on salad.
3. In the same skillet cook broccoli in the remaining 1 tablespoon garlic butter over medium heat for 4 to 6 minutes or until tender. Place on salad. Drizzle salad with blue cheese vinaigrette. If desired, sprinkle with blue cheese. Makes 4 main-dish servings.
*NOTE: If mango is underripe, saute it with the broccoli to enhance its flavor.
EACH SERVING: *381 cal., 22 g total fat (5 g sat. fat), 59 mg chol., 469 mg sodium, 26 g carbo., 6 g fiber, 24 g pro. Daily Values: 115% vit. A, 137% vit. C, 7% calcium, 11% iron.*

FRUIT SALAD WITH A KICK

PREP: 15 minutes **CHILL:** 1 hour

- 1 6-oz. carton plain low-fat yogurt
- ¼ cup red jalapeño jelly
- ¼ cup pickled sushi ginger, finely chopped (optional)
- 3 medium apples, cored and cut into bite-size pieces
- 2 cups red seedless grapes, halved
- ½ cup dried cherries
- ¼ cup raisins
- ¼ cup chopped walnuts, toasted

1. In a large bowl combine yogurt, jelly, and, if desired, ginger. Stir until well combined. Add apple pieces, grapes, cherries, and raisins. Toss to coat.
2. Cover and chill for 1 hour. To serve, top with walnuts. Makes 10 side-dish servings.

EACH SERVING: *207 cal., 2 g total fat (0 g sat. fat), 1 mg chol., 16 mg sodium, 48 g carbo., 4 g fiber, 3 g pro. Daily Values: 4% vit. A, 12% vit. C, 7% calcium, 21% iron.*

PEPPER JACK PASTA SALAD

PREP: 25 minutes **CHILL:** up to 4 hours

- 6 oz. dried tri-color rotini pasta (2 cups)
- ½ cup bottled cucumber ranch salad dressing
- 1 Tbsp. yellow mustard
- ¼ tsp. salt
- 1 small cucumber, halved, seeded, and cut into 1-inch pieces
- 1 small yellow summer squash, cut into 1-inch pieces
- ¼ of a medium sweet onion, very thinly sliced
- 1 small tomato, chopped
- 1 cup frozen peas, thawed
- 6 cups torn mixed salad greens
- 3 oz. Monterey Jack cheese with jalapeño peppers, shredded (¾ cup) Bottled cucumber ranch salad dressing

1. Cook pasta according to package directions; drain. Rinse pasta with cold water; drain again.
2. In a large bowl stir together the ½ cup salad dressing, mustard, and salt. Stir in pasta, cucumber, squash, onion, tomato, and peas; toss to coat. Cover; chill for up to 4 hours.
3. Serve pasta mixture on mixed greens. Sprinkle with cheese. Pass additional dressing. Makes 8 side-dish servings.

EACH SERVING: *291 cal., 19 g total fat (4 g sat. fat), 11 mg chol., 419 mg sodium, 24 g carbo., 2 g fiber, 7 g pro. Daily Values: 21% vit. A, 15% vit. C, 11% calcium, 8% iron.*

HONEY-THYME SALAD

PREP: 45 minutes **COOK:** 25 minutes **COOL:** 10 minutes

- 7 fresh ripe nectarines
- 1½ cups water
- 2 sprigs fresh lemon thyme or thyme
- 3 Tbsp. lemon juice
- 3 Tbsp. honey
- 2 Tbsp. Dijon-style mustard
- ⅓ cup extra virgin olive oil
- ½ tsp. salt
- ¼ tsp. ground black pepper
- 6 cups torn mixed salad greens
- 1 cup fresh red and/or black raspberries
- ¼ cup snipped fresh chives
- 2 Tbsp. finely chopped shallot
- ¼ cup pine nuts, toasted
- 2 tsp. snipped fresh lemon thyme or thyme

1. For dressing, halve and pit nectarines, reserving pits. Coarsely chop one of the nectarines; set aside remaining nectarines. In a medium saucepan combine nectarine pits, chopped nectarine, water, and thyme sprigs. Bring to boiling; reduce heat. Simmer, uncovered, about 25 minutes or until liquid is reduced to ⅔ cup. Strain mixture through a fine-mesh sieve; discard solids in strainer. Let syrup cool for 10 minutes.
2. Whisk lemon juice, honey, and mustard into syrup. Slowly whisk in oil, salt, and pepper; set aside.
3. Slice remaining nectarines. In a very large salad bowl combine sliced nectarines, greens, raspberries, chives, and shallot. Drizzle with desired amount of dressing (cover and chill remaining dressing for up to 3 days); toss to coat. Divide salad among 6 salad plates. Sprinkle with pine nuts and snipped fresh thyme. Makes 6 side-dish servings.

EACH SERVING: *275 cal., 17 g total fat (2 g sat. fat), 0 mg chol., 322 mg sodium, 32 g carbo., 5 g fiber, 3 g pro. Daily Values: 19% vit. A, 35% vit. C, 3% calcium, 8% iron.*

WATERMELON AND BABY GREENS SALAD

PREP: 25 minutes **CHILL:** 6 hours

- 1 small red onion, halved and thinly sliced
- ¼ cup lime juice
- 6 cups coarsely chopped watercress or mesclun mix
- 5 cups cubed, seeded watermelon (about ½ of a 4- to 5-lb. watermelon)
- 1 cup crumbled feta cheese (4 oz.)
- ¼ cup pine nuts, toasted
- ½ cup bottled raspberry vinaigrette salad dressing

1. Place onion in a shallow baking dish; add lime juice. Cover and chill for 6 to 24 hours.
2. In a very large bowl toss together onion and lime juice, watercress, and watermelon. Arrange salad on a large serving platter. Top with feta and pine nuts. Drizzle with dressing. Makes 10 to 12 side-dish servings.

EACH SERVING: *120 cal., 8 g total fat (2 g sat. fat), 13 mg chol., 225 mg sodium, 11 g carbo., 1 g fiber, 4 g pro. Daily Values: 29% vit. A, 29% vit. C, 11% calcium, 3% iron.*

PORK AND PENNE SALAD

PREP: 30 minutes **CHILL:** 2 hours

- 2 cups dried penne pasta
- 2 cups broccoli florets
- 2 cups chopped or shredded cooked pork
- 1 cup frozen white whole kernel corn (shoe peg), thawed
- ½ cup pine nuts or slivered almonds, toasted
- ½ cup chopped red and/or green sweet pepper
- ½ cup sliced green onion
- ¾ cup bottled Parmesan ranch salad dressing
- 1 2.25-oz. can sliced, pitted ripe olives, drained

1. Cook pasta according to package directions, adding broccoli florets the last 3 minutes of cooking; drain. Rinse with cold water; drain pasta mixture again.
2. In a large bowl combine pasta mixture, pork, corn, pine nuts, sweet pepper, green onion, salad dressing, and olives. Cover and chill for 2 hours. Stir gently before serving. Makes 6 main-dish servings.

EACH SERVING: *530 cal., 36 g total fat (8 g sat. fat), 63 mg chol., 402 mg sodium, 33 g carbo., 3 g fiber, 22 g pro. Daily Values: 14% vit. A, 89% vit. C, 6% calcium, 17% iron.*

PICNIC DESSERTS

CHOCO-ZUCCHINI CUPCAKES

PREP: 30 minutes **BAKE:** 25 minutes **COOL:** 5 minutes

    Nonstick cooking spray (optional)
  2 cups shredded zucchini (8 oz.)
  3 eggs
  2 cups granulated sugar
  ¾ cup cooking oil
  2 tsp. vanilla
  2 cups all-purpose flour
  ⅔ cup unsweetened cocoa powder
  1 tsp. baking soda
  1 tsp. salt
  ½ tsp. baking powder
  ¾ cup milk chocolate pieces (optional)
  1 recipe Peanut Butter Frosting

1. Preheat oven to 325°F. Line twenty-four 2½-inch muffin cups with double or single layer of paper bake cups or lightly coat with nonstick cooking spray; set aside.

2. In a large bowl stir together zucchini, eggs, granulated sugar, oil, and vanilla. Add flour, cocoa powder, baking soda, salt, baking powder, and, if desired, chocolate pieces; stir until combined. Spoon batter into prepared pans, filling cups about half full.

3. Bake about 25 minutes or until a wooden toothpick inserted near centers comes out clean. Cool in pans on wire racks for 5 minutes. Remove from cups. Cool completely on wire racks. Frost with Peanut Butter Frosting. Makes 24 cupcakes.

PEANUT BUTTER FROSTING: In a medium mixing bowl beat ½ cup peanut butter; ⅓ cup butter, softened; 1 tablespoon milk; and ½ teaspoon vanilla with an electric mixer on medium speed until smooth. Gradually add 1½ cups powdered sugar, beating until combined. If necessary, stir in 1 to 2 teaspoons additional milk until frosting reaches desired consistency. Makes about 1½ cups.

EACH CUPCAKE: *263 cal., 13 g total fat (4 g sat. fat), 33 mg chol., 207 mg sodium, 35 g carbo., 1 g fiber, 4 g pro. Daily Values: 3% vit. A, 3% vit. C, 1% calcium, 6% iron.*

KID FRIENDLY

MALTED MILK BALL COOKIES

PREP: 35 minutes **BAKE:** 8 minutes per batch **COOL:** 2 minutes

  ¾ cup butter, softened
  1¼ cups packed brown sugar
  1 cup granulated sugar
  1½ tsp. baking soda
  ½ tsp. salt
  3 eggs
  ¼ cup cooking oil
  1½ tsp. vanilla
  3½ cups all-purpose flour
  1½ cups whole bran cereal
  3 cups malted milk balls, crushed (12 oz.)

1. Preheat oven to 375°F. In a very large mixing bowl beat butter with an electric mixer on medium to high speed for 30 seconds. Add brown sugar, granulated sugar, baking soda, and salt. Beat until well combined, scraping sides of bowl occasionally. Beat in eggs, oil, and vanilla. Beat in as much of the flour as you can with the mixer. Stir in any remaining flour and the cereal. Reserve ½ cup of the crushed malted milk ball candies to sprinkle on top of cookies. Stir remaining candies into dough.

2. Shape dough into 1½-inch balls. Place balls 2 inches apart on an ungreased cookie sheet. Bake for 8 to 10 minutes or until golden. Place cookie sheet on a wire rack. Immediately sprinkle tops of warm cookies with reserved crushed candies. Cool on cookie sheet for 2 minutes. Transfer cookies to a wire rack and cool completely. Makes about 60 cookies.

EACH COOKIE: *122 cal., 5 g total fat (2 g sat. fat), 17 mg chol., 100 mg sodium, 19 g carbo., 1 g fiber, 1 g pro. Daily Values: 3% vit. A, 2% calcium, 6% iron.*

APPLE CRISP PIE

PREP: 30 minutes **BAKE:** 45 minutes

8 cups sliced, cored, peeled apples
½ cup packaged regular pancake mix
½ cup packed brown sugar
¼ cup granulated sugar
2 tsp. apple pie spice
¾ cup milk
2 eggs
2 Tbsp. butter, softened
1 cup packaged regular pancake mix
¾ cup crushed rich round crackers
½ cup packed brown sugar
¼ cup butter, chilled

1. Preheat oven to 350°F. In a very large bowl toss apple slices with the ½ cup pancake mix, ½ cup brown sugar, the granulated sugar, and apple pie spice. In a small bowl stir together milk and eggs; add to apple mixture and stir to coat. Transfer to a 13×9×2-inch baking pan; dot with the 2 tablespoons butter. Set aside.
2. In a medium bowl stir together the 1 cup pancake mix, rich round crackers, and the ½ cup brown sugar; cut in the ¼ cup butter until crumbly. Sprinkle over apple mixture.
3. Bake for 45 to 50 minutes or until apples are soft and topping is golden. Cool. If desired, serve with ice cream and caramel topping. Makes 16 servings.
EACH SERVING: *212 cal., 7 g total fat (3 g sat. fat), 41 mg chol., 232 mg sodium, 36 g carbo., 2 g fiber, 3 g pro. Daily Values: 5% vit. A, 5% vit. C, 7% calcium, 6% iron.*

PICNIC PEANUT BUTTER BARS

PREP: 20 minutes **BAKE:** 35 minutes

3 cups all-purpose flour
1 cup salted peanuts, finely chopped
1 cup sugar
1 cup peanut butter
¾ cup butter
2 tsp. vanilla
3 cups tiny marshmallows
1 cup semisweet chocolate pieces

1. Preheat oven to 350°F. Grease a 15×10×1-inch baking pan; set aside. In a very large bowl stir together flour, peanuts, sugar, and ¼ teaspoon *salt*. Using a pastry blender, cut in peanut butter and butter until crumbly. Stir in vanilla. Firmly pat 6 cups of the crumb mixture into bottom of prepared pan.
2. Bake for 20 minutes. Top evenly with marshmallows, chocolate, and remaining crumb mixture. Bake 15 minutes more or until marshmallows are toasted and crumbs are golden. Cool in pan on wire rack. Cut into bars (bars will be slightly crumbly). Makes 32 bars.
EACH BAR: *221 cal., 12 g total fat (5 g sat. fat), 11 mg chol., 104 mg sodium, 23 g carbo., 2 g fiber, 5 g pro. Daily Values: 3% vit. A, 1% calcium, 4% iron.*

LOW FAT

APPLE-RHUBARB CRUNCH

PREP: 25 minutes **BAKE:** 30 minutes

Nonstick cooking spray
3 cups chopped fresh or frozen rhubarb
¾ cup sugar
3 medium apples, peeled, cored, and sliced
½ cup dried cranberries
1 cup all-purpose flour
¾ cup sugar
1 tsp. baking powder
1 egg, lightly beaten
1 Tbsp. sugar
¼ tsp. ground cinnamon

1. Preheat oven to 350°F. Lightly coat a 2-quart rectangular baking dish with cooking spray; set aside. In a medium saucepan combine rhubarb, the ¾ cup sugar, and ⅔ cup *water*. Bring to boiling; reduce heat. Simmer, uncovered, for 15 minutes or until mixture is slightly thickened. Place apple slices in dish; sprinkle with cranberries. Top with rhubarb mixture.
2. In a medium bowl combine flour, the ¾ cup sugar, and baking powder. Stir in egg until mixture is crumbly; spoon evenly on top of fruit. Lightly coat surface of crumb mixture with cooking spray. Sprinkle with a mixture of the 1 tablespoon sugar and the cinnamon. Bake for 30 to 40 minutes or until browned and bubbly. Makes 6 to 8 servings.
EACH SERVING: *373 cal., 1 g total fat (0 g sat. fat), 35 mg chol., 76 mg sodium, 90 g carbo., 4 g fiber, 4 g pro. Daily Values: 3% vit. A, 11% vit. C, 20% calcium, 9% iron.*

KID FRIENDLY

CANDY BAR-GRAHAM CAKE

PREP: 25 minutes **BAKE:** 55 minutes
CHILL: 10 minutes

Nonstick cooking spray
1¼ cups graham cracker crumbs
¼ cup sugar
⅓ cup butter
4 2.1-oz. bars chocolate-covered crisp peanut butter candy bars, chilled and crushed
1 pkg. 2-layer-size Swiss chocolate or devil's food cake mix
½ cup cooking oil
3 eggs
1 cup milk chocolate pieces

1. Preheat oven to 350°F. Line a 13×9×2-inch baking pan with heavy foil; lightly coat foil with cooking spray. Set aside.
2. In a medium bowl combine graham cracker crumbs and sugar. Using a pastry blender, cut in butter until mixture resembles coarse

---

crumbs. Press crumb mixture into bottom of pan. Bake for 10 minutes. Remove from oven and sprinkle with half of the crushed candy.
3. In a large mixing bowl combine cake mix, oil, eggs, and 1¼ cups *water*. Beat with an electric mixer on low speed for 30 seconds, scraping sides of bowl. Beat on high speed for 2 minutes. Spread batter into prepared pan. Bake about 45 minutes or until a wooden toothpick inserted near the center comes out clean. Remove from oven and immediately sprinkle with remaining crushed candy and milk chocolate pieces. Cool completely on a wire rack. Chill for 10 minutes or until chocolate is firm. Using foil, lift cake from pan. Cut into pieces. Makes 12 servings.
EACH SERVING: *592 cal., 31 g total fat (12 g sat. fat), 72 mg chol., 500 mg sodium, 72 g carbo., 2 g fiber, 7 g pro. Daily Values: 3% vit. A, 10% calcium, 9% iron.*

SUMMER GARDEN CAKE

PREP: 35 minutes **BAKE:** 50 minutes for loaves; 20 minutes for cupcakes

3 cups all-purpose flour
2 tsp. ground cinnamon
1 tsp. baking soda
1 tsp. salt
½ tsp. baking powder
¼ tsp. ground allspice
3 eggs, beaten
1½ cups granulated sugar
1 cup cooking oil
1 cup very finely shredded zucchini
1 cup finely chopped, seeded tomato
¼ cup finely shredded carrot
1 tsp. vanilla
1 recipe Citrus Glaze (optional)

1. Preheat oven to 350°F. Grease bottoms and ½ inch up sides of two 8×4×2-inch loaf pans or twenty-four 2½-inch muffin cups or line muffin cups with paper bake cups; set aside.
2. In a very large bowl stir together flour, cinnamon, baking soda, salt, baking powder, and allspice; set aside. In a large bowl stir together eggs, sugar, oil, zucchini, tomato, carrot, and vanilla. Add egg mixture to flour mixture; stir until moistened. Divide evenly between loaf pans or among muffin cups.
3. Bake loaves for 50 to 60 minutes or cupcakes about 20 minutes or until a wooden toothpick inserted in centers comes out clean. Cool in pans for 10 minutes. Remove from pans and cool completely on wire racks. If desired, drizzle with Citrus Glaze. Makes 24 servings.
EACH SERVING (WITHOUT GLAZE): *199 cal., 10 g total fat (1 g sat. fat), 26 mg chol., 168 mg sodium, 25 g carbo., 1 g fiber, 3 g pro. Daily Values: 6% vit. A, 3% vit. C, 2% calcium, 5% iron.*
CITRUS GLAZE: In a small bowl stir together ½ cup powdered sugar, 2 teaspoons lime or lemon juice, and enough milk (½ to 2 teaspoons) to reach drizzling consistency.

CHICKEN ON THE BARBECUE

TEX-THAI CHICKEN BREASTS

PREP: 30 minutes **MARINATE:** 1 hour **GRILL:** 12 minutes

- ¾ cup bottled green salsa
- ¼ cup unsweetened coconut milk
- 1 green onion, chopped (2 Tbsp.)
- ½ tsp. finely shredded lime peel
- 1 Tbsp. lime juice
- 1 Tbsp. chopped fresh cilantro
- 1 Tbsp. chopped fresh mint
- 1 tsp. green curry paste
- 1 tsp. grated fresh ginger
- 1 tsp. soy sauce
- 1 clove garlic, minced
- 4 skinless, boneless chicken breast halves (1¼ lb. total)
  Chopped mango and chopped cucumber
  Fresh mint (optional)

1. In a blender or food processor combine salsa, coconut milk, green onion, lime peel and juice, cilantro, the 1 tablespoon mint, curry paste, ginger, soy sauce, and garlic. Cover and blend or process until nearly smooth. Remove ⅓ cup of the salsa mixture for sauce; cover. Chill until serving time.

2. Place chicken in a large resealable plastic bag set in a shallow dish. Pour remaining salsa mixture over chicken; seal bag. Marinate in the refrigerator for 1 to 2 hours, turning bag occasionally. Drain chicken, reserving marinade.

3. For a charcoal grill, grill chicken on the rack of an uncovered grill directly over medium coals for 12 to 15 minutes or until chicken is no longer pink (170°F), turning once and brushing with reserved marinade halfway through grilling. (For a gas grill, preheat grill. Reduce heat to medium. Cover and grill as above.) Serve chicken with chopped mango and cucumber. Drizzle with the reserved ⅓ cup salsa mixture. If desired, garnish with mint. Makes 4 servings.

EACH SERVING: *226 cal., 6 g total fat (3 g sat. fat), 82 mg chol., 465 mg sodium, 8 g carbo., 1 g fiber, 34 g pro. Daily Values: 10% vit. A, 26% vit. C, 4% calcium, 11% iron.*

SMOKY CHEDDAR WRAPS

PREP: 25 minutes **GRILL:** 12 minutes

- 2 Tbsp. raw sugar or 1 Tbsp. packed brown sugar
- 2 Tbsp. Old Bay seasoning
- ½ tsp. paprika
- ¼ tsp. ground chipotle chile pepper
- ⅛ tsp. ground black pepper
- 1½ lb. skinless, boneless chicken breasts
- 6 8-inch chipotle and chile pepper flour tortillas
- 1 6-oz. carton plain low-fat yogurt
- ¼ cup light mayonnaise or salad dressing
- 2 Tbsp. cider vinegar
- 1 tsp. pure maple syrup
- 3 oz. baby romaine lettuce leaves (about 4 cups)
- 3 oz. smoked cheddar cheese, shredded (¾ cup)

1. In a small bowl combine sugar, Old Bay seasoning, paprika, chile pepper, and black pepper. Remove and reserve 1 teaspoon of the spice mixture. Place remaining spice mixture in a large resealable plastic bag. Add chicken to bag. Seal bag and turn to coat chicken.

2. For a charcoal grill, grill chicken on the rack of an uncovered grill directly over medium coals for 12 to 15 minutes or until chicken is no longer pink (170°F), turning once halfway through grilling. (For a gas grill, preheat grill. Reduce heat to medium. Cover; grill as above.)

3. Wrap tortillas tightly in heavy foil. Add to grill the last 10 minutes of grilling time, turning once halfway through grilling. Remove chicken from grill and thinly slice.

4. Meanwhile, in a small bowl combine the reserved 1 teaspoon spice mixture, yogurt, mayonnaise, vinegar, and syrup. Spread mixture over one side of each tortilla. Top with lettuce, cheese, and sliced chicken. Roll up tortillas. Makes 6 servings.

EACH SERVING: *349 cal., 12 g total fat (5 g sat. fat), 86 mg chol., 1,013 mg sodium, 24 g carbo., 1 g fiber, 34 g pro. Daily Values: 27% vit. A, 6% vit. C, 21% calcium, 12% iron.*

ASIAN GLAZED CHICKEN WINGS

PREP: 25 minutes **MARINATE:** 8 hours
GRILL: 20 minutes

- ½ cup packed brown sugar
- ½ cup oyster sauce
- ¼ cup fish sauce
- ¼ cup sweet soy sauce*
- 2 green onions, coarsely chopped
- 4 cloves garlic, quartered
- 1 to 3 tsp. crushed red pepper
- ½ tsp. salt
- ½ to 1 tsp. ground black pepper
- 1 2½- to 3-lb. pkg. frozen chicken wing drummettes, thawed and drained

1. For marinade, in a blender combine brown sugar, oyster sauce, fish sauce, soy sauce, green onion, garlic, crushed red pepper, salt, and black pepper. Cover and blend until nearly smooth. (Or finely chop green onions and garlic; in a small bowl combine with remaining marinade ingredients.)

2. Place drummettes in a large resealable plastic bag; add marinade. Seal bag and turn to coat chicken. Place bag in a deep bowl. Marinate in the refrigerator for 8 to 24 hours, turning bag occasionally. Drain drummettes, discarding marinade.

3. For a charcoal grill, arrange medium-hot coals around a drip pan. Test for medium heat above pan. Place drummettes on grill rack over the drip pan. Cover and grill for 20 to 25 minutes or until chicken is no longer pink (180°F), turning once halfway through grilling. (For a gas grill, preheat grill; adjust for indirect cooking. Reduce heat to medium. Place chicken on grill rack not over heat. Cover and grill as above.) Makes about 20 drummettes.

*NOTE: If you cannot find sweet soy sauce, substitute 2 tablespoons soy sauce and 1 tablespoon packed brown sugar.

EACH DRUMMETTE: *131 cal., 9 g total fat (2 g sat. fat), 58 mg chol., 197 mg sodium, 2 g carbo., 0 g fiber, 10 g pro.*

CHICKEN WITH FETA CREAM SAUCE

PREP: 30 minutes **MARINATE:** 1 hour
GRILL: 12 minutes

- 4 skinless, boneless chicken breast halves (about 1¼ lb. total)
- 1 cup bottled feta cheese or Mediterranean salad dressing
- 3 Tbsp. butter
- 1 clove garlic, minced
- 1 cup crumbled feta cheese
- ½ cup whipping cream
- ½ of a medium cucumber, seeded and chopped
- 1½ tsp. lemon juice
- ¼ tsp. dried dillweed
- 2 cups hot cooked couscous

1. Place chicken in a large resealable plastic bag set in a shallow bowl. Pour salad dressing over chicken; seal bag. Marinate in the refrigerator for 1 hour. Drain chicken, discarding marinade.

2. For a charcoal grill, grill chicken on the rack of an uncovered grill directly over medium coals for 12 to 15 minutes or until chicken is no longer pink (170°F), turning once halfway through grilling. (For a gas grill, preheat grill. Reduce heat to medium. Place chicken on grill rack over heat. Cover and grill as above.) Transfer chicken to a serving platter; cover and keep warm.

3. For feta cream sauce, in a medium saucepan melt butter over medium heat. Add garlic; cook for 30 seconds. Stir in feta cheese. Cook and stir over medium heat until cheese starts to melt. Stir in whipping cream; heat through. Remove from heat and add cucumber, lemon juice, and dillweed.

4. Serve chicken with hot cooked couscous and feta cream sauce. Makes 4 servings.

EACH SERVING: *761 cal., 55 g total fat (20 g sat. fat), 166 mg chol., 1,219 mg sodium, 27 g carbo., 2 g fiber, 42 g pro. Daily Values: 22% vit. A, 7% vit. C, 13% calcium, 8% iron.*

LOW FAT

ISLAND HOPPER GRILLED CHICKEN

PREP: 20 minutes **MARINATE:** 2 hours
GRILL: 45 minutes

- 1½ cups mango or papaya nectar
- 1 cup pineapple juice
- ½ cup snipped fresh basil
- 2 cloves garlic, minced
- 4 tsp. grated fresh ginger
- 1 Tbsp. Asian chile sauce
- ½ tsp. salt
- ½ tsp. ground black pepper
- 3 to 3½ lb. chicken thighs (bone-in), skinned
- 1½ tsp. cornstarch
  Hot cooked rice

1. For marinade, in a medium bowl combine nectar, pineapple juice, basil, garlic, ginger, chile sauce, salt, and pepper. Reserve 1¼ cups of the mixture for sauce.

2. Place chicken in a large resealable plastic bag set in a large bowl; pour remaining marinade over chicken. Seal bag. Marinate in the refrigerator for 2 to 24 hours, turning bag occasionally. Drain chicken thighs, discarding marinade.

3. For a charcoal grill, arrange medium-hot coals around a drip pan. Test for medium heat above pan. Place chicken on grill rack over drip pan. Cover and grill for 45 to

50 minutes or until chicken is no longer pink (180°F). (For a gas grill, preheat grill; adjust for indirect cooking. Reduce heat to medium. Place chicken on grill rack not over heat. Cover and grill as above.)

4. Meanwhile, for sauce, place reserved marinade in a small saucepan. Stir in cornstarch. Cook and stir over medium heat until thickened and bubbly. Cook and stir for 2 minutes more. Serve chicken with sauce and cooked rice. Makes 6 servings.

EACH SERVING: *319 cal., 5 g total fat (1 g sat. fat), 107 mg chol., 252 mg sodium, 37 g carbo., 1 g fiber, 28 g pro. Daily Values: 7% vit. A, 18% vit. C, 4% calcium, 16% iron.*

ORANGE-GLAZED CHICKEN AND PEPPERS

PREP: 15 minutes **GRILL:** 50 minutes

- 2 lb. meaty chicken pieces (breast halves, thighs, and drumsticks), skinned, if desired
  Salt
  Ground black pepper
- ½ cup orange marmalade
- ¼ cup cider vinegar
- 3 Tbsp. soy sauce
- 2 Tbsp. frozen orange juice concentrate, thawed
- ⅛ tsp. cayenne pepper
- 2 medium green and/or red sweet peppers, quartered (seeds and membranes removed)

1. Sprinkle chicken pieces lightly with salt and black pepper.

2. For a charcoal grill, arrange medium-hot coals around a drip pan. Test for medium heat above pan. Place chicken pieces, meaty sides down, on the grill rack over the drip pan. Cover and grill for 40 minutes. (For a gas grill, preheat grill; adjust for indirect cooking. Reduce heat to medium. Cover; grill as above.)

3. Meanwhile, in a small saucepan combine orange marmalade, vinegar, soy sauce, orange juice concentrate, and cayenne pepper. Bring to boiling; reduce heat and simmer, uncovered, for 3 minutes. Remove from heat.

4. After grilling for 40 minutes, turn chicken meaty sides up; add sweet peppers, cut sides down, to grill directly over heat. Brush chicken and peppers with orange mixture. Cover and grill for 10 to 15 minutes more or until chicken is no longer pink (170°F for breast pieces, 180°F for thighs and drumsticks) and sweet peppers are crisp-tender. Brush with any remaining glaze before serving. Makes 4 servings.

EACH SERVING: *392 cal., 13 g total fat (4 g sat. fat), 104 mg chol., 879 mg sodium, 33 g carbo., 1 g fiber, 36 g pro. Daily Values: 7% vit. A, 104% vit. C, 5% calcium, 10% iron.*

STAR-SPANGLED SUMMER DRINKS

PRIZE TESTED RECIPES® $400 WINNER

JOLENE GENSHEIMER, BELLEVUE, WASH.

PRIZE TESTED RECIPES® $200 WINNER

ELEANOR J. FROEHLICH, ROCHESTER HILLS, MICH.

COCONUT LEMONADE

PREP: 10 minutes **CHILL:** 4 hours

  3 cups water
 ⅔ cup lemon juice
 ½ cup sugar
  2 Tbsp. coconut beverage flavoring syrup or cream of coconut
 ½ cup frozen unsweetened blueberries
 ½ cup frozen red raspberries
  1 small fresh carambola (star fruit), thinly sliced crosswise
     Ice cubes (optional)

1. In a large bowl combine the water, lemon juice, sugar, and coconut syrup. Stir until sugar dissolves. Cover and chill for 4 to 24 hours.
2. To serve, transfer lemon juice mixture to a serving bowl or pitcher. Add blueberries, raspberries, and carambola. If desired, serve over ice in glasses. Makes 4 (8-ounce) servings.
EACH SERVING: *150 cal., 0 g total fat (0 g sat. fat), 0 mg chol., 7 mg sodium, 39 g carbo., 2 g fiber, 1 g pro. Daily Values: 1% vit. A, 52% vit. C, 1% calcium, 1% iron.*

SPICED FRUIT TEA

PREP: 15 minutes **CHILL:** 4 hours **FREEZE:** 4 hours

  5 cups boiling water
  5 bags orange-flavored spiced herb tea
 ⅓ cup sugar
 ¼ tsp. ground cinnamon
  1 46-oz. can unsweetened pineapple juice
  2 cups cranberry juice
 ⅓ cup lime juice
     Assorted fresh fruit, such as fresh pineapple chunks, orange slices, kumquat slices, and/or lime slices (optional)
     Fresh mint leaves (optional)

1. Pour the boiling water into a very large bowl. Add tea bags; let steep for 5 minutes. Remove and discard tea bags. Stir in sugar and cinnamon until sugar dissolves. Stir in pineapple juice, cranberry juice, and lime juice. Remove 3 cups of the tea mixture. Cover and chill the remaining tea mixture for 4 hours or up to 3 days.
2. Pour the 3 cups tea mixture into two clean ice cube trays, adding fruit, if desired. Cover and freeze for 4 hours or until firm.
3. To serve, divide prepared ice cubes among glasses. Add chilled tea mixture. If desired, garnish with fresh fruit and/or mint. Makes 8 to 10 (about 8-ounce) servings.
EACH SERVING: *157 cal., 0 g total fat (0 g sat. fat), 0 mg chol., 9 mg sodium, 39 g carbo., 0 g fiber, 1 g pro. Daily Values: 77% vit. C, 3% calcium, 4% iron.*

RASPBERRY MOJITO PUNCH

START TO FINISH: 15 minutes

⅓ cup sugar
¼ cup lightly packed fresh mint leaves
3 cups cold water
1 12 oz. can frozen raspberry juice
 blend concentrate, thawed
½ cup fresh lime juice, chilled
24 oz. (3 cups) club soda, chilled
1 cup ice cubes
1 lime, thinly sliced
1 cup fresh raspberries

1. In a punch bowl combine sugar and mint. Using the back of a wooden spoon, lightly mash the mint by pressing it against the side of the bowl. Add water, raspberry juice blend, and lime juice, stirring until sugar dissolves.
2. Stir in club soda, ice cubes, lime slices, and raspberries. Serve immediately. Makes 8 (8-ounce) servings.
EACH SERVING: *139 cal., 0 g total fat (0 g sat. fat), 0 mg chol., 38 mg sodium, 34 g carbo., 1 g fiber, 0 g pro. Daily Values: 106% vit. C, 2% calcium, 5% iron.*

FAST!

REFRESHING GREEN MANGO SIPPER

PREP: 15 minutes **COOK:** 5 minutes

1 medium mango, green and firm to
 the touch
2 cups cold water
½ to ¾ cup sugar
2 Tbsp. lemon juice
1 cup ice cubes
 Sugar (optional)
 Ice cubes

1. Peel and remove seed from mango. Cut mango into large pieces. In a medium saucepan cook mango in a small amount of boiling water for 5 to 20 minutes or until the mango pieces are fork tender. Drain.
2. In a blender combine cooked mango, the cold water, the ½ to ¾ cup sugar, lemon juice, and 1 cup ice cubes. Cover and blend until smooth. If desired, stir in additional sugar to taste. Serve over ice in glasses. Makes 4 (8 ounce) servings.
EACH SERVING: *133 cal., 0 g total fat (0 g sat. fat), 0 mg chol., 4 mg sodium, 35 g carbo., 1 g fiber, 0 g pro. Daily Values: 8% vit. A, 30% vit. C, 1% calcium.*

RHUBARB ICED TEA

PREP: 10 minutes **COOK:** 10 minutes
CHILL: several hours

4 cups 1-inch pieces fresh or frozen
 rhubarb
1¼ cups cranberry-apple juice
¾ cup sugar
4 cups water
5 bags black tea, such as orange pekoe
 Ice cubes

1. In a medium saucepan combine rhubarb, cranberry-apple juice, and sugar. Bring to boiling; reduce heat. Simmer, covered, for 10 minutes or until rhubarb is very tender. Remove from heat; cool.
2. Place cooled rhubarb mixture in a blender or food processor. Cover and blend or process until nearly smooth.* Transfer to a large bowl; set aside.
3. Meanwhile, bring the water to boiling. Remove from heat. Add tea bags and let stand, covered, for 3 to 5 minutes. Remove and discard the tea bags. Transfer tea to a large pitcher or punch bowl. Stir in rhubarb mixture. Cover and chill thoroughly. Stir before serving. Serve over ice in glasses. Makes 8 (8-ounce) servings.
*NOTE: If desired, strain blended rhubarb mixture through a fine-mesh sieve, discarding pulp. Add strained rhubarb mixture to the tea. This yields 6 (8-ounce) servings.
EACH SERVING: *110 cal., 0 g total fat (0 g sat. fat), 0 mg chol., 6 mg sodium, 28 g carbo., 1 g fiber, 1 g pro. Daily Values: 1% vit. A, 33% vit. C, 6% calcium, 1% iron.*

SOUTHERN PEACH SWIZZLE

PREP: 15 minutes **FREEZE:** overnight
STAND: 30 minutes **CHILL:** several hours

1 large peach, peeled, pitted, and
 coarsely chopped, or 1 cup frozen
 peach slices, thawed and coarsely
 chopped
½ cup Southern Comfort or bourbon
4 cups water
1 2-inch piece fresh ginger, sliced
2 Tbsp. packed brown sugar
1 32-oz. jar peach nectar, chilled
1 12-oz. can frozen lemonade
 concentrate, thawed
1 1-liter bottle ginger ale, chilled

1. In a small bowl toss chopped peach with 2 tablespoons of the Southern Comfort; divide peach mixture between two ice cube trays. Fill the ice cube trays with water; cover and freeze overnight.
2. For syrup, in a medium saucepan combine the 4 cups water, ginger, and brown sugar. Bring to boiling; reduce heat. Simmer, uncovered, for 5 minutes. Remove from heat; let stand for 30 minutes. Strain and discard ginger. Cover; chill syrup for several hours.
3. Just before serving, in a large punch bowl combine syrup, peach nectar, lemonade concentrate, remaining Southern Comfort, and chilled ginger ale. Serve over prepared ice cubes in glasses. Makes 14 (about 8-ounce) servings.
EACH SERVING: *136 cal., 0 g total fat (0 g sat. fat), 0 mg chol., 13 mg sodium, 30 g carbo., 1 g fiber, 0 g pro. Daily Values: 4% vit. A, 14% vit. C, 1% calcium, 3% iron.*

PRIZE TESTED RECIPES® $400 WINNER

GRACE SAMMARTINO, TEGA CAY, S.C.

PRIZE TESTED RECIPES® $200 WINNER

MARGIE TYLER, MURFREESBORO, TENN.

FAST!

FRANKS WITH NAPA SLAW

PREP: 10 minutes **STAND:** 15 minutes

    3 cups shredded napa cabbage or green cabbage
    ½ cup packaged coarsely shredded fresh carrot
    ⅓ cup thinly sliced sweet onion
    ¼ cup rice vinegar
    1 Tbsp. lime juice
    1 Tbsp. salad oil
    1 Tbsp. honey
    1 tsp. minced garlic
    ½ tsp. ground ginger
    ½ tsp. dried dillweed
    8 frankfurters
    8 frankfurter buns, split

1. In a large bowl toss together cabbage, carrot, and onion; set aside. In a small bowl whisk together vinegar, lime juice, oil, honey, garlic, ginger, and dillweed. Pour vinegar mixture over cabbage mixture; toss to coat. Let stand at room temperature for 15 minutes, stirring occasionally, or cover and refrigerate in an airtight container for up to 24 hours before serving.

2. Meanwhile, prepare frankfurters according to package directions. Place franks in buns. Top with cabbage mixture. Makes 8 servings.

EACH SERVING: *306 cal., 17 g total fat (6 g sat. fat), 24 mg chol., 729 mg sodium, 29 g carbo., 2 g fiber, 10 g pro. Daily Values: 24% vit. A, 17% vit. C, 8% calcium, 13% iron.*

KID FRIENDLY

SEASHELL HOT DOG BAKE

PREP: 25 minutes **BAKE:** 35 minutes

    8 oz. dried medium shell macaroni
    1 cup chopped onion (1 large)
    1 clove garlic, minced
    1 Tbsp. butter
    1 16-oz. pkg. beef frankfurters, halved lengthwise and sliced
    1½ cups purchased spaghetti sauce
    1 cup chopped tomato (1 large)
    1 4-oz. can (drained weight) mushroom stems and pieces, drained
    1 8-oz. carton dairy sour cream
    2 oz. provolone cheese, shredded (½ cup)
    2 oz. mozzarella cheese, shredded (½ cup)

1. Preheat oven to 350°F. Prepare macaroni according to package directions; drain and set aside.

2. In a large skillet cook onion and garlic in hot butter over medium heat until nearly tender. Stir in frankfurters and cook until lightly browned. Stir in spaghetti sauce, tomato, and mushrooms. Bring to boiling. Remove from heat. Stir in sour cream and half of the cheeses. Stir mixture into the drained pasta. Spoon into a 2-quart casserole.

3. Bake, covered, about 30 minutes or until hot. Uncover and sprinkle with remaining cheeses. Bake, uncovered, 5 minutes more or until cheese melts. Makes 6 servings.

EACH SERVING: *600 cal., 38 g total fat (18 g sat. fat), 73 mg chol., 1,411 mg sodium, 46 g carbo., 4 g fiber, 21 g pro. Daily Values: 22% vit. A, 18% vit. C, 23% calcium, 19% iron.*

ASIAN-SPICED FRANKS

START TO FINISH: 30 minutes

- 3 oz. rice noodles
- 1 cup chopped onion (1 large)
- 1 cup chopped red and/or green sweet pepper
- 2 Tbsp. cooking oil
- 1 16-oz. pkg. frankfurters, diagonally sliced ½ inch thick
- ¼ tsp. anise seeds, crushed
- 1 cup unsweetened pineapple juice
- 1 Tbsp. Asian chili sauce (such as Sriracha chili sauce)
- 1 Tbsp. soy sauce
- 2 tsp. cornstarch
- 1 Tbsp. sesame seeds, toasted

1. In a large bowl soak rice noodles according to package directions. Drain. Snip into 2- to 3-inch lengths. Set aside.

2. In a large skillet cook and stir onion and sweet pepper in hot oil until onion is tender. Add frankfurters and anise seeds; cook for 2 minutes more.

3. Combine pineapple juice, chili sauce, soy sauce, and cornstarch; add to skillet along with soaked rice noodles. Cook and stir until thickened and rice noodles are tender. Sprinkle with sesame seeds. If desired, pass additional soy sauce. Makes 4 servings.

EACH SERVING: *570 cal., 40 g total fat (13 g sat. fat), 55 mg chol., 1,596 mg sodium, 36 g carbo., 2 g fiber, 16 g pro. Daily Values: 26% vit. A, 133% vit. C, 4% calcium, 12% iron.*

SWEET SAUERKRAUT TOPPER

PREP: 20 minutes **COOK:** 5 minutes
CHILL: overnight

- 1 14- to 15-oz. can sauerkraut, rinsed and drained
- 1 cup chopped green, red, and/or yellow sweet pepper
- 1 cup chopped onion (1 large)
- ⅓ cup cider vinegar
- 2 Tbsp. olive oil
- ⅓ cup sugar
- ¼ tsp. celery salt

1. In a large bowl combine sauerkraut, sweet pepper, and onion; set aside. In a small saucepan combine vinegar, oil, sugar, and celery salt; heat to boiling, stirring to dissolve sugar. Pour over sauerkraut mixture. Cover and refrigerate overnight.

2. To serve, drain sauerkraut mixture or serve with a slotted spoon. Serve with hot frankfurters, bratwurst, or hamburgers. Makes 16 (¼-cup) servings.

EACH SERVING: *43 cal., 2 g total fat (0 g sat. fat), 0 mg chol., 190 mg sodium, 7 g carbo., 1 g fiber, 0 g pro. Daily Values: 1% vit. A, 20% vit. C, 1% calcium, 2% iron.*

FRANK AND VEGETABLE SKILLET

PREP: 20 minutes **COOK:** 15 minutes

- 1 16-oz. pkg. frankfurters, sliced ½ inch thick
- 1 cup chopped onion (1 large)
- 2 cups button or cremini mushrooms, quartered
- 2 Tbsp. butter
- 2 Tbsp. cornstarch
- 1 14-oz. can chicken broth
- 2 Tbsp. lemon juice
- ½ tsp. dried thyme, crushed
- ¼ tsp. ground black pepper
- 2½ cups cooked brown or white rice
- 1½ cups sugar snap peas, trimmed and halved horizontally
- 1 large red sweet pepper, coarsely chopped
- ¼ cup finely shredded Parmesan cheese

1. In a very large skillet cook frankfurters, onion, and mushrooms in hot butter over medium heat until onion is tender, stirring occasionally. Stir in cornstarch; add chicken broth, lemon juice, thyme, and black pepper. Cook and stir until thickened and bubbly.

2. Stir in rice, peas, and sweet pepper. Cover and cook for 3 to 5 minutes, stirring once, until heated through. Sprinkle with Parmesan cheese. Makes 6 servings.

EACH SERVING: *421 cal., 27 g total fat (11 g sat. fat), 50 mg chol., 1,202 mg sodium, 31 g carbo., 4 g fiber, 14 g pro. Daily Values: 21% vit. A, 113% vit. C, 8% calcium, 11% iron.*

SOUTH-OF-THE-BORDER CHILI DOGS

PREP: 20 minutes **COOK:** 3 hours (low)

- 2 lb. ground beef
- 1½ cups chopped onion (3 medium)
- 1 16-oz. jar salsa
- 1 10-oz. can mild enchilada sauce
- ¼ cup bottled sliced pickled jalapeño peppers
- 2 Tbsp. yellow mustard
- 24 frankfurters
- 24 frankfurter buns, split
- 6 oz. Monterey Jack cheese with jalapeño peppers or Monterey Jack cheese, shredded (1½ cups)

1. In a very large skillet cook beef and onion until beef is no longer pink and onion is tender. Drain. Stir in salsa, enchilada sauce, jalapeño slices, and mustard.

2. In a 6-quart slow cooker arrange frankfurters to fit in the bottom. Top with ground beef mixture. Cover and cook on low-heat setting for 3 to 4 hours.

3. Remove franks from slow cooker with tongs and place in buns. Spoon meat mixture over franks. Sprinkle with cheese. Makes 24 chili dogs.

EACH CHILI DOG: *417 cal., 27 g total fat (11 g sat. fat), 62 mg chol., 1,022 mg sodium, 25 g carbo., 2 g fiber, 18 g pro. Daily Values: 9% vit. A, 3% vit. C, 13% calcium, 15% iron.*

STIR-FRIED FRANKS WITH RICE

START TO FINISH: 30 minutes

- 3 Tbsp. reduced-sodium soy sauce
- 1 Tbsp. rice vinegar or cider vinegar
- 2 tsp. sesame seeds
- ½ tsp. packed brown sugar
- ⅛ tsp. chili powder
- ⅛ tsp. ground black pepper
- 1 Tbsp. minced fresh ginger or ½ tsp. ground ginger
- 2 tsp. bottled minced garlic
- 1 Tbsp. cooking oil
- 3 cups broccoli florets, thinly bias-sliced carrots, and/or thinly bias-sliced celery
- 1 small onion, halved and thinly sliced
- 1 small red or green sweet pepper, seeded and cut into bite-size strips
- 12 oz. frankfurters, bias-sliced
- 3 cups hot cooked rice
   Snipped fresh cilantro

1. In a small bowl stir together soy sauce, vinegar, sesame seeds, brown sugar, chili powder, and black pepper; set aside.

2. In a wok or very large nonstick skillet cook ginger and garlic in hot oil over medium-high heat for 30 seconds. Add broccoli, onion, and sweet pepper. Cook and stir for 5 to 7 minutes or until vegetables are crisp-tender. Transfer vegetables to a bowl; set aside.

3. Add frankfurters to hot wok or skillet (add more oil as necessary during cooking). Cook and stir for 1 to 2 minutes or until franks start to brown. Return vegetables to wok or skillet. Add soy sauce mixture. Cook and stir until heated through. Serve over rice. Sprinkle with cilantro. Makes 6 servings.

EACH SERVING: *336 cal., 19 g total fat (7 g sat. fat), 28 mg chol., 942 mg sodium, 30 g carbo., 2 g fiber, 11 g pro. Daily Values: 18% vit. A, 111% vit. C, 6% calcium, 13% iron.*

FROZEN DESSERTS

PRIZE TESTED RECIPES® $400 WINNER

MARY ALICE GRAVES, KEMPTON, IND.

PRIZE TESTED RECIPES® $200 WINNER

JANET HASENKAMP, PENDLETON, ORE.

COFFEE-MALLOW TORTE

PREP: 30 minutes **FREEZE:** 6 hours **STAND:** 10 minutes

- 2 cups crushed chocolate wafer cookies (about 35 cookies)
- ⅓ cup butter, melted
- ⅔ cup hot fudge ice cream topping
- 1 tsp. instant coffee crystals
- ½ of a 7-oz. jar marshmallow crème
- 1 8-oz. container frozen whipped dessert topping, thawed
- 1 qt. coffee ice cream
- ⅓ cup chopped pecans, toasted
- ½ oz. semisweet chocolate, grated
- ⅓ cup caramel-flavor ice cream topping
- ¼ oz. semisweet chocolate, shaved
  Pecan halves (optional)

1. In a medium bowl combine cookie crumbs and butter. Press into the bottom and about 1½ inches up the sides of a 9-inch springform pan; set aside.

2. In a small saucepan combine hot fudge topping and coffee crystals. Heat and stir just until smooth; cool slightly. Spread topping over crumb mixture in the springform pan. In a large bowl fold marshmallow crème into whipped dessert topping until combined; set aside.

3. In a chilled large bowl stir ice cream with a wooden spoon until softened. Fold in whipped topping mixture. Spoon into crust. Sprinkle with chopped pecans and grated chocolate. Cover and freeze for 6 hours or until firm. Before serving let stand at room temperature for 10 minutes. Drizzle with caramel topping and sprinkle with shaved chocolate. If desired, garnish with pecan halves. Makes 12 to 16 servings.

EACH SERVING: *433 cal., 26 g total fat (15 g sat. fat), 96 mg chol., 210 mg sodium, 44 g carbo., 1 g fiber, 5 g pro. Daily Values: 13% vit. A, 13% calcium, 2% iron.*

BLACK RASPBERRY CREAM PIE

PREP: 10 minutes **BAKE:** 5 minutes **FREEZE:** 4 hours

- 1 purchased 9-inch graham cracker crumb pie shell
- 1 egg white, beaten
- 1 cup whipping cream
- 1 8-oz. pkg. cream cheese, softened
- 1 10-oz. jar black raspberry spread
  Fresh black raspberries, lemon peel twist, and/or mint leaves (optional)

1. Preheat oven to 375°F. Brush pie shell with beaten egg white. Bake for 5 minutes. Cool on a wire rack.

2. In a medium mixing bowl beat whipping cream with an electric mixer on medium-high speed until stiff peaks form; set aside.

3. In a large mixing bowl beat cream cheese with an electric mixer on medium-high speed until smooth. Add black raspberry spread. Beat on low speed just until combined. Fold in whipped cream. Spoon mixture into pie shell. Cover and freeze for 4 to 24 hours or until firm. If desired, garnish with fresh raspberries, lemon peel twist, and/or mint. Makes 8 servings.

EACH SERVING: *294 cal., 21 g total fat (13 g sat. fat), 83 mg chol., 114 mg sodium, 23 g carbo., 0 g fiber, 7 g pro. Daily Values: 17% vit. A, 5% calcium, 4% iron.*

STRAWBERRY CAKE ROLL

PREP: 30 minutes **BAKE:** 12 minutes
FREEZE: 4 hours

- 1 cup all-purpose flour
- 1 tsp. baking powder
- ¼ tsp. salt
- ¾ cup finely chopped fresh strawberries
- ¼ cup frozen mixed berry juice concentrate, thawed
- 3 eggs
- ½ cup granulated sugar
- ¾ cup finely chopped pecans
  Powdered sugar
- 1 pt. strawberry ice cream

1. Preheat oven to 375°F. Grease a 15×10×1-inch baking pan; line pan with waxed paper. Set aside. In a small bowl combine flour, baking powder, and salt; set aside.

2. In a small saucepan combine strawberries and juice concentrate. Bring mixture to boiling; reduce heat to low. Cook, stirring and mashing with a spoon, about 4 minutes or until slightly thickened. Remove from heat; cool to room temperature. Set aside.

3. In a large mixing bowl beat eggs with an electric mixer on high speed about 5 minutes or until thick and lemon color. Gradually add strawberry mixture and granulated sugar, beating on medium speed until sugar is almost dissolved. Sprinkle flour mixture over egg mixture; fold in gently just until combined. Spread batter evenly in prepared pan. Sprinkle with nuts.

4. Bake for 12 to 15 minutes or until top springs back when lightly touched. Immediately loosen edges of cake; turn out onto a towel sprinkled with powdered sugar. Carefully remove waxed paper. Starting with a narrow end, roll up warm cake and towel together. Cool on a wire rack.

5. Unroll cake. Stir ice cream to soften; carefully spread on cake to within 1 inch of edges. Reroll cake without towel. Trim ends of cake. Place on a baking sheet; cover and freeze for 4 to 24 hours. Slice to serve. Makes 10 servings.

EACH SERVING: *233 cal., 10 g total fat (2 g sat. fat), 71 mg chol., 104 mg sodium, 33 g carbo., 2 g fiber, 5 g pro. Daily Values: 3% vit. A, 26% vit. C, 5% calcium, 7% iron.*

CARDAMOM-NUT CHEESECAKE ICE CREAM

PREP: 40 minutes **COOK:** 6 minutes
COOL: 1 hour **CHILL:** 4 hours
FREEZE: 4½ hours

- 1 cup coarsely chopped walnuts
- ½ cup sugar
- 2 Tbsp. butter
- 2 tsp. ground cardamom
- 3 8-oz. pkg. cream cheese, softened
- 2 cups sugar
- 5 cups half-and-half or light cream
- 3 egg yolks
- 2 Tbsp. lemon juice
- 2 tsp. vanilla

1. In a heavy 8-inch skillet combine walnuts, ½ cup sugar, butter, and cardamom. Cook over medium heat, stirring constantly, for 6 to 8 minutes or until sugar melts, turns a rich brown color, and coats nuts. Remove from heat. Spread nuts on a buttered baking sheet or foil; separate into clusters. Cool. Break clusters into small chunks; cover and set aside.

2. In a very large mixing bowl beat cream cheese and 1 cup of the sugar with an electric mixer on medium speed until mixture is smooth. Set aside.

3. In a medium saucepan combine 3 cups of the half-and-half, remaining 1 cup sugar, and egg yolks; cook and stir over medium heat until mixture coats a metal spoon. Gradually beat into cream cheese mixture; stir in the remaining 2 cups half-and-half, the lemon juice, and vanilla. Cover and chill for 4 hours or overnight.

4. Pour chilled cream mixture and nut mixture into a 4- to 5- quart ice cream freezer container. Freeze according to manufacturer's directions. Ripen 4 hours before serving. Makes 24 (½-cup) servings.

EACH SERVING: *294 cal., 20 g total fat (11 g sat. fat), 78 mg chol., 112 mg sodium, 25 g carbo., 0 g fiber, 5 g pro. Daily Values: 12% vit. A, 2% vit. C, 8% calcium, 3% iron.*

MELON SHERBET

PREP: 25 minutes **CHILL:** 2 hours
FREEZE: 4½ hours

- 1¼ cups sugar
- 1 envelope unflavored gelatin
- 8 cups cubed cantaloupe or honeydew melon
- 1 cup milk
- 2 tsp. finely shredded lemon peel

1. In a medium saucepan combine sugar and gelatin. In a blender or food processor puree half of the melon at a time; stir 2 cups of the pureed fruit into mixture in saucepan. Cook and stir until sugar and gelatin dissolve and mixture just bubbles. Remove from heat. Stir in remaining pureed fruit, milk, and lemon peel. (Mixture may appear curdled.) Cover and chill for 2 to 4 hours.

2. Pour chilled mixture into a 4-quart ice cream freezer container; freeze according to manufacturer's directions. Ripen 4 hours before serving. Makes 20 (½-cup) servings.

EACH SERVING: *81 cal., 0 g total fat (0 g sat. fat), 1 mg chol., 18 mg sodium, 18 g carbo., 1 g fiber, 2 g pro. Daily Values: 44% vit. A, 40% vit. C, 2% calcium, 1% iron.*

ORANGE SHERBET CHEESECAKE SQUARES

PREP: 25 minutes **BAKE:** 12 minutes
FREEZE: 1 hour + 8 hours
STAND: 10 minutes

- 2 cups crushed vanilla wafers
- ½ cup butter, melted
- 2 8-oz. pkg. cream cheese, softened
- 1 14-oz. can sweetened condensed milk
- 1 qt. orange sherbet
- 3 medium oranges, peeled, sectioned, and chopped
- 1 cup flaked coconut, toasted
- ⅓ cup dried tart cherries, chopped
- 1 8-oz. container frozen whipped dessert topping, thawed

1. Preheat oven to 350°F. In a medium bowl combine crushed wafers and butter. Press into the bottom of a 13×9×2-inch baking pan. Bake for 12 to 15 minutes or until browned and set. Cool on a wire rack.

2. In a large mixing bowl beat cream cheese until smooth; gradually beat in sweetened condensed milk. Stir sherbet to soften;* fold into cream cheese mixture. Cover and freeze for 1 to 2 hours or until almost firm.

3. In a small bowl combine chopped oranges, half of the coconut, and the cherries. Fold into sherbet mixture. Spread over crust in pan. Top with whipped dessert topping and sprinkle with remaining coconut.

4. Cover and freeze for 8 to 24 hours. Before serving, let stand 10 minutes at room temperature. Cut into squares. Makes 12 to 15 servings.

*NOTE: To soften sherbet, place sherbet in a chilled bowl; use a wooden spoon to press sherbet against sides of bowl until softened.

EACH SERVING: *591 cal., 35 g total fat (22 g sat. fat), 73 mg chol., 321 mg sodium, 63 g carbo., 3 g fiber, 8 g pro. Daily Values: 20% vit. A, 20% vit. C, 17% calcium, 7% iron.*

PRIZE TESTED RECIPES® $400 WINNER

JENNIFER HONEYCUTT, NASHVILLE, TENN.

 FAST!

SALMON, APPLES, AND FENNEL

START TO FINISH: 30 minutes

- ¼ cup all-purpose flour
- ¼ tsp. salt
- ¼ tsp. ground black pepper
- 2 eggs
- 1 Tbsp. water
- ⅔ cup fine dry bread crumbs
- 4 4- to 5-oz. skinless salmon fillets, ½ to ¾ inch thick
- ¼ cup butter
- 2 Tbsp. olive oil
- 2 medium fennel bulbs, trimmed, cored, and cut into thin wedges
- 4 medium cooking apples, cored and cut into thin wedges
- ¼ cup honey
  Snipped fresh parsley

1. In a shallow dish combine flour, salt, and pepper. In another shallow dish whisk together eggs and water. In a third shallow dish place bread crumbs. Rinse salmon; pat dry. Dip salmon into flour mixture, then egg mixture, then into bread crumbs to coat; set aside.

2. In a very large skillet heat 2 tablespoons of the butter and the oil over medium heat until butter melts. Add fennel. Cook and stir for 4 minutes. Add apple wedges. Cook and stir for 3 to 4 minutes more or until apples and fennel are tender. Stir in honey. Transfer the mixture to a bowl; set aside.

3. In the same skillet heat remaining 2 tablespoons butter over medium heat. Add salmon. Cook for 8 to 10 minutes or until fish flakes easily when tested with a fork, turning once (if fish browns too quickly, reduce heat to medium-low). Transfer fish and apple mixture to serving plates. Garnish with parsley. Makes 4 servings.

EACH SERVING: *602 cal., 26 g total fat (10 g sat. fat), 195 mg chol., 534 mg sodium, 64 g carbo., 8 g fiber, 31 g pro. Daily Values: 20% vit. A, 38% vit. C, 14% calcium, 21% iron.*

PRIZE TESTED RECIPES® $200 WINNER

JEAN BURNETT, FORKED RIVER, N.J.

FAST! LOW FAT

SWEET APPLE DESSERT GAZPACHO

START TO FINISH: 20 minutes

- 3 6-oz. cartons vanilla low-fat yogurt
- 2 medium Granny Smith apples, peeled, cored, and cut up
- 1 medium cucumber, peeled, halved, seeded, and cut up
- ¾ cup apple juice or apple cider
- 1 Tbsp. packed fresh mint leaves
- 1 fresh jalapeño chile pepper, seeded and cut up* (optional)
- ¼ tsp. salt
  Fresh mint (optional)
  Purchased pizzelles or other cookies (optional)

1. In a food processor or blender combine yogurt, cut-up apples, cucumber, apple juice, mint, jalapeño pepper (if desired), and salt. Cover and process or blend until mixture is nearly smooth. (If container is too full, process or blend half of the mixture at a time.) If desired, garnish with mint and serve with pizzelles. Makes 8 servings.

*NOTE: Because hot chile peppers, such as jalapeños, contain volatile oils that can burn your skin and eyes, avoid direct contact with chiles as much as possible. When working with chile peppers, wear plastic or rubber gloves. If your bare hands touch the chile peppers, wash your hands well with soap and water.

EACH SERVING: *89 cal., 1 g total fat (1 g sat. fat), 3 mg chol., 117 mg sodium, 18 g carbo., 1 g fiber, 3 g pro. Daily Values: 2% vit. A, 6% vit. C, 12% calcium, 2% iron.*

APPLEDORF SALAD WITH CREAMY DRESSING

START TO FINISH: 30 minutes

- 1 cup apple cider or apple juice
- 1 cup dried cranberries
- 4 medium red apples, cored and cut into bite-size pieces
- 1 Tbsp. lemon juice
- 4 stalks celery, sliced
- ½ cup dry roasted sunflower kernels
- 1 cup plain low-fat yogurt
- 1 cup cottage cheese
- 1 Tbsp. honey
- 4 tsp. lemon juice
- ½ cup finely chopped red apple
- 6 cups torn mixed salad greens

1. In a small saucepan heat cider until simmering; remove from heat. Add cranberries. Cover and let stand for 5 minutes. Drain cranberries; discard liquid. In a very large bowl toss the 4 cut-up apples with 1 tablespoon lemon juice. Add cranberries, celery, and sunflower kernels; stir to combine. Set aside.

2. For dressing, in a blender or food processor combine yogurt, cottage cheese, honey, and 4 teaspoons lemon juice. Cover and blend or process until smooth. Transfer to a small bowl; stir in finely chopped apple.

3. To serve, divide salad greens among 8 salad plates. Top with apple-cranberry mixture. Spoon dressing over salads. Makes 8 servings.

EACH SERVING: *202 cal., 5 g total fat (1 g sat. fat), 3 mg chol., 192 mg sodium, 32 g carbo., 4 g fiber, 7 g pro. Daily Values: 11% vit. A, 16% vit. C, 11% calcium, 5% iron.*

HARVEST RAVIOLI

START TO FINISH: 30 minutes

- 1 cup chopped onion (1 large)
- 4 cloves garlic, minced
- 1 Tbsp. olive oil
- 1 1-lb. butternut squash, halved, seeded, peeled, and cut into 1-inch cubes (about 3 cups)
- 1 14-oz. can chicken broth
- 1 Tbsp. snipped fresh sage or 1 tsp. dried sage, crushed
- ½ cup apple cider or apple juice
- 1 Tbsp. cornstarch
- 3 medium Granny Smith apples, cored and cut into thin wedges
- 1 20- to 24-oz. pkg. frozen cheese-filled ravioli
- ½ cup walnuts, toasted and chopped
- 2 Tbsp. grated Parmesan cheese
- ¼ tsp. cracked black pepper
  Snipped fresh sage (optional)

1. In a very large skillet cook onion and garlic in hot oil over medium heat for 5 minutes or until tender, stirring occasionally. Add squash, broth, and dried sage (if using). Bring to boiling; reduce heat. Simmer, covered, for 10 minutes. Combine apple cider and cornstarch; add to skillet along with apple wedges and fresh sage (if using). Cook, stirring gently, until thickened and bubbly. Cook, uncovered, 2 minutes more.

2. Meanwhile, cook ravioli according to package directions. Drain. Add ravioli to hot apple mixture; toss gently to combine. To serve, top with walnuts, Parmesan cheese, pepper, and, if desired, additional fresh sage. Makes 6 servings.

EACH SERVING: *366 cal., 12 g total fat (2 g sat. fat), 31 mg chol., 532 mg sodium, 57 g carbo., 5 g fiber, 11 g pro. Daily Values: 141% vit. A, 33% vit. C, 17% calcium, 8% iron.*

ROAST CHICKEN WITH APPLE TRIO

PREP: 25 minutes **ROAST:** 1¾ hours
STAND: 10 minutes

- 1 24-oz. pkg. sauerkraut, drained
- 1 large yellow onion, halved and thinly sliced
- 4 large Granny Smith apples, cored and sliced
- 6 small red potatoes (about 1 lb.)
- 2 cups packaged peeled fresh baby carrots, halved lengthwise
- 2 cloves garlic, minced
- 1 3- to 4-lb. whole broiler-fryer chicken*
- 1 cup apple cider or apple juice
- 1 Tbsp. snipped fresh marjoram or 1 tsp. dried marjoram, crushed
- 1 tsp. salt
- 1 tsp. ground black pepper
- ½ tsp. caraway seeds
- 1 24- to 25-oz. jar applesauce

1. Preheat oven to 375°F. In a roasting pan layer sauerkraut, onion, apple slices, potatoes, carrots, and garlic.

2. Place chicken, breast side up, on vegetables. Combine apple cider, marjoram, salt, pepper, and caraway seeds; pour over chicken. Cover with heavy foil. Roast for 1¼ hours. Uncover and cut string between legs; roast for 30 to 45 minutes more or until an instant-read thermometer inserted in thigh registers 180°F. Let chicken rest, covered, for 10 minutes before carving. Transfer chicken and vegetables to platter.

3. Meanwhile, heat applesauce. Serve applesauce with chicken. Makes 6 servings.

*NOTE: Some chickens are sold ready to roast. If not already done, pull neck skin of chicken to the back and fasten with a short skewer. Tie drumsticks to tail with kitchen string. Twist wing tips under the back.

EACH SERVING: *576 cal., 15 g total fat (5 g sat. fat), 198 mg chol., 1,447 mg sodium, 56 g carbo., 10 g fiber, 54 g pro. Daily Values: 159% vit. A, 77% vit. C, 16% calcium, 55% iron.*

FRENCH APPLE DESSERT RISOTTO

PREP: 25 minutes **COOK:** 30 minutes

- 3 Tbsp. butter
- 3 large cooking apples, peeled, cored, and sliced (about 6 cups)
- 2 tsp. ground cinnamon
- 1 Tbsp. maple syrup
- 4 cups milk
- 1¼ cups uncooked Arborio rice
- ½ cup apple cider
- 1 Tbsp. sugar
  Dash salt
- ¼ to ½ cup whipping cream, half-and-half, or light cream
- 2 oz. white baking chocolate, chopped
- 2 tsp. vanilla

1. In a large skillet melt 2 tablespoons of the butter over medium heat. Add apple slices and cinnamon. Cook and stir about 4 minutes or until apple slices are tender but still hold their shape. Remove from heat. Stir in syrup and set aside.

2. In a medium saucepan heat milk over medium heat until simmering (do not boil); keep warm.

3. In a large saucepan melt remaining 1 tablespoon butter over medium heat. Add rice. Cook and stir until rice is coated with butter. Stir in cider, sugar, and salt. Cook and stir until cider is absorbed. Add ½ cup of the warm milk. Continue to cook and stir over medium heat until milk is absorbed. Add remaining milk, ½ cup at a time, until the rice is tender and liquid is absorbed but mixture is still creamy (this should take about 25 minutes). Remove from heat.

4. Stir in ¼ cup cream, the chocolate, and vanilla until chocolate melts. Stir in half of the cooked apple mixture. If desired, stir in additional cream until desired consistency. Spoon into a serving dish. Top with remaining apple mixture. Makes 8 servings.

EACH SERVING: *325 cal., 12 g total fat (8 g sat. fat), 33 mg chol., 111 mg sodium, 47 g carbo., 3 g fiber, 7 g pro. Daily Values: 10% vit. A, 7% vit. C, 17% calcium, 7% iron.*

EASY PASTA TOSSES

PRIZE TESTED RECIPES® $400 WINNER

NANETTE PORTERFIELD, WARREN, MICH.

FAST!

EASY ITALIAN MAC

START TO FINISH: 30 minutes

    8 oz. dried bow tie pasta
    1 fennel bulb, trimmed and cored
    8 oz. fresh asparagus spears
    1 Tbsp. butter
    1 Tbsp. olive oil
    1 clove garlic, minced
    ½ cup mascarpone cheese
    ½ cup shredded mozzarella cheese (2 oz.)
    ¼ cup finely shredded Pecorino Romano cheese (1 oz.)
    1 cup frozen peas, thawed
       Salt
       Ground black pepper
    1 Tbsp. finely chopped fresh Italian (flat-leaf) parsley

1. Cook pasta according to package directions. Drain pasta, reserving ½ cup of the pasta water; set aside.
2. Chop fennel into 1-inch pieces. Snap off and discard woody bases from asparagus. Cut asparagus into 1-inch pieces. In a large skillet cook and stir fennel and asparagus in hot butter and olive oil over medium heat for 5 to 7 minutes or until nearly tender. Add garlic and cook 1 minute more.
3. Add cooked pasta, mascarpone cheese, and reserved pasta water to skillet. Gently stir to combine. Stir in mozzarella, Romano, and peas. Season to taste with salt and pepper. Transfer to a serving dish; sprinkle with parsley. Makes 4 servings.
EACH SERVING: *449 cal., 19 g total fat (9 g sat. fat), 41 mg chol., 430 mg sodium, 55 g carbo., 6 g fiber, 19 g pro. Daily Values: 28% vit. A, 28% vit. C, 23% calcium, 21% iron.*

PRIZE TESTED RECIPES® $200 WINNER

KARIN WOLD-PARISH, LINCOLN, NEB.

CHICKEN FAJITA PASTA

START TO FINISH: 35 minutes

    12 oz. dried pappardelle pasta or egg noodles
     1 8-oz. carton dairy sour cream
     ½ cup chipotle liquid meat marinade
     2 Tbsp. lime juice
     1 tsp. chili powder
     1 tsp. ground cumin
     ½ tsp. crushed red pepper
     1 medium onion, halved and thinly sliced (½ cup)
     1 medium red sweet pepper, seeded and cut into thin
        bite-size strips (1 cup)
     1 fresh Anaheim chile pepper, seeded and cut into thin
        bite-size strips (⅓ cup) (See Note, page 306)
     2 Tbsp. olive oil
     3 large skinless, boneless chicken breast halves, cut into
        thin bite-size strips (1 to 1¼ lb. total)
     1 Tbsp. snipped fresh cilantro (optional)
        Lime wedges (optional)

1. In a 4- to 5-quart Dutch oven cook pasta in boiling lightly salted water according to package directions. Drain and return pasta to pan; keep warm. Meanwhile, in a medium bowl combine sour cream, marinade, lime juice, chili powder, cumin, and crushed red pepper. Set aside.
2. In a large skillet cook and stir onion, sweet pepper, and Anaheim pepper in 1 tablespoon of the hot oil over medium heat for 4 to 5 minutes or until crisp-tender. Remove vegetables from skillet; set aside. Add remaining oil to skillet. Add half of the chicken; cook and stir over medium-high heat for 2 to 3 minutes or until chicken is no longer pink. Remove from skillet. Repeat with remaining chicken, adding additional oil if necessary. Add chicken, vegetables, and sour cream mixture to pasta. Toss to coat. Heat through over low heat. If desired, sprinkle with cilantro and serve with lime wedges. Makes 6 to 8 servings.
EACH SERVING: *453 cal., 15 g total fat (6 g sat. fat), 60 mg chol., 589 mg sodium, 53 g carbo., 3 g fiber, 27 g pro. Daily Values: 22% vit. A, 98% vit. C, 7% calcium, 13% iron.*

CAJUN SHRIMP PASTA WITH ANDOUILLE CREAM SAUCE

START TO FINISH: 40 minutes

    1 lb. fresh or frozen peeled, deveined
       large shrimp
    1 lb. dried bow tie pasta
    1 cup chopped sweet onion (1 large)
    1 Tbsp. olive oil
    3 to 4 tsp. Cajun seasoning
    1 10-oz. container refrigerated Alfredo
       pasta sauce
    ½ cup milk
    4 oz. smoked cheddar cheese,
       shredded (1 cup)
    4 oz. cooked andouille sausage,
       chopped
    1 cup chopped tomato
       Grated Parmesan cheese
       Sliced green onion

1. Thaw shrimp, if frozen. Set aside. Cook pasta according to package directions. Drain and return pasta to pan; keep warm.
2. Meanwhile, in a very large skillet cook onion in hot oil over medium heat for 5 to 10 minutes or until onion is tender, stirring occasionally. Stir in Cajun seasoning. Add shrimp. Cook for 2 to 4 minutes or until shrimp are opaque, stirring occasionally. Reduce heat to low.
3. Stir in Alfredo sauce, milk, and cheddar cheese. Cook and stir over low heat until cheese melts. Stir in cooked sausage and tomato. Add shrimp mixture to hot pasta; toss gently to coat. Sprinkle with Parmesan and green onion. Makes 8 servings.

EACH SERVING: *473 cal., 17 g total fat (8 g sat. fat), 136 mg chol., 629 mg sodium, 51 g carbo., 3 g fiber, 29 g pro. Daily Values: 16% vit. A, 11% vit. C, 25% calcium, 22% iron.*

FAST!
CHIPOTLE SHRIMP PASTA

START TO FINISH: 30 minutes

    1 cup chicken broth
    1 cup whipping cream
    1 tsp. finely chopped chipotle pepper
       in adobo sauce
    1 lb. medium shrimp in shells, peeled
       and deveined
    8 oz. dried linguine
    2 Tbsp. grated Parmesan cheese
    1 Tbsp. snipped fresh parsley
       Lime wedges

1. In a medium saucepan stir together broth, cream, and chipotle pepper. Bring to boiling; reduce heat. Boil gently, uncovered, for 15 minutes or until thickened and reduced by half, stirring occasionally. Add shrimp; return to boiling. Reduce heat and cook, uncovered, 2 minutes more or until shrimp are opaque, stirring occasionally.

2. Meanwhile, cook linguine according to package directions. Drain and return to pan.
3. Add shrimp mixture and Parmesan cheese to pasta; toss to coat. Transfer to a serving dish. Sprinkle with parsley and serve with lime wedges. Makes 4 servings.

EACH SERVING: *556 cal., 26 g total fat (15 g sat. fat), 257 mg chol., 478 mg sodium, 46 g carbo., 2 g fiber, 33 g pro. Daily Values: 24% vit. A, 11% vit. C, 14% calcium, 27% iron.*

SPINACH AND PANCETTA PASTA

START TO FINISH: 40 minutes

    2 oz. pancetta, chopped
    ½ cup chopped onion (1 medium)
    2 cloves garlic, minced
    ½ cup pine nuts
    ½ cup tub-style cream cheese spread
       with chive and onion
    ¼ tsp. salt
    ¼ tsp. ground black pepper
    8 oz. dried penne pasta
    1 8- to 9-oz. pkg. frozen artichoke
       hearts
    1 5- to 7-oz. pkg. fresh baby spinach
    ¼ cup finely shredded Parmesan
       cheese

1. In a large skillet cook pancetta and onion over medium-low heat about 15 minutes or until pancetta and onion are golden brown, stirring occasionally. Add garlic and pine nuts; cook and stir for 1 minute. Stir in cream cheese spread, salt, and pepper. Heat until the cheese melts.
2. Meanwhile, in a 5- to 6-quart Dutch oven cook penne according to package directions, adding artichoke hearts for the last 4 minutes of cooking. Drain, reserving ½ cup of the pasta cooking water. Return pasta mixture to Dutch oven. Add pancetta mixture; toss to coat. Add pasta water to make desired consistency. Toss in spinach. Transfer to a large serving bowl; sprinkle with Parmesan cheese. Makes 4 servings.

EACH SERVING: *555 cal., 29 g total fat (10 g sat. fat), 44 mg chol., 695 mg sodium, 56 g carbo., 7 g fiber, 17 g pro. Daily Values: 77% vit. A, 28% vit. C, 19% calcium, 23% iron.*

HONEY MUSTARD PASTA SALAD

PREP: 25 minutes   **CHILL:** 4 hours

    8 oz. dried mostaccioli pasta
    8 oz. cheddar cheese, cut into
       ½-inch cubes
    8 oz. cooked ham, cut into
       ½-inch cubes
    1 6-oz. can pitted ripe olives, drained
       and halved
    4 medium green onions, sliced
    ⅓ cup honey mustard
    ¼ cup olive oil
    ¼ cup red wine vinegar
    ¼ tsp. salt
    ¼ tsp. ground black pepper

1. Cook pasta according to package directions. Drain; rinse with cold water. Transfer to a large bowl. Add cheese, ham, olives, and sliced onion.
2. For dressing, in a small bowl whisk together honey mustard, olive oil, vinegar, salt, and pepper. Pour dressing over pasta mixture; toss to coat. Cover and chill for 4 to 24 hours. Toss before serving. Makes 5 servings.

EACH SERVING: *579 cal., 34 g total fat (13 g sat. fat), 74 mg chol., 1,386 mg sodium, 42 g carbo., 3 g fiber, 25 g pro. Daily Values: 14% vit. A, 7% vit. C, 38% calcium, 21% iron.*

FAST!
ASIAN NOODLE TOSS

START TO FINISH: 25 minutes

    8 oz. dried linguine
    1 16-oz. pkg. frozen broccoli stir-fry
       vegetable blend
    ¼ cup chicken broth
    ¼ cup rice vinegar
    2 Tbsp. toasted sesame oil
    1 Tbsp. soy sauce
    2 tsp. grated fresh ginger
    ⅛ to ¼ tsp. crushed red pepper
       (optional)
    2 cups chopped cooked pork, chicken,
       or turkey
    ¼ cup snipped fresh cilantro or mint
       Chopped peanuts (optional)

1. Cook linguine according to package directions, adding the vegetable blend for the last 4 minutes of cooking; drain and remove from pan.
2. In the same pan combine chicken broth, rice vinegar, sesame oil, soy sauce, ginger, and, if desired, crushed red pepper. Heat to boiling. Stir in cooked meat. Add cooked pasta mixture; toss to coat and heat through. Transfer to a serving bowl and sprinkle with cilantro. If desired, sprinkle with peanuts. Makes 4 to 6 servings.

EACH SERVING: *534 cal., 20 g total fat (6 g sat. fat), 70 mg chol., 407 mg sodium, 50 g carbo., 5 g fiber, 34 g pro. Daily Values: 26% vit. A, 31% vit. C, 6% calcium, 20% iron.*

WHAT'S NEW IN MEAT LOAF

WENDY A. TUTTLE, ALBUQUERQUE, N.M.

RACHAEL BLEYMAIER, VILLE PLATTE, LA.

ENCHILADA MEAT LOAF

PREP: 20 minutes **BAKE:** 50 minutes **STAND:** 10 minutes

- 1 egg, lightly beaten
- ½ finely chopped onion (1 medium)
- ¼ cup bottled salsa
- 2 Tbsp. chili powder
- 3 cloves garlic, minced
- ½ tsp. salt
- 1 lb. ground beef
- 1 8.5-oz. pkg. corn muffin mix
- 2 oz. sharp cheddar cheese, sliced
  Bottled salsa (optional)

1. Preheat oven to 350°F. In a large bowl combine egg, onion, ¼ cup salsa, chili powder, garlic, and salt; add ground beef and mix well. Shape into a ball and place in a 9-inch pie plate. Flatten the meat mixture to a 6-inch circle; set aside.

2. Prepare corn muffin mix according to package directions. Spread corn muffin batter over meat in pie plate. Bake about 50 minutes or until an instant-read thermometer inserted into the side of the meat loaf registers 160°F. Remove from oven. Halve cheese slices and arrange on top of the corn muffin mixture. Cover loosely and let stand 10 minutes before serving. If desired, serve with additional salsa. Makes 6 servings.

EACH SERVING: *573 cal., 33 g total fat (13 g sat. fat), 161 mg chol., 1,069 mg sodium, 46 g carbo., 3 g fiber, 23 g pro. Daily Values: 22% vit. A, 6% vit. C, 16% calcium, 20% iron.*

LOW FAT
GINGER-SESAME MEAT LOAF

PREP: 35 minutes **BAKE:** 1 hour **STAND:** 10 minutes

    Nonstick cooking spray
- 2 eggs, lightly beaten
- 1 cup chopped green onion
- 1 cup finely shredded carrot
- ¼ cup reduced-sodium soy sauce
- 4 cloves garlic, minced
- 2 Tbsp. sesame seeds
- 1 Tbsp. finely chopped lemongrass or
  2 tsp. finely shredded lemon peel (optional)
- 1 Tbsp. grated fresh ginger
- 2 tsp. chili powder
- 1½ lb. uncooked ground chicken
- 8 oz. pad thai noodles (rice noodles)
- ⅔ cup purchased pad thai stir-fry sauce
- 2 Tbsp. chicken broth
  Sliced green onion and/or sesame seeds (optional)

1. Preheat oven to 350°F. Lightly coat an 84×2-inch loaf pan with cooking spray; set aside.

2. In a large bowl combine eggs, green onion, carrot, soy sauce, garlic, sesame seeds, lemongrass or lemon peel (if using), ginger, and chili powder; add ground chicken. Mix well. Pat into prepared pan.

3. Bake for 60 to 70 minutes or until an instant-read thermometer inserted into center of meat loaf registers 165°F. Remove from oven. Let stand for 10 minutes; remove from pan.

4. Meanwhile, prepare noodles according to package directions; drain. Toss with ⅓ cup of the pad thai sauce. Return mixture to pan and heat through. In a small saucepan heat remaining pad thai sauce and broth just to boiling. To serve, divide noodles among plates; top with sliced meat loaf. Drizzle with broth mixture. If desired, sprinkle with green onion and/or sesame seeds. Makes 8 servings.

EACH SERVING: *308 cal., 8 g total fat (2 g sat. fat), 112 mg chol., 723 mg sodium, 33 g carbo., 3 g fiber, 24 g pro. Daily Values: 56% vit. A, 12% vit. C, 7% calcium, 11% iron.*

MEAT LOAF ITALIANO

PREP: 35 minutes **BAKE:** 55 minutes
STAND: 10 minutess

- ¼ cup dried tomatoes (not oil pack)
- 2 eggs, lightly beaten
- ½ cup finely chopped onion (1 medium)
- 1 15-oz. can pizza sauce
- ½ cup seasoned fine dry bread crumbs
- 2 cloves garlic, minced
- ½ tsp. salt
- ¼ tsp. ground black pepper
- 1 lb. lean ground beef
- 1 lb. lean ground pork
- 4 oz. smoked or regular provolone cheese or smoked mozzarella cheese, shredded
- 1 cup small-curd cream-style cottage cheese
- 2 Tbsp. purchased basil pesto
- ½ of a medium red sweet pepper, finely chopped

1. In a small bowl add enough hot water to dried tomatoes to cover; let stand for 30 minutes or until softened. Drain well; finely snip tomatoes.

2. Preheat oven to 350°F. In a very large bowl combine eggs, onion, ½ cup of the pizza sauce, bread crumbs, garlic, salt, and black pepper. Add beef and pork; mix well. Pat half of the meat mixture into a 9×9×2-inch baking pan.

3. In a medium bowl combine half of the shredded cheese, the cottage cheese, pesto, sweet pepper, and snipped tomatoes. Spread mixture over meat in pan. Top with remaining meat mixture.

4. Bake, uncovered, for 55 to 65 minutes or until an instant-read thermometer inserted into center of meat loaf registers 160°F. Remove from oven. Carefully drain off fat. Sprinkle the loaf with remaining shredded cheese; let stand for 10 minutes.

5. Meanwhile, in a small saucepan heat remaining pizza sauce until warm. Cut meat loaf into squares. Pass heated sauce. Makes 9 servings.

EACH SERVING: *301 cal., 16 g total fat (7 g sat. fat), 117 mg chol., 702 mg sodium, 12 g carbo., 2 g fiber, 25 g pro. Daily Values: 15% vit. A, 26% vit. C, 17% calcium, 13% iron.*

MEAT LOAF WITH RED CURRANT SAUCE

PREP: 25 minutes **BAKE:** 65 minutes
STAND: 10 minutes

- 1 lb. lean ground beef
- 1 lb. ground ham
- 1 cup finely chopped onion (1 large)
- 1 cup cooked wild rice
- ½ cup tart dried cherries, snipped
- ¼ cup fine dry bread crumbs
- 2 eggs, lightly beaten
- ½ tsp. ground sage
- 1 cup red currant jelly
- 3 Tbsp. rice vinegar or white wine vinegar
- 1 Tbsp. butter
- 1 Tbsp. yellow mustard
- ½ tsp. paprika
- ¼ tsp. salt

1. Preheat oven to 350°F. Line a shallow baking pan with foil; set aside. In a very large bowl combine beef, ham, onion, cooked rice, cherries, bread crumbs, eggs, and sage; mix well. Shape mixture into an 8½×4½-inch oval loaf in prepared pan.

2. Bake for 65 to 75 minutes or until an instant-read thermometer inserted in center of meat loaf registers 160°F. Remove from oven; cover and let stand for 10 minutes.

3. Meanwhile, for sauce, in a small saucepan whisk together jelly, vinegar, butter, mustard, paprika, and salt. Bring to boiling, whisking constantly. Reduce heat; simmer, uncovered, for 12 to 15 minutes or until reduced to ¾ cup. Sauce thickens as it cools. Serve warm with meat loaf. Makes 8 servings.

EACH SERVING: *416 cal., 14 g total fat (5 g sat. fat), 126 mg chol., 941 mg sodium, 50 g carbo., 3 g fiber, 24 g pro. Daily Values: 6% vit. A, 7% vit. C, 5% calcium, 15% iron.*

GREEK-INSPIRED MEAT LOAF ROLL

PREP: 25 minutes **BAKE:** 1¼ hours
STAND: 10 minutes

- 2 eggs, lightly beaten
- ¼ cup tomato juice
- ¾ cup soft bread crumbs
- 1 tsp. Greek seasoning
- ½ tsp. salt
- 1 lb. ground lamb or beef
- 1 lb. uncooked ground turkey
- ½ of a 10-oz. pkg. frozen chopped spinach, thawed and well drained
- 2 oz. feta cheese, crumbled (½ cup)
- ¼ cup oil-packed dried tomatoes, patted dry and chopped
  Chopped fresh tomato (optional)
  Crumbled feta cheese (optional)

1. Preheat oven to 350°F. In a large bowl stir together eggs, tomato juice, bread crumbs, Greek seasoning, and salt. Add ground lamb and turkey; mix well. On parchment paper or foil pat meat into a 12×8-inch rectangle.

Leaving a ½-inch border, sprinkle meat with spinach, 2 ounces feta, and dried tomatoes. Starting from a short side, carefully roll up meat, using paper to lift; seal edges and ends. Place roll, seam side down, in a 13×9×2-inch baking pan, reshaping loaf as necessary.

2. Bake, uncovered, for 1¼ hours or until an instant-read thermometer inserted into center registers 165°F. Remove from oven. Let stand, covered with foil, for 10 minutes.

3. To serve, slice meat loaf. If desired, sprinkle slices with chopped fresh tomato and additional crumbled feta cheese. Makes 8 servings.

EACH SERVING: *303 cal., 21 g total fat (7 g sat. fat), 145 mg chol., 403 mg sodium, 4 g carbo., 1 g fiber, 23 g pro. Daily Values: 45% vit. A, 15% vit. C, 9% calcium, 14% iron.*

KID FRIENDLY

MEAT AND POTATO LOAVES

PREP: 25 minutes **BAKE:** 35 minutes

- 1 egg, lightly beaten
- ⅓ cup fine dry bread crumbs
- ¼ cup finely chopped onion
- ¼ cup beef broth
- ¼ tsp. salt
- ¼ tsp. ground black pepper
- 1 lb. ground beef
- 1¼ cups frozen shredded hash brown potatoes, thawed
- 1 cup shredded Mexican cheese blend
- ¾ cup chunky salsa

1. Preheat oven to 350°F. In a large bowl combine egg, bread crumbs, onion, broth, salt, and pepper. Add ground beef; mix well. Divide into four portions.

2. In a medium bowl combine potatoes, ½ cup of the cheese, and ¼ cup of the salsa. Set mixture aside.

3. On foil pat each portion of meat mixture into a 5-inch square. Place one-fourth of the potato mixture down the center of each square, leaving a 1-inch border at sides and ends. Shape meat mixture around potato mixture, pressing to seal. Place loaves, seam sides down, in a 13×9×2-inch baking pan.

4. Bake, uncovered, for 30 minutes or until an instant-read thermometer inserted in centers registers 160°F. Top with remaining salsa and cheese; bake loaves 5 minutes more. Makes 4 servings.

EACH SERVING: *612 cal., 45 g total fat (19 g sat. fat), 166 mg chol., 863 mg sodium, 23 g carbo., 2 g fiber, 27 g pro. Daily Values: 10% vit. A, 12% vit. C, 27% calcium, 19% iron.*

CREATIVE BROWNIES

JENNIFER CODUTO, KENT, OHIO

COFFEE AND COOKIE BROWNIES

PREP: 20 minutes **BAKE:** 40 minutes

    1   16.5- to 18-oz. pkg. refrigerated sugar cookie dough
    2   eggs, lightly beaten
    1   19.5-oz. pkg. milk chocolate brownie mix
    ½   cup cooking oil
    ⅓   cup coffee liqueur or cooled strong coffee
    1   cup semisweet or bittersweet chocolate pieces

1. Preheat oven to 350°F. Press sugar cookie dough into the bottom of a 13×9×2-inch baking pan; set aside.
2. In a large bowl stir eggs, brownie mix, oil, and liqueur just until combined. Spread brownie mixture over sugar cookie dough. Sprinkle with chocolate pieces.
3. Bake for 40 minutes or until edges are set. Cool completely in pan on a wire rack. Cut into bars. Makes 24 bars.
EACH BAR: *279 cal., 15 g total fat (3 g sat. fat), 23 mg chol., 159 mg sodium, 36 g carbo., 1 g fiber, 3 g pro. Daily Values: 1% vit. A, 2% calcium, 6% iron.*

KRISTINE KELLY, SALEM, WIS.

KID FRIENDLY

BUTTERSCOTCH BROWNIES

PREP: 30 minutes **BAKE:** 20 minutes **COOL:** 2 hours

    ⅓   cup butter
    ⅔   cup packed brown sugar
    1⅓ cups flaked or shredded coconut
    ¾   cup chopped pecans
    ½   cup butter, softened
    1   cup packed brown sugar
    ½   tsp. baking soda
    ¼   tsp. salt
    3   eggs
    ½   tsp. vanilla
    1½ cups all-purpose flour
    ½   cup chopped pecans
    ½   cup tiny marshmallows
        Caramel-flavor ice cream topping (optional)

1. Preheat oven to 350°F. Grease a 13×9×2-inch baking pan; set aside. In a small saucepan melt ⅓ cup butter; stir in ⅔ cup brown sugar, coconut, and ¾ cup pecans. Pat evenly into prepared pan. Set aside.
2. In a large mixing bowl beat ½ cup butter with an electric mixer on medium to high speed for 30 seconds. Add 1 cup brown sugar, baking soda, and salt; beat until combined. Beat in eggs and vanilla until combined. Add flour and beat until combined. Stir in ½ cup pecans and marshmallows. Spoon small mounds of mixture over coconut mixture in pan. Carefully spread to cover.
3. Bake about 20 minutes (mixture should be evenly brown; center may jiggle slightly when shaken). Cool in pan on a wire rack.
4. Cut into bars. If desired, drizzle with caramel ice cream topping. Makes 24 bars.
EACH BAR: *211 cal., 13 g total fat (6 g sat. fat), 43 mg chol., 113 mg sodium, 23 g carbo., 1 g fiber, 2 g pro. Daily Values: 5% vit. A, 2% calcium, 6% iron.*

APPLE BROWNIES WITH DULCE DE LECHE FROSTING

PREP: 35 minutes **BAKE:** 25 minutes

- ½ cup shortening
- 1¼ cups sugar
- 2 eggs
- ½ cup applesauce
- 2 oz. unsweetened chocolate, melted and cooled
- 1 tsp. vanilla
- 1¼ cups all-purpose flour
- 1 tsp. baking powder
- ½ tsp. salt
- 1 cup finely shredded, peeled, cored cooking apple
- 1 cup chopped walnuts, toasted
- 1 14-oz. can sweetened condensed milk
- 2 Tbsp. butter
- 1 tsp. vanilla

1. Preheat oven to 350°F. Line a 13×9×2-inch baking pan with foil, extending foil beyond ends of pan. Grease foil or lightly coat with nonstick cooking spray. Set aside.

2. In a large mixing bowl beat shortening and sugar with an electric mixer on medium speed until combined. Beat in eggs until combined. Beat in applesauce, chocolate, and 1 teaspoon vanilla until combined. Stir together flour, baking powder, and salt; stir into creamed mixture just until combined. Gently stir in apple and ½ cup of the walnuts. Spread batter into prepared pan. Bake for 25 minutes or until center is set and sides start to pull away from the pan. Cool about 20 minutes or until slightly warm.

3. Meanwhile, for frosting, in a medium saucepan combine sweetened condensed milk and butter. Cook and stir over medium heat until butter melts and mixture bubbles. Reduce heat to medium-low; cook about 5 minutes or until mixture thickens to the consistency of a thin pudding, stirring constantly to prevent scorching. Remove from heat; stir in 1 teaspoon vanilla. Immediately pour frosting over brownies, spreading evenly; sprinkle with remaining nuts. Cool completely in pan on a wire rack. Use foil to lift from pan. Cut into bars. Makes 24 bars.

EACH BAR: *221 cal., 12 g total fat (4 g sat. fat), 26 mg chol., 98 mg sodium, 28 g carbo., 1 g fiber, 3 g pro. Daily Values: 2% vit. A, 1% vit. C, 7% calcium, 6% iron.*

BENGAL BROWNIES

PREP: 20 minutes **BAKE:** 30 minutes

- 4 oz. unsweetened chocolate
- 1 cup butter
- 1 cup granulated sugar
- 1 cup packed brown sugar
- 1 tsp. vanilla
  Dash salt
- 1 cup all-purpose flour
- ½ tsp. ground cardamom
- 3 eggs
- 1 recipe Spiced Pecans
- ⅓ cup hot fudge ice cream topping

1. Preheat oven to 350°F. Line a 3-quart rectangular baking dish with foil, extending foil beyond ends of dish. Grease foil or lightly coat with nonstick cooking spray. Set aside.

2. In a medium saucepan heat and stir chocolate and butter over low heat until smooth. Remove from heat. Beat in granulated sugar, brown sugar, vanilla, and salt. Set the mixture aside.

3. Stir together flour and cardamom; set aside. In a large mixing bowl beat eggs until foamy. Add chocolate and flour mixtures and mix well. Gently stir in Spiced Pecans. Spread batter into prepared baking dish. Drizzle fudge topping evenly in a thin stream over batter. Use a narrow spatula to zigzag topping through batter.

4. Bake for 30 minutes. Cool completely in pan on a wire rack. Use foil to lift from dish. Cut into bars. Makes 18 to 24 bars.

SPICED PECANS: In a heavy skillet heat and stir 1 cup chopped pecans, 1 tablespoon butter, 1 teaspoon sugar, ¼ teaspoon ground cardamom, and ⅛ teaspoon ground cloves over medium heat until nuts are golden. Cool on paper towels. Makes 1 cup.

EACH BAR: *319 cal., 20 g total fat (10 g sat. fat), 64 mg chol., 118 mg sodium, 35 g carbo., 2 g fiber, 3 g pro. Daily Values: 8% vit. A, 4% calcium, 11% iron.*

CARAMEL HAZELNUT BROWNIES

PREP: 20 minutes **BAKE:** 30 minutes

- 24 vanilla caramels (½ of a 14-oz. package), unwrapped
- ⅔ cup sweetened condensed milk
- 1⅔ cups all-purpose flour
- 1 tsp. baking powder
- ½ tsp. salt
- ⅔ cup butter, softened
- ½ cup chocolate-hazelnut spread
- 1⅔ cups sugar
- 4 eggs
- 3 oz. unsweetened chocolate, melted and cooled
- 1 cup hazelnuts, toasted and coarsely chopped

1. Preheat the oven to 350°F. Line a 15×10×1-inch baking pan with heavy foil, extending foil beyond ends of pan. Grease foil or lightly coat with cooking spray. Set aside. In a medium saucepan combine caramels and condensed milk. Cook and stir over medium-low heat until caramels melt and mixture is smooth; set aside.

2. In a medium bowl combine flour, baking powder, and salt; set aside. In a large mixing bowl combine butter and chocolate-hazelnut spread; beat with an electric mixer on medium speed for 30 seconds. Gradually beat in sugar. Add eggs, 1 at a time, beating well after each addition. Stir in unsweetened chocolate. Stir in flour mixture. Stir in hazelnuts. Spread batter into prepared pan. Drizzle caramel mixture over brownies. Use a knife to swirl caramel mixture into brownie mixture.

3. Bake for to 30 to 35 minutes or until center is set and edges begin to pull away from sides of pan. Cool in pan on a wire rack. Use foil to lift from pan. Cut into bars. Makes 32 bars.

EACH BAR: *211 cal., 11 g total fat (4 g sat. fat), 39 mg chol., 148 mg sodium, 28 g carbo., 1 g fiber, 3 g pro. Daily Values: 3% vit. A, 1% vit. C, 5% calcium, 6% iron.*

CHOCO-CHERRY BROWNIES

PREP: 25 minutes **BAKE:** 30 minutes

- Nonstick cooking spray
- ½ cup dried tart cherries
- 2 Tbsp. orange juice
- 1 cup semisweet chocolate pieces
- 6 Tbsp. butter
- ½ cup packed brown sugar
- 2 eggs
- 1 tsp. vanilla
- ¾ cup all-purpose flour
- ½ cup plain granola
- ¼ cup quick-cooking rolled oats
- ¼ tsp. baking soda
- ¼ teaspoon salt

1. Preheat oven to 325°F. Line a 9×9×2-inch baking pan with foil, extending foil beyond ends of pan. Lightly coat foil with cooking spray. Set aside. In a small microwave-safe bowl combine cherries and orange juice; microwave, uncovered, on 100% power (high) for 1 minute, stirring once. Set aside.

2. Meanwhile, in a medium saucepan melt chocolate and butter over low heat, stirring constantly. Remove from heat; stir in brown sugar. Stir in eggs and vanilla. In a small bowl stir together flour, granola, oats, undrained cherries, baking soda, and salt; stir into chocolate mixture until combined. Spread batter into prepared pan.

3. Bake for 30 minutes. Cool completely in pan on a wire rack. Use foil to lift from pan. Cut into bars. Makes 16 bars.

EACH BAR: *179 cal., 9 g total fat (5 g sat. fat), 38 mg chol., 102 mg sodium, 24 g carbo., 1 g fiber, 2 g pro. Daily Values: 6% vit. A, 2% vit. C, 2% calcium, 6% iron.*

WINTER SOUPS

SPLIT PEA SOUP WITH BARLEY

PREP: 20 minutes **COOK:** 65 minutes

- 10 cups water
- 1 lb. dry yellow split peas, rinsed and drained (about 2 cups)
- ½ cup regular (not quick-cooking) barley
- 2 Tbsp. instant chicken bouillon granules
- 1 bay leaf
- 1 cup finely chopped celery (2 stalks)
- 1 cup finely chopped carrot (2 medium)
- ½ cup finely chopped onion (1 medium)
- 5 ounces cooked ham, chopped (1 cup)
- ½ tsp. ground black pepper
  Salt and ground black pepper

1. In a 4- to 5-quart Dutch oven or pot combine the water, split peas, barley, bouillon granules, and bay leaf. Bring to boiling; reduce heat. Simmer, covered, for 30 minutes.

2. Stir in celery, carrot, and onion. Return to boiling; reduce heat. Simmer, covered, for 30 minutes more or until vegetables, peas, and barley are tender. Stir in ham and ½ teaspoon pepper. Cook for 5 minutes more or until ham is heated through. Remove and discard bay leaf. Season to taste with salt and pepper. Makes 8 servings.

EACH SERVING: *279 cal., 3 g total fat (1 g sat. fat), 10 mg chol., 1,131 mg sodium, 47 g carbo., 18 g fiber, 19 g pro. Daily Values: 54% vit. A, 6% vit. C, 6% calcium, 16% iron.*

GINGER-CARROT SOUP

PREP: 30 minutes **COOK:** 50 minutes

- 2 Tbsp. cooking oil
- 3 cups thinly sliced onion
- 2 Tbsp. sugar
- ⅛ tsp. freshly ground black pepper
- 2 Tbsp. grated fresh ginger
- 8 carrots (about 1¼ lb.)
- 1 sweet potato
- 6 cups chicken broth
- 1 cup half-and-half or light cream
  Salt and ground black pepper

1. For caramelized onion, in a large skillet heat oil over medium heat. Add onion, sugar, and ⅛ teaspoon pepper; reduce heat to low. Cook, covered, for 30 minutes, stirring twice. Add ginger; cook, uncovered, for 20 to 30 minutes more or until onion is golden brown, stirring occasionally. Divide onion mixture in half.

2. Meanwhile, peel carrots and sweet potato; cut into 1-inch pieces. In a large saucepan or Dutch oven combine broth, carrot pieces, and sweet potato. Bring to boiling; reduce heat. Simmer, covered, for 40 minutes or until vegetables are very tender. Add half of the caramelized onion to vegetables in saucepan. With a handheld blender puree until mixture is nearly smooth (or process 2 cups at a time in a food processor). Add half-and-half; heat through. Season to taste with salt and additional ground black pepper. Top servings with remaining caramelized onion. Makes 12 servings.

EACH SERVING: *105 cal., 5 g total fat (2 g sat. fat), 9 mg chol., 524 mg sodium, 13 g carbo., 2 g fiber, 2 g pro. Daily Values: 169% vit. A, 10% vit. C, 5% calcium, 2% iron.*

CREAM OF CHILE POBLANO SOUP

PREP: 20 minutes **ROAST:** 25 minutes
STAND: 20 minutes

- 5 poblano chile peppers
- 2 Tbsp. cooking oil
- ¾ cup sliced celery
- ½ cup chopped onion (1 medium)
- 4 cloves garlic, minced
- 2 Tbsp. all-purpose flour
- 2 14-oz. cans chicken broth
- 1 cup loosely packed cilantro leaves
- 1 12-oz. can evaporated milk
  Salt and ground black pepper
  Lime wedges

1. Preheat oven to 425°F. Halve poblanos; discard seeds, stems, and membranes (see Note, page 318). Place pepper halves, cut sides down, on a foil-lined baking sheet. Roast, uncovered, for 25 minutes or until skins are charred. Wrap in the foil; let stand for 20 minutes.

2. Meanwhile, in a large saucepan heat oil over medium heat. Add celery, onion, and garlic; cook until tender. Stir in flour. Remove from heat.

3. Peel peppers. In a blender or large food processor combine 4 of the pepper halves, the onion mixture, and ½ cup of the broth. Cover and blend or process until nearly smooth. Add cilantro; cover and blend or process until combined. Return mixture to saucepan. In blender or food processor puree remaining peppers with ½ cup of the broth. Add to mixture in saucepan along with remaining broth. Cook and stir until slightly thickened and bubbly. Stir in evaporated milk; heat through. Season to taste with salt and black pepper. Serve with lime wedges. Makes 8 servings.

EACH SERVING: *139 cal., 7 g total fat (2 g sat. fat), 13 mg chol., 531 mg sodium, 15 g carbo., 1 g fiber, 5 g pro. Daily Values: 27% vit. A, 346% vit. C, 15% calcium, 14% iron.*

CREAMY BROCCOLI-CAULIFLOWER SOUP

PREP: 25 minutes **COOK:** 40 minutes

- 1 Tbsp. olive oil
- ¾ cup chopped sweet onion
- 2 14-oz. cans chicken broth
- ¾ cup water
- 4½ cups cauliflower florets
- 2 small potatoes, peeled and chopped
- 1 Tbsp. Dijon-style mustard
  Dash freshly ground black pepper
- 2¼ cups broccoli florets
- 4 oz. Gruyére or Gouda cheese, finely shredded

1. In a 4-quart Dutch oven heat olive oil over medium heat. Add onion; cook for 5 minutes or until tender. Stir in broth, the water, 2¼ cups of the cauliflower florets, and the chopped potato. Bring mixture to boiling; reduce heat. Simmer, covered, for 20 minutes or until cauliflower is very tender.

2. Cool mixture slightly. In a blender or food processor blend or process mixture, half at a time, until smooth. Return all mixture to the Dutch oven. Stir in mustard and pepper. Stir in remaining cauliflower florets and broccoli. Bring mixture to boiling; reduce heat. Simmer, covered, for 20 minutes or until cauliflower is tender. Stir in cheese. Cook and stir until cheese melts. Makes 8 servings.

EACH SERVING: *126 cal., 7 g total fat (3 g sat. fat), 17 mg chol., 517 mg sodium, 10 g carbo., 3 g fiber, 7 g pro. Daily Values: 6% vit. A, 90% vit. C, 17% calcium, 4 iron.*

LOW FAT

SAVORY BARLEY, BEAN, AND MUSHROOM SOUP

PREP: 20 minutes **COOK:** 45 minutes

- ½ cup dried shiitake mushrooms
- 2 cups boiling water
- 1 Tbsp. olive oil
- 1 cup chopped onion (1 large cup)
- ½ cup chopped celery (1 stalk)
- ½ cup chopped carrot (1 medium)
- 2 cloves garlic, minced
- ½ tsp. dried thyme, crushed
- ½ tsp. dried oregano, crushed
- 1 bay leaf
- 2 14-oz. cans vegetable broth
- 1 15-oz. can navy beans or cannellini beans (white kidney beans), rinsed and drained
- ½ cup regular (not quick-cooking) barley
- ½ tsp. salt
- ¼ tsp. ground black pepper
- 1 cup sliced fresh mushrooms
- ½ cup sliced zucchini
- 1 Tbsp. olive oil
- 1 cup shredded fresh spinach
- ¼ cup chopped fresh parsley (optional)
- 1 Tbsp. cider vinegar (optional)

1. In a medium bowl cover shiitake mushrooms with the boiling water. Let stand for 15 to 20 minutes or until tender. Drain, reserving liquid. Strain liquid and set aside. Chop mushrooms and set aside.

2. In a large saucepan heat 1 tablespoon olive oil over medium heat. Add onion, celery, and carrot; cook about 8 minutes or until tender, stirring occasionally. Stir in garlic, thyme, oregano, and bay leaf; cook and stir 2 minutes more. Stir in broth, reserved mushroom liquid, soaked mushrooms, beans, barley, salt, and pepper. Bring to boiling; reduce heat. Simmer, covered, for 35 minutes or until barley is tender.

3. In a large skillet cook fresh mushrooms and zucchini in 1 tablespoon hot oil over medium heat until tender. Add mushrooms and zucchini to soup along with spinach and, if desired, parsley and vinegar. Heat through. Discard bay leaf. Makes 4 or 5 servings.

EACH SERVING: *304 cal., 9 g total fat (1 g sat. fat), 0 mg chol., 1,616 mg sodium, 51 g carbo., 18 g fiber, 13 g pro. Daily Values: 68% vit. A, 18% vit. C, 10% calcium, 23% iron.*

LOW FAT

SWEET POTATO AND ROSEMARY SOUP

PREP: 25 minutes **COOK:** 25 minutes
COOL: 10 minutes

- 1 Tbsp. olive oil
- ⅓ cup chopped onion (1 small)
- 2 cloves garlic, minced
- 1 cup chopped carrot (2 medium)
- ½ chopped celery (1 stalk)
- 1 tsp. dried thyme, crushed
- 1 tsp. dried rosemary, crushed
- 2 medium (about 1 lb.) sweet potatoes, peeled and chopped (3½ cups)
- 1 large (10 oz.) russet potato, peeled and chopped (1½ cups)
- 2 14-oz. cans reduced-sodium chicken broth

1. In a large saucepan heat oil over medium heat. Add onion and garlic; cook and stir about 5 minutes or until onion is tender. Add carrot, celery, thyme, and rosemary. Cook and stir for 3 minutes more. Add chopped potatoes and broth. Bring to boiling; reduce heat. Simmer, covered, for 25 minutes. Cool slightly.

2. Remove half of the mixture (about 3½ cups) to a large heatproof bowl. Place half of the mixture from the bowl in a blender or food processor. Cover and blend or process until smooth. Return to mixture in saucepan. Place remaining half in blender or food processor. Process until smooth; return to saucepan. Heat through. Makes 6 servings.

EACH SERVING: *118 cal., 2 g total fat (0 g sat. fat), 0 mg chol., 361 mg sodium, 21 g carbo., 3 g fiber, 3 g pro. Daily Values: 192% vit. A, 22% vit. C, 4% calcium, 6% iron.*

STUFFINGS AND DRESSINGS

PRIZE TESTED RECIPES® $400 WINNER

PATRICIA A. HARMON, BADEN, PA.

PRIZE TESTED RECIPES® $200 WINNER

MERI VILLANE, COLORADO SPRINGS, COLO.

SOUL SISTER'S CORN BREAD DRESSING

PREP: 30 minutes **BAKE:** 45 minutes

- 2 medium sweet potatoes
- 4 slices bacon
  Butter
- ¾ cup chopped onion
- 1 clove garlic, minced
- 2 cups chopped fresh collard greens or Swiss chard
- 3 cups corn bread stuffing mix
- ½ cup coarsely chopped pecans
- 1 Tbsp. snipped fresh parsley
- ¼ tsp. coarsely ground black pepper
- 1 to 1¼ cups chicken broth

1. Preheat oven to 325°F. Wash sweet potatoes; prick several times with a fork. Place on a microwave-safe plate. Microwave on 100% power (high) for 4 to 6 minutes or until tender. Cool at least 20 minutes. Peel potatoes and cut into ½-inch cubes. Set aside.

2. Meanwhile, in a large skillet cook bacon until crisp; drain on paper towels, reserving drippings in skillet. Crumble bacon and set aside. Measure drippings; if necessary, add butter to drippings to make 3 tablespoons. Cook onion in reserved drippings over medium heat just until tender. Add garlic and cook for 30 seconds. Add collard greens and cook about 5 minutes more or until tender.

3. In a large bowl combine sweet potato, bacon, greens mixture, stuffing mix, pecans, parsley, and pepper. Add enough broth to moisten, tossing lightly to combine. Transfer to a 2-quart casserole or square baking dish; cover. Bake about 45 minutes or until heated through (170°F). Or use to stuff an 8- to 10-pound turkey. Makes 8 to 10 servings.

EACH SERVING: *310 cal., 16 g total fat (4 g sat. fat), 17 mg chol., 669 mg sodium, 35 g carbo., 2 g fiber, 7 g pro. Daily Values: 106% vit. A, 10% vit. C, 4% calcium, 9% iron.*

CHORIZO CORN BREAD STUFFING

PREP: 40 minutes **BAKE:** 30 minutes

- 15 to 16 oz. uncooked chorizo sausage (casings removed, if present)
- ½ cup butter
- 2 cups chopped onion (2 large)
- 2 medium fennel bulbs, trimmed, cored, and cut into thin wedges, or 2 large apples, cored and chopped (2 cups)
- ¾ cup chopped celery
- 2 cloves garlic, minced
- 1 16-oz. pkg. corn bread stuffing mix
- 1 cup dry-roasted salted pistachio nuts
- ¾ cup dried cranberries
- 1 14-oz. can reduced-sodium chicken broth
- 2 eggs, lightly beaten

1. Preheat oven to 350°F. Grease twelve 8- to 10-ounce casseroles or a 13×9×2-inch baking pan or dish; set aside. In a large skillet cook sausage until no longer pink, stirring to break up sausage; drain off fat. Transfer sausage to a very large bowl. Set aside.

2. Carefully wipe out skillet. In the skillet melt butter over medium heat. Add onion, fennel (if using), celery, and garlic. Cook for 10 to 15 minutes or until tender, stirring occasionally. Add apple (if using); cook and stir 2 minutes more. Add vegetable mixture, stuffing mix, nuts, and cranberries to sausage in bowl; toss to combine. In a medium bowl combine broth and eggs; add to sausage mixture. Toss to combine. (For moister stuffing, add ½ cup water.)

3. Transfer mixture to prepared dish(es) or pan. Bake, covered, for 20 minutes for individual casseroles or 35 minutes for large pan or dish. Uncover and bake for 10 to 15 minutes more or until heated through (170°F) and top is light brown. Makes 12 servings.

EACH SERVING: *504 cal., 30 g total fat (11 g sat. fat), 356 mg chol., 1,054 mg sodium, 42 g carbo., 3 g fiber, 17 g pro. Daily Values: 7% vit. A, 7% vit. C, 7% calcium, 18% iron.*

CAROLINA LOW COUNTRY DRESSING

PREP: 45 minutes **BAKE:** 45 minutes

- 1 pint shucked oysters
- ½ cup butter
- ½ cup chopped celery (1 stalk)
- ½ cup chopped onion (1 medium)
- 1 tsp. dried sage, crushed
- ½ tsp. salt
- ½ tsp. ground black pepper
- 8 cups crumbled corn bread*
- 6 2¼-inch baked flaky biscuits, torn into bite-size pieces (about 3 cups)
- 1 cup cooked white or brown rice
- 2 eggs, lightly beaten
- ½ to 1 cup chicken broth

1. Preheat oven to 350°F. Drain oysters, reserving liquid. Coarsely chop oysters; set the oysters aside.

2. In a large skillet melt butter over medium heat. Add celery, onion, sage, salt, and pepper; cook about 5 minutes or until celery and onion are tender. Add chopped oysters; cook and stir for 2 minutes more.

3. In a very large bowl combine corn bread, biscuits, rice, oyster mixture, and eggs. Toss until just combined. Drizzle with reserved oyster liquid and enough broth to moisten; toss lightly to combine. Transfer mixture to a 3-quart rectangular baking dish.

4. Bake, covered, for 30 minutes. Uncover and bake about 15 minutes more or until heated through (170°F) and light brown. Makes 16 servings.

*NOTE: To make 8 cups crumbled corn bread, prepare two 8.5-ounce packages corn muffin mix according to package directions.

EACH SERVING: *319 cal., 14 g total fat (6 g sat. fat), 90 mg chol., 808 mg sodium, 39 g carbo., 2 g fiber, 9 g pro. Daily Values: 9% vit. A, 4% vit. C, 19% calcium, 28% iron.*

[LOW FAT]

CHESTNUT AND ANDOUILLE SAUSAGE STUFFING

PREP: 30 minutes **BAKE:** 30 minutes

- 1 10-oz. can whole, peeled chestnuts, drained
- 8 oz. cooked andouille or smoked sausage, chopped
- 3 cups soft bread crumbs (about 4 slices)
- 3 cups crumbled corn bread
- 2 Tbsp. snipped fresh parsley
- 1 Tbsp. snipped fresh thyme
- ½ tsp. salt
- ¼ to ½ tsp. ground black pepper
- ¼ cup butter
- ½ cup finely chopped shallot
- ¼ to ½ cup water

1. Place chestnuts in a very large bowl. Coarsely mash with a potato masher. Stir in sausage, bread crumbs, corn bread, parsley, thyme, salt, and pepper; set aside.

2. In a small skillet melt butter over medium heat. Add shallot; cook for 4 to 5 minutes or until tender, stirring occasionally. Add shallot mixture to chestnut mixture; toss to combine. Add enough water to moisten.

3. Use to stuff a whole broiler-fryer chicken, turkey, or pork chops. Place extra stuffing in a casserole dish. Bake, covered, along with poultry or meat in a 325°F oven for 30 to 45 minutes or until heated through (170°F). Makes 16 servings.

EACH SERVING: *116 cal., 5 g total fat (2 g sat. fat), 24 mg chol., 324 mg sodium, 14 g carbo., 0 g fiber, 5 g pro. Daily Values: 7% vit. A, 5% vit. C, 7% calcium, 5% iron.*

TROPICAL FRUIT STUFFING

PREP: 20 minutes **BAKE:** 45 minutes

- ⅓ cup butter
- 2 medium Granny Smith apples, cored and chopped (2 cups)
- 1 cup sliced celery (2 stalks)
- ½ cup chopped onion (1 medium)
- 1 tsp. poultry seasoning
- 1 tsp. ground sage
- ½ tsp. seasoned salt
- 9 cups dry cinnamon-raisin bread cubes* (12 slices)
- ½ cup chopped walnuts, toasted
- ¾ cup tropical blend mixed dried fruit bits
- 2 Tbsp. cider vinegar
- ¾ to 1 cup chicken broth

1. Preheat oven to 350°F. In a large saucepan melt butter over medium heat. Add apple, celery, and onion; cook about 5 minutes or until tender. Stir in poultry seasoning, sage, and seasoned salt.

2. In a very large bowl combine bread cubes, walnuts, and dried fruit. Add apple mixture to bread cube mixture; toss to combine. Drizzle vinegar and enough chicken broth over mixture to moisten, tossing lightly to combine. Transfer to 2-quart baking dish. Bake, covered, for 45 minutes or until heated through (170°F). Makes 8 servings.

*NOTE: To make dry bread cubes, cut fresh bread into ½-inch cubes. Spread bread cubes in two 15×10×1-inch baking pans. Bake in a 300°F oven for 10 to 15 minutes or until cubes are dry, stirring twice; cool. (Cubes will continue to dry and crisp as they cool.) Or let bread cubes stand, loosely covered, at room temperature for 8 to 12 hours.

EACH SERVING: *346 cal., 15 g total fat (6 g sat. fat), 28 mg chol., 463 mg sodium, 47 g carbo., 4 g fiber, 7 g pro. Daily Values: 8% vit. A, 5% vit. C, 4% calcium, 9% iron.*

SWEET AND SAVORY ORANGE-CRANBERRY STUFFING

PREP: 15 minutes **BAKE:** 40 minutes

- ⅓ cup butter
- ½ cup chopped red onion
- 2 tsp. chopped pickled ginger or 1 Tbsp. grated fresh ginger (optional)
- 1 tsp. dried thyme, crushed
- 1 tsp. snipped fresh rosemary
- 1 tsp. Dijon-style mustard
- ½ tsp. salt
- ¼ tsp. freshly ground black pepper
- 8 slices whole wheat bread, cubed and dried*
- ½ cup orange-flavored sweetened dried cranberries, chopped
- ¾ to 1¼ cups orange juice

1. Preheat oven to 350°F. In a large saucepan melt butter over medium heat. Add onion; cook and stir for 5 minutes or until tender. Stir in ginger (if desired), thyme, rosemary, mustard, salt, and pepper; cook and stir for 1 minute. Remove from heat.

2. In a very large bowl combine bread cubes and cranberries; stir in onion mixture. Drizzle with enough orange juice to moisten, tossing lightly to combine. Transfer the mixture to a 1½-quart casserole.

3. Bake, covered, for 30 minutes. Uncover and bake 10 to 15 minutes more or until heated through (170°F) and top is slightly crisp. Makes 6 servings.

*NOTE: To make dry bread cubes, cut fresh bread into ½-inch cubes. Spread bread cubes in a shallow baking pan. Bake in a 300°F oven for 10 to 15 minutes or until cubes are dry, stirring twice; cool. (Cubes will continue to dry and crisp as they cool.) Or let bread cubes stand, loosely covered, at room temperature for 8 to 12 hours.

EACH SERVING: *314 cal., 14 g total fat (7 g sat. fat), 27 mg chol., 499 mg sodium, 44 g carbo., 5 g fiber, 6 g pro. Daily Values: 8% vit. A, 27% vit. C, 3% calcium, 13% iron.*

SLOW COOKER IDEAS

MOROCCAN CHICKEN STEW

PREP: 30 minutes **COOK:** 6½ hours (low) or 3½ hours (high)

     4 carrots, peeled and sliced
     2 large onions, halved and thinly sliced
     3 lb. meaty chicken pieces (breast halves, thighs,
          and drumsticks), skinned
     ½ tsp. salt
     ½ cup raisins
     ½ cup dried apricots, coarsely chopped
     1 14-oz. can chicken broth
     ¼ cup tomato paste
     2 Tbsp. all-purpose flour
     2 Tbsp. lemon juice
     2 cloves garlic, minced
  1½ tsp. ground cumin
  1½ tsp. ground ginger
     1 tsp. ground cinnamon
     ¾ tsp. ground black pepper
          Hot cooked couscous
          Pine nuts, toasted
          Fresh cilantro (optional)

1. In a 5- to 6-quart slow cooker place carrot and onion slices. Sprinkle chicken with salt; add to cooker. Top chicken with raisins and apricots. In a medium bowl whisk together broth, tomato paste, flour, lemon juice, garlic, cumin, ginger, cinnamon, and pepper. Add to cooker.
2. Cover; cook on low-heat setting for 6½ to 7 hours or on high-heat setting for 3½ to 4 hours. Serve in shallow bowls with couscous. Sprinkle with pine nuts and, if desired, garnish with cilantro. Makes 4 servings.
EACH SERVING: *600 cal., 15 g total fat (3 g sat. fat), 139 mg chol., 997 mg sodium, 65 g carbo., 8 g fiber, 52 g pro. Daily Values: 222% vit. A, 29% vit. C, 11% calcium, 25% iron.*

CURRIED CHICKEN

PREP: 20 minutes
COOK: 8½ hours (low) or 4 hours (high) + 15 minutes (high)

  1¼ lb. skinless, boneless chicken thighs
     1 red sweet pepper, chopped
     1 yellow sweet pepper, chopped
     1 small onion, sliced
     1 fresh jalapeño chile pepper, seeded and finely chopped*
     2 cloves garlic, minced
     1 cup reduced-sodium chicken broth
     ½ cup golden raisins
     ½ cup shredded coconut
     3 Tbsp. curry powder
     1 tsp. salt
     ¼ tsp. ground cinnamon
     ¼ tsp. cayenne pepper (optional)
     ½ cup unsweetened coconut milk
     1 Tbsp. cornstarch
          Hot cooked rice (optional)
     ¾ cup coarsely chopped lightly salted cashews
          Whole green onions (optional)

1. In a 3½- to 4-quart slow cooker place chicken, sweet peppers, onion, jalapeño, garlic, broth, raisins, coconut, curry powder, salt, cinnamon, and, if desired, cayenne. Cover; cook on low-heat setting for 8½ to 9 hours or on high-heat setting for 4 to 4½ hours.
2. Stir together coconut milk and cornstarch until smooth. Stir into chicken mixture. If cooking on low-heat setting, adjust to high-heat setting. Cover; cook for 15 to 20 minutes more or until slightly thickened. If desired, serve with rice. Sprinkle with cashews. If desired, garnish with green onions. Makes 4 servings.
***NOTE:** Because hot chile peppers, such as jalapeños, contain volatile oils that can burn your skin and eyes, avoid direct contact with chiles as much as possible. When working with chile peppers, wear plastic or rubber gloves. If your bare hands do touch the chile peppers, wash your hands well with soap and water.
EACH SERVING: *489 cal., 23 g total fat (8 g sat. fat), 118 mg chol., 868 mg sodium, 39 g carbo., 6 g fiber, 35 g pro. Daily Values: 24% vit. A, 214% vit. C, 8% calcium, 32% iron.*

ASIAN CHICKEN AND RICE

PREP: 25 minutes **COOK:** 6 hours (low) or 3 hours (high) + 20 minutes (high)

- 3 lb. meaty chicken pieces (breasts, thighs, and drumsticks), skinned
  Salt and ground black pepper
- 1 Tbsp. cooking oil
- 2 medium onions, sliced
- ¼ cup sliced almonds
- 1 Tbsp. minced fresh ginger
- 4 cloves garlic, minced
- 1 tsp. ground coriander
- 1 tsp. ground turmeric
- ¼ cup chicken broth
- 1 Tbsp. finely shredded lemon peel
- 1 cup coconut milk
- 1 Tbsp. chili garlic sauce
- 1½ tsp. soy sauce
- 1 tsp. packed brown sugar
  Hot cooked brown or white rice

1. Season chicken with salt and pepper. In a large skillet brown chicken, half at a time, on all sides in hot oil. Remove chicken, reserving drippings. Place chicken in a 3½- to 4-quart slow cooker; set aside.

2. In the same skillet cook onion in drippings for 5 minutes or until tender. Stir in sliced almonds, ginger, garlic, coriander, and turmeric. Cook and stir for 1 minute. Remove from heat. Stir in chicken broth; cool slightly. Transfer mixture to a food processor or blender. Cover and process or blend until mixture is nearly smooth. Stir in lemon peel. Spoon mixture over chicken in slow cooker.

3. Cover; cook on low-heat setting for 6 to 8 hours or on high-heat setting for 3 to 4 hours. If cooking on low-heat setting, adjust to high-heat setting. In bowl combine coconut milk, chili garlic sauce, soy sauce, and brown sugar. Pour over chicken mixture. Cover; cook for 20 minutes more. Serve chicken with sauce and rice. Makes 6 servings.

EACH SERVING: *464 cal., 22 g total fat (11 g sat. fat), 92 mg chol., 353 mg sodium, 31 g carbo., 4 g fiber, 34 g pro. Daily Values: 10% vit. C, 6% calcium, 15% iron.*

[LOW FAT]

ITALIAN ROUND STEAK DINNER

PREP: 20 minutes
COOK: 9 hours (low) or 4½ hours (high)

- 2¼ lb. boneless beef round steak
- 1 Tbsp. cooking oil
- 1 large fennel bulb, cut into thin wedges
- 1 large onion, halved and thinly sliced
- 1 cup packaged fresh julienned carrots
- 1 28-oz. can crushed tomatoes
- 1 15-oz. can tomato sauce
- ½ cup beef broth
- 2 tsp. dried Italian seasoning, crushed
- ⅛ tsp. crushed red pepper
- 6 cups hot cooked pasta
- ¼ cup finely shredded Parmesan cheese

1. Cut meat into 8 serving-size pieces; sprinkle lightly with *salt* and *ground black pepper*. In a large skillet brown steak, half at a time, in hot oil. In a 4- to 4½-quart slow cooker place fennel, onion, and julienned carrots. Add browned beef. In a large bowl combine undrained crushed tomatoes, tomato sauce, beef broth, Italian seasoning, and crushed red pepper. Pour over meat in cooker.

2. Cover; cook on low-heat setting for 9 to 10 hours or on high-heat setting for 4½ to 5 hours.

3. Divide pasta among 8 serving plates; top each with a steak portion and sauce. Sprinkle with cheese. Makes 8 servings.

EACH SERVING: *434 cal., 9 g total fat (3 g sat. fat), 72 mg chol., 764 mg sodium, 47 g carbo., 6 g fiber, 38 g pro. Daily Values: 53% vit. A, 26% vit. C, 12% calcium, 29% iron.*

[LOW FAT]

TURKEY SAUSAGE AND BEAN SOUP

PREP: 20 minutes **COOK:** 10 hours (low) or 5 hours (high) + 1 hour (high)

- 1 lb. dried beans (cranberry, kidney, Great Northern, and/or pinto beans)
- 8 cups water
- 4 cups water
- 1 32-oz. carton chicken broth
- 3 medium red-skinned potatoes, cubed
- 4 cloves garlic, minced
- 1 Tbsp. chili powder
- 1 16-oz. link smoked turkey sausage, halved and sliced ½ inch thick
- 2 cups frozen cut green beans
- 1 tsp. salt

1. Rinse dried beans; drain. In a Dutch oven place beans and 8 cups water. Bring to boiling; reduce heat. Simmer, uncovered, for 10 minutes. Cover and let stand for 1 hour. (Or cool; transfer to a very large bowl. Cover and chill the beans for up to 24 hours.) Drain and rinse beans.

2. In a 6- to 7-quart slow cooker combine beans, 4 cups water, broth, potato, garlic, and chili powder. Cover; cook on low-heat setting for 10 hours or on high-heat setting for 5 hours. Mash slightly with a potato masher or the back of a wooden spoon.

3. Add sausage, green beans, and salt. If cooking on low-heat setting, adjust to high-heat setting. Cover and cook 1 hour more. Makes 10 to 12 servings.

EACH SERVING: *270 cal., 5 g total fat (2 g sat. fat), 25 mg chol., 1,038 mg sodium, 39 g carbo., 13 g fiber, 19 g pro. Daily Values: 8% vit. A, 42% vit. C, 9% calcium, 40% iron.*

PEPPERY ITALIAN BEEF SANDWICHES

PREP: 30 minutes
COOK: 10 hours (low) or 5 hours (high)

- 1 2½- to 3-lb. boneless beef chuck pot roast
- 4 tsp. garlic-pepper seasoning
- 1 Tbsp. cooking oil
- 1 14-oz. can beef broth
- 1 0.7-oz. envelope Italian dry salad dressing mix
- 1 tsp. onion salt
- 1 tsp. dried oregano, crushed
- 1 tsp. dried basil, crushed
- 1 tsp. dried parsley
- 1 12- to 16-oz. jar pepperoncini salad peppers, drained
- 8 hoagie buns or kaiser rolls, split and toasted
- 2 cups shredded mozzarella cheese

1. Trim fat from meat. Coat meat with garlic-pepper seasoning. In a Dutch oven brown meat on all sides in hot oil.

2. In a 3½- to 4-quart slow cooker place meat. (If necessary, cut meat in half to fit in slow cooker.) In a medium bowl whisk together beef broth, dressing mix, onion salt, oregano, basil, and parsley. Pour over meat in slow cooker. Top with pepperoncini peppers.

3. Cover; cook on low-heat setting for 10 hours or on high-heat setting for 5 to 6 hours. Transfer meat to a cutting board. Using two forks, pull meat apart into shreds. Using a slotted spoon, remove peppers from cooking liquid and transfer to a serving bowl. Skim fat from cooking liquid and transfer cooking liquid to a serving bowl.

4. To serve, spoon some shredded meat on the bottom halves of buns. Sprinkle with cheese and, if desired, spoon desired amount of cooking liquid over cheese. Top with pepperoncini peppers and bun tops. Makes 8 servings.

EACH SERVING: *560 cal., 17 g total fat (6 g sat. fat), 94 mg chol., 2,358 mg sodium, 53 g carbo., 2 g fiber, 46 g pro. Daily Values: 3% vit. A, 32% calcium, 26% iron.*

FESTIVE HOLIDAY COOKIES

CINNAMON WREATHS

PREP: 30 minutes **CHILL:** 1 hour **BAKE:** 10 minutes per batch
COOL: 2 minutes

- ¾ cup butter, softened
- ½ cup granulated sugar
- ½ cup packed brown sugar
- ½ tsp. baking soda
- 1½ tsp. ground cinnamon
- ½ tsp. ground ginger
- 1 egg
- 1 tsp. vanilla
- 2¼ cups all-purpose flour
- 2 Tbsp. granulated sugar
  Red and/or green miniature candy-coated
  semisweet chocolate pieces
- 1 recipe Frosting

1. In a large mixing bowl beat butter with an electric mixer for 30 seconds. Beat in ½ cup granulated sugar, the brown sugar, baking soda, ½ teaspoon of the cinnamon, the ginger, and ⅛ teaspoon *salt* until combined. Beat in egg and vanilla until combined. Beat in as much flour as you can with the mixer; stir in any remaining flour. Divide dough in half. Cover and chill about 1 hour or until easy to handle.
2. Preheat oven to 350°F. Combine 2 tablespoons granulated sugar and remaining 1 teaspoon cinnamon. On a lightly floured surface, roll half of the dough at a time until ¼ inch thick. Cut with a 3-inch scalloped round cookie cutter. Cut out centers using a 1-inch scalloped cutter. Place cutouts on an ungreased cookie sheet. Sprinkle with sugar mixture. Carefully press candy pieces into dough.
3. Bake for 10 to 12 minutes or until edges are firm and bottoms are very light brown. Cool on cookie sheet for 2 minutes. Transfer to wire racks; cool. Decorate with Frosting. Makes 18 to 20 cookies.
FROSTING: In a small saucepan stir 3 ounces white baking chocolate and ½ teaspoon shortening over low heat just until melted and smooth. Remove from heat. Stir in a few drops green food coloring to desired shade. Decorate cookies as desired.
EACH COOKIE: *216 cal., 10 g total fat (6 g sat. fat), 33 mg chol., 118 mg sodium, 29 g carbo., 1 g fiber, 1 g pro. Daily Values: 5% vit. A, 2% calcium, 6% iron.*

CHOCO-BERRY THUMBPRINTS

PREP: 30 minutes **BAKE:** 10 minutes **COOL:** 15 minutes

- 1 cup bittersweet chocolate pieces
- ½ of a 14-oz. can (⅔ cup) sweetened condensed milk
- ½ cup seedless red raspberry jam
- ½ cup coconut, toasted
- ½ cup butter, softened
- ¾ cup granulated sugar
- 1 egg
- 1½ tsp. vanilla
- 1⅔ cups all-purpose flour
- ⅓ cup unsweetened cocoa powder
- ¼ tsp. baking powder
- ¼ tsp. baking soda
- ¼ tsp. salt
  Powdered sugar (optional)

1. For filling, in a medium saucepan combine chocolate and milk. Stir over low heat just until chocolate is melted and smooth; remove from heat. Stir in jam. Carefully stir in coconut. Cover; set aside. Preheat oven to 350°F. Grease thirty-six 1¾-inch muffin cups (metal muffin pans work best); set aside.
2. For dough, in a large mixing bowl beat butter with an electric mixer on medium to high speed for 30 seconds. Add granulated sugar, egg, and vanilla. Beat on medium speed until well combined, scraping sides of the bowl occasionally. Add flour, cocoa powder, baking powder, baking soda, and salt. Beat on medium speed just until combined. Divide dough into 36 equal pieces; shape into 1-inch balls. Press a ball evenly on bottom and up the sides of each muffin cup. Divide filling among muffin cups.
3. Bake for 10 to 12 minutes or until crust is set and just dry. Cool in pan on wire rack for 15 minutes. Carefully remove tarts; cool completely on rack. If desired, sprinkle with powdered sugar. Store in airtight container at room temperature for up to 3 days or for 1 week in the refrigerator. Makes 36 cookies.
EACH COOKIE: *122 cal., 6 g total fat (3 g sat. fat), 15 mg chol., 57 mg sodium, 18 g carbo., 1 g fiber, 1 g pro. Daily Values: 2% vit. A, 1% vit. C, 2% calcium, 4% iron.*

CANDIED CHERRY BROWNIES

PREP: 25 minutes **BAKE:** 40 minutes

- ¾ cup butter
- 3 oz. bittersweet chocolate, chopped
- 2 cups granulated sugar
- ½ tsp. peppermint extract or almond flavoring
- 3 eggs
- 1 cup all-purpose flour
- ¼ cup unsweetened cocoa powder
- ½ tsp. baking powder
- ¼ tsp. salt
- ½ cup red and/or green candied cherries, coarsely chopped
- 1 cup lightly salted pistachio nuts, chopped
  Powdered sugar

1. Preheat oven to 325°F. Line a 13×9×2-inch baking pan with foil; grease and flour foil.
2. In a heavy medium saucepan combine butter and chocolate. Stir over low heat until melted. Remove from heat. Stir in granulated sugar and extract. Add eggs, 1 at a time, beating with a wooden spoon after each addition just until combined. In a small bowl combine flour and cocoa powder; remove and set aside 1 tablespoon of the mixture. Stir baking powder and salt into remaining flour mixture; stir into butter mixture. In the small bowl combine reserved flour mixture and candied cherries, stirring to coat and separate cherries. Stir into chocolate mixture along with nuts. Spread batter evenly into prepared pan.
3. Bake for 40 minutes. Cool completely in pan on a wire rack. Use foil to lift brownies from pan. Invert and peel off foil; invert again. Cut into bars. Sprinkle with powdered sugar. Makes 48 brownies.
EACH BROWNIE: *103 cal., 5 g total fat (3 g sat. fat), 21 mg chol., 50 mg sodium, 14 g carbo., 1 g fiber, 1 g pro. Daily Values: 2% vit. A, 1% calcium, 3% iron.*

CHOCOLATE JEWELS

PREP: 25 minutes **BAKE:** 8 minutes

- About 20 large gumdrops (no spiced or black candies)
- ½ cup butter, softened
- 1 cup packed brown sugar
- ½ tsp. baking soda
- ½ tsp. salt
- ⅓ cup unsweetened cocoa powder
- 1 egg
- ¼ cup milk
- 1¾ cups all-purpose flour
- ¾ cup chopped pecans
- ½ cup dried cranberries
- ½ cup miniature semisweet chocolate pieces

1. Preheat oven to 350°F. Cut gumdrops into ¼- to ½-inch pieces; set aside.
2. In a large mixing bowl beat butter with an electric mixer on medium to high speed for 30 seconds. Add brown sugar, baking soda, and salt; beat until combined. Add cocoa

powder and beat well. Beat in egg and milk. Beat in as much flour as you can with the mixer; stir in any remaining flour. Stir in pecans, cranberries, and chocolate pieces.
3. Drop dough from a rounded teaspoon onto ungreased cookie sheets. Press several gumdrop pieces on top of each cookie. Bake for 8 to 10 minutes or until set. Cool 1 minute on cookie sheet. Transfer to a wire rack; cool completely. Makes about 36 cookies.
EACH COOKIE: *117 cal., 5 g total fat (2 g sat. fat), 13 mg chol., 74 mg sodium, 17 g carbo., 1 g fiber, 1 g pro. Daily Values: 2% vit. A, 1% calcium, 4% iron.*

COFFEE CUPS

PREP: 30 minutes **CHILL:** 1 hour
BAKE: 22 minutes

- ½ cup butter, softened
- 1 3-oz. pkg. cream cheese, softened
- 1 cup all-purpose flour
- 24 milk chocolate kisses with stripes
- 1 egg white, lightly beaten
- ¼ cup sugar
- 1 tsp. unsweetened cocoa powder
- 1 tsp. instant coffee crystals

1. In a mixing bowl beat butter and cream cheese with electric mixer on medium speed until combined. Beat in flour. Cover; chill for 1 hour or until firm and easy to handle.
2. Preheat oven to 325°F. Divide dough into 24 equal pieces; shape into 1-inch balls. Press a ball evenly on bottom and up the sides of 24 ungreased 1¾-inch muffin cups. Place a chocolate kiss in the bottom of each cup.
3. In a small bowl combine egg white, sugar, cocoa powder, and instant coffee crystals. Spoon ½ teaspoon of the mixture into each cup. Bake for 22 to 25 minutes or until lightly puffed and golden brown. Cool in pan on wire rack for 15 minutes. Carefully remove tarts; cool completely on rack. Makes 24 cookies.
EACH COOKIE: *100 cal., 7 g total fat (4 g sat. fat), 15 mg chol., 44 mg sodium, 9 g carbo., 0 g fiber, 1 g pro. Daily Values: 3% vit. A, 1% calcium, 2% iron.*

ITALIAN RICOTTA COOKIES

PREP: 25 minutes **BAKE:** 10 minutes

- 1 cup butter, softened
- 1 cup granulated sugar
- ½ tsp. salt
- ½ tsp. baking soda
- ¾ cup ricotta cheese
- 2 eggs
- 1 tsp. vanilla
- 2¼ cups all-purpose flour
- ½ cup lightly salted pistachio nuts, chopped
- ⅓ cup dried currants
- 1½ cups powdered sugar
- 1 to 2 Tbsp. milk
  Red and green paste food coloring
  Finely chopped pistachio nuts (optional)

1. Preheat oven to 350°F. In a very large mixing bowl beat butter with an electric mixer on medium to high speed for 30 seconds. Add granulated sugar, salt, and baking soda. Beat until combined, scraping sides of bowl occasionally. Beat in ricotta cheese, eggs, and vanilla. (Mixture will look curdled.) Beat in as much flour as you can with the mixer; stir in any remaining flour. Stir in ½ cup pistachio nuts and the currants. Drop dough from teaspoons 2 inches apart onto ungreased cookie sheets.
2. Bake for 10 to 12 minutes or until set and light brown on bottom. Transfer to wire rack; cool completely. In a small bowl stir together powdered sugar and enough milk to make a drizzling consistency. Divide in half; tint one half red and the other half green. Drizzle over cookies. If desired, sprinkle with nuts. Makes about 48 cookies.
EACH COOKIE: *104 cal., 5 g total fat (3 g sat. fat), 21 mg chol., 71 mg sodium, 13 g carbo., 0 g fiber, 1 g pro. Daily Values: 3% vit. A, 1% calcium, 2% iron.*

PECAN-CRUSTED MOJITO BARS

PREP: 15 minutes **BAKE:** 40 minutes

- 1¾ cups all-purpose flour
- 1 cup chopped pecans
- ¾ cup granulated sugar
- 1 cup butter, cut into slices
- 4 eggs, lightly beaten
- 1½ cups granulated sugar
- 2 Tbsp. finely shredded lime peel
- ½ cup lime juice
- ¼ cup all-purpose flour
- 2 Tbsp. milk
- 1 Tbsp. snipped fresh mint
- ½ tsp. baking powder
  Powdered sugar
  Finely shredded lime peel (optional)
  Small fresh mint leaves (optional)

1. Preheat oven to 350°F. Line a 13×9×2-inch baking pan with foil, extending foil beyond ends; set aside. In a food processor combine 1¾ cups flour, pecans, and ¾ cup granulated sugar. Add butter slices. Cover and pulse with several on/off turns until mixture resembles coarse crumbs. Press crumb mixture into the bottom of the prepared pan. Bake for 20 to 22 minutes or until crust is light brown.
2. For filling, in a bowl whisk together eggs, 1½ cups sugar, lime peel and juice, ¼ cup flour, milk, mint, baking powder, and ¼ teaspoon *salt* until combined. Pour over hot crust.
3. Bake for 20 to 25 minutes more or until filling is set and edges just begin to brown. Cool completely in pan on a wire rack. Use foil to lift from pan. Cut into bars. Sift powdered sugar over bars. Cover; store in refrigerator. If desired, garnish with lime peel and mint leaves. Makes 36 bars.
EACH BAR: *150 cal., 8 g total fat (4 g sat. fat), 37 mg chol., 64 mg sodium, 19 g carbo., 1 g fiber, 1 g pro. Daily Values: 4% vit. A, 3% vit. C, 1% calcium, 3% iron.*

ANNUAL Recipes 2007

D-E

F

H

I–K

L

Q-R

S

Nutrition information.
With each recipe, we give important nutrition information you easily can apply to your own needs. You'll find the calorie count of each serving and the amount, in grams, of fat, saturated fat, cholesterol, sodium, carbohydrates, fiber, and protein to help you keep tabs on what you eat. You can check the levels of each recipe serving for vitamin A, vitamin C, calcium, and iron, if they are present. These are noted in percentages of the Daily Values. The Daily Values are dietary standards determined by the Food and Drug Administration (FDA). To stay in line with the nutrition breakdown of each recipe, follow the suggested number of servings.

How we analyze.
The Better Homes and Gardens® Test Kitchen computer analyzes each recipe for the nutritional value of a single serving.
- The analysis does not include optional ingredients.
- We use the first serving size listed when a range is given. For example: If we say a recipe "Makes 4 to 6 servings," the nutrition information is based on 4 servings.
- When ingredient choices (such as butter or margarine) appear in a recipe, we use the first one mentioned for analysis. The ingredient order does not mean we prefer one ingredient over another.
- When milk and eggs are recipe ingredients, the analysis is calculated using 2 percent (reduced-fat) milk and large eggs.

What you need.
The dietary guidelines below suggest nutrient levels that moderately active adults should strive to eat each day. There is no real harm in going over or under these guidelines in any single day, but it is a good idea to aim for a balanced diet over time.

Calories: About 2,000
Total fat: Less than 65 grams
Saturated fat: Less than 20 grams
Cholesterol: Less than 300 milligrams
Carbohydrates: About 300 grams
Sodium: Less than 2,400 milligrams
Dietary fiber: 20 to 30 grams

Low Fat icon.
Certain recipes throughout the book have an icon next to the nutrition information that indicates the recipe is low fat. For a recipe to earn this icon, it must meet certain nutritional requirements. For a main dish one serving should have 12 grams of fat per serving or less, one serving of a side dish should have 5 grams of fat or less, an appetizer serving should have 2 grams of fat or less, and cookies and desserts should have 2 grams of fat or less per serving. Occasionally the fat level will slightly exceed one of the recommended numbers, but typically they remain below the listed amounts.

Metric Information

The charts on this page provide a guide for converting measurements from the U.S. customary system, which is used throughout this book, to the metric system.

Product Differences

Most of the ingredients called for in the recipes in this book are available in most countries. However, some are known by different names. Here are some common American ingredients and their possible counterparts:

- Sugar (white) is granulated, fine granulated, or castor sugar.
- Powdered sugar is icing sugar.
- All-purpose flour is enriched, bleached or unbleached white household flour. When self-rising flour is used in place of all-purpose flour in a recipe that calls for leavening, omit the leavening agent (baking soda or baking powder) and salt.
- Light-colored corn syrup is golden syrup.
- Cornstarch is cornflour.
- Baking soda is bicarbonate of soda.
- Vanilla or vanilla extract is vanilla essence.
- Green, red, or yellow sweet peppers are capsicums or bell peppers.
- Golden raisins are sultanas.

Volume and Weight

The United States traditionally uses cup measures for liquid and solid ingredients. The chart below shows the approximate imperial and metric equivalents. If you are accustomed to weighing solid ingredients, the following approximate equivalents will be helpful.

- 1 cup butter, castor sugar, or rice = 8 ounces= ½ pound = 250 grams
- 1 cup flour = 4 ounces = ¼ pound = 125 grams
- 1 cup icing sugar = 5 ounces = 150 grams

Canadian and U.S. volume for a cup measure is 8 fluid ounces (237 ml), but the standard metric equivalent is 250 ml.

1 British imperial cup is 10 fluid ounces.

In Australia, 1 tablespoon equals 20 ml, and there are 4 teaspoons in the Australian tablespoon.

Spoon measures are used for smaller amounts of ingredients. Although the size of the tablespoon varies slightly in different countries, for practical purposes and for recipes in this book, a straight substitution is all that's necessary. Measurements made using cups or spoons always should be level unless stated otherwise.

Common Weight Range Replacements

Imperial / U.S.	Metric
½ ounce	15 g
1 ounce	25 g or 30 g
4 ounces (¼ pound)	115 g or 125 g
8 ounces (¼ pound)	225 g or 250 g
16 ounces (1 pound)	450 g or 500 g
1¼ pounds	625 g
1½ pounds	750 g
2 pounds or 2¼ pounds	1,000 g or 1 Kg

Oven Temperature Equivalents

Fahrenheit Setting	Celsius Setting*	Gas Setting
300°F	150°C	Gas Mark 2 (very low)
325°F	160°C	Gas Mark 3 (low)
350°F	180°C	Gas Mark 4 (moderate)
375°F	190°C	Gas Mark 5 (moderate)
400°F	200°C	Gas Mark 6 (hot)
425°F	220°C	Gas Mark 7 (hot)
450°F	230°C	Gas Mark 8 (very hot)
475°F	240°C	Gas Mark 9 (very hot)
500°F	260°C	Gas Mark 10 (extremely hot)
Broil	Broil	Grill

*Electric and gas ovens may be calibrated using celsius. However, for an electric oven, increase celsius setting 10 to 20 degrees when cooking above 160°C. For convection or forced air ovens (gas or electric) lower the temperature setting 25°F/10°C when cooking at all heat levels.

Baking Pan Sizes

Imperial / U.S.	Metric
9×1½-inch round cake pan	22- or 23×4-cm (1.5 L)
9×1½-inch pie plate	22- or 23×4-cm (1 L)
8×8×2-inch square cake pan	20×5-cm (2 L)
9×9×2-inch square cake pan	22- or 23×4.5-cm (2.5 L)
11×7×1½-inch baking pan	28×17×4-cm (2 L)
2-quart rectangular baking pan	30×19×4.5-cm (3 L)
13×9×2-inch baking pan	34×22×4.5-cm (3.5 L)
15×10×1-inch jelly roll pan	40×25×2-cm
9×5×3-inch loaf pan	23×13×8-cm (2 L)
2-quart casserole	2 L

U.S. / Standard Metric Equivalents

⅛ teaspoon = 0.5 ml	
¼ teaspoon = 1 ml	
½ teaspoon = 2 ml	
1 teaspoon = 5 ml	
1 tablespoon = 15 ml	
2 tablespoons = 25 ml	
¼ cup = 2 fluid ounces = 50 ml	
⅓ cup = 3 fluid ounces = 75 ml	
½ cup = 4 fluid ounces = 125 ml	
⅔ cup = 5 fluid ounces = 150 ml	
¾ cup = 6 fluid ounces = 175 ml	
1 cup = 8 fluid ounces = 250 ml	
2 cups = 1 pint = 500 ml	
1 quart = 1 liter	